Causes and Symptoms of Socio-Cultural Polarization

Israr Qureshi • Babita Bhatt • Samrat Gupta
Amit Anand Tiwari
Editors

Causes and Symptoms of Socio-Cultural Polarization

Role of Information and Communication Technologies

Springer

Editors
Israr Qureshi
Research School of Management
Australian National University
Canberra, ACT, Australia

Babita Bhatt
Research School of Management
Australian National University
Canberra, ACT, Australia

Samrat Gupta
Information Systems Area
Indian Institute of Management Ahmedabad
Ahmedabad, Gujarat, India

Amit Anand Tiwari
Marketing Management Area
Indian Institute of Management Rohtak
Rohtak, Haryana, India

ISBN 978-981-16-5267-7 ISBN 978-981-16-5268-4 (eBook)
https://doi.org/10.1007/978-981-16-5268-4

This Springer imprint is published by the registered company Springer Nature Singapore Pte Ltd.
The registered company address is: 152 Beach Road, #21-01/04 Gateway East, Singapore 189721, Singapore

Dedicated to the people who lost their lives or livelihoods due to polarization

Acknowledgement

We acknowledge MHRD (India) for supporting this work through Scheme for Promotion of Academic Research and Collaboration (SPARC) grant #P495 and Australian National University for providing support through Grand Challenge project on Social Cohesion, Integration and Diversity.

Contents

Introduction to the Role of Information and Communication Technologies in Polarization 1
Israr Qureshi, Babita Bhatt, Samrat Gupta, and Amit Anand Tiwari

Part I Techniques and Methods

A Schelling-Opinion Model Based on Integration of Opinion Formation with Residential Segregation 27
Victoria Arcón, Juan Pablo Pinasco, and Inés Caridi

The Dynamics of Online Opinion Formation: Polarization Around the Vaccine Development for COVID-19 51
Gaurav Jain, Avinash Bapu Sreenivas, Samrat Gupta, and Amit Anand Tiwari

Investigating Dynamics of Polarization of YouTube True and Fake News Channels 73
Manideepto Das, Priya Singh, and Adrija Majumdar

Part II Social Aspects of Polarization

Political Polarization in Australia: A Case Study of Brushfires in Australia 115
Zhiwen Zheng and Babita Bhatt

(De)polarizing ICT Debates of Reservations and Affirmative Action Policy: A Plea for Reparations in India and the U.S. 133
Kofi-Charu Nat Turner, Nagaraju Gundemeda, and Sabiha Sultana

Part III Cultural Aspects of Polarization

Impact of ICT on Literary Censorship: A Study of Selected Controversial Texts in Contemporary India 151
Fujeena Abdul Kader and Upender Gundala

Investigating Social Media Induced Polarization on National Education Policy 2020 177
Bhavna Sharma and Kirti Vasuja

Media Bias and Bollywood: An Untold Story 211
Gaurav Jain, Snehanshu Suman, Samrat Gupta, and Amit Anand Tiwari

Part IV Consequences and Outcomes of Polarization: Trends and Future Research Directions

Polarisation in Information Ethics: The Debates Between Privacy and Common Goods in the Chinese Social Credit System 233
Zhiwen Zheng and Babita Bhatt

A Comprehensive Review on Countering Rumours in the Age of Online Social Media Platforms 253
Amir Ebrahimi Fard and Trivik Verma

Future Research Directions in Polarization 285
Israr Qureshi, Babita Bhat, Samrat Gupta, and Amit Anand Tiwari

Index 297

Contributors

Victoria Arcón Universidad de Buenos Aires, Buenos Aires, Argentina

Babita Bhatt Australian National University, Canberra, Australia

Inés Caridi Universidad de Buenos Aires, Buenos Aires, Argentina

Manideepto Das Indian Institute of Management Ahmedabad, Ahmedabad, Gujarat, India

Amir Ebrahimi Fard Delft University of Technology, Delft, the Netherlands

Upender Gundala National Institute of Technology Rourkela, Rourkela, Odisha, India

Nagaraju Gundemeda University of Hyderabad, Hyderabad, India

Samrat Gupta Information Systems Area, Indian Institute of Management Ahmedabad, Ahmedabad, Gujarat, India

Gaurav Jain Indian Institute of Management Ahmedabad, Ahmedabad, Gujarat, India

Fujeena Abdul Kader National Institute of Technology Rourkela, Rourkela, Odisha, India

Adrija Majumdar Indian Institute of Management Ahmedabad, Ahmedabad, Gujarat, India

Juan Pablo Pinasco Universidad de Buenos Aires, Buenos Aires, Argentina

Israr Qureshi Australian National University, Canberra, Australia

Bhavna Sharma BPS Women University, Sonipat, Haryana, India

Priya Singh Indian Institute of Management Ahmedabad, Ahmedabad, Gujarat, India

Avinash B. Sreenivas Indian Institute of Management Ahmedabad, Ahmedabad, Gujarat, India

Sabiha Sultana Directorate of Secondary and Higher Education, Ministry of Education, Dhaka, Bangladesh

Snehanshu Suman Indian Institute of Management Ahmedabad, Ahmedabad, Gujarat, India

Amit Anand Tiwari Marketing Management Area, Indian Institute of Management Rohtak, Rohtak, Haryana, India

K. C. Nat Turner University of Massachusetts, Amherst, MA, USA

Kirti Vasuja BPS Women University, Sonipat, Haryana, India

Trivik Verma Delft University of Technology, Delft, the Netherlands

Zhiwen Zheng Australian National University, Canberra, Australia

Introduction to the Role of Information and Communication Technologies in Polarization

Israr Qureshi, Babita Bhatt, Samrat Gupta, and Amit Anand Tiwari

1 Introduction

The year 2020 has been a testing ground for the progress towards a cohesive and sustainable future envisaged through the advancement in Information and Communication Technologies (ICTs) (UN ECOSOC 2021). In a time of uncertainty, helplessness, and growing frustrations, we, as a society, found that ICTs can be a mixed blessing. We witnessed the power of ICTs in connecting people across the globe in their collective trauma and desperation (Garfin 2020), forming online mutual aid groups to offer help and support to those in need (Knearem et al. 2021) and building solidarity, and increasing outreach of movements for social justice (Frankfurt 2020). However, these positive trends were marred by the increase in information chaos (Forum on Information and Democracy (2021), the formation of echo chambers (Boutyline and Willer 2017), and the consolidation of extreme views and ideologies (Zeller 2021). These polarizing forces threaten the development-oriented nature of information society and deteriorate social cohesion, which is composed of trust, sense of belonging, and participation in community life (Chan et al. 2006). Social cohesion is the glue that holds the community together and is necessary for collaborative problem solving (Friedkin 2004).

I. Qureshi · B. Bhatt
Australian National University, Canberra, Australia
e-mail: israr.qureshi@anu.edu.au; babita.bhatt@anu.edu.au

S. Gupta (✉)
Information Systems Area, Indian Institute of Management Ahmedabad, Ahmedabad, Gujarat, India
e-mail: samratg@iima.ac.in

A. A. Tiwari
Marketing Management Area, Indian Institute of Management Rohtak, Rohtak, Haryana, India
e-mail: amit.tiwari@iimrohtak.ac.in

I. Qureshi et al. (eds.), *Causes and Symptoms of Socio-Cultural Polarization*,
https://doi.org/10.1007/978-981-16-5268-4_1

For this reason, social cohesion has been at the centre of global policy as we transition towards a post-pandemic world, and was reflected in Davos agenda 2021 - A Great Reset (World Economic Forum 2021). It has also been acknowledged that ICT-based platforms increasingly shape how and with whom we interact, which has broader implications on social cohesion or lack thereof. ICTs facilitate or constrain our interactions with various socio-cultural groups and our access to various opinions; thus, they have the potential to exacerbates social divides. Therefore, we need a better understanding of the factors that drive polarization. One of our purposes in call for the book chapter was to initiate the process of developing scholarly insight to the causes and symptoms of ICTs induced polarization. We start the book chapter with an overview of the ICTs, its potential, and threat for developing an inclusive, people-centric, cohesive society.

In the modern era of technological advancement, the prime focus is on transformation facilitated by digital technologies (Lyytinen and Rose 2003; Yoo 2010). With the rise in the integration of technological artifacts into various socio-cultural domains such as education, politics, economics, healthcare, agriculture, entertainment, among others, more emphasis is placed on improving the efficient transfer of data and information to the end-user via various channels (Yoo 2010). This transformation requires governing and managing various technological and communication processes that leverage the internet, networks, computing devices, social networking applications, video conferencing, and other media applications and services collectively referred to as *Information and Communication Technology* (ICT) (Shachaf 2008). ICT facilitates accessibility, retrieval, transmission, and manipulation of information for various users in a digital format. In recent years, ICT is playing a significant role in disrupting and transforming socio-cultural environment and in shaping business and society (Kinuthia 2009; Odendaal 2003; Qureshi et al. 2021; Shirazi 2012). However, the impact of ICTs on these areas remains controversial (Qureshi et al. 2018a) and is described as a *double-edged sword* (Qureshi 2009; Qureshi et al. 2021).

It is difficult to deny that the socio, economic and cultural benefits of ICTs have been substantial. ICTs play a vital role in providing communication channels for most people worldwide and connecting government entities with citizens (Welch and Feeney 2014). It is increasingly becoming important even in the less economically developed contexts (Parthiban et al. 2020, 2021; Qureshi et al. 2018a; Riaz and Qureshi 2017; Shalini et al. 2021). ICT is also enabling citizens to raise social issues such as child hunger, women empowerment, mental health, and racial disparity and bringing issues of social cohesion, collective organizing to the forefront (Escobedo et al. 2021; Pillai et al. 2021a; Shirazi 2012; Torero and Von Braun 2006). Additionally, ICT-enabled feedback mechanisms are helping government and non-government organizations assess the need and efficacy of their schemes and policies around various socio-cultural issues (Hota et al. 2021; Jacobs and Weaver 2015). For instance, a social media campaign led by Marcus Rashford – a Manchester United football player, spurred the British government to take a political U-turn and continue its scheme of providing free meals to children (Moore 2021). ICTs provide the potential to bring about technology-based social change by making important information available to the public and hence if used properly, reducing cultural stigma, bias, and ethnic prejudice (Shirazi 2012; Kinuthia 2009; Qureshi et al. 2020, 2021). The integration of ICTs in the transportation sector has opened up an enormous avenue for the public by making global travel affordable, quick, and hassle-free. This facilitates people's global movement, thus promoting the intermix of cultures, food, and art (Law et al. 2019), which has implications for increasing social cohesion.

Moreover, ICT platforms, such as YouTube – an online video-sharing and viewing platform, have provided an ecosystem for creating culture-based content that is made available to the public. Travel vlogs, cultural programs, cultural documentaries, and food vlogs help sensitizing viewers to different cultures (Park et al. 2017). In the same vein, to a large extent, socio-cultural aspects of the world are reflected through ICTs enabled transmission of movies, TV shows, and books (Gorbunova and Petrova 2019). The cable services provide more options to the viewers to look for channels that satisfy their cultural needs. This results in competition within the entertainment industry to provide global content to their viewers. Due to this transition, socio-cultural issues have taken center stage in content consumption by the general public around the globe.[1] Therefore, audio-visual content, such as movies, TV shows, documentaries, and eBooks, has become a powerful medium of engaging people and having a strong influence on shaping our society (Valkenburg and Piotrowski 2017). However, this can have a mixed effect on social cohesion. The choice of channels to find the content palatable to viewers' taste result in individuals globally connected but locally disengaged. For example, critics have argued that expatriates, migrants, and refugees use ICTs to remain connected with their native cultures and might find it difficult to integrate with their host cultures. In such situations, ICTs could increase the social cohesion within these diasporas but weakens the social cohesion within the (geographic) communities they live.

Development through ICT also promotes social innovation (Qureshi et al. 2021). Advances in ICT have led to innovations in a variety of services ranging from healthcare, market linkages to social intermediation (Andreassen et al. 2015; Ferro et al. 2013; Kistruck et al. 2013; Pillai et al. 2021b). In the healthcare system, ICT facilitates a transparent mechanism for accessibility, storage and transmission of vital individual health information such as blood group, medical conditions, allergies and so on. This facilitates a better identification and dispatching of the closest healthcare providers and telemedicine services to suffering individuals. Also, based on the personalized information of users' suitable eHealth and mHealth services could also be provided to them (Crean 2010). In the education system, ICT-enabled services have led to the transformation of the classroom environment,

[1] Understanding Media and Culture: An Introduction to Mass Communication (2010). The eLearning Support Initiative. Creative Commons Attribution. Retrieved from https://open.lib.umn.edu/mediaandculture/chapter/9-2-the-relationship-between-television-and-culture/ (accessed on 12 May 2021).

thereby enabling engaging learning activities such as multimedia-based learning (Bhattacharjee and Deb 2016). Various synchronous and asynchronous online courses provide a platform for a more interactive exchange of learning between teacher and student. The penetration of ICT into governance processes provides a common ground where dialogues between citizens and local government authorities can be exchanged, ultimately leading to sustainable development (Qureshi et al. 2021) through two-way communication mechanisms such as e-voting and e-petition (Tomor et al. 2019). These examples illustrate the potential of ICTs in building vertical linages and facilitating trust and good governance.

The foundation of ICT-enabled social interactions is *the* idea of *social platforms* (Escobedo et al. 2021; Kenney and Zysman 2016; Pandey et al. 2021; Pillai et al. 2021b). These ICT-*enabled platforms* leverage webservice and applications, which users can create, share and express a variety of content that enable social networking (Qureshi 2009; Qureshi et al. 2018b; Taprial and Kanwar 2012). The fundamental aspect of ICT-enabled platforms is to create a strong base of global connectivity amongst large user demographics, to provide a virtual podium where dialogues/viewpoints can be exchanged on a range of topics (Qiu et al. 2021; Qureshi et al. 2020). ICT-enabled platforms also open up avenues for businesses to have an open and direct relationship with their customers, thus facilitating improved business decisions and profitability (Setia et al. 2020). ICT-enabled platforms also help maximize public awareness with regards to health issues, emergency services, and disaster-related information, to name a few. Moreover, government bodies can leverage ICTs to have regular citizen engagement, thereby improving the transparency and efficiency of their operations (Bonsón et al. 2012; Qiu et al. 2021). There are various ICT-enabled platforms that serve a broad spectrum of user-defined needs, some of which are shown in Fig. 1.

As discussed above, ICT-enabled platforms have covered almost every aspect of today's societal and business world due to their unparalleled advantages. However, ICT-enabled platforms also have detrimental consequences for society, such as the spread of misinformation, cyberbullying, cybercrime, and the dark web, as described subsequently. In the next sections, we elaborate on these aspects of ICT-enabled platforms as they provide rich insights on the causes and symptoms of polarization in social media and could help in formulating solutions to mitigate excessive divisions.

1.1 Spread of Misinformation

Any false or inaccurate information that is broadcasted, posted, or relayed on social media is termed misinformation. Misinformation can be broadly classified into an unintentional spread of misinformation and an intentional spread of misinformation (Tandoc Jr et al. 2018; Wu et al. 2019). Unintentional spread of misinformation is defined as the type of information that gets disseminated on ICT-enabled platforms by users who trust their source, such as their family members, friends, colleagues,

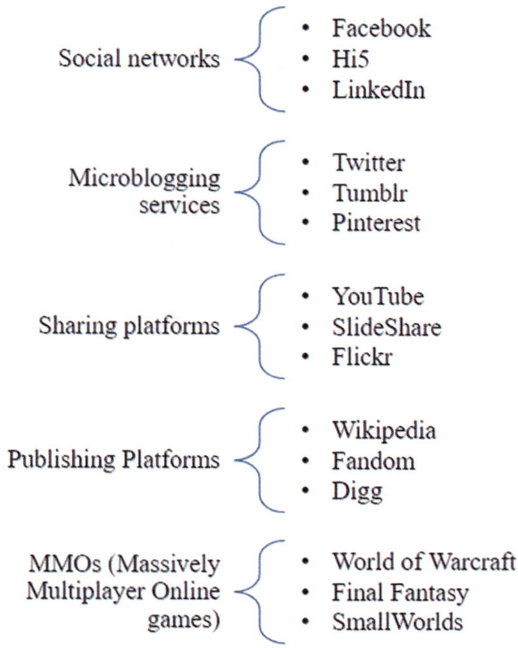

Fig. 1 Various ICT-enabled platforms

and or various social media influencers. Intentional spread of misinformation is a type of information that has premeditated intentions of deceiving the public. The intentional spread of misinformation has an adverse effect on society as it triggers hatred, conspiracy, and propaganda-based mentality in public. In the business sphere, misinformation promotes disseminating false, unverified information regarding a brand, business entity, or organization that aims to tarnish the brand or entity, leading to financial and reputational losses (Ryan et al. 2020). In recent years, many ICT-enabled platforms have come under scrutiny for spreading fake news and promoting certain political and religious propaganda (Farkas et al. 2018; Ghai et al. 2021; Tandoc Jr et al. 2018). Our aim in the call for book chapter was to develop more understanding of all types of misinformation, its role in exacerbating social divisions and mistrust, and the actions required to eradicate all types of misinformation.

1.2 Cyberbullying

Cyberbullying is electronic communication-based bullying targeted at individuals using e-mail services, ICT-enabled platforms, online gaming platforms, and other digital-based messaging applications (Kowalski et al. 2012). Today, ICT-enabled platforms are a breeding ground for numerous trolls - a person who intentionally wants to provoke an emotional response from others by posting messages on social media is termed as a *troll*. Trolling has a negative impact on people's mental health and also increases the risk of worry and distress (Golf-Papez and Veer 2017). Due to increasing concern of mental health amongst the younger generation, ICT-enabled platforms are directing more resources towards AI-based (automated) intelligent systems to detect texts, pictures, and videos containing violent, harmful, hate-related messages (Van Hee et al. 2018). For instance, linear support vector machines are employed that automate cyberbully identification and make it feasible to clean up ICT-enabled platforms from such negative influences/intentions (Van Hee et al. 2018). Evidence shows that causing emotional distress and cyberbullying are the techniques through which Trolls engage in polarizing behavior (Tucker et al. 2018). Trolls are also producers of disinformation, and hence providing critical insights on the processes by which trolls create content and spread it on ICT-enabled platforms has been our goal in this call for book chapters.

1.3 Fraud and Cybercrime

Cyberattacks have taken the highest priority with respect to the national security agenda worldwide and are now treated as a criminal offense, thus leading to a term known as *cybercrime* (Wall and Williams 2017). Cybercrime can be classified into type I cybercrimes and type II cybercrimes (Gordon and Ford 2006). Type I cybercrimes are technology-based such as phishing, hidden Uniform Resource Locators (URLs), and hidden charges. For instance, phishing-related issues on these platforms involve a link that looks very similar to the page an individual wants to visit but actually, the landing page is fake (Chiew et al. 2018). So, once personal details are entered on such dubious websites, the cybercriminals have access to the personal email address, password, and other personal or financial details. Also, these morphed URLs have the potential to install malware on computers/smartphones once they are visited by any user.[2] On the other hand, type II cybercrimes relate more to human-based involvement such as identity theft, and tailgating to name a few (Gordon and Ford 2006). Identity theft is a cybercrime that involves gaining personal information such as tax numbers, health insurance, and other banking-related information so that the criminal can open other bank accounts with such details and use these fake accounts to divert funds and other resources (van de Weijer et al. 2019). Tailgating is a social engineering-based attack wherein cyber threat actor(s) trick employees to gain software-controlled access into company premises (Gordon and Ford 2006). Deibert (2019) notes how polarizing leaders or leaders with authoritarian tendencies have used cheap yet effective digital social-engineering campaigns to shape public opinions and advanced their divisive agenda.

[2] Top 5 social media scams (April 24, 2019), NortonLifeLock, retrieved from https://us.norton.com/internetsecurity-online-scams-top-5-social-media-scams.html?aid=social_media_scams

Consequently, in our call for chapters, we sought to bring attention to the actors and the processes of socio-cultural polarization.

1.4 Dark Web

The dark web is defined as a world wide web in which the client and user communication channels are initiated via unique, customized communications protocols, specific software, configurations, and authorization (Weimann 2016). The dark web facilitates the concealment of critical user information such as geographic location and IP identification. This is made possible because the dark web is a subset of the unindexed part of the worldwide web, generally referred to as the deep web (Chertoff and Simon 2015). Today, the rise of social media popularity has indirectly attracted the penetration of dark web members to provide Crimeware-as-a-Service, which allows renting goods or services from other cybercriminals as needed (Sood and Enbody 2013). Thus, ICT-enabled platforms have brought the dark web services closer than ever before to cybercriminals. The anonymity aspect of social media has led to an increase in dark web activities. It is surprising to note that approximately $3.25 billion was generated by the cybercrime economy worldwide in 2018, out of which illegal pharmaceutical trading, stolen data sales, and financial crimes accounted for nearly 78.5% of the total annual cybercrime economy (McGuire 2019). The dark web shows the growing vulnerability of contemporary institutions to online crime and manipulation.

Social media is in a perilous state today not only because of all the aforementioned concerns but also how they have given rise to the phenomenon known as *polarization* (Prasetya and Murata 2020). The unparalleled access to information and diversity of discourse that social media provides engender partisan news and polarized debates amongst the users (Qureshi et al. 2020). For instance, today's environment of growing civil wars, military coup, corruption, and highly unstable state of governance in multiple countries has led to an influx of immigrants in various countries wherein different political parties are contradicting each other on the issue of accepting these immigrants (Van der Brug and Van Spanje 2009). These contradicting opinions have spilled onto mainstream ICT-enabled platforms where citizens with different political ideologies are partaking in such debates, thus polarizing the sentiments around the issue (Ekman 2019; Ohme 2020).

2 Polarization

Polarization refers to a phenomenon in which "a small number of groups become highly homogenized internally, but increasingly different and opposed to each other externally" (Lucas and Warman 2018, p 988). It amplifies intra-community viewpoints, exacerbates prejudices and grievances, and divides society into two

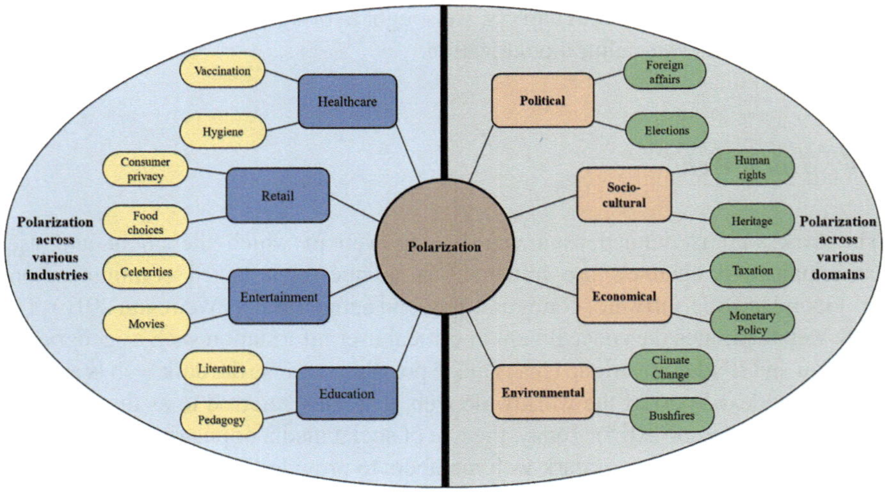

Fig. 2 Representation of polarization in various industries and domains

(bipolar) or more (multipolar) opposing extremes (Grover et al. 2019; O'Hara and Stevens 2015). As such, polarization is a threat to democracy and democratic values (Deibert 2019). Well-functioning democracies thrive on public participation, and independent news channels and media platforms that keep powerful entities accountable and create spaces for expressing differences of opinions (Grover et al. 2019). However, these spaces become a cause of concern when like-minded users get entrapped in their own informational bubble around the topics of critical concerns such as gun laws, societal inequality, and immigration. Figure 2 depicts an overview of polarization across different industries and domains.

2.1 Polarization in Different Domains and Industries

A major cause of polarization in contemporary society is news media (Bolsen and Shapiro 2018). The agenda of a media outlet may be aligned with the ideology of an influential figure in a particular domain, which might result in reporting partisan news (Stroud and Curry 2015). As a result, the news broadcasted to the public through print and social media may be biased (Shultziner and Stukalin 2019). The synergistic effect of homophilic structures on social media-enabled social networks and partisan news leads to the formation of *echo chambers* wherein individuals are largely exposed to conforming opinions (Flaxman et al. 2016). Therefore, individuals with a set of beliefs harbor a high affinity to an agenda that aligns with their views and builds up a no-compromise mentality towards any kind of opposing information.

In the field of politics, polarization stems mainly from the ideological divides between various political parties (Druckman and Levendusky 2019). In a multi-party system, political polarization is highly evident due to the ideological identity. On the one hand, political polarization is associated with some positive benefits, such as keeping the party accountable and using party affiliations to gain support for an agenda that might align with the overall national benefits, such as economic benefits and job creation.[3] On the other hand, political polarization has adversely affected policymaking by creating an environment where negotiation and compromise with other parties are seen as a betrayal of the party's identity.

For instance, following the aftermath of one of the deadliest mass shootings in Las Vegas, the USA, in 2017, the debate on gun laws in the senate and the public eye has ever been more polarized. Gun ownership in the USA has now become a representation of one's political affiliation. In a poll conducted by Pew research center on various topics, gun laws took center stage with a 54-point gap that was deemed as the largest gap witnessed with respect to various other societal issues.[4]

In the healthcare field, polarization can lead to severe adverse effects. For instance, the global COVID-19 vaccine acceptance rates are heavily skewed, with Ecuador having an acceptance rate of 97% while the acceptance rate of Kuwait is only 23.60% (Sallam 2020). There may be several reasons for varying vaccine acceptance rates across nations, but one of the major reasons is ICTs-induced polarization which provides a platform for anti-vaxxers to continue their efforts to hinder the national vaccination program by spreading misinformation (Ashton 2021).

Climate change and environmental sustainability have been a growing concern among scientists and environmental activists due to the depletion of polar ice caps and the rise in sea levels causing severe atmospheric conditions. However, debates in various parliaments around the world have shown polarizing opinions wherein some politicians deem climate change as a hoax created by other countries to derail political agendas (Hoffarth and Hodson 2016). Such polarizing opinions on climate change have spilled over onto social media and have resulted in the formation of echo chambers that insulate people from opposing views (Williams et al. 2015). For instance, 13 federal agencies published a volume on National Climate Assessment and clearly indicated a rise of 7–8 inches of global sea level due to various factors.

---

[3] Rettig, J. (May 27, 2010). Why Political Polarization Might be Good for America: Author Alan Abramowitz discusses why polarization can be healthy for democracy. US NEWS. Retrieved from https://www.usnews.com/opinion/articles/2010/05/27/why-political-polarization-might-be-good-for-america

[4] Harry Enten, Harry (Oct 4, 2017). The U.S. Has Never Been So Polarized On Guns. FiveThi tyEight. Retrieved from https://fivethirtyeight.com/features/the-u-s-has-never-been-so-polarized-on-guns/

However, the former U.S president Donald Trump denied all findings and said, "I don't believe it. No, no, I don't believe it".[5]

Global entertainment industry has also fallen prey to polarization, especially when it comes to the topic surrounding books, cultural festivals, celebrities, and censorship (Matakos et al. 2017; Wojcieszak 2011; Baum and Groeling 2008). The dissemination of misinformation by various media outlets has led to convoluted stories about the events, content, and figures that attract significant attention from the youth (Kahne and Bowyer 2017). Social media enabled thriving online communities wherein individuals interact with other like-minded users lead to reinforcement of users' existing viewpoints. The political ideologies also influence film censorship boards, thus indirectly controlling the representation of critical issues communicated through movies and television serials (Pang 2011).

3 Processes That Lead to Polarization

In order to make sense of the root causes of polarization in various aspects of society, it is essential to understand the processes that lead to polarizing opinions around a certain topic. These processes can be categorized as sociological, psychological, communication, selection and ICT induced processes. We also give specific attention to ICTs induced processes. Although ICTs induced processes of polarization have socio-psychological roots, they also have distinct characteristics. In subsequent subsections, we elaborate on each of these processes by highlighting their theoretical underpinnings:

3.1 Sociological Process

Game theory helps to understand the divergence in policy-motivated voter groups and exhibit out-of-equilibrium belief (Woon 2018). Therefore, behavioral game theory establishes a relation between voter behavior and strategic expectations. Game theory also sheds light on the polarizing standpoint/position of a candidate (Woon 2018).

Muted group theory refers to the lack of ability exhibited by a group to express themselves due to inequity in the language (Korn 2016). The muted group theory is categorized as a communication theory that emphasizes how a group is muted/excluded based on the usage of a particular language resulting in loss of information and thus polarization (Korn 2016).

[5] Sangomla, A. (03 November 2020) . US Elections 2020: A history of Trump's climate change denial. Down to Earth. Retrieved from https://www.downtoearth.org.in/news/climate-change/us-elections-2020-a-history-of-trump-s-climate-change-denial-74075

Social identity theory focuses on intergroup behavior and social attachment (Iyengar et al. 2012). This intergroup behavior has a lasting effect on an individual, which shapes one's identity. Therefore, a strong attachment to a group inflicts a strong group's philosophy and ideology on a group member (Wojcieszak and Garrett 2018).

Protracted social conflict refers to interactions among communal groups based on sensitive topics such as religion, race, ethnicity, and culture (Azar and Moon 1986). These communities are plagued with deep-rooted mindsets that have generally existed over a long period of time. These types of communal interactions are polarized to such an extent that they tend to spread violence, hatred, and fear in society (Azar and Moon 1986).

3.2 Psychological Process

Cognitive dissonance is a phenomenon that explains how those individuals who have negative feelings about themselves experience opinion-reinforcing information (Mullainathan and Washington 2009). These individuals seek opinion reinforcement to overcome feelings such as diminishing self-esteem and self-value, leading to polarized opinions/polarization.

Confirmation bias is another approach that explains how individuals search and favor selective information that tends to support their preconceived notions or beliefs (Westerwick et al. 2017). This selective information-seeking process exhibits a high level of bias in opinion formation as they are interpreted and tailored towards solidifying one's thought process resulting in polarized viewpoints.

Skepticism is defined as an individual attitude that is predominantly based upon the doubting of knowledge, system or a process (Han and Federico 2018). In terms of understanding the polarization process, motivated skepticism is the combination of an individual's tendency to cast doubts over selective information which does not align with their ideology and at the same time reinforcing their preconceived beliefs by accepting only certain information (McCright 2016).

Motivated reasoning is a phenomenon in which individuals indulge in biased reasoning to make decisions that are consistent with their preferred outcomes rather than making decisions based on objective evidence (Taber and Lodge 2006).

3.3 Communication Process

Agenda setting theory refers to a phenomenon adopted by the media industry to manipulate public opinions and concerns about certain issues leading to polarized opinion formation (Hyun and Moon 2016).

Cultivation theory describes how society is influenced by the social reality portrayed on television and media (Shanahan and morgan 1999). Thus, the over-exposure to media shapes the perception of reality and influences one's ability to raise questions on certain issues.

Flaming refers to the hostile online communication and exchange of ideas on various social media-enabled artifacts such as community chat rooms and forums, leading to polarized beliefs between people of different cultures (Cho and Kwon 2015).

Spiral of silence refers to self-censoring of views in a disagreeable opinions climate. This phenomenon is common in political and mass communication spheres (Clemente and Roulet 2015). The fear of isolation silences individuals having opposing views, thus resulting in limitation of the range of public opinions (Kushin et al. 2019).

3.4 Selection Process

Homophily refers to the tendency of certain individuals to form strong bonds with other like-minded individuals on social networks (McPherson et al. 2001). Homophily contributes towards the formation of echo chambers, thus leading to polarized individual opinion (Boutyline and Willer 2017).

Selective exposure refers to biased consumption, retention, and perception of media content (Arceneaux et al. 2013). According to this theory, individuals consume specific content that reinforces their preconceived viewpoint while avoiding contradictory content.

Groupthink is a phenomenon that sheds light on individual behavior and how it affects the group decision-making process (Baron 2005). According to groupthink, individuals confirm to each other as they don't have any exposure to critical evaluation around a certain topic or issue. This leads to minimum conflict within the group as they always arrive at a consensus irrespective of the topic of discussion (Janis 2008).

Herd behavior helps in understanding how individuals act together in a group without any planned direction (Hamilton 1964). Herd behavior is common in strikes, riots and mob violence.

3.5 ICTs Induced Process

Echo chambers refer to information bubbles wherein individuals hear similar voices to their own (Flaxman et al. 2016). Echo Chambers on ICT-enabled platforms may coarsen the online debate, thus distorting the psychosocial lives of individuals (O'Hara and Stevens 2015).

Cyberbalkanization, also known as splinternet, refers to the fragmentation of the internet into various sub-groups or sub-sections based on shared interests (Van

Alstyne and Brynjolfsson 2005). The process of cyberbalkanization is common across nations wherein the web is fenced off into a series of national internets.

Filter bubbles refer to a phenomenon wherein ICT-enabled platforms algorithmically process individual search history, cookies, and location to provide the preferred information to the users (Pariser 2011). Therefore, algorithms inadvertently amplify ideological segregation by automatically recommending agreeable content to users, thus leading to polarization (Flaxman et al. 2016).

Ghettoization is the process of segregation of members of a particular community that has underprivileged social status and a position of lesser power to a restricted area (Wright and Jacobs 1994). In social media ghettos, freedom of speech is curtailed, and only the topics that align with ghetto philosophy are encouraged, thus leading to polarization (Bright 2018).

4 Polarization Due to ICT-Enabled Platformization

The presence of various ICT-enabled platforms has broadened the scope of content creation and consumption. The unique principles of various ICT-enabled platforms allow individuals to engage in a particular forum depending on mood, interest, and requirements. Social media employs algorithms for populating user's feeds wherein user's search history, time spent on each topic, interaction with other users and communities are some of the algorithmic input parameters (Eslami et al. 2015). These parameters support more user engagement as they help in featuring the interest of users (Kumar et al. 2019).

Generally, the use of ICT-enabled platforms has two objectives. The first one lies with how an individual uses ICT-enabled platforms for his/her own benefits, such as receiving news feeds, the latest information on a plethora of products and services, and growing one's social network connections (Baumöl et al. 2016; Warner-Søderholm et al. 2018). The second objective lies in using ICT-enabled platforms by businesses, political parties, and other such entities to influence individuals' decisions such as voting, purchasing, and vaccination (Kushin and Yamamoto 2010; Cao et al. 2014; Ortiz et al. 2019). ICT-enabled platforms exert user influence by employing persuasive algorithms (Beck 2016). A persuasive algorithm is defined as a technology that is based on the idea of modifying an individual's behavior, attitude, or socio-psychological beliefs (Stibe 2015).

Facebook uses a persuasive algorithm with numerous data points as input parameters to analyze the user behavior based on their preferences such as *like and comment* feature on pages, time spent on a particular page, and *reaction* feature as it has more weightage in comparison to *like* feature (Kaur et al. 2019).

Twitter also uses a technique based on the philosophy of a persuasive algorithm (Young 2010). The input parameters to analyze user preferences and behavior are different on Twitter because of the nature of the platform. Twitter is a social networking, micro-blogging platform that allows users to send a 140-character based message, also known as a tweet. As a result, the user interface on Twitter mainly revolves around *retweets* and mentions (Conover et al. 2011). Retweets are ways of endorsing tweets posted by other users, whereas mentions allow the user to direct the conversation to a specific user or community.

Instagram is an ICT-enabled platform that works on the principle of sharing pictures and videos through a mobile application. Instagram employs a machine learning algorithm based on a ranking system that has the ability to customize the users' feed based on factors such as user's interest, timestamp of posts, frequency of usage of an application, and followership as input parameters (Giannoulakis and Tsapatsoulis 2016).

YouTube facilitates video promotion via *watch time* which implies that YouTube algorithm prioritizes videos with longer total viewing sessions over the number of clicks received (Bessi et al. 2016). In the case of YouTube, the algorithm is based on interest-agnostic content discovery, which refers to the means through which highly active users get highly-tailored content (Sun et al. 2016). YouTube engages its users through algorithms based on the *ranking system* and recommendation system (Fyfield et al. 2020; Zhou et al. 2010). Ranking based system determines how a video is performing based on various performance analytics such as the number of clicks, watch time, likes, dislikes, comments, and the upload schedule by content creators. Recommendation system profiles users based on their content history, interaction with a content creators' channel, and genre preference. Therefore, similar profiles are grouped under different categories, and then individual users get video recommendations based on videos watched by similar profiles (Toderici et al. 2010). Since the video recommendations are based on several dependent factors, there are high chances of engaging a user into one particular genre or content (Bessi et al. 2016). Therefore, when liked-minded users get similar recommendations, the process of communication amongst them via the help of the videos can result in the formation of echo chambers.

LinkedIn, a professional social networking platform, segregates news feeds, updates, and posts based on a coupled-system of ranks, interest, timestamp, and user interactions such as likes and comments (Gerard 2012). Various artifacts of LinkedIn encourage users, influencers, public figures, and government officials to participate in exchanging dialogues over numerous topics. As news around work, vacancies, and business are highly tailored to an individual's profile, it influences user's viewpoints (Lee et al. 2014).

In conjunction with algorithmic input parameters on various ICT-enabled platforms, another important factor that affects what a user sees in their feed is a hashtag. As hashtag(s) are attached with social media content, individuals make use of hashtags as search parameters to view and categorize posts. The most trending hashtag in the realm of user's interest shows up first as a result influencing a user's feed.

Therefore, content promotion on ICT-enabled platforms generally follows a broad philosophy of persuasive algorithm and is narrowed down by the implementation of respective features of platforms. Also, such type of algorithm-based content promotion is the leading cause of ICT induced polarization and eventually leads to polarized communities in the socio-cultural realm (Cohen 2018).

During the recent years, research on polarization with a particular focus on social media data has gained traction (Grover et al. 2019; O'Hara and Stevens 2015; Qureshi et al. 2020). Some methodological attempts have also been made to detect fake news, communities and quantify polarization in social networks (Gupta and Deodhar 2021; Gupta and Kumar 2016, 2020, 2021; Gupta et al. 2016; Gupta et al. 2019; Guerra et al. 2013; Kumar et al. 2017; Yang et al. 2019). However, understanding the role of ICTs in causing socio-cultural polarization and symptoms of socio-cultural polarization due to ICTs largely remains underexplored. In our views, understanding these technological aspects, their theoretical underpinnings and their impact on social cultural polarization holds great relevance particularly when technology enabled social media usage has increased exponentially. We believe that processes such as the proliferation of extreme views around socio-cultural activities through cyberbalkanization, and their reinforcement through echo chambers need further investigation so as to evaluate their impact on society at large. Consequently, in our call for papers, we sought to advance the systematic knowledge in ICT induced polarization and to facilitate a meaningful conversation to counteract such polarization.

5 Overview of the Book Chapters

In line with the above argument, we see the chapters in this book as an effort to investigate the causes and symptoms of socio-cultural polarization in the context of Information and Communication Technology. In addition to the overview and concluding chapters, this book is organized into four sections consisting of ten chapters. These chapters have been written by scholars from various countries such as Argentina, Australia, India, Netherlands, and the USA. The first section consists of three chapters related to methods that can be used to model and analyze the processes related to polarization. The second section which is about social aspects of polarization, consists of two chapters covering issues such as bushfires and reservations policy. The third section is related to cultural aspects of polarization such as literary censorship, national education policy, and media bias in Bollywood. Finally, the fourth section of this book discusses aspects related to polarization in information ethics and dealing with misinformation on ICT-enabled platforms. The book concludes with trends and future research issues in the field of socio-cultural polarization.

Chapter 2 deals with the modification of the Schelling opinion model for residential segregation. The chapter describes how the addition of opinion states gives rise to a variant that allows us to combine social influence and mobility dynamics. The proposed model imitates the movement of agents and change of opinion by modelling the behavior of their neighbors. The chapter provides insights into how these mechanisms are responsible for the creation and sustenance of segregation and polarization.

Chapter 3 focuses on ICTs induced polarization which is a result of the widespread misinformation on vaccine inefficacy and the side effects of the COVID-19 vaccine. The chapter explains how, due to the misinformation spread on the Covid-19 vaccines, a section of the society exhibited hesitancy towards vaccines. This chapter employs simulation-based model of dynamical co-evolution in adaptive networks to explain polarization around vaccination. The opinion formation on social media is modelled on comments posted under COVID-19 related YouTube videos. The experiments reveal that the degree of polarization on online discourse increases with recency in time.

Chapter 4 demonstrates the rise and propagation of fake news by various YouTube channel owners with a complete focus on the materialistic goals of increasing viewership and subscribers. An increase in fake news viewership results in the emergence of polarizing opinions amongst viewers and subscriber base. This chapter helps to understand the behavior of users (viewers and subscribers) by employing epidemiological modeling.

Chapter 5 uses the Australian bushfire (2019–2020) as a case study to demonstrates the social and environmental cost of political polarization. This chapter brings attention to social media echo-chambers in reinforcing and perpetuating extreme political positions on the causes and mitigation of bushfires. The chapter uses narrative analysis and identifies polarization rooted in economic vs environment logic and short terms vs long term time horizon. The paper proposes a hybrid logic to address polarization around environmental issues.

Chapter 6 aims to understand how ICTs have been responsible for the formation of public opinion around the issue of Indian reservation policies and the affirmative action policies in the U.S. The central argument of this paper is that even though ICT facilitated idea mediation with respect to equality and justice, it failed in recognition of racial and caste oppression over centuries (cf. Bhardwaj et al. 2021; Bhatt et al. 2022; Sutter et al. 2022).

Chapter 7 sheds light on literary censorship in modern India. The first part of the chapter investigates fundamental reasons behind the cyber-attacks on literary authors and texts. The second part of the chapter deals with understanding the role of ICT that shapes the modern trends of literary censorship in India. The insights gained from this chapter reveal that among various socio-cultural issues, literary censorship is also one of the major issues that leads to polarization.

Chapter 8 aims at understanding the reasons for social media-induced polarization and opinion formation on the National Education Policy (NEP) 2020 in India. The outcome of this chapter consisting of a two-step process of data acquisition and data monitoring reveals an increased use of phrases about NEP 2020 on Twitter while indicating an existence of attitudinal change by social media users towards NEP 2020.

Chapter 9 pertains to media bias in Bollywood- an Indian film industry based in Mumbai. This chapter identifies main controversial topics and key media outlets publishing about them on their online portals. Based on the sentiment score, percentages of negative and positive words of each of the controversies, media outlets were found to be belonging to two clusters exhibiting opposing bias.

Chapter 10 discusses the ethical aspects of big data and the increasing polarization in information ethics. It employs two ethical approaches, the common good approach and the individual liberty approach to conceptualize two extreme views on big data uses. Using the Chinese social credit system (CSC) as a case study, this chapter demonstrates how big data is either seen as an innovation to promote the common good (i.e., good governance, fairness, and social harmony) or as a tool to increase surveillance and control in society. The paper proposes contextual integrity theory as a theoretical concept to bridge these opposing views.

Chapter 11 discusses how online social media has become a vehicle for spreading rumors and demonstrates its implications on individuals, organizations, and social institutions. This chapter designs a systematic framework to address the spread of rumors on social media. The chapter identifies various forms of false and unverified information, such as, gossip, legends, propaganda, conspiracy theory, fake news, pseudoscience, and misinformation, and discusses their relevance and impact on multiple stakeholders. This chapter also provides insights on various perspectives that enable the exploration of epidemic management and their role in addressing rumors.

Chapter 12 provides insights on the current status of the research in polarization and discusses avenues for future research.

Overall, the breadth and depth of the topics on polarization explored in these book chapters, the methodological diversity employed to examine the phenomena, and the solutions proposed to bridge division and extremism make the book a timely scholarly contribution. It is our hope that this book will bring more awareness to the causes, symptoms, and consequences of ICT-induced polarization and will create a dialogue among multiple stakeholders to build digital social infrastructure for promoting cross-cutting ties and social cohesion.

References

Andreassen HK, Kjekshus LE, Tjora A (2015) Survival of the project: a case study of ICT innovation in health care. Soc Sci Med 132:62–69

Arceneaux K, Johnson M, Cryderman J (2013) Communication, persuasion, and the conditioning value of selective exposure: like minds may unite and divide but they mostly tune out. Polit Commun:213–231

Ashton J (2021) COVID-19 and the anti-vaxxers. J R Soc Med 114(1):42–43

Azar EE, Moon CI (1986) Managing protracted social conflicts in the third world: facilitation and development diplomacy. Millennium 15(3):393–406

Baron RS (2005) So right it's wrong: groupthink and the ubiquitous nature of polarized group decision making. In: Advances in experimental social psychology, pp 219–253

Baum MA, Groeling T (2008) New media and the polarization of American political discourse. Polit Commun 25(4):345–365

Baumöl U, Hollebeek L, Jung R (2016) Dynamics of customer interaction on social media platforms. Electron Mark 26(3):199–202

Beck E (2016) A theory of persuasive computer algorithms for rhetorical code studies. Enculturation 23

Bessi A, Zollo F, Del Vicario M, Puliga M, Scala A, Caldarelli G, Uzzi B, Quattrociocchi W (2016) Users polarization on Facebook and Youtube. PLoS One 11(8):e0159641
Bhardwaj A, Mishra SK, Qureshi I, Kumar KK, Konrad AM, Seidel MDL, Bhatt B (2021) Bridging caste divides: middle-status ambivalence, elite closure, and lower-status social withdrawal. J Manag Stud 58(8):2111–2136
Bhatt B, Qureshi I, Sutter C (2022) How do intermediaries build inclusive markets? The role of the social context. J Manag Stud
Bhattacharjee B, Deb K (2016) Role of ICT in 21st century's teacher education. Int J Edu Inf Stud 6:1–6
Bolsen T, Shapiro MA (2018) The US news media, polarization on climate change, and pathways to effective communication. Environ Commun 12(2):149–163
Bonsón E, Torres L, Royo S, Flores F (2012) Local e-government 2.0: social media and corporate transparency in municipalities. Gov Inf Q 29(2):123–132
Boutyline A, Willer R (2017) The social structure of political echo chambers: variation in ideological homophily in online networks. Polit Psychol:551–569
Bright J (2018) Explaining the emergence of political fragmentation on social media: the role of ideology and extremism. J Comput-Mediat Commun 23(1):17–33
Cao P, Meister S, Klante O (2014) How social media influence apparel purchasing behavior. Mark Rev St Gallen 31(6):77–86
Chan J, To, H. P, Chan E (2006) Reconsidering social cohesion: developing a definition and analytical framework for empirical research. Soc Indic Res 75(2):273–302
Chertoff M, Simon T (2015) The impact of the dark web on internet governance and cyber security.
Chiew KL, Yong KSC, Tan CL (2018) A survey of phishing attacks: their types, vectors and technical approaches. Expert Syst Appl 106:1–20
Cho D, Kwon KH (2015) The impacts of identity verification and disclosure of social cues on flaming in online user comments. Comput Hum Behav 51:363–372
Clemente M, Roulet TJ (2015) Public opinion as a source of deinstitutionalization: a "spiral of silence" approach. Acad Manag Rev 40(1):96–114
Cohen JN (2018) Exploring echo-systems: how algorithms shape immersive media environments. J Media Lit Educ 10(2):139–151
Conover MD, Ratkiewicz J, Francisco M, Gonçalves B, Menczer F, Flammini A (2011) Political polarization on twitter. In: Fifth international AAAI conference on weblogs and social media. ICWSM, Barcelona
Crean KW (2010) Accelerating innovation in information and communication technology for health. Health Aff 29(2):278–283
Deibert RJ (2019) The road to digital unfreedom: three painful truths about social media. J Democr 30(1):25–39
Druckman JN, Levendusky MS (2019) What do we measure when we measure affective polarization? Public Opin Q 83(1):114–122
Ekman M (2019) Anti-immigration and racist discourse in social media. Eur J Commun 34(6):606–618
Escobedo M, Zheng Z, Bhatt B (2021) Socially oriented sharing economy platform in regional Australia: a Polanyian analysis. In: Edited volume: sharing economy at the base of the pyramid: opportunities and challenges. Springer. eBook ISBN 978-981-16-2414-8, Singapore. https://doi.org/10.1007/978-981-16-2414-8
Eslami M, Aleyasen A, Karahalios K, Hamilton K, Sandvig C (2015, February) Feedvis: a path for exploring news feed curation algorithms. In: Proceedings of the 18th ACM conference companion on Computer Supported Cooperative Work & Social Computing, pp 65–68
Farkas J, Schou J, Neumayer C (2018) Cloaked Facebook pages: exploring fake Islamist propaganda in social media. New Media Soc 20(5):1850–1867
Ferro E, Caroleo B, Leo M, Osella M, Pautasso E (2013, May) The role of ICT in smart cities governance. In: Proceedings of 13th international conference for E-democracy and open government. Donau-Universität Krems, pp 133–145

Flaxman S, Goel S, Rao JM (2016) Filter bubbles, echo chambers, and online news consumption. Public Opin Q 80(S1):298–320
Forum on Information and Democracy (2021) Working group on infodemics: policy framework, November 2020. ForumID_Report-on-infodemics_101120.pdf (informationdemocracy.org)
Frankfurt T 2020 How technology is fueling social justice during a pandemic, Forbers (Aug 20, 2020). https://www.forbes.com/sites/forbestechcouncil/2020/08/20/how-technology-is-fueling-social-justice-during-a-pandemic/?sh=2cdc6d564c18
Friedkin NE (2004) Social cohesion. Annu Rev Sociol 30(1):409–425. https://doi.org/10.1146/annurev.soc.30.012703.110625
Fyfield M, Henderson M, Phillips M (2020) Navigating four billion videos: teacher search strategies and the YouTube algorithm. Learn Media Technol 46:1–13
Garfin DR (2020) Technology as a coping tool during the coronavirus disease 2019 (COVID-19) pandemic: implications and recommendations. Stress Health 36(4):555–559
Gerard JG (2012) Linking in with LinkedIn®: three exercises that enhance professional social networking and career building. J Manag Educ 36(6):866–897
Ghai A, Kumar P, Gupta S (2021) A deep-learning-based image forgery detection framework for controlling the spread of misinformation. Inf Technol People.
Giannoulakis S, Tsapatsoulis N (2016) Evaluating the descriptive power of Instagram hashtags. J Innov Digit Ecosyst 3(2):114–129
Golf-Papez M, Veer E (2017) Don't feed the trolling: rethinking how online trolling is being defined and combated. J Mark Manag 33(15–16):1336–1354
Gorbunova IB, Petrova NN (2019) Music computer technologies, supply chain strategy and transformation processes in socio-cultural paradigm of performing art: using digital button accordion. Int J Supply Chain Manag 8(6):436–445
Gordon S, Ford R (2006) On the definition and classification of cybercrime. J Comput Virol 2(1):13–20
Grover P, Kar AK, Dwivedi YK, Janssen M (2019) Polarization and acculturation in US election 2016 outcomes–can twitter analytics predict changes in voting preferences. Technol Forecast Soc Chang 145:438–460
Guerra P, Meira Jr W, Cardie C, Kleinberg R (2013, June) A measure of polarization on social media networks based on community boundaries. In: Proceedings of the international AAAI conference on web and social media, vol 7, no. 1
Gupta S, Deodhar S (2021) Understanding digitally enabled complex networks: a plural granulation based hybrid community detection approach. Inf Technol People
Gupta S, Kumar P (2016, August) Community detection in heterogenous networks using incremental seed expansion. In: 2016 international conference on data science and engineering (ICDSE), pp 1–5. IEEE
Gupta S, Kumar P (2020) An overlapping community detection algorithm based on rough clustering of links. Data Knowl Eng 125:101777
Gupta S, Kumar P (2021) A constrained agglomerative clustering approach for unipartite and bipartite networks with application to credit networks. Inf Sci 557:332–354
Gupta S, Kumar P, Bhasker B (2016, September) A rough connectedness algorithm for mining communities in complex networks. In: International conference on big data analytics and knowledge discovery. Springer, Cham, pp 34–48
Gupta S, Kumar P, Perfilieva I (2019) A community detection algorithm based on granulation of links. ALLDATA 2019:41
Hamilton W (1964) The genetical evolution of social behaviour. J Theor Biol:17–52
Han J, Federico CM (2018) The polarizing effect of news framing: comparing the mediating roles of motivated reasoning, self-stereotyping, and intergroup animus. J Commun 68(4):685–711
Hoffarth MR, Hodson G (2016) Green on the outside, red on the inside: perceived environmentalist threat as a factor explaining political polarization of climate change. J Environ Psychol 45:40–49

Hota PK, Qiu S, Bhatt B (2021) Ethitrade: countering challenges of sharing economy at the base of the pyramid using technology. In: Qureshi I, Bhatt B, Shukla DM (eds) Sharing economy at the base of the pyramid: opportunity and challenges. Springer, Singapore
Hyun KD, Moon SJ (2016) Agenda setting in the partisan TV news context: attribute agenda setting and polarized evaluation of presidential candidates among viewers of NBC, CNN, and Fox News. J Mass Commun Q 93(3):509–529
Iyengar S, Sood G, Lelkes Y (2012) Affect, not ideology a social identity perspective on polarization. Public Opin Q 76(3):405–431
Jacobs AM, Weaver RK (2015) When policies undo themselves: self-undermining feedback as a source of policy change. Governance 28(4):441–457
Janis IL (2008) Groupthink. IEEE Eng Manag Rev 36(1):36
Kahne J, Bowyer B (2017) Educating for democracy in a partisan age: confronting the challenges of motivated reasoning and misinformation. Am Educ Res J 54(1):3–34
Kaur W, Balakrishnan V, Rana O, Sinniah A (2019) Liking, sharing, commenting and reacting on Facebook: user behaviors' impact on sentiment intensity. Telematics Inform 39:25–36
Kenney M, Zysman J (2016) The rise of the platform economy. Iss Sci Technol 32(3):61
Kinuthia W (2009) Educational development in Kenya and the role of information and communication technology. Int J Edu Dev Using ICT 5(2)
Kistruck GM, Beamish PW, Qureshi I, Sutter CJ (2013) Social intermediation in base-of-the-pyramid markets. J Manag Stud 50(1):31–66
Knearem T, Jo J, Tsai C, Carroll J (2021) Making space for support: an exploratory analysis of pandemic-response mutual aid platforms. In: C&T '21: Proceedings of the 10th international conference on Communities & Technologies – wicked problems in the age of tech (C&T '21), June 20–25, 2021, Seattle, WA, USA. ACM, New York, NY, USA 6 pages
Korn JU (2016) 'Genderless' online discourse in the 1970s: muted group theory in early social computing. Morgan & Claypool Publishers, New York, NY, pp 213–230
Kowalski RM, Giumetti GW, Schroeder AN, Reese HH (2012) Cyber bullying among college students: evidence from multiple domains of college life. In: Misbehavior online in higher education. Emerald Group Publishing Limited
Kumar P, Gupta S, Bhasker B (2017) An upper approximation based community detection algorithm for complex networks. Decis Support Syst 96:103–118
Kumar A, Salo J, Li H (2019) Stages of user engagement on social commerce platforms: analysis with the navigational clickstream data. Int J Electron Commer 23(2):179–211
Kushin MJ, Yamamoto M (2010) Did social media really matter? College students' use of online media and political decision making in the 2008 election. Mass Commun Soc 13(5):608–630
Kushin MJ, Yamamoto M, Dalisay F (2019) Societal majority, Facebook, and the spiral of silence in the 2016 US presidential election. Social Media+Society 5(2):1–11
Law R, Leung D, Chan ICC (2019) Progression and development of information and communication technology research in hospitality and tourism. Int J Contem Hosp Manag
Lee JK, Choi J, Kim C, Kim Y (2014) Social media, network heterogeneity, and opinion polarization. J Commun 64(4):702–722
Lucas C, Warman R (2018) Disrupting polarized discourses: can we get out of the ruts of environmental conflicts? Environ Plan C: Politics Space 36(6):987–1005
Lyytinen K, Rose GM (2003) The disruptive nature of information technology innovations: the case of internet computing in systems development organizations. MIS Q:557–596
Matakos A, Terzi E, Tsaparas P (2017) Measuring and moderating opinion polarization in social networks. Data Min Knowl Disc 31(5):1480–1505
McCright AM (2016) Anti-reflexivity and climate change skepticism in the US general public. Hum Ecol Rev 22(2):77–108
McGuire M (2019) Social media platforms and the cybercrime economy: the next chapter of into the web of profit. Bromium Report
McPherson M, Smith-Lovin L, Cook JM (2001) Birds of a feather: homophily in social networks. Annu Rev Sociol 27(1):415–444

Moore K (2021) Football is not 'a matter of life and death'. It is far less important than that. Football and the COVID-19 pandemic in England. Soccer Soc 22(1–2):43–57
Mullainathan S, Washington E (2009) Sticking with your vote: cognitive dissonance and political attitudes. Am Econ J Appl Econ 1(1):86–111
O'Hara K, Stevens D (2015) Echo chambers and online radicalism: assessing the Internet's complicity in violent extremism. Policy Internet 7(4):401–422
Odendaal N (2003) Information and communication technology and local governance: understanding the difference between cities in developed and emerging economies. Comput Environ Urban Syst 27(6):585–607
Ohme J (2020) Algorithmic social media use and its relationship to attitude reinforcement and issue-specific political participation–the case of the 2015 European immigration movements. J Inf Technol Politics:1–19
Ortiz RR, Smith A, Coyne-Beasley T (2019) A systematic literature review to examine the potential for social media to impact HPV vaccine uptake and awareness, knowledge, and attitudes about HPV and HPV vaccination. Hum Vaccines Immunother 15(7–8):1465–1475
Pandey M, Bhati M, Shukla DM, Qureshi I (2021) Resourcing and value creation: a case of sharing economy model at the base of the pyramid. In: Qureshi I, Bhatt B, Shukla DM (eds) Sharing economy at the base of the pyramid: opportunity and challenges. Springer, Singapore
Pang L (2011) The state against ghosts: a genealogy of China's film censorship policy. Screen 52(4):461–476
Pariser E (2011) The filter bubble: what the internet is hiding from you. Penguin UK
Park M, Park J, Baek YM, Macy M (2017) Cultural values and cross-cultural video consumption on YouTube. PLoS One 12(5):e0177865
Parthiban R, Qureshi I, Bandyopadhyay S, Bhatt B, Jaikumar S (2020) Leveraging ICT to overcome complementary institutional voids: insights from institutional work by a social enterprise to help marginalized. Inf Syst Front:1–21
Parthiban R, Qureshi I, Bandyopadhyay S, Jaikumar S (2021) Digitally mediated value creation for non-commodity base of the pyramid producers. Int J Inf Manag 56:102256
Pillai V, Pandey M, Bhatt B (2021a) Social sustainability at the BOP through building inclusive social capital: a case study of Drishtee. In: Edited volume: sharing economy at the base of the pyramid: Opportunities and challenges. Springer, Singapore. eBook ISBN 978-981-16-2414-8. https://doi.org/10.1007/978-981-16-2414-8.
Pillai V, Shukla DM, Qureshi I (2021b) Social intermediation using sharing economy in India: A case study of Farmizen. In: Qureshi I, Bhatt B, Shukla DM (eds) Sharing economy at the base of the pyramid: opportunity and challenges. Springer, Singapore
Prasetya HA, Murata T (2020) A model of opinion and propagation structure polarization in social media. Comput Soc Netw 7(1):1–35
Qiu S, Xu Z, Bhatt B (2021) The sharing economy platforms in rural China: bridging institutional voids through institutional entrepreneurship. In: Sharing economy at the base of the pyramid. Springer, Singapore, pp 75–99
Qureshi I (2009) Influence of computer mediated communication on social capital: a disaggregated approach (Doctoral Dissertation University of Western Ontario, London, Canada)
Qureshi I, Sutter C, Bhatt B (2018a) The transformative power of knowledge sharing in settings of poverty and social inequality. Organ Stud 39(11):1575–1599
Qureshi I, Fang Y, Haggerty N, Compeau DR, Zhang X (2018b) IT-mediated social interactions and knowledge sharing: role of competence-based trust and background heterogeneity. Inf Syst J 28(5):929–955
Qureshi I, Bhatt B, Gupta S, Tiwari AA (2020) Call for papers: causes, symptoms and consequences of social media induced polarization (SMIP). Inf Syst J. Available at: https://onlinelibrary.wiley.com/pb-assets/assets/13652575/ISJ_SMIP_CFP_3-1614604498620.pdf
Qureshi I, Pan SL, Zheng Y (2021) Digital social innovation: an overview and research framework. Inf Syst J
Riaz S, Qureshi I (2017) Emergence of a new institutional logic: shaping the institutionally complex field of community radio in India. Res Sociol Organ 50:383–418

Ryan CD, Schaul AJ, Butner R, Swarthout JT (2020) Monetizing disinformation in the attention economy: the case of genetically modified organisms (GMOs). Eur Manag J 38(1):7–18
Sallam M (2020) COVID-19 vaccine hesitancy worldwide: a systematic review of vaccine acceptance rates. medRxiv. https://doi.org/10.1101/2020.12.28.20248950
Setia P, Soh F, Deng K (2020) Platformizing organizations: a synthesis of the literature. Oxford Research Encyclopedia of Business and Management
Shachaf P (2008) Cultural diversity and information and communication technology impacts on global virtual teams: an exploratory study. Inf Manag 45(2):131–142
Shalini, Manoharan B, Parthiban R, Qureshi I, Bhatt B, Rakshit K (2021) Digital technology-enabled transformative consumer responsibilisation: a case study. Eur J Mark
Shanahan J, Morgan M (1999) Television and its viewers: cultivation theory and research. Cambridge University Press
Shirazi F (2012) Information and communication technology and women empowerment in Iran. Telematics Inform 29(1):45–55
Shultziner D, Stukalin Y (2019) Distorting the news? The mechanisms of partisan media bias and its effects on news production. Polit Behav:1–22
Sood AK, Enbody RJ (2013) Crimeware-as-a-service—a survey of commoditized crimeware in the underground market. Int J Crit Infrastruct Prot 6(1):28–38
Stibe A (2015, June) Advancing typology of computer-supported influence: moderation effects in socially influencing systems. In: International conference on persuasive technology. Springer, Cham, pp 253–264
Stroud NTJ, Curry A (2015) The polarizing effects of partisan and mainstream news. American Gridlock: The Sources, Character, and Impact of Political Polarization:337–354
Sun L, Wang X, Wang Z, Zhao H, Zhu W (2016) Social-aware video recommendation for online social groups. IEEE Trans Multimed 19(3):609–618
Sutter C, Bhatt B, Qureshi I (2022) What makes resource provision an effective means of poverty alleviation? A resourcing perspective. Organ Sci. https://doi.org/10.1287/orsc.2021.1570
Taber CS, Lodge M (2006) Motivated skepticism in the evaluation of political beliefs. Am J Polit Sci 50(3):755–769
Tandoc EC Jr, Lim ZW, Ling R (2018) Defining “fake news” a typology of scholarly definitions. Digit Journal 6(2):137–153
Taprial V, Kanwar P (2012) Understanding social media. Bookboon
Toderici G, Aradhye H, Pasca M, Sbaiz L, Yagnik J (2010, June) Finding meaning on Youtube: tag recommendation and category discovery. In: 2010 IEEE computer society conference on computer vision and pattern recognition. IEEE, pp 3447–3454
Tomor Z, Meijer A, Michels A, Geertman S (2019) Smart governance for sustainable cities: findings from a systematic literature review. J Urban Technol:3–27
Torero M, Von Braun J (eds) (2006) Information and communication technologies for development and poverty reduction: the potential of telecommunications. The International Food Policy Research Institute
Tucker JA, Guess A, Barberá P, Vaccari C, Siegel A, Sanovich S, Stukal D, Nyhan B (2018) Social media, political polarization, and political disinformation: a review of the scientific literature. Political polarization, and political disinformation: A review of the scientific literature (March 19, 2018)
UN ECOSOC (2021) Progress made in the implementation of and follow-up to the outcomes of the world summit on the information society at the regional and international levels. United Nations, New York
Valkenburg PM, Piotrowski JT (2017) Plugged in: how media attract and affect youth. Yale University Press
Van Alstyne M, Brynjolfsson E (2005) Global village or cyber-balkans? Modeling and measuring the integration of electronic communities. Manag Sci 51(6):851–868
van de Weijer SG, Leukfeldt R, Bernasco W (2019) Determinants of reporting cybercrime: a comparison between identity theft, consumer fraud, and hacking. Eur J Criminol 16(4):486–508

Van der Brug W, Van Spanje J (2009) Immigration, Europe and the 'new' cultural dimension. Eur J Polit Res 48(3):309–334
Van Hee C, Jacobs G, Emmery C, Desmet B, Lefever E, Verhoeven B, Daelemans W, Hoste V (2018) Automatic detection of cyberbullying in social media text. PLoS One 13(10):e0203794
Wall DS, Williams M (eds) (2017) Policing cybercrime: networked and social media technologies and the challenges for policing. Routledge
Warner-Søderholm G, Bertsch A, Sawe E, Lee D, Wolfe T, Meyer J, Fatilua UN (2018) Who trusts social media? Comput Hum Behav 81:303–315
Weimann G (2016) Going dark: Terrorism on the dark web. Stud Confl Terror 39(3):195–206
Welch EW, Feeney MK (2014) Technology in government: how organizational culture mediates information and communication technology outcomes. Gov Inf Q 31(4):506–512
Westerwick A, Johnson BK, Knobloch-Westerwick S (2017) Confirmation biases in selective exposure to political online information: source bias vs. content bias. Commun Monogr 84(3):343–364
Williams HT, McMurray JR, Kurz T, Lambert FH (2015) Network analysis reveals open forums and echo chambers in social media discussions of climate change. Glob Environ Chang 32:126–138
Wojcieszak M (2011) Deliberation and attitude polarization. J Commun 61(4):596–617
Wojcieszak M, Garrett RK (2018) Social identity, selective exposure, and affective polarization: how priming national identity shapes attitudes toward immigrants via news selection. Hum Commun Res 44(3):247–273
Woon J (2018) Primaries and candidate polarization: behavioral theory and experimental evidence. Am Polit Sci Rev 112(4):826–843
World Economic Forum (2021) World leaders urge mindset change to build trust, foster collective action in the year ahead. 29th June, 2021, https://www.weforum.org/press/2021/01/world-leaders-urge-mindset-change-to-build-trust-foster-collective-action-in-the-year-ahead/
Wright R, Jacobs J (1994) Male flight from computer work: a new look at occupational resegregation and ghettoization. Am Sociol Rev:511–536
Wu L, Morstatter F, Carley KM, Liu H (2019) Misinformation in social media: definition, manipulation, and detection. ACM SIGKDD Explorations Newslett 21(2):80–90
Yang S, Shu K, Wang S, Gu R, Wu F, Liu H (2019, July) Unsupervised fake news detection on social media: a generative approach. In: proceedings of the AAAI conference on artificial intelligence, Vol 33, No. 01, pp 5644–5651
Yoo Y (2010) Computing in everyday life: a call for research on experiential computing. MIS Q:213–231
Young MM (2010, June) Twitter me: Using micro-blogging to motivate teenagers to exercise. In: International conference on design science research in information systems. Springer, Berlin/Heidelberg, pp 439–448
Zeller M (2021) Extremists thrive in times of crisis: the COVID-19 pandemic is no exception, Open Democracy, 12 May 2020 https://www.opendemocracy.net/en/global-extremes/extremists-strive-times-crisis-covid-19-pandemic-no-exception/
Zhou R, Khemmarat S, Gao L (2010, November) The impact of YouTube recommendation system on video views. In: Proceedings of the 10th ACM SIGCOMM conference on internet measurement, pp 404–410

Part I
Techniques and Methods

A Schelling-Opinion Model Based on Integration of Opinion Formation with Residential Segregation

Victoria Arcón, Juan Pablo Pinasco, and Inés Caridi

Abstract Residential segregation is a social and economic issue of concern, with implications at the economic, educational, and health levels. Fifty years ago, Schelling introduced a model of interacting agents of two types to warn that mild discriminatory mechanisms can still generate high global segregation levels. That work gave rise to many variants and was a pioneer in the agent-based approach to model social phenomena. In this work, we add a second feature to agents, their opinion state, giving rise to a variant that allows us to combine two mechanisms (social influence and mobility dynamics), which could relate to the emergence of polarized neighborhoods. Here, unhappy agents can move to another place (as in the classical Schelling model) or change opinions by imitating one of their neighbors. We show that these mechanisms create and sustain both segregation and polarization, by creating echo-chambers dynamically. We present results about the patterns in which clusters of different types and opinions arise under this model's rules and study their variation depending on the model's weight parameter, which determines the importance of each feature on the agent's level of satisfaction with its neighborhood.

Keywords Residential segregation · Schelling model · Opinion formation · Agent-based model · Opinion polarization

---

V. Arcón (✉) · I. Caridi
Instituto de Cálculo UBA-CONICET, Facultad de Ciencias Exactas y Naturales, Universidad de Buenos Aires, Buenos Aires, Argentina
e-mail: victoria.e.arcon@gmail.com

J. P. Pinasco
Depto. de Matemática and IMAS UBA-CONICET, Facultad de Ciencias Exactas y Naturales, Universidad de Buenos Aires, Buenos Aires, Argentina

I. Qureshi et al. (eds.), *Causes and Symptoms of Socio-Cultural Polarization*,
https://doi.org/10.1007/978-981-16-5268-4_2

1 Introduction

Residential segregation is the concentration of individuals by ethnicity, nationality, or socioeconomic group in different regions of an urban area. This phenomenon is currently present in many cities (Cable, 2013) and comes with an increasing cultural and social diversity product of migrations of the last decades (Quillian, 1999). According to data from censuses and surveys, previous works have shown that residential segregation is associated with ethnic and/or income-level membership (Bischoff and Reardon, 2014; Iceland et al., 2002). Also, urban infrastructure and the development of neighborhoods and suburbs have, in some cases, intensified segregation (Fox, 2017; Sherman, 2014; Wilson, 2009), deepening physical separation of the different socioeconomic groups.

Although it may represent some advantages, residential segregation has negative implications for some of the usual minority and vulnerable groups. It reinforces inequalities in access to job opportunities (Swanstrom et al., 2002), education (Gotham, 2014), health care (Crandall et al., 2013), transportation (Sanchez et al., 2003), and other services (Green et al., 2017). Some experts also pointed out that ethnic residential segregation may help develop racist attitudes and radicalize views regarding migration and minority cultures (Semyonov and Glikman, 2009), contributing to increase the polarization of society.

Socio-cultural behaviors arise from the exchange of information between individuals and, therefore, they are closely linked to how the information flows among the population. In particular, the social ties built and maintained in the local neighborhood are useful to solve concrete local problems (Sampson et al., 1997) and affect the spread of information and behaviors, playing a key role in integrating social groups at higher scales (Granovetter, 1973). Residential segregation directly impacts how these social ties of physical proximity are displayed, drawing boundaries on the structure of information flows. We can think of the segregation process as a dynamical formation of echo-chambers: social fragmentation over the residential space encourages individuals within a group to interact only with their peers. In this case, the collective behaviors of the socio-cultural space that emerge could collide at higher scales, as polarized positions may arise.

Then, it is relevant to understand the residential segregation process along with the formation of habits, practices, norms, or beliefs (hereafter referred to as *opinion*, for consistency with the existing literature). Moreover, it is interesting to explore how social influence at the local level of physical proximity and individual preferences of being surrounded by similar peers, affect each other.

The question of how residential segregation may relate to the polarization of opinions has already been proposed and analyzed previously from theoretical and empirical perspectives (Feliciani et al., 2017; Morales et al., 2019; Waal et al., 2013). Opinion polarization is commonly defined as the process by which, in a given space of opinions, a population gradually divides into groups with an increasing affinity or coincidence of opinions and, at the same time, with an increasing differentiation of opinions between groups (Esteban and Ray, 1994). When polarization is high, the number of opinion groups of significant size is usually small and, in many cases, only two antagonistic opinions can be distinguished.

In this work, we study mechanisms that give rise to groupings of individuals in the physical space for two attributes of different nature: a feature of individuals that is unalterable and traditionally associated with residential segregation (as is the case of ethnicity) and a socio-cultural attribute that is an opinion (with two opposing positions) that can change by the effect of social influence at the local scale.

While we do not analyze how opinions have become polarized into two extremes, our work represents a contribution to polarization studies. The way groupings of people who share socio-cultural values emerge in the residential space can be thought of as a pre-polarization state. In this frame, a region of the territory is polarized when it is occupied almost exclusively by individuals with the same opinion, as opposed to intermediate mixed compositions in which individuals with different opinions live nearby. The polarization of neighborhood composition dynamically creates echo-chambers (Flaxman et al., 2016), as individuals are exposed at the local scale to information consistent with their own views and positions are reinforced.

Thomas Schelling model of segregation (Schelling, 1969, 1971) is a pioneer in the formalization of residential segregation. In this work, we modified his original model by adding a binary opinion state to agents. Thus, each agent has two binary variables: the original one related to the type membership and the new one related to opinion state. We consider an individual level of satisfaction that is a weighted average between the importance of being surrounded by a local vicinity of agents of the same type or by agents of the same opinion. We present rules that define how to update the locations and opinions of the agents trying to improve their satisfaction. This model aims to contribute to segregation and opinion formation research exploring how the mechanisms of social influence and mobility dynamics may relate and contribute to emerging patterns in the physical space.

On the other hand, our model provides a novel mechanism which creates polarized states in a society without introducing negative feedback. It is known that segregation does not arise in opinion models without additional mechanisms, even though it is a widespread social phenomenon.

2 Literature Review

In the late 1960s, Thomas Schelling introduced an agent-based social segregation model (Schelling, 1969, 1971). In this model, agents belong to two different types, representing a binary classification of the population (racial, religious, by income, etc.). Each agent has a preference regarding the composition of its neighborhood: an agent is satisfied when the proportion of agents of the same type surrounding it is at least equal to its tolerance threshold, a general parameter τ. Initially, both kinds of agents are randomly distributed in the physical space. During the dynamics, if an agent becomes dissatisfied, it has an incentive to find another empty space that fits its preference. In the final states, clusters grouping agents by type arise, even for slightly discriminatory preferences.

From a theoretical point of view, Schelling's model showed how the preference of individuals to be surrounded by similar neighbors constitutes an essential element of the segregation process. This partiality can lead to highly segregated collective results, even without being strongly discriminatory. In this sense, he contributed to a new perspective from which to understand residential segregation. Instead of being exclusively subject to strongly direct or centralized discriminatory actions, Schelling opened the debate on the role of the individual preferences in the resulting collective patterns (Clark, 1986; Galster, 1988). Up to that time, most social studies pointed to housing discrimination forms, such as zoning ordinances and restrictive covenants of the real estate market (Mitchell and Franco, 2018), as the main force in explaining residential segregation (Massey and Denton, 1987). The advancement of civil rights legislation and the prohibition of overt forms of discrimination made this explanation re-evaluated. Schelling model was useful to support new hypotheses focused on individual preferences (Clark, 1991). His model has been widely studied from different areas of knowledge (Clark and Fossett, 2008; O'Sullivan, 2009; Pollicott and Weiss, 2001; Vinković and Kirman, 2007), and many variants have been formulated by partially modifying their rule.

In particular, in Caridi et al. (2013, 2017), we interpolate the Schelling model of social segregation with the Voter model, another well-known agent-based model introduced by Holley and Liggett (1975). In the Voter model, agents of two-state opinion can change their mind depending on their nearest neighbor's opinions by following different types of interaction rules (Castellano et al., 2007). We applied this mixed model to the language competition problem, where each agent has associated a binary variable that represents its language. When the agent is surrounded by more individuals of the other language than some tolerance threshold, it may change its place of residence (Schelling strategy) or change its language (Voter strategy). We analyzed the dynamic process and defined measures to characterize the segregation phenomena observed in the stationary states. In the present work, we are taking a similar approach but distinguishing two features of agents separately: opinion, which may change, and type, which is fixed.

In Feliciani et al. (2017), the authors analyzed another merge between the Schelling model and opinion dynamics to address the conditions under which spatial segregation induces opinion polarization. In the model, both dynamics were not simultaneously but successively implemented. Initially, they use a Schelling model to create different segregation levels for a binary type membership variable. Then, they simulate two processes of opinion dynamics (negative influence (Flache and Macy, 2011) and persuasive arguments (Mäs and Flache, 2013; Mäs et al., 2013)) that take into account similarity based on opinion and type membership to update the agent's continuous opinion state. They studied the difference of the spatial patterns of the opinion distribution obtained under each dynamic, focusing on the alignments of type membership and opinion values, in the same spirit that we do in Sect. 4.2.3.

In Klašnja and Novta (2014) the authors use a similar approach and propose a game-theoretic model to analyze the impact of ethnic segregation and polarization in the raising of conflicts. For a binary ethnic classification of the population, high polarization is identified with the presence of two ethnic groups of equal size, while low polarization refers to the situation where one group is a global minority. Authors run the original Schelling model to create samples of hypothetical countries with different levels of ethnic polarization, and then test their conflict model. They show how segregation has a positive effect on conflict when ethnic polarization is low and negative effect when polarization is high. They describe empirical examples (Hindu–Muslim riots in India and the ethnic civil war of Bosnia) that support their findings.

The work in Valdez (2014) addresses the relationship between residential segregation and polarization from an empirical approach. The author analyzes how residential segregation impacts political polarization linked to an increase in votes for anti-immigrant parties. Using data from the 2010 parliamentary election in Sweden, she performed a spatial analysis that reveals that voting for an anti-immigrant party was highly spatially dependent. She correlated the variation in the election's results with the percent of non-western residents in adjacent neighborhoods. Results support the contact hypothesis for which superficial inter-group contact relates to a polarizing increasing political anti-immigrant attitude since segregation decreases the likelihood of meaningful inter-group contact.

Mechanisms involved in processes of socio-cultural polarization have been analyzed by proposing models for culture and opinion formation. In the influential Axelrod model for disseminating culture (Axelrod, 1997) individuals belonging to different cultures can develop q distinct opinions about f different topics. The dynamic rules of opinion updates put into practice the idea that social influence is homophilic, that is, that the probability of a cultural trait (opinion) spreading from one agent to another depends on how many other traits (opinions) they share. The resulting dynamics converge into a global monocultural state when initial cultural diversity is below a critical value, and to the asymptotical persistence of segregated multicultural patterns in another case.

In Gracia-Lázaro et al. (2009) authors explored a variation of the Axelrod model incorporating a Schelling dynamic rule for agent's mobility. They studied how the density of empty spaces in the territory can affect the convergence to a unique global culture. For low values of the density of empty sites, the mobility enhances the convergence to a monocultural global culture. In contrast, for sufficiently high values of density of empty sites, the dynamics can lead to the coexistence of disconnected domains of different cultures.

Another model of global opinion formation combined with a socio-cultural class membership is presented in Galam (2005) for a two-state binary opinion and heterogeneous beliefs. In this model, agents are attached to a social-cultural class characterized by a bias value k, which is the mean value of all individual heterogeneous beliefs within the class. At each step, agents are distributed randomly in different groups within their respective classes to evolve locally by majority rule. In case of a tie, the group adopts one or another opinion with respective probabilities k and $1-k$. This process leads to a full polarization of each class around one opinion. However, the authors also show how the segregation of subclasses of agents living in the same area within a socio-cultural class may produce a coexistence of opinions at the class level.

Authors proposed in Mäs et al. (2010) a model to explain the emergence of clustering of opinions in the actual populations. They added an individualization force to the usual homophilic rules of social influence. An agent's strive for individualization is weak if there are only a few others with similar opinions to its own, while on the contrary, agents are more motivated to differentiate themselves if many others hold a similar opinion. The results show that individualization has disintegrative effects because when clusters grow too large, individualization increases and promotes their splitting.

In Starnini et al. (2016) authors studied a model that combines mobility with opinion formation. Agents are endowed with a continuous opinion variable. They perform random walks of fixed step length and interact with agents they find within a certain distance d. This mobility scheme is intended to reproduce face-to-face interactions in a social gathering. According to the rules of interaction, agents tend to become more similar to the individuals surrounding them and have a higher probability of moving away from dissimilar peers. This feedback between mobility and social dynamics leads to the emergence of a stable dynamical scenario in which groups of like-minded individuals are segregated in physical space, while single individuals constantly leave or join them.

Voter type models converge to a monocultural state. In the opinion dynamics literature, polarization appears due to repulsive effects, bias, or lack of communication among agents with different opinions (due to echo-chambers or epistemic bubbles), see for instance (Baldassarri and Bearman, 2007; Bessi et al., 2015; Deffuant et al., 2002; Mäs et al., 2013; Salzarulo, 2006). Recently, in Saintier et al. (2020); Vazquez et al. (2020), the propensity of agents to support one of the opinions generates quickly a polarized state, which can decay to a single dominant opinion or persist forever. Here, we are introducing a new mechanism for polarization, in the context of mobility and with the possibility of involving mechanisms of segregation.

3 Research Methodology

Thomas Schelling's model of segregation is a suitable starting point for our analysis. The model gives an abstract and general perspective from which it is possible to study the fundamental mechanisms involved in the emergence of individual's groupings in the physical space. Although the model is based on simple interaction rules between agents that are easy to interpret, emergent results are not easy to understand from the individual behaviors.

Agent-based modeling for social dynamics (Epstein and Axtell, 1996; Gaylord and d'Andria, 1999) is an attractive methodological framework for generating and analyzing complex systems (Bar-yam, 2019; Mitchell, 2009). In those systems, the interaction of individuals gives rise to the emergence of collective properties that cannot be easily anticipated from individual behavior. Therefore, this approach provides useful information on the dynamics of the system, and it is appropriate for the study of the macroscopic effects arising from simple microscopic rules of interaction.

We focus on the effect of certain forms of homophilic attitudes whereby individuals prefer to relate to and reside near others with similar characteristics (Boutyline and Willer, 2016). We analyze the patterns in which the resulting groupings from both feature levels unfold in the physical space. We explore whether it is possible to establish a relationship between them.

The implementation of computer simulations is relatively straightforward and provides a convenient technique for analyzing the model under different controllable scenarios and systematically exploring the rules and parameters involved. We ran the simulations in the C language program, and performed the statistical analysis using the software R (R Core Team, 2017). We use the R *ggplot* package (Wickham, 2016) to create graphs and data visualizations.

3.1 *Model Parameters and Rules*

This section presents the two-dimensional agent-based model we work with and introduces their rules and parameters.

Residential Space

A square lattice of side L represents the system's space. Each site means a residential location that can be occupied by an agent. The lattice has periodic boundary conditions, i.e., it represents a torus containing L^2 sites. These periodic boundary conditions allow all sites, both within and at the edges of the lattice, to have exactly eight adjacent sites surrounding them. There are some empty sites. The parameter $\rho \in (0, 1)$ is the density of empty sites and, therefore, $N = (1 - \rho) \times L^2$ is the total number of agents.

Agent's Type and Opinion

An agent's state is characterized by a two-dimensional vector (c, o). Variable c represents its *type* and it is identified with a color: *red* $(+1)$ or *black* (-1). This agent's feature is defined initially and remains fixed throughout the dynamics; we could interpret it as the ethnicity or some anthropological characteristic of the individual set from birth or inheritance, and unchangeable. Variable o refers to the agent's *opinion* and it is also a discrete binary variable that takes values in $\{-1, +1\}$. This feature is allowed to switch during the dynamics. We could interpret it as to be in favor of or against certain socio-cultural beliefs, habits or consumption, new activities, or laws under discussion in the city.

Initially, agents are randomly distributed over the residential space, and the type and the opinion are assigned to agents independently. The parameter R is the proportion of *red* agents, and the parameter Y refers to the initial ratio of agents with an opinion equivalent to 1.

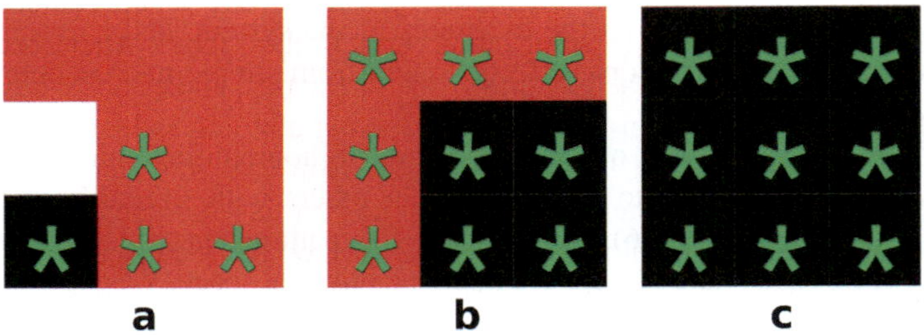

Fig. 1 Three possible neighborhood compositions. There are *red* (+1) and *black* (−1) types of agents. Empty sites are in *white*. *Green marks* correspond to agents who have an opinion *in favor* (+1) and the *absence of the green mark* means opinion *against* (−1). We calculate the level of satisfaction of the central agent i for $\alpha = 0.5$: (**a**) $c_i = 1, o_i = 1, S(i) = 2/7$; (**b**) $c_i = -1, o_i = 1, S(i) = 3/8$; (**c**) $c_i = -1, o_i = 1, S(i) = 1$

Satisfaction and Tolerance
We consider an agent's neighborhood as the eight sites surrounding its location (that is, the Moore neighborhood). We define the level of *satisfaction* of an agent i as:

$$S(i) = \frac{1}{|n(i)|} \sum_{j \in n(i)} \alpha\, c_j c_i + (1 - \alpha)\, o_j o_i, \tag{1}$$

where $n(i)$ refers to the set of i's neighboring agents and parameter $\alpha \in [0, 1]$. The notation c_j refers to the type of agent j and o_j to its opinion. Note that $S(i) \in [-1, 1]$ takes its maximum value when all the neighbors are of the same type and have the same opinion of i, independently of α. On the contrary, the minimum value of the satisfaction corresponds to all neighboring agents of opposite type and opinion. $S(i)$ represents the similarity between an agent and its neighborhood. It is a weighted average where the weight parameter α indicates which feature has more impact on agent's satisfaction: for $\alpha > 1/2$, neighboring agents of the same type are preferred, while for $\alpha < 1/2$, the opinion of neighbors is more relevant. To clarify, we include in Fig. 1 examples of possible neighborhoods and calculate the level of satisfaction of the central agent.

An agent is *happy* if its level of satisfaction is greater or equal to the threshold value τ, which is called the *tolerance* and is the same for all agents. Otherwise, the agent is *unhappy*.

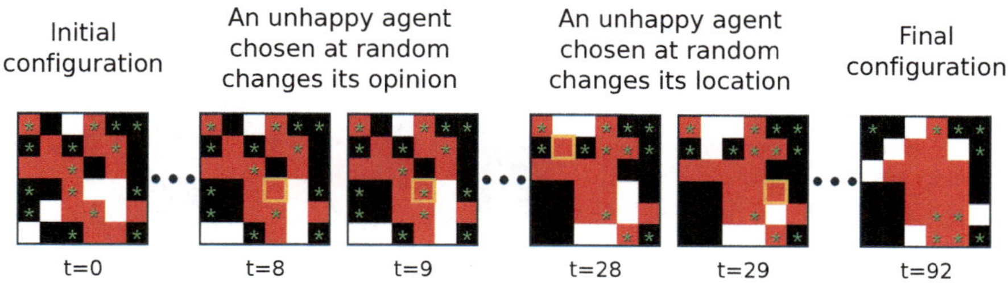

Fig. 2 Residential space configurations for different time steps of a single realization. The side of the lattice is of length $L = 6$, and there are 5 empty sites. The parameters are $\alpha = 0.5$, $p = 0.5$, tolerance $\tau = 0.25$, and $R = Y \approx 0.48$. The initial random configuration is observed at $t = 0$ and the final stable configuration with no unhappy agents is reached when $t = 92$. Time step $t = 8$ is an example of an unhappy agent changing its opinion and $t = 28$, of an unhappy agent changing its location

Dynamic Rules of Interaction
At each time step, an *unhappy* agent is chosen randomly, and it could follow two different strategies:

- With probability p, the agent tries to change its location, selecting a new one at random among the empty sites.
- With probability $1 - p$, the agent attempts to change its opinion.

We can interpret probability p as a balance between the difficulty of migrating and that of changing beliefs or opinions. In both cases, the change is not mandatory. It could fail if the agent does not get happy with the corresponding strategy. We present in Fig. 2 configurations of the residential space corresponding to different time steps of a realization of the model on a lattice of side $L = 6$.

The system evolves until the number of unsatisfied agents is zero or the process stabilizes. We focus on the characterization of the patterns observed in the final configurations, that is, the patterns in which agents are displayed over the residential space once the system reaches equilibrium.

4 Results

We present some results from simulations implemented for $L = 50$, $\tau = 0.25$, $\rho = 0.15$ and different combinations of the values α and p. We also explore other values of tolerance, τ, and density of empty spaces, ρ, not included here.

In the beginning, we randomly choose N sites to fill with agents, and then we assign labels corresponding to their type and their opinion independently. From the initial configuration, we check all agent's satisfaction levels and initialize the set of unhappy agents. At each time step, an (unhappy) agent is randomly selected over that set. The agent tries to change its location (with probability p) or its opinion

Fig. 3 Final configuration for $\alpha = 0.5$, $p = 0.5$, tolerance $\tau = 0.25$ and $R = Y = 0.5$. The lattice size is 50×50 and the proportion of empty sites is $\rho = 0.15$

(with probability $1 - p$). We update the set of unhappy agents according to the change that eventually occurs. The simulation ends when there are no unhappy agents or it reaches the maximum of 900,000 iterations.

For each condition of the parameters, we simulated 50 independent realizations with different initial random configurations. Mean values and standard deviations are taken over those realizations, and we use the notation $\bar{X}$ to refer to the mean value of variable X. The time of execution for each realization is approximately 0, 05 s. We present in Fig. 3 an example of a final distribution of agents obtained for a simulation of the model over a lattice of side $L = 50$.

4.1 Findings

Our model allows us to compare the impact of mobility and the local social influence dynamics over the segregation process. To that end, we measure which of the two proposed strategies at each time step is most frequently taken by agents, particularly regarding their balance parameter p. For this purpose, we defined two measures that synthesize aspects of the dynamic behavior:

- M (moves) is the ratio between the total number of location changes and the number of agents. It represents the number of moves per capita needed to reach the final configuration.
- A (adaptations) is the ratio between the total number of opinion changes and the number of agents. It represents the changes of opinion per capita needed to reach the final configuration.

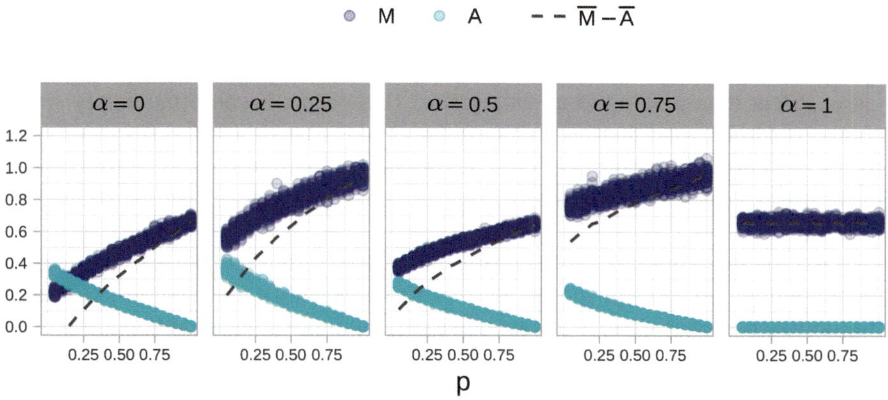

Fig. 4 Points represent moves per capita (M) and adaptations (changes of opinion) per capita (A) needed to reach the final configuration from 50 independent realizations with different initial uniformly random configurations. The dashed line is the difference between the mean values of M and A taken over those 50 realizations, $\bar{M} - \bar{A}$. The parameters of the simulations are $L = 50$, $\rho = 0.15$, $\tau = 0.25$, $R = Y = 0.5$

We refer to opinion changes as an adaptation since each switch of agent's opinion consists of fitting the environment by adopting the majority opinion among neighboring agents. Notice that an agent i changes its opinion if it increases its satisfaction, $S(i)$, to exceed the threshold tolerance value τ. Considering two consecutive times t and $t+1$ and assuming agent i changes its opinion at time t, we have

$$\begin{aligned} S^{t+1}(i) - S^{t}(i) &> 0 \\ \frac{1-\alpha}{|n(i)|} \sum_{j \in n(i)} o_j(o_i^{t+1} - o_i^{t}) &> 0 \\ \frac{1-\alpha}{|n(i)|} \sum_{j \in n(i)} o_j(o_i^{t+1} + o_i^{t+1}) &> 0 \\ \frac{2(1-\alpha)}{|n(i)|} \sum_{j \in n(i)} o_j o_i^{t+1} &> 0 \end{aligned} \tag{2}$$

as $o_i^t = -o_i^{t+1}$. The sum in Eq. (2) counts the difference between the number of neighbors with the same opinion as agent i and the number of neighbors whose opinion is different from i. Then, it is direct to see from the last inequality in Eq. (2) that the agent's i opinion belongs to the local majority at time $t+1$ (as to the minority at t).

In Fig. 4 we show the relation between M and A for different values of p and α. In most instances, the number of movements M is higher than the adaptations

A, even for the lower values of p, where the probability of moving is minimal. This is due to the asymmetry of the reward of following each dynamic. Adopting the local majority opinion is a strategy that satisfies the agent's preference to a lesser extent than moving to an empty site. This occurs because the empty site is chosen randomly, and there is a chance that the new neighborhood fits in with the preferences not only for the opinions but also for the types present. Therefore, agents reject much more frequently the strategy of changing opinion than the strategy of mobility.

Based on the difference of the mean values $\bar{M} - \bar{A}$ for low values of p in Fig. 4, the Schelling dynamics of movements dominate in almost all the cases. However, this domination is of smaller impact when the opinions of the neighbors have more relevance than the types in agent's satisfaction ($\bar{M} - \bar{A}$ is less for $\alpha < 0.5$, than for $\alpha > 0.5$).

4.2 *Final Configurations*

We refer as *initial configuration* to the random distribution of agents over the lattice corresponding to time step $t = 0$. The *final configuration* corresponds to the system's resulting distribution of agents once the simulation finishes (and there are no unhappy agents or the simulation reaches the maximum of iterations).

Besides the differences observed in the dynamics for different values of p, the patterns in which agents are spatially distributed in the final configurations do not vary substantially by modifying this parameter. For this reason, in our characterization of the final configurations, we focus on the results obtained for $p = 0.5$.

In Fig. 5, there are some examples of final configurations. Note that extreme values of α correspond to systems where a single feature is involved in the agent's satisfaction. Consequently, the spatial patterns observed relate only to opinion ($\alpha = 0$) or to type ($\alpha = 1$). For intermediate values of α, agents are grouped to a lesser and greater extent by both type and opinion. In what follows, we define some measures that better characterize this kind of groupings by feature.

4.2.1 Non-mixed Neighborhoods

We consider that a neighborhood is non-mixed when all the agents who reside there are of the same type and/or opinion. As a local grouping measure, we look at the proportions of non-mixed neighborhoods present in the final configurations. In this respect, we distinguish three cases:

- $Unique_c$: Proportion of neighborhoods with agents of the same type but mixed opinions.

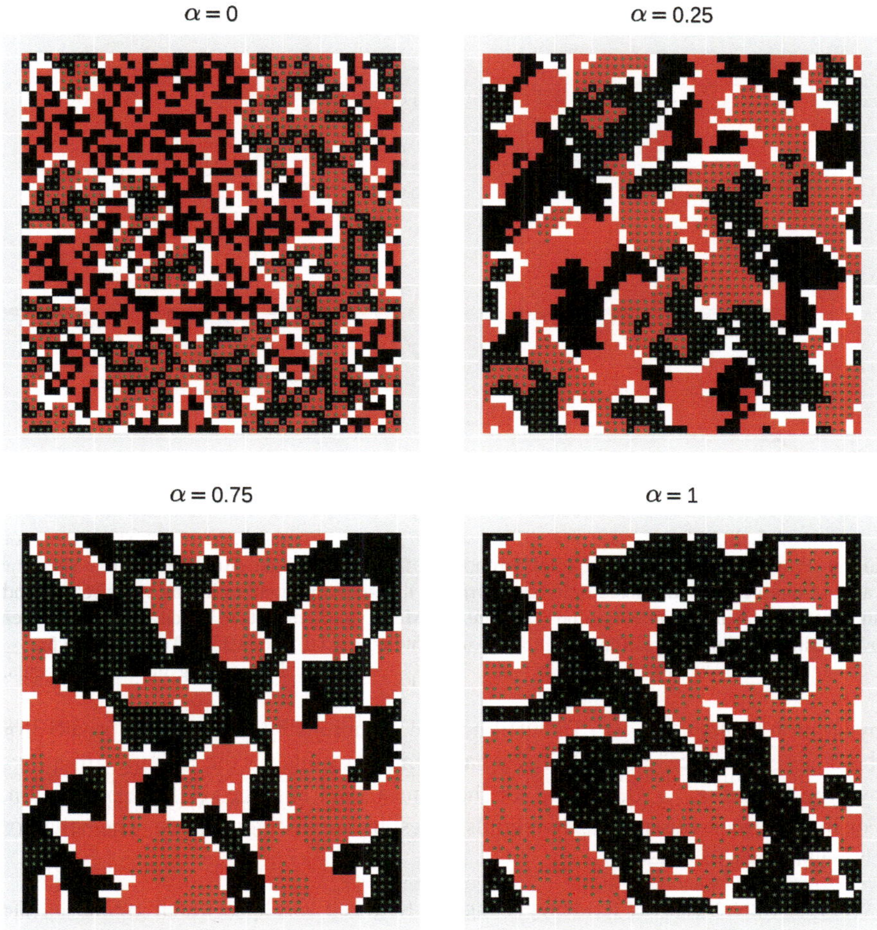

Fig. 5 Four final configurations for $\alpha = 0, 0.25, 0.75, 1$ and $p = 0.5$, and parameters $L = 50$, $\rho = 0.15$, $\tau = 0.25$, $R = Y = 0.5$. Different spatial patterns of segregation emerge: agents are grouped to a lesser and greater extent by both type (*red—black*) and opinion (*green marked—not green marked*)

- $Unique_o$: Proportion of neighborhoods with agents of the same opinion but mixed types.
- $Unique_{c,o}$: Proportion of neighborhoods with agents of the same type and opinion.

The study of these three measures gives a guideline on the kind of local clustering (by type and/or by opinion) that is more frequent in the final segregation pattern.

We show in Fig. 6 the mean values and standard deviations of $Unique_c$, $Unique_o$ and $Unique_{c,o}$ for $p = 0.5$ and various values of α. We see how for the extreme value of $\alpha = 0$, more than 0.75 of the neighborhoods show groupings exclusively

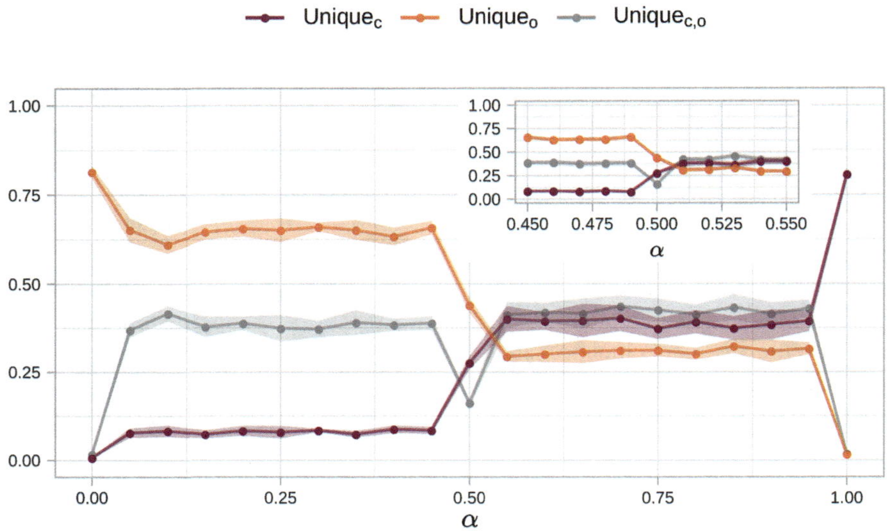

Fig. 6 Proportion of non-mixed neighborhoods in the final configuration. We distinguished the cases of unique type but mixed opinions ($Unique_c$), unique opinion but mixed types ($Unique_o$) and unique type and unique opinion ($Unique_{c,o}$). Mean values and standard deviations are taken over 50 independent realizations for $p = 0.5$, $L = 50$, $\rho = 0.15$, $\tau = 0.25$ and $R = Y = 0.5$

by opinion ($Unique_o > 0.75$), but almost no groupings by type. Symmetrically, for the other extreme case of $\alpha = 1$, we have similar results for the existing groupings by type ($Unique_c > 0.75$) and for the almost total absence of those of opinion. For intermediate values of α, two kinds of results are distinguishable. The behavior change occurs for $\alpha = 0.5$.

For $0 < \alpha < 0.5$, the tendency of agents to group locally is much greater by the similarity of opinion than by type. Slightly more than 0.6 of the neighborhoods present exclusive groupings by opinion. The total local groupings by opinion is close to 0.9 (if we also consider those neighborhoods in which both features are unique: $Unique_o + Unique_{c,o} \approx 0.9$). Local groupings only by type do not exceed 0.13 and, therefore, the difference $Unique_o - Unique_c$ is around 0.5.
For $0.5 < \alpha < 1$, we do not observe an analogous behavior to that described above. Although the number of exclusive local groupings by type exceeds the opinion ones, the measures $Unique_c$ and $Unique_o$ are much closer, with a difference approximately less than 0.25.

For non-mixed neighborhoods, the similarity between an agent and its neighborhood is maximum for one or both features. In particular, this identification between the features of an agent and those of its neighbors allows us to affirm that knowing the composition of an agent's neighborhood provides clear information about its features (and vice versa). It is worth asking if a comparable statement can be made for the general case, including the neighborhoods where the similarity is not maximum. To do this, in Sect. 4.2.2, we use tools from information theory to study this scenario in detail.

On the other hand, neighborhoods with agents of the same type and opinion indicate a local overlap of type and opinion clusters. In Sect. 4.2.3, we propose a more detailed analysis of this phenomenon by introducing a measure of overlapping that is maximum for the cases of non-mixed neighborhoods with unique type and unique opinion, and extends to other possible neighborhood compositions.

4.2.2 Mutual Information

To further understand how the groupings of agents by the similarity of their features allows us to draw conclusions about spatially close agents, we explore to what extent a feature of an agent is related to its neighbors. We calculate the mutual information between the type of an agent and the types of its neighbors (MI_c). Besides, we calculate the mutual information between an agent's opinion and the opinion of its neighbors (MI_o).

The mutual information of two variables X and Y is defined as in Cover and Thomas (2006):

$$
\begin{aligned}
MI(X,Y) &= H(X) - H(X|Y) \\
&= \sum_{x,y} P(X=x, Y=y)\, log_2 \frac{P(X=x)P(Y=y)}{P(X=x, Y=y)}
\end{aligned}
\qquad (3)
$$

where $H(X|Y)$ is the conditional entropy of variable X given that Y is known and $H(X)$ is the entropy of variable X. Mutual information is a measure of the mutual dependence between the two variables. It quantifies the amount of information obtained about one random variable by observing the other random variable and vice versa.

We calculate the mutual information index $MI_c = MI(X,Y)$ with variable X taking values -1 or 1 according to the type of a randomly chosen agent and variable Y is the proportion of its 1-type agents. In our model, the distribution of this variable X is known: R is the probability of $\{X = 1\}$ and $1 - R$ is the probability of $\{X = -1\}$. We calculate the other mutual information index $MI_o = MI(X,Y)$ in an analogous way, where the variables X and Y are defined as before but with respect to the opinions of the agents. We compute both mutual information indexes (MI_c, MI_o) by approximating marginal and joint probabilities of the possible outputs of the variables in Eq. (3) by the empirical frequencies obtained from the simulations.

The extreme scenario corresponds to the maximum value of the mutual information, which in this case is equivalent to 1. The variable X can only take two values. Thus $H(X)$ has 1 as maximum, and the mutual information is maximized when $H(X|Y) = 0$, meaning that the knowledge of a random variable determines the other random variable unequivocally and vice versa.

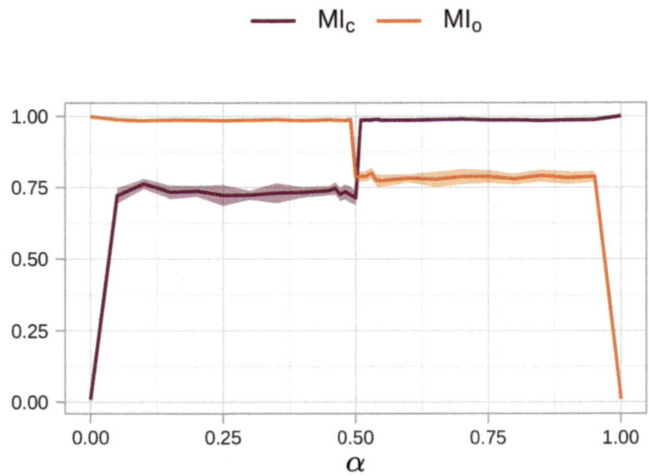

Fig. 7 Mutual information between the type of an agent and the types of its neighbors (MI_c) and mutual information between an agent's opinion and the opinion of its neighbors (MI_o). Mean values and standard deviations are taken over 50 independent realizations for $p = 0.5$, $L = 50$, $\rho = 0.15$, $\tau = 0.25$ and $R = Y = 0.5$

We show in Fig. 7 the values of the mutual information indexes as a function of α for $p = 0.5$. The observed result is remarkable. For $\alpha < 0.5$, values of MI_o are close to 1, indicating that the knowledge of the opinions of the agent's neighborhood gives almost complete information about its own opinion and vice versa. Symmetrically, for $\alpha > 0.5$, the value of MI_c is near 1, pointing that knowing the types of agent's neighborhood gives almost total information about its own type and vice versa.

Nevertheless, in instances where mutual information indexes move away from 1, they maintain a high value around 0.75 (except only at the extremes values of $\alpha = 0$ and $\alpha = 1$, as expected) showing also a close relationship between the agent and its neighbors for the corresponding lower weighted feature.

4.2.3 Overlapping

Finally, it would also be interesting to explore how these spatial patterns of groupings by the features are related. Following the concepts introduced in Feliciani et al. (2017) when measuring local alignment, we quantify to what extent a correspondence on a local scale can be established between the type membership and opinions. We examine the overlapping of opinion clusters and type clusters in the residential space. When we compare a couple of neighboring agents, we assert that there is local overlapping of the clusters if they are of the same type and opinion (overlapping by continuity) or if they differ in both features (overlapping by rupture or jump). If the two neighbors coincide in one feature but differ in the other, there is no overlapping.

According to this idea, we define the overlap index for the site occupied by agent i as:

$$Overlap\ (i) = \frac{1}{|n(i)|} \sum_{j \in n(i)} \frac{c_j c_i\ o_j o_i + 1}{2}, \tag{4}$$

where $n(i)$ refers to the set of i's neighboring agents. Note that $Overlap\ (i) \in [0, 1]$ and it reaches the maximum value 1 when there is an overlapping between agent i and all of its neighbors. The minimum value 0 corresponds to the case where there is no overlapping with any of its neighbors.

We exhibit in Fig. 8 examples of the *Overlap* index for various local clustering configurations extracted from a final state of the system for $\alpha = 0.25$ and $p = 0.5$. Considering the spatial pattern, we observe that the maximum value of the overlap index is reached either in sites located in the interior of type and opinion clusters to which they belong or in sites located at the boundaries of both kinds of clusters.

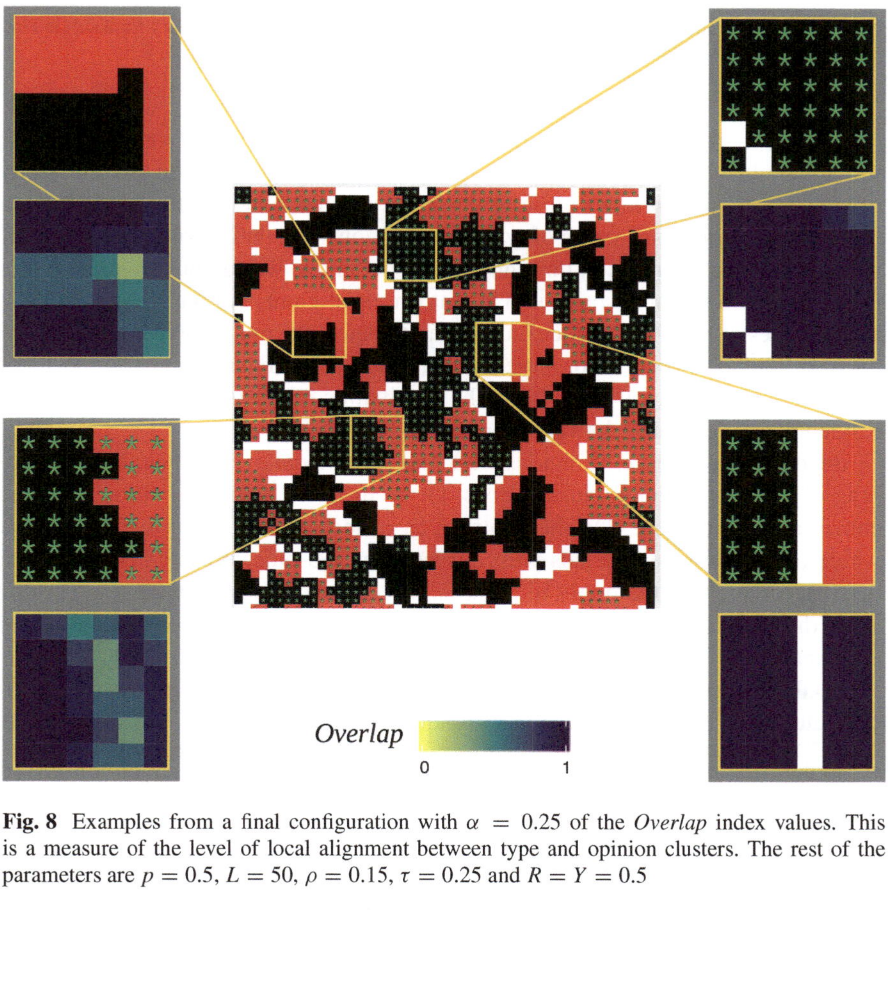

Fig. 8 Examples from a final configuration with $\alpha = 0.25$ of the *Overlap* index values. This is a measure of the level of local alignment between type and opinion clusters. The rest of the parameters are $p = 0.5$, $L = 50$, $\rho = 0.15$, $\tau = 0.25$ and $R = Y = 0.5$

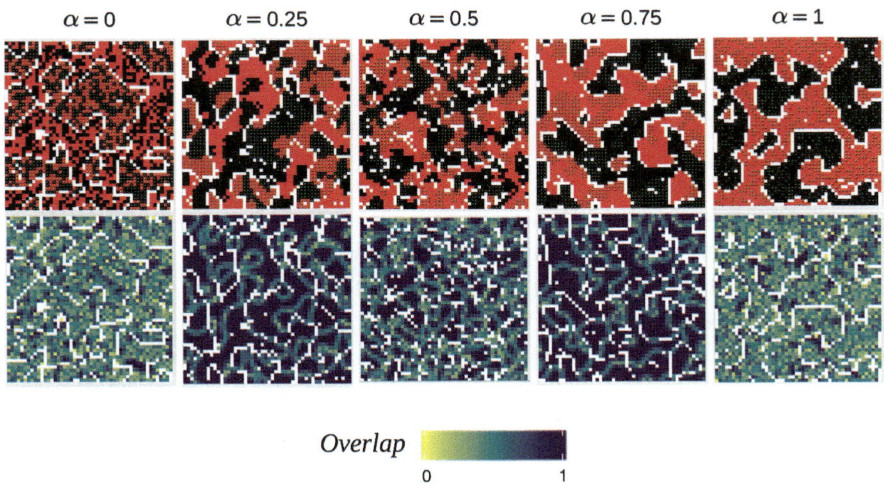

Fig. 9 Five final configurations for $\alpha = 0, 0.25, 0.5, 0.75, 1$ and $p = 0.5$ and their corresponding spatial distribution of the index *Overlap*. Dark areas correspond to high values of local overlapping of clusters of type and opinion, and light areas indicate the presence of a boundary for a single kind of cluster. The rest of the parameters are $L = 50$, $\rho = 0.15$, $\tau = 0.25$, $R = Y = 0.5$

In Fig. 9 there are final configurations with their corresponding *Overlap* index for different values of α. For the extreme values $\alpha = 0$ and $\alpha = 1$, the great majority of sites have *Overlap* index close to 0.5, the expected value for this measure in a uniformly random distribution of types and opinions. For the intermediate values of α, we get better information through the overlap index: we can clearly identify the regions of the residential space with the maximum alignment of the clusters, and the lower values of the *Overlap* index are useful to detect the presence of a boundary of a single kind of cluster. Also, if we compare the five configurations in Fig. 9, there seems to be symmetrical behavior in the distribution of the *Overlap* index over the residential space around the value $\alpha = 0.5$.

Beyond the existence of regions with maximum local overlapping, the overlapping of type and opinion clusters does not occur in the same way throughout the entire residential space. On the contrary, in a final configuration there are areas where a specific type overlaps with one opinion and other areas where the same type coincides with the opposite opinion. There is no global overlapping (in this sense that a particular type of agent associates with a specific opinion) for any of the combinations of parameters explored.

Finally, we present a brief summary of the measures defined in this section to characterize the final configuration's segregation patterns.

- To describe groupings at the local level, we analyze the frequency of non-mixed neighborhoods. We calculate the proportion of neighborhoods with agents that share the value of one feature ($Unique_c$ for type and $Unique_o$ for opinion) or of both ($Unique_{c,o}$).

- To describe groupings at the global level and understand how each agent's feature is related to that of its neighbors, we implement information theory measures. We calculate the mutual information between the type of an agent and the types of its neighbors (MI_c) and, analogously, the mutual information between the opinion of an agent and the opinions of its neighbors (MI_o).
- To describe a correspondence or alignment between the groupings by feature, both at the global and local level, we calculate the *Overlap* index for each agent.

5 Discussion

We propose an agent-based model that combines Schelling segregation dynamic with a simple dynamic of opinion formation for agents characterized by two binary features: their type (fixed) and their opinion (changeable). Results show that spatial groupings by type and by opinion emerge during the dynamics. Of the two mechanisms involved in the emergence of polarized neighborhoods available in our model, we find that moving to a neighborhood where others with similar socio-cultural values reside is a more convenient strategy for unsatisfied individuals than adapting to their environment by changing opinion. Also, we note that comparatively, neighborhood's compositions get more polarized for the opinions than for the types, although there are high linkages in both features for spatially close agents.

Our segregation model contributes to Schelling's original model since it extends its dynamic rule and introduces the effect of social influence at the local scale on an opinion feature that agents can change. This variant of the model allows comparing two mechanisms that simultaneously intervene in the socio-cultural segregation process and captures how the emerging social fragmentation restricts information flows through local interactions. We show that mobility is preferred by the agents and prevails over local social influence dynamics shaping their opinions. This statement holds even for those cases in which the similarity with neighbors linked to the unchangeable feature type has little or no relevance to agent's satisfaction level. On the other hand, our model enables us to study the emergence of spatial clusters at multiple levels (one for each feature) and to explore the possible links between them.

Different measures describe the resulting spatial patterns depending on the weight parameter α, which determines the importance of each feature on the agent's level of satisfaction. We leave aside the extreme cases $\alpha = 0$ and $\alpha = 1$ because of the absence of groupings for one of the two features.

We analyze the proportion of non-mixed neighborhoods in the final configurations to measure local groupings and the degree of polarization of the neighborhoods. We observe that in systems where the neighboring agent's opinion has a greater incidence in satisfaction, there is a high proportion of neighborhoods with unique opinions. This proportion is also much more significant than the observed for the neighborhoods with unique type in the analogous systems where the type of agents is the most relevant. In comparison, we conclude that neighborhoods become more polarized for the opinions than for the types of agents.

We analyze the relationship between the agent's type or the agent's opinion and the proportion in its neighborhood for each feature by introducing two mutual information indexes. The results show intense associations between an agent and its neighbors for the most weighty feature. However, there is also a close connection between an agent and its neighbors for the lower weighting feature. Therefore, we detect high linkages in both features for spatially close agents in all cases, indicating the presence of strong local social influences on opinions and a strong local association for types.

Finally, we analyzed the local overlapping of type and opinion clusters. We note that the pattern of local overlapping behaves in a very similar way regardless of which of the two features has a greater incidence in the satisfaction of the agents, except for the systems in which both features have equal weight ($\alpha = 0.5$), where lower values of overlapping are observed.

According to our results, the patterns in which both kinds of clusters are distributed over the residential space are different for low and high values of α. The results are mainly affected by which of the two features is the most influential for the satisfaction (i.e., if α is greater, less, or equal to 0.5). Still, we do not observe significantly different behaviors depending on how much more weight one feature has over the other.

Further analysis is required to better understand the relationship between type and opinion of agents according to the variation of other parameters of the model, such as the tolerance threshold τ and the proportion of empty locations ρ. Changing to a continuous variable for the opinion state (or including a more complex dynamic for the opinions) may also contribute to opinion polarization analysis.

The model proposed in this work and the findings suggested by our analysis are a theoretical contribution from which to understand the phenomenon of socio-cultural polarization of neighborhood compositions. It generalizes forms of homophilic selection, compares their scopes, and articulates a quantitative analysis of the emerging polarization effect that spatially concentrates individuals who share certain socio-cultural values and dynamically creates echo-chambers. From a complementary perspective and to show our work's practical implications, we conclude with a description of concrete examples that may fall within our model.

In Morales et al. (2019), the authors study how existing physical segregation affects the social fragmentation of opinions displayed in the online virtual space. They apply a clustering algorithm to geolocated hashtags from Twitter to characterize topics of conversations and analyze their polarization over different neighborhoods for Chicago, Dallas, Detroit, Istambul, Los Angeles, New York City, and Philadelphia. They measure how the popularity of topics is mutually exclusive among wealthier and poorer areas of each city. This polarization of interests corresponds to a strong geographically segregated pattern between central and peripheral neighborhoods (dot maps shown in Morales et al. (2019)). They conclude that the physical separation of individuals segregated by income reflects polarized behaviors of cultural interests. With the lens of our model, in this example, income level represents the agent's type and the degree of interest in a specific topic, their opinions. The physical segregation in terms of type is related to the segregation observed in the opinion space. It also makes sense to think about the overlapping concept as we defined in Sect. 4.2.3 to conclude that their results show that there appears to be global overlapping of both kinds of clustering.

In Dottle (2019), authors analyzed another concrete example of two linked segregation processes. First, they measure political segregation in the United States urban areas by calculating a two-partisan segregation index as proposed in Brown and Enos (2017). To compute it, they use data from 2016 voter files, take the residential location of registered Democrats and Republicans voters and calculate a spatially weighted exposure to their 1000 nearest neighbors. This index is useful to describe how separated in the physical space are Republicans and Democrats. The authors noticed that the U.S. cities that exhibit higher political segregation were also cities with the highest proportions of black residents (the top five are Jackson, Mississippi; New Orleans, Louisiana; Baton Rouge, Louisiana; Birmingham, Alabama; and Shreveport, Louisiana). This result motivates them to show how the two-partisan segregation index and the racial segregation index, measured according to the U.S. Census Bureau data, are correlated. They suggest that this relationship may be because black voters are almost uniformly Democratic. Therefore, high racial residential segregation translates into high political segregation levels in the physical space (Igielnik and Budiman, 2020; Abramowitz, 2014). The same holds when they consider groups of all non-white voters in the same category, though the correlation isn't as strong. From our model's perspective, the type of agents is represented here by ethnicity and the binary opinion state is associated with their support for the Democratic or Republican party. The study shows a significant overlap in the territory between type and opinion and that both segregation processes are strongly linked.

In Martin and Webster (2018), authors examine the extent to which spatial political segregation in the United States is associated with individual mobility preferences. They use data of Florida voters between 2006 and 2012 who moved their residences between 2008 and 2010, along with population characteristics from the U.S. Census Bureau at the census tract level. They find that the preferences of voters who move from one residence to another are related to party affiliation. However, voters appear to be sorting by non-political neighborhood attributes (such as affordability of housing or quality of schools) that relate to party preferences rather than explicitly seeking out politically similar neighbors. Furthermore, they demonstrate through simulations that the estimated partisan bias in mobility choices is too small to sustain the current political polarization in the territory. Therefore, they suggest that location and social influences must impact individual political preferences, not the other way around.

Finally, if we understand the opinion variable in a broad sense, as the language in Caridi et al. (2013), we can cite (Christopher, 2004), where both racial and language segregation were measured in South Africa during the Apartheid. The Afrikaans (55%) and English (40%) speaking populations were highly segregated among the white population; similarly, non-white population was segregated in urban settlements according to their native languages. We can argue that Afrikaans and English languages were introduced by Europeans, and even inside the white population the religion, history, and the Boer Wars could cause this segregation. However, it is interesting in this case that also sports become segregated, with the white population playing mainly rugby, and non-white population, mainly supporting football. Let us remark that racial segregation was enforced by law, while racially homogeneous neighbors evolved to language-segregated configurations.

References

Abramowitz AI (2014) How race and religion have polarized American voters. https://www.washingtonpost.com/news/monkey-cage/wp/2014/01/20/how-race-and-religion-have-polarized-american-voters/. Accessed 25 Sept 2020

Axelrod R (1997) The dissemination of culture: A model with local convergence and global polarization. J Confl Resolut 41:203–226

Baldassarri D, Bearman P (2007) Dynamics of political polarization. Am Sociol Rev 72(5):784–811

Bar-yam Y (2019) Dynamics of complex systems. Routledge Taylor and Francis, New York

Bessi A, Petroni F, Del Vicario M, Zollo F, Anagnostopoulos A, Scala A, Caldarelli G, Quattrociocchi W (2015) Viral misinformation: The role of homophily and polarization. In: Proceedings of the 24th international conference on World Wide Web, pp 355–356

Bischoff K, Reardon S (2014) Residential segregation by income, 1970–2009. Russell Sage Foundation, New York, pp 208–234

Boutyline A, Willer R (2016) The social structure of political echo chambers: Variation in ideological homophily in online networks: Political echo chambers. Polit Psychol 38:551–569

Brown J, Enos R (2017) Partisan segregation project. http://ryandenos.com/partisan-segregation. Accessed 20 Sept 2020

Cable D (2013) Racial dot map. Weldon Cooper Center for Public Service, Rector and Visitors of the University of Virginia, Virginia

Caridi I, Nemiña F, Pinasco J, Schiaffino P (2013) Schelling-voter model: An application to language competition. Chaos, Solitons Fractals 56:216–221

Caridi I, Pinasco J, Saintier N, Schiaffino P (2017) Characterizing segregation in the Schelling-voter model. Physica A Stat Mech Appl 487:125–142

Castellano C, Fortunato S, Loreto V (2007) Statistical physics of social dynamics. Rev Mod Phys 81(2):591

Christopher AJ (2004) Linguistic segregation in urban South Africa, 1996. Geoforum 35(2):145–156

Clark W (1986) Residential segregation in American cities: A review and interpretation. Popul Res Policy Rev 5(2):95–127

Clark W (1991) Residential preferences and neighborhood racial segregation: A test of the Schelling segregation model. Demography 28:1–19

Clark W, Fossett M (2008) Understanding the social context of the Schelling segregation model. Proc Natl Acad Sci USA 105:4109–4114

Cover TM, Thomas JA (2006) Elements of information theory. Wiley-Interscience, London

Crandall M, Sharp D, Unger E, Straus D, Brasel K, Hsia R, Esposito T (2013) Trauma deserts: Distance from a trauma center, transport times, and mortality from gunshot wounds in Chicago. Am J Public Health 103(6):1103–1109

Deffuant G, Amblard F, Weisbuch G, Faure T (2002) How can extremism prevail? a study based on the relative agreement interaction model. J Artif Soc Soc Simul 5(4). https://www.jasss.org/5/4/1.html
Dottle R (2019) Where democrats and republicans live in your city. https://projects.fivethirtyeight.com/republicans-democrats-cities/. Accessed 20 Sept 2020
Epstein J, Axtell R (1996) Growing artificial societies: Social science from the bottom up. MIT Press and Brookings Institution Press, New York
Esteban J, Ray D (1994) On the measurement of polarization. Econometrica 62:819–851
Feliciani T, Flache A, Tolsma J (2017) How, when and where can spatial segregation induce opinion polarization? two competing models. J Artif Soc Social Simul 20(2). https://www.jasss.org/20/2/6.html
Flache A, Macy M (2011) Small worlds and cultural polarization. J Math Sociol 35:146–176
Flaxman S, Goel S, Rao J (2016) Filter bubbles, echo chambers, and online news consumption. Public Opin Q 80(S1):298–320
Fox W (2017) Segregation along highway lines: How the Kensington Expressway Reshaped Buffalo, New York. University at Buffalo, New York
Galam S (2005) Heterogeneous beliefs, segregation, and extremism in the making of public opinions. Phys Rev E Stat Nonlinear Soft Matter Phys 71:046123
Galster G (1988) Residential segregation in American cities: A contrary review. Popul Res Policy Rev 7(2):93–112
Gaylord R, d'Andria L (1999) Simulating society: A Mathematica toolkit for modeling socioeconomic behavior. Springer, Berlin
Gotham K (2014) Missed opportunities, enduring legacies: School segregation and desegregation in Kansas city, Missouri. In: The pursuit of racial and ethnic equality in American public schools: Mendez, Brown, and Beyond, pp 221–245
Gracia-Lázaro C, Lafuerza L, Floría L, Moreno Y (2009) Residential segregation and cultural dissemination: An Axelrod-Schelling model. Phys Rev E Stat Nonlinear Soft Matter Phys 80:046123
Granovetter M (1973) The strength of weak ties. Am J Sociol 78(6):1360–1380
Green S, Turner MA, Gourevitch R (2017) Racial residential segregation and neighborhood disparities. US Partnership on Mobility from Poverty, Washington
Holley R, Liggett T (1975) Ergodic theorems for weakly interacting infinite systems and the voter model. Ann Probability 3:643–663
Iceland J, Weinberg D, Steinmetz E (2002) Racial and ethnic residential segregation in the United States: 1980–2000. U.S. Census Bureau, Suitland
Igielnik R, Budiman A (2020) The changing racial and ethnic composition of the U.S. electorate. Pew Research Center, Washington. https://www.pewresearch.org/2020/09/23/the-changing-racial-and-ethnic-composition-of-the-u-s-electorate/. Accessed 25 Sept 2020
Klašnja M, Novta N (2014) Segregation, polarization, and ethnic conflict. J Confl Resolut 60(5):927–955
Martin G, Webster S (2018) Does residential sorting explain geographic polarization? Polit Sci Res Methods 8:1–17
Mäs M, Flache A (2013) Differentiation without distancing explaining bi-polarization of opinions without negative influence. PloS One 8:e74516
Mäs M, Flache A, Helbing D (2010) Individualization as driving force of clustering phenomena in humans. PLoS Comput Biol 6:e1000959
Mäs M, Flache A, Takacs K, Jehn K (2013) In the short term we divide, in the long term we unite: Demographic crisscrossing and the effects of fault lines on subgroup polarization. Organ Sci 24:716–736
Massey D, Denton N (1987) Trends in the residential segregation of blacks, Hispanics, and Asians: 1970-1980. Am Sociol Rev 52(6):802–825
Mitchell M (2009) Complexity—A Guided Tour. Oxford University, Oxford
Mitchell R, Franco J (2018) HOLC "Redlining" maps: The persistent structure of segregation and economic inequality. In: National community reinvestment coalition report

Morales A, Dong X, Bar-Yam Y, Pentland A (2019) Segregation and polarization in urban areas. R Soc Open Sci 6:190573
O'Sullivan A (2009) Schelling's model revisited: Residential sorting with competitive bidding for land. Reg Sci Urban Econ 39:397–408
Pollicott M, Weiss H (2001) The dynamics of Schelling-type segregation models and a nonlinear graph Laplacian variational problem. Adv Appl Math 27:17–40
Quillian L (1999) Migration patterns and the growth of high-poverty neighborhoods, 1970–1990. Am J Sociol 105(1):1–37
R Core Team (2017) R: A language and environment for statistical computing. R Foundation for Statistical Computing, Vienna. https://www.R-project.org/
Saintier N, Pablo Pinasco J, Vazquez F (2020) A model for the competition between political mono-polarization and bi-polarization. Chaos: An Interdisciplinary J Nonlinear Sci 30(6):063146
Salzarulo L (2006) A continuous opinion dynamics model based on the principle of meta-contrast. J Artif Soc Soc Simul 9(1). https://www.jasss.org/9/1/13.html
Sampson R, Raudenbush S, Earls F (1997) Neighborhoods and violent crime: A multilevel study of collective efficacy. Science 277(5328): 918–924
Sanchez TW, Stolz R, JMa (2003) Moving to equity: Addressing inequitable effects of transportation policies on minorities. The Civil Rights Project at Harvard University, Cambridge
Schelling TC (1969) Models of segregation. In American economic review, papers and proceedings, vol 59, pp 488–493
Schelling TC (1971) Dynamic models of segregation. J Math Sociol 1:143–186
Semyonov M, Glikman A (2009) Ethnic residential segregation, social contacts, and anti-minority attitudes in European societies. Eur Sociol Rev 25(6):693–708
Sherman B (2014) Racial bias and interstate highway planning: a mixed methods approach. CUREJ: College Undergraduate Research Electronic Journal, University of Pennsylvania, Pennsylvania
Starnini M, Frasca M, Baronchelli A (2016) Emergence of metapopulations and echo chambers in mobile agents. Sci Rep 6(1):1–8
Swanstrom T, Dreier P, Mollenkopf J (2002) Economic inequality and public policy: The power of place. City Community 1:349–372
Valdez S (2014) Visibility and votes: A spatial analysis of anti-immigrant voting in Sweden. Migr Stud 2:162–188
Vazquez F, Saintier N, Pinasco JP (2020) Role of voting intention in public opinion polarization. Phys Rev E 101(1):012101
Vinković D, Kirman A (2007) A physical analogue of the Schelling model. Proc Natl Acad Sci USA 103:19261–19265
Waal J, De Koster W, Achterberg P (2013) Ethnic segregation and radical right-wing voting in Dutch cities. Urban Aff Rev 49(5):748–777
Wickham H (2016) ggplot2: Elegant graphics for data analysis. Springer, New York. https://ggplot2.tidyverse.org
Wilson W (2009) The political and economic forces shaping concentrated poverty. Political Sci Q 123:555–571

The Dynamics of Online Opinion Formation: Polarization Around the Vaccine Development for COVID-19

Gaurav Jain, Avinash Bapu Sreenivas, Samrat Gupta, and Amit Anand Tiwari

Abstract According to the World Health Organization (WHO), social media-induced polarization caused due to the spread of misinformation related to the efficacy and side effects of a COVID-19 vaccine is potentially leading to vaccine hesitancy, one of the top ten threats to global health. In this study, we investigate the dynamics of social media polarization around COVID-19 vaccine which could be one of the causes of vaccine hesitancy. We use a simulation-based model of dynamical co-evolution in adaptive networks wherein interacting individuals influence each other's opinions to arrive at a final network state. The opinion formation model simulates the temporal dynamics of social media polarization on the comments posted on different COVID-19 vaccine-development-related YouTube videos. The experimental results suggest that the degree of polarization in the online discourse, as measured by the time taken to form consensus, increases with recency in time. This finding significantly contributes to the highly contested debate around whether the flow of information on social media fosters or counteracts polarization.

Keywords Polarization · COVID-19 pandemic · COVID-19 vaccine · Online opinion formation · Consensus formation · Social media

---

G. Jain (✉) · A. B. Sreenivas · S. Gupta
Indian Institute of Management Ahmedabad, Ahmedabad, Gujarat, India
e-mail: ep19gauravj@iima.ac.in; avinash@iima.ac.in; samratg@iima.ac.in

A. A. Tiwari
Marketing Management Area, Indian Institute of Management Rohtak, Rohtak, Haryana, India
e-mail: amit.tiwari@iimrohtak.ac.in

I. Qureshi et al. (eds.), *Causes and Symptoms of Socio-Cultural Polarization*,
https://doi.org/10.1007/978-981-16-5268-4_3

1 Introduction

COVID-19 was not only declared as a pandemic but was also termed as an "infodemic" by the United Nations.[1] COVID-19 led to the creation of enormous information on the web. For instance, there were more than 8000 papers in PubMed that included the word "COVID-19" by 30th April 2020 (Gonzalez-Padilla and Tortolero-Blanco 2020). In addition to the rapid spread of the coronavirus, the information (and misinformation) on social media about the virus spread equally rapidly thus creating a panic in the society (Depoux et al. 2020; Laato et al. 2020). The panic created by social media was more contagious than the virus itself (Depoux et al. 2020; Wilson and Chen 2020). This unprecedented spread of information (and misinformation) influenced our society's response to the virus[2] (Papakyriakopoulos et al. 2020). As there was no scientific and social knowledge about the origin and the impact of COVID-19, many conspiracy theories emerged and spread quickly while claiming to provide credible explanations to the impact and the cure of the virus (Shahsavari et al. 2020). Public belief in these conspiracy theories prospectively predicted a resistance to the preventive measures and vaccination (Romer and Jamieson 2020). These conspiracy theories, coupled with the partisan differences, led to polarization in the society (Bail et al. 2018; Qureshi et al. 2020). For example, prominent republican government officials in the US, including the outgoing President Trump, have sent conflicting messages saying that the crisis caused by the coronavirus is less severe, but the Democrats emphasized the grave dangers of the pandemic.[3] Moreover, the partisan media have echoed this divide thus causing differences between the right and left leaning people to the extent that it could have far reaching impacts on human health and the economy (Allcott et al. 2020; Gupta et al. 2021). These biased media opinions spread rapidly over social media and led to echo chamber effect whereby the individuals who were exposed to the opinions, beliefs and attitudes consistent to their own became polarized (Justwan et al. 2018).

In general, access to unsupervised social media usage allows individuals to share content without any editorial review and users can self-select the content that may contribute to ideological isolation (Fard and Verma 2021; Puri et al. 2020). In the context of coronavirus, anti-vaccination messaging on social media has raised considerable public health concerns, misinformation regarding the medical composition and adverse effects of vaccination potentially leading to vaccine hesitancy, a patient level reluctance to receive vaccines (Puri et al. 2020). Due to the continued resurgence of vaccine preventable diseases, WHO has included

[1] https://www.un.org/en/un-coronavirus-communications-team/un-tackling-%E2%80%98infodemic%E2%80%99-misinformation-and-cybercrime-covid-19

[2] https://www.theatlantic.com/technology/archive/2018/08/how-misinfodemics-spread-disease/568921/

[3] https://www.vox.com/policy-and-politics/2020/3/12/21177135/coronavirus-covid-19-pandemic-trump-biden-speeches

vaccine hesitancy as one of the top ten threats to global health in 2019 (Puri et al. 2020). Misinformation and rumors related to COVID-19 vaccination on social media platforms started eroding the public confidence well before the release of an effective COVID-19 vaccine (Donovan 2020; Puri et al. 2020). For example, in India, leader of one political party (Samajwadi party)[4] has termed a COVID-19 vaccine, approved for emergency use by the Indian Council for Medical Research as the ruling party's (BJP's)[5] vaccine hence casting doubts in the minds of his followers about the efficacy of the vaccination and eventually leading to polarization between the followers of these political parties. This polarization has led to vaccine hesitancy among Indian masses to some extent (Khan et al. 2020). Another example is that of the outgoing US President Trump who repeated the debunked theory that vaccines cause autism while communicating that he slowed his son Barron's vaccination schedule.[6] Research around the propagation of vaccine content on social media shows that the anti-vaccine content garners more user engagement than the neutral content (Blankenship et al. 2018; Puri et al. 2020). Some of the examples are:

1. Analysis of tweets between 2010 to 2016 containing the hashtag "vaccine" found that the anti-vaccine tweets were 4.13 times more likely to be retweeted than the neutral tweets (Blankenship et al. 2018; Puri et al. 2020).
2. Analysis of 150 Instagram posts containing the hashtag "HPV" suggested that the anti-vaccine posts had a significantly higher number of likes as compared to the neutral posts (Basch and MacLean 2019; Puri et al. 2020).
3. Another related research on 87 YouTube videos containing "vaccine safety" and "vaccines and children" in 2017 showed that 65% of the videos expressed an anti-vaccine sentiment (Basch et al. 2017; Puri et al. 2020).
4. Analysis of the top YouTube videos containing "COVID-19" and "coronavirus" identified that 27.5% of videos contained non-factual data around the disease but garnered over 60 million views (Li et al. 2020; Puri et al. 2020).

Anti-vaccine groups use different methods like bots and trolls that generate anti-vaccination messages in social network sites to quickly spread their messages arguing the possible harmful effects and distrust of pharmaceuticals (Ortiz-Sánchez et al. 2020). As more and more people get exposed to this anti-vaccine related misinformation on social media, it becomes increasingly difficult for the healthcare agencies and the political system of a country to convince people to get vaccinated. Though, polarization around the use and efficacy of the vaccines tends to change with time as increasingly reliable information becomes available on social media and the positive health outcomes of vaccination are communicated to the public, social media induced polarization and spread of (mis)information considerably affects the resurgence of vaccine curable diseases.

---

[4] Samajwadi Party is a political party in India headquartered in New Delhi.

[5] BJP- The Bharatiya Janata Party is one of two major political parties in India, along with Indian National Congress. It has been the ruling political party of the Republic of India since 2014

[6] https://www.nytimes.com/2020/12/18/us/politics/trump-vaccine-skeptics.html

This spread of misinformation on social media causing polarization around vaccine development and administration during an ongoing pandemic motivates us to study the opinion formation process of social media users, who participate in the online discourse related to COVID-19 vaccine development, using an adaptive network modelling approach. We use the concept of dynamical co-evolution in adaptive network with interacting individuals who influence each other's opinions to arrive at a final network state (Das et al. 2021). We believe that this model is better suited to study the evolution of the opinions among the social media users, as compared to the opinion evolution model in the static networks, because the opinions of the users in social media are not independent of other users' opinions. Therefore, we study the dynamics of opinion formation in the form of a consensus formation process between the users where the extent of polarization among the users is determined by how soon a consensus is reached. A faster consensus formation depicts lesser polarization among the users. This process is executed on different subsets of users segregated in different bins based on the timestamp of their comments on a particular YouTube video. The experiments help in understanding the temporal dynamics of the users' opinion/consensus formation and hence the change in the degree of polarization over time. A study of this change in the degree of polarization around the use of vaccines is critical for the healthcare agencies and governments to understand how much effort should be spent to curb the social media induced polarization around the vaccine development during pandemics, COVID-19 in our case.

2 Background

The late 1990s saw the rise of polarized opinions around vaccination specifically with respect to Measles-Mumps-Rubella (MMR) vaccines. For instance, a study published by a British physician led to highly polarizing opinions amongst many parents because the study linked MMR vaccine to autism and other gastrointestinal diseases in children (Wakefield 1999). This research led to huge controversy among several communities around the world. The polarized opinions with respect to MMR vaccines transformed into "echo chamber" effects which are observable even today. Though the findings of this research were retracted in 2010 and deemed as "most damaging medical hoax of the last 100 years" (Flaherty 2011)" by medical fraternity,[7] the fraudulent claims relating MMR vaccine to autism in children have gained momentum in the recent years thus strengthening the preconceived opinions of the anti-vaccinationists specifically in north America and western Europe. The rise of vaccine hesitation can be clearly observed during a 6-year span between 1996 and 2002 in the United Kingdom. The MMR vaccination rates dropped

[7] https://www.healio.com/news/pediatrics/20120325/wakefield-study-linking-mmr-vaccine-autism-uncovered-as-complete-fraud

from 92% in 1996 to 84% in 2002. In the following year (2003), vaccination rates plummeted to an alarming 61% in various parts of London. In the United States between 1999–2000, the vaccination rates saw a drop of 2% as the parents were simultaneously influenced by the publication linking MMR vaccine to autism and various other scientific papers emphasizing on the fact that there was no link between the two (Hussain et al. 2018). The resulting echo chamber effects impacted the governmental activities such as creating awareness, successful and organized vaccination programs in the society. This impact can be summarized through following instances:

1. In 2000, the Irish government reported various clusters of measle cases throughout the country. 1500 cases and 3 deaths were registered due to the outbreak. The primary reason for the measles outbreak was traced back to the publication that had created a controversial situation as it linked MMR vaccine to autism in children (Pepys 2007).
2. In 2006, the United Kingdom reported a mammoth 701.8% increase in measles cases in comparison to the reported cases in the year 1998 (56 cases in 1998; 449 cases in 2006). Also, in the same year of 2006, there was 1 registered case of death due to measles. This was the first reported death since 1992 (Asaria and MacMahon 2006).
3. In 2008, due to the increase in measles cases the United Kingdom government declared measles as endemic despite the presence of the MMR vaccine (Godlee et al. 2011).
4. Over the course of 3 years i.e. 2008–2011, French government reported an alarming rise in measles cases which accounted for 22,000 cases (Antona et al. 2013).

In the modern world, the existence of polarization around critical issues specifically around vaccines is very dangerous and has adverse effects on society because of the presence of information and communication technology (ICT) such as social media (Qureshi et al. 2018, 2021). Today, social media platforms are on the rise due to the influx of over 3.81 billion users in 2020 in comparison to 970 million in 2010.[8] Social media tends to have a massive and long-lasting impact on general public about various topics that are endorsed by social media influencers, celebrities and various verified accounts as they tend to have a wider reach.[9] Hence, critical issues such as polarization around vaccines have gained momentum on various social media platforms as celebrities are promoting/endorsing various anti-vaccination drives in various countries around the world. For instance, in the California, USA SB 276 (Senate Bill) a strict new vaccine legislation was introduced which aims to combat against medical exemption surrounding immunization without being

[8] https://backlinko.com/social-media-users

[9] https://influencermarketinghub.com/what-is-an-influencer/https://influencermarketinghub.com/what-is-an-influencer/

approved by a recognized public health officer.[10] SB 276 helps support a process known as "community immunity". This process promotes the basic idea that individuals unable to self-immunize against a vaccine-preventable disease must be protected by following various protocols set by the immunization program.[11] This bill gained social media traction when Hollywood superstar Jessica Biel joined hands with famous anti vaxxer Robert F. Kennedy Jr. to oppose the passing of SB 276. She used social media platform -Instagram in order to get her polarizing opinion across to her massive 9.2 million[12] followers. This is one instance where a famous personality or influencer can cause the rise of "echo chamber" effects with the help of social media.

2.1 History of Vaccine Hesitation

Even after the pioneering effort by father of immunology Edward Jenner in 1798 to introduce the world's first ever vaccine against smallpox, there is numerous evidence of vaccine hesitation that has plagued the medical fraternity. The earliest instance of vaccine hesitation dates back to 1853 when a strict act was passed in England and Wales that made vaccination of infants below the age of 4 months a compulsion. This act of 1853 gave rise to the first vaccine hesitancy in Leicester, England where the opposition members decided against the immunization program (Ross 1968).

More recent instances of vaccine hesitation are the hesitancy towards Human Papilloma Virus (HPV) vaccine mainly concentrated in Japan around 2012–2013. HPV vaccination rates plummeted to less than 1% from over 70% in Japan when an unconfirmed report about the adverse effect of HPV immunization was broadcasted on Japanese national media (Simms et al. 2020). In relation to the ongoing pandemic, in China, their immunization program has gained negative publicity as the public has conveyed their consensus of distrust with respect to the domestically-manufactured vaccines. Due to the hesitation towards domestically-manufactured vaccines, the core principles of immunization programs are being compromised as the public have shown inclination towards foreign-manufactured vaccines and foreign-based vaccination programs (Lin et al. 2020).

---

[10] https://www.hollywoodreporter.com/news/jessica-biels-vaccine-lobbying-draws-ire-california-legislators-1218309

[11] https://trackbill.com/bill/california-senate-bill-276-immunizations-medical-exemptions/1688024/

[12] https://www.instagram.com/jessicabiel/?hl=en

2.2 Polarization and Echo Chambers around Vaccines

Social media is defined as information and communication technology that aims at providing a platform for its users to share/broadcast ideas, thoughts and various kinds of information with the help of virtual communities and networks. Therefore, social media provides a perfect platform to voice one's opinion and also have the transparency to view the opinion of fellow social media users. There are 2 sides of the coin with respect to social media. One the positive aspects, social media provides a strong platform to businesses of various sizes to spread the information to a wider audience. Since dissemination of information is way faster to a larger pool of users, social media is a key tool for government agencies during the course of a natural disaster (Ulvi et al. 2019). The dark side of social media leads to family intimacy issues as members spend more time on these platforms than quality time with family. Social media is a breeding ground for various trolls and trolling has an adverse effect on mental health. Finally, the rise of "echo chamber" effect in today's world is associated or stems mainly from social media (Sasahara et al. 2020). "Echo chamber" effects around critical topics such as vaccines, national election and various conspiracy theories (flat earth movement) has created a scenario of misinformation taking center stage and hampering the ability of the public to differentiate between correct information and misinformation.

On one hand the general public looks up to social media (especially in today's scenario of ongoing pandemic) to gain vital information from various government and medical agencies surrounding COVID-19 such as symptoms, self-quarantine rules and regulation, lockdown rules and immunization programs. On the other hand, certain sections of society are disseminating misinformation such as anti-lockdown protests,[13] anti-mask protest[14] and mainly anti-vax content[15] on social media. These dual effects of social media are furthered by polarization and formation of echo chambers.

Polarization is defined as the phenomenon in which certain opinions surrounding a topic are opposed, disagreed and also debated by individuals with different mindset (Kozma and Barrat 2008). Echo chamber can be described as a bubble in which one's belief and or opinion is reinforced to such an extent that it reflects their own mindset. Echo chambers stems mainly from a process known as confirmation bias (Del Vicario et al. 2017).

Echo chambers can be summarized with the help of a proverb "Birds of a feather flock together" (Sunstein 2017). This basically translates to individuals with similar characters, thoughts, beliefs and interest tending to stick together and reinforcing their own beliefs.

---

[13] https://www.theguardian.com/technology/2020/apr/20/facebook-anti-lockdown-protests-bans

[14] https://www.vox.com/the-goods/2020/8/7/21357400/anti-mask-protest-rallies-donald-trump-covid-19

[15] https://www.telegraph.co.uk/news/2020/12/02/take-anti-vaccine-conspiracy-posts-face-consequences-ministers

In the context of vaccination, polarization has a completely adverse effect on global health care (Schmidt et al. 2018). Polarization around vaccination brings out the negative impact of social media and how the power of social media can be exploited to spread misinformation, unverified sources disseminating inaccurate precautionary measures and rise of anti-vaxxers getting unnecessary limelight to spread their philosophy. For instance, various anti-vax hashtags like #vaccinescauseautism and #vaccinesarepoison that promote vaccine hoax propaganda and misinformation are now being blocked by social media companies like Instagram. Any hashtag that appears with misinformation around vaccines is being tracked by social media companies and being banned immediately. Also, the presence of echo chambers hinders and limits the flow of accurate information by verified government agencies on social media due to overshadowing role played by "fake"/misinformation.[16] For instance, the misinformation that was being spread and shared by millions of Vietnamese regarding shortage of anti-bacterial gels, wipes, toilet paper and grocery had created a pseudo-inflation of prices thus affecting the middle and lower-income level communities (Phuong et al. 2020).

3 Methodology: Using Network Simulation

The evolution of the participating individuals' states or opinions determines the changing topology of an adaptive network (Kozma and Barrat 2008). Opinion formation dynamics and the dissemination of cultural information have been studied using statistical physics models (Kozma and Barrat 2008). These statistical models try to characterize the essential features of developing social behaviors by studying the mechanisms of opinion formation in which the individuals evolve their opinions through interaction with other neighboring individuals, thus following a local majority (Glauber 1963; Galam et al. 1982; Gupta and Kumar 2020; Krapivsky and Redner 2003; Kumar et al. 2017). Without any supervision on the random encounters between the nodes (individuals), the network self-regulates possibly leading to a global consensus where the opinions of all the individuals converge. Alternatively, networks can reach a state of polarization where multiple different opinions survive. Later models of opinion dynamics also introduced a bounded confidence concept where individuals interact with others only if their opinions are close enough. This bounded confidence or the closeness is described by a tolerance parameter that controls the evolution of the network towards different polarization states based on the value of the tolerance parameter (Kozma and Barrat 2008). Many studies have focused on the scenario where all individuals interact with all the others in a network which is mostly possible in a network with a smaller number of individuals (Kozma and Barrat 2008). However, recent

[16] https://news.harvard.edu/gazette/story/2020/05/social-media-used-to-spread-create-covid-19-falsehoods/

studies of complex social networks models suggests that the network topology in which the individuals interact may not be regular (Pastor-Satorras and Vespignani 2004; Newman 2003; Dorogovtsev and Mendes 2003; Dorogovtsev and Mendes 2002; Albert and Barabási 2002). Therefore, the evolution of these adaptive models and their implication on the corresponding dynamical behavior on more realistic networks has been explored in various studies (Castellano et al. 2005; Gupta and Deodhar 2021; Gupta and Kumar 2016; Sood and Redner 2005.

This research uses a simulation-based technique of consensus formation in the random networks to model the problem of social media polarization. The comments on a particular YouTube video, along with their polarity scores, are divided into subsets based on their timestamps and are used as an input to the simulation to determine the evolution of users' opinions. Our focus in this research is the opinion formation in the adaptive networks. Prior research has used various techniques to understand the different aspects of the cultural behavior of the individuals on social media platforms. One such technique is the study of the dynamics of opinion formation (Deffuant et al. 2000; Jin et al. 2017; Kozma and Barrat 2008; Ju et al. 2020). Our simulation modelling is borrowed from this work where the users' opinions are evolved when random binary encounters take place within a network whenever the difference in the polarity of their opinions is within a threshold limit of tolerance parameter.

The initial random graph is built by connecting a pair of nodes with probability p among the k users who comment on the particular YouTube video. This random graph corresponds to an Erdős–Rényi random network model. The expected number of connections between the nodes in this graph will be $kC_2 \times p$. On an average, any node in this network will have $k \times p$ neighbors. One of the limitations of this model is that it treats the initial connections between the nodes as independent of other connections. While this assumption of network independence may be tenable for the supervised lab experiments carried out on various statistical models, it is less realistic in the real-world social networks where the connections between the users may not be independent of each other (Cranmer et al. 2017; Robins et al. 2012; Fredrickson and Chen 2019; Krackhardt 1988). Interdependence between the individuals within a network is fundamental to the theory of social processes and social influence. For example, we may be influenced by the opinions of our friends or co-workers or catch an illness through friendship with an infected acquaintance (Robins et al. 2012). However, the initial network structural independence assumption taken for this experiment is due to the lack of available information regarding the dependent/independent variables that describe the users and the relationships between the users who have commented on our chosen social media platform, i.e., YouTube.

At each step of the consensus formation simulation, one user is randomly chosen, and its polarity score is compared with that of the rest of the users in the network. The mean of the absolute differences of all their polarity scores is taken if the polarity scores are within a tolerance limit (TL). Thereafter, the chosen user's polarity score (aka. opinion) is adjusted based on the Eq. 1 below:

$$x_i = \mu\left(x_i + \mu\left(\sum\nolimits_{j=1}^{k} |x_i - x_j| < TL\right)\right) \tag{1}$$

where,

- x_i is the polarity score of user i and x_j is the polarity score of user j where i and j span from 1 .... k and $i \neq j$, as the same user cannot interact with oneself.
- $\mu \in (0, 0.5)$ is the convergence parameter which controls the speed of convergence of the opinions. A value of $\mu = 0$ is rare to observe in the real world social networks. $\mu = 0$ means the adjusted polarity score of a user becomes zero which implies that the user becomes unpolarized after a single interaction with other users. This phenomenon is rare in the real-world social networks as individuals are less likely to completely agree with the opinions of their connections and abandon their own beliefs and interpretations in a single interaction. On conducting a sensitivity analysis on μ by increasing its value in increments of 0.1, we concluded that the changes in the value of μ only impact the consensus formation time but not the dynamics of opinion formation (Appendix 1). Hence, we have taken the value of $\mu = 0.5$ for simplicity as it corresponds to x_i and x_j converging to the average of their opinions after the interaction (Kozma and Barrat 2008; Ben-Naim et al. 2004; Deffuant et al. 2000).
- The tolerance limit (TL) determines if the two users or opinions will interact with each other or not. Any two users will interact with each other only when the difference in their polarity scores is within this TL. This threshold condition is specified to consider a real-world social interaction between the users where they only interact if their opinions are *close enough*. There could be various reasons like social pressure, lack of understanding or conflict of interest for exhibiting such a behavior (Deffuant et al. 2000). There is a possibility that the TL for each set of interacting individuals is different and it could change over time. For our experiments, we have used a TL value of 0.3 after doing a sensitivity analysis.[17] This update of opinions in random binary encounters towards a single or multiple consensus is an iterative process. (We conjecture that our overall results as explained in Sect. 3 would remain similar by keeping a different tolerance level for the experiment).

The result of this simulation could be a converged network with a single opinion for all the users or multiple clusters representing fragmented opinion clusters (Gupta and Kumar 2020; Gupta et al. 2016; Gupta and Kumar 2021). This methodology tells us the number of iterations taken to form a consensus when used on the input data of different timestamps. Higher number of iterations taken to form a consensus suggests high polarization and a lower number of iterations suggest less polarization.

[17] Smaller values of TL (0.1,0.2) revealed that the network almost never evolve to a consensus. Alternatively, larger values of TL (0.4,0.5,0.6) didn't provide any meaningful insights as a broader level consensus was formed.

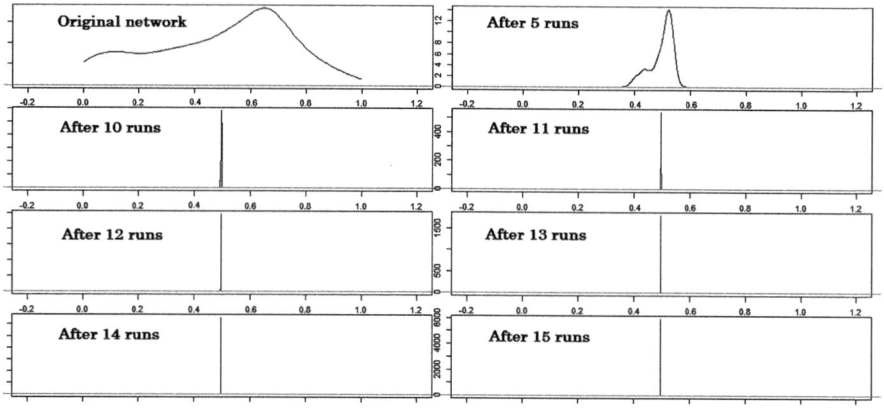

Fig. 1 An illustration of consensus formation with N = 1000, TL = 0.3, p = 0.1 and μ = 0.5

We illustrate the working of this methodology using a YouTube video captioned as "The Race To Develop A Coronavirus Vaccine".[18] This video talks about the chaos that the coronavirus outbreak is causing in the global economy, freezing supply chains and forcing companies across the world to ban travels and look at business continuity plans. However, at drug companies and research labs, the race is on to develop a vaccine for the virus. There are 8179 comments on this video as of 23rd October 2020. For demonstration of our approach, we extracted a sample of 1000 comments which were posted on this video in the third week of April 2020, computed their polarity scores and obtained their opinion formation using the methodology described above. Please note that these 1000 comments and the period chosen is only for methodology demonstration purposes and is not a representative of the findings of this study.

Figure 1 shows the consensus formation process on these 1000 comments. In the sub-figures, the X-axis shows the polarity scores over a scale of 0 to 1 and the Y-axis shows the density of comments. The graph in sub-figure titled "Original network" shows the initial state of the spread of opinions on a scale of 0 to 1. Two random comments are selected and the difference in their polarity scores is taken. If the difference in their polarity scores is less than the tolerance limit, polarity scores of each of the comments are updated according to Eq. 1. If the difference in their polarity scores is greater than the tolerance limit, the polarity score of the first comment will be compared with that of another randomly selected comment from the network. The first iteration completes when this process is repeated for all the 1000 comments in the data. The graph in sub-figure titled "After 5 runs" shows the spread of users' polarity after 5 such iterations are completed. As the spread of the polarity scores is reduced in this sub-figure, it shows that the opinions have converged but the opinions have still not reached a consensus. As the number

[18] https://www.youtube.com/watch?v=ek3T8xiu1Fw

of iterations increase, a consensus is formed in 12 iterations depicted by a straight vertical line.

We conducted similar experiments on various YouTube videos related to COVID-19 vaccine and it provided us an insight into the evolution of users' polarization over time. We have provided a detailed discussion of these experiments in the next section.

4 Experiments and Results

4.1 Process of Data Preparation

The primary step in the data preparation process is the selection of YouTube videos related to vaccines that meet the essential and basic criteria i.e., number of comments and relevance to the study. Table 1 summarizes the videos selected for experimentation. After having established and selected the videos, the next step is the extraction of all vital data pertaining to each of the videos. This step is achieved with the help of a python script and YouTube's well - integrated Application Programming Interface (API). The general interaction or discourse of the viewers with respect to a video is bifurcated into.

Seed Comments – They are referred to as the primary or direct comments a user posts under the comment section of the respective videos.

Secondary Comments – These are referred to as the replies posted to the seed comments by the user.

Establishing the focus point of any study is vital to achieve the best results. Hence, this study focuses mainly on seed comments (by eliminating secondary comments) as it highlights polarizing comments and also evolution of the same with respect to each video. Also, in order to encapsulate the originality of seed comments, the edited original comments are eliminated from the dataset. This marks the cleaning of the dataset for a selected video. The final step of data preparation is the classification of the cleaned dataset into various subsets based on the published dates of the comments. This facilitates a better understanding of polarization and/or consensus formation. Figure 2 part (a) depicts the entire process of data cleaning.

4.2 Experimental Setup

The cleaned data obtained from the previous step is subjected to sentiment analysis using Microsoft Azure, a text analytical machine learning API available as an add-on in Microsoft Excel. The principal functionality of this API is the ability to arrive at a sentiment score (between 0 and 1) for each comment by using an advanced

Table 1 COVID-19 vaccine development related YouTube videos on which the experiment was performed

Sl. No	Title	Description	Duration
1	The Race to Develop A Coronavirus Vaccine	This video briefly explains the spread of coronavirus and how it has affected people's livelihood. Plus, it also stresses the need for vaccines. Vaccine development for emergency pandemic is not sustainable for investors of a drug company in comparison to the established diseases due to short term requirement.	10 minutes14 seconds
2	The Coronavirus Vaccine Explained I COVID-19	This video explains in detail the role and effectiveness of different types of vaccines on a human immune system. Coronavirus strain is explained with the various phases of clinical trials for a vaccine. Also, pinpoints the constraints faced during vaccine development and testing before mass production.	10 minutes39 seconds
3	The Exciting Covid-19 Vaccine!	At a testing center in Abu Dhabi, a Chinese-made COVID-19 vaccine (Seal) is in its most crucial stage of clinical trial i.e., phase 3. Various nationals who volunteered for the clinical trials are responding in a positive manner and hence provides hope to the entire world.	3 minutes34 seconds
4	Bill Gates on How Quickly We Could See A Coronavirus VaccineI MSNBC	Bill Gates, the co-founder of Microsoft provides a detailed explanation of the timeline for the vaccine to fight against COVID-19. Also, Bill Gates pinpoints the various reasons behind the inefficient testing in the US.	4 minutes01 seconds

(continued)

Table 1 (continued)

Sl. No	Title	Description	Duration
5	WHO on Oxford-AstraZeneca coronavirus vaccine data: It is good news	This video shows the WHO personnel applauding a newly published data by the researchers at Oxford university and AstraZeneca on a potential coronavirus vaccine. However, they cautioned that it's still early days and further evidence of the vaccine's effectiveness is needed to conclude the research.	6 minutes20 seconds
6	The risky way to speed up a coronavirus vaccine	This video explains the time stricken (traditional) clinical trial (phase-3) and a controversial model to quicken the process of phase-3 human trial of the COVID-19 vaccine. Human challenge trial and the stages are explained via the help of interviews with epidemiologists and challenge trial volunteers. Also indicates the problems surrounding COVID-19 and human challenge trials.	9 minutes12 seconds

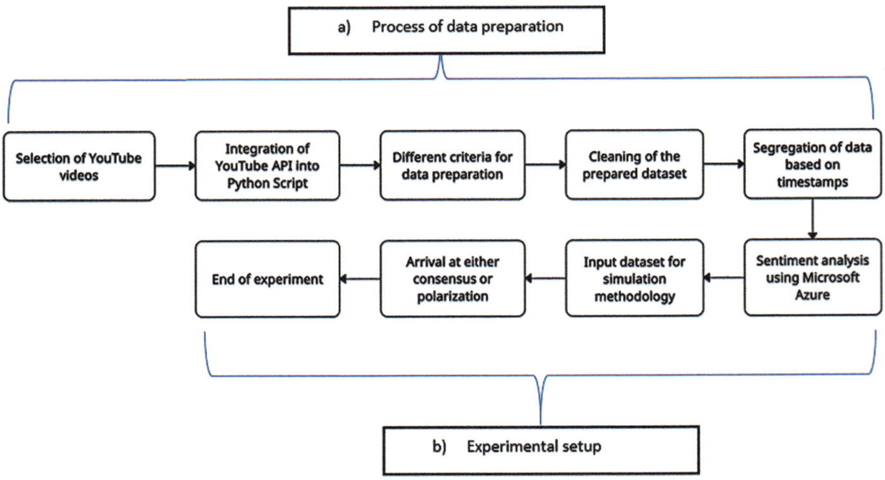

Fig. 2 Integrated steps showing data preparation and experimental setup

Natural Language Processing (NLP) algorithm. Apart from the sentiment score, Microsoft Azure also labels each comment as positive, negative or neutral. So, finally, the cleaned, segregated (subset based on timestamp) dataset along with the results obtained from Microsoft Azure forms the input dataset in order to run the simulation as explained in the methodology section. Figure 2 part (b) summarizes the experimental setup.

4.3 Experimental Results

This section describes the experimental results obtained on the datasets that comprise the subsets of comments of different timestamps. These datasets pertain to the YouTube videos related to the online discourse on the COVID-19 vaccine. Table 2 shows the consolidated experimental results on all the YouTube videos related to the discussions around COVID-19 vaccine on which we conducted the experiment. For example, for the video captioned as "Bill Gates On How Quickly We Could See A Coronavirus Vaccine | MSNBC", the consensus formation took 13 iterations on the 7072 user comments posted on the video in the third week of May. Similarly, it took 23 iterations to form a consensus on the 91 comments posted in the third week of June and 65 iterations to form a consensus on the 27 comments posted in the third week of July. This result points to a delayed consensus formation as the time goes by and hence shows an increase in the degree of polarization with time on various topics related to the development and the availability of COVID-19 vaccine.

5 Discussion

Our selection of the YouTube videos to conduct experiments was based on our objective to capture as much variation as possible in the online public discourse related to the development of COVID-19 vaccine and the associated controversies around that. For example, we chose one of the videos which talks about the chaos that COVID-19 has caused in the global economy where companies are forced to freeze their supply chains, ask employees to permanently work from home, and ban all global or domestic travel. The video also discusses how fast the countries, especially the US, have mobilized their resources to develop a vaccine. Despite a huge market for vaccines, vaccine development for emergency situations like disease outbreaks is usually not seen as a good business opportunity by the pharmaceutical industry as the vaccine is planned to be used for a shorter duration of time in such situations. The video also shows the medical fraternity talking about the different phases of the trial and the ethical, medical and other considerations associated with the trials so as to be sure that it is safe to vaccinate the normal public. The comments initially posted on this video blame the companies for linking the development of the vaccine with a business opportunity rather than doing

Table 2 Experimental results of consensus formation on COVID-19 vaccine development related YouTube videos

Videos	Time	# comments	#Iterations for convergence
The Race To Develop A Coronavirus Vaccine	Third week of April	3207	13
	Third week of May	812	17
	Third week of June	29	80
The Coronavirus Vaccine Explained I COVID-19	Third week of May	3401	13
	Third week of June	49	25
	Third week of July	25	70
The Exciting Covid-19 Vaccine!	Third week of August	8486	12
	Third week of September	1455	13
	Fourth week of September	45	30
	First week of October	52	45
Bill Gates On How Quickly We Could See A Coronavirus Vaccine I MSNBC	Third week of May	7072	13
	Third week of June	91	23
	Third week of July	27	65
WHO on Oxford-AstraZeneca coronavirus vaccine data: It is good news	First week of August	491	12
	First week of September	33	60
The risky way to speed up a coronavirus vaccine	First week of August	1134	10
	First week of September	392	11

it for the public good. With time, we observed a shift in users' behavior when they started raising doubts over the coronavirus genome sequence developed by the Chinese and the discourse became more polarized. Spread of misinformation around the genome sequence, which acts as an input in the vaccine development process, is partly to blame for this increased polarization. Another video that we chose for our experiment features an interview with Bill Gates, cofounder of Microsoft and the Bill and Melinda Gates foundation, on how quickly we could see a coronavirus vaccine. Bill talks about how an investment of billions of dollars in vaccine development could save a potential loss of trillions of dollars caused due to lockdowns etc. When asked about his assessment on how the US has done in terms of testing and what could have been better, he mentions that the access to testing is chaotic even though the testing capacity has gone up. Users who commented on this video seem to be frustrated for a few reasons, such as a person not related to the medical field discussing the availability of the vaccine and success of the public health policies. Users also casted doubts on whether Bill has some hidden agenda as he is an investor in many pharmaceutical companies, some of which are in the race to develop a vaccine for COVID-19. While the general response to this video was negative towards the start, few users also supported Bill's point of view as the time went by. This is evident from the increased polarization that was seen among the users who commented on this video. Similarly, the other videos that we used for our experiments garnered unusual responses from the users and hence depict a very different online social behavior during a pandemic situation and thus induce polarization in the society.

One interesting observation from this study is that the polarization among the social media users on a COVID-19 vaccine related video increases with time. As the time goes by, a larger number of iterations taken to form a consensus demonstrates this outcome. One of the reasons we consider this observation as significant in the study of social media polarization, particularly around topics that lead to a political debate and COVID-19 vaccination is one of such topics, is that it is still a highly contested debate whether the flow of information on social media fosters or counteracts polarization (Kligler-Vilenchik et al. 2020). There are studies that suggest that the selective exposure in echo chambers may lead users to falsely construe the available information and majority opinion to reinforce their own beliefs and interpretations by which they consider increasingly extreme positions (Müller et al. 2017; Wojcieszak 2011; Gaffney et al. 2013). On the contrary, some recent studies suggest that as the users regularly get exposed to opposing opinions on the social media, the homophilic effect in their network gets weakened by this cross-cutting exposure with time (Yardi and Boyd 2010). Various studies (Garimella et al. 2017a, b) have been conducted to study how the polarization in social media can be reduced by balancing information exposure and connecting the opposing views. Thus, our experimental outcome that shows an increase in users' polarization with time, when they participate in a public discourse on a COVID-19 vaccine related topic on social media (YouTube in our case), contributes to the wider ongoing research around the social media induced polarization (SMIP).

There could be a few possible explanations of this phenomenon. One could be that the online social media users who have extreme views on any topic continue to comment on the videos while the users with moderate to neutral views lose interest to comment with time. This explanation is also corroborated by a decrease in the number of comments on the videos as the recency of the discourse increases (shown in Table 2). Another explanation is related to the evolution of the opinions in the adaptive networks, where two users reach a consensus when there is a path of users in between them, each having their opinion within the tolerance limit of the previous user's opinion (Kozma and Barrat 2008). Having a larger number of comments presents a higher possibility of getting such a path between two users in a network and hence it takes a smaller number of iterations to form a consensus. However, our observation of increased polarization with time on COVID-19 vaccine related videos on YouTube still holds true despite the explanations above.

6 Conclusion

Our study suggests that the social media induced polarization on the discussion around COVID-19 vaccine has increased over time. This observation is contrary to the findings of the previous studies on polarization around socio-cultural issues which suggest a decrease in social media induced polarization over time (Amendola et al. 2015). Alternatively, studies conducted on Facebook users who belong to pro-vaccine and anti-vaccine communities suggest that the anti-vaccination group consumes more coherent sources with their views and has a more cohesive growth (i.e., pages liked by the same people) than the pro-vaccine groups (Schmidt et al. 2018). This echo chamber effect may eventually give rise to vaccine hesitancy, and the social media campaigns that advocate the importance of vaccination may only reach the pro-vaccination groups (Schmidt et al. 2018). Our study strengthens the view that as time goes by, social media fosters polarization among the users. However, our observations are limited to the users who commented on the COVID-19 vaccine-related YouTube videos selected for our study.

Predominantly around the COVID-19 vaccine debate, the inability of the countries, including that of the developed nations, to control the outbreak has triggered a greater interest in the discovery of a vaccine and this could be a potential reason for why the society is becoming more polarized around this topic. Political establishments of various countries have promised a free vaccination of COVID-19 for all if they are voted to power. This use of COVID-19 vaccine to gain a political mileage is one of the major causes of polarization in the society. One of the possible use cases of this study is to minimize the societal divide around the availability of the cure during pandemics. Government and healthcare agencies of various countries could intervene as soon as possible to curb the spread of misinformation on social media by running online social awareness campaigns that are targeted to reach anti-vaccination communities, thus making people aware of the ill-effects of falling prey to the fake news around the cure and the discovery of a vaccine.

While we have tried to capture the dynamics of opinion formation on a diverse set of YouTube videos that are related to the development of COVID-19 vaccine, our work has its own limitations. Our first limitation is the use of Azure sentiment analysis methodology which doesn't consider the contextual polarity of a word. Our second limitation is that the possible impact of user's polarization around one YouTube video on the opinion of the users of other YouTube videos is not considered i.e. all the YouTube videos are considered independent of each other. In addition to this, we also don't have a prior knowledge of the users' connections with each other to establish the effect of homophily and interdependence on the starting state of our network. Lastly, we have only considered YouTube videos for our experiments and hence our findings are limited to just a single social media platform.

This study could open several interesting directions for future work. One would be to increase the scope of this work to include the study of opinion dynamics around the economic impact of the lockdowns during COVID-19. Secondly, the study of polarization on other social media platforms (such as Twitter and Facebook) may provide some useful insights into how the opinions of the users evolve over time during pandemics.

A.1 Appendix

Sensitivity analysis results of the convergence parameter μ showing that the consensus formation gets delayed as μ increases but the end result remains the same:

Number of comments	μ	# of iterations for consensus formation
91	0.1	6
91	0.2	6
91	0.3	7
91	0.4	10
91	0.5	20

References

Albert R, Barabási A-L (2002) Statistical mechanics of complex networks. Rev Mod Phys 74:47

Allcott H, Boxell L, Conway JC, Gentzkow M, Thaler M, Yang DY (2020) Polarization and public health: partisan differences in social distancing during the coronavirus pandemic. National Bureau of Economic Research. Working Paper No. 26946

Amendola L, Marra V, Quartin M (2015) The evolving perception of controversial movies. Palgrave Commun 1(1):1–9

Antona D, Lévy-Bruhl D, Baudon C, Freymuth F, Lamy M, Maine C et al (2013) Measles elimination efforts and 2008–2011 outbreak, France. Emerg Infect Dis:357–364

Asaria P, MacMahon E (2006) Measles in the United Kingdom: can we eradicate it by 2010? BMJ 333:890–895

Bail CA, Argyle LP, Brown TW, Bumpus JP, Chen H, Hunzaker M, Volfovsky A (2018) Exposure to opposing views on social media can increase political polarization. Proc Natl Acad Sci U S A 115:9216–9221

Basch CH, MacLean SA (2019) A content analysis of HPV related posts on Instagram. Hum Vaccines Immunother 15(7–8):1476–1478

Basch, C. H., Zybert, P., Reeves, R. and Basch, C E. (2017). What do popular YouTube videos say about vaccines? Child Care Health Dev. Wiley Online Library. Doi:https://doi.org/10.1111/cch.12442.

Ben-Naim E, Krapivsky PL, Redner S (2004) Bifurcations and patterns in compromise processes. Physica D 183:190

Blankenship EB, Goff ME, Yin J, Tse Z, Fu KW, Liang H, Saroha N, Fung IC (2018) Sentiment, contents, and retweets: a study of two vaccine-related twitter datasets. Perm J 22:17–138

Castellano C, Loreto V, Barrat A, Cecconi F, Parisi D (2005) Comparison of voter and Glauber ordering dynamics of networks. Phys Rev E 71:066107

Cranmer SJ, Leifeld P, McClurg SD, Rolfe M (2017) Navigating the range of statistical tools for inferential network analysis. American Journal of Political Science 61(1):237–251
Das M, Singh P, Mazumdar A (2021) Investigating dynamics of polarization of Youtube true and fake news channels. In: Qureshi I, Bhatt B, Gupta S, Tiwari AA (eds) Causes and symptoms of socio-cultural polarization: role of information and communication technologies. Springer
Deffuant G, Neau D, Amblard F, Weisbuch G (2000) Mixing beliefs among interacting agents. Adv Complex Syst 3(01n04):87–98
Del Vicario M, Scala A, Caldarelli G, Eugene Stanley H, Quattrociocchi W (2017) Modeling confirmation bias and polarization. Sci Rep 7:40391
Depoux A, Martin S, Karafillakis B, Preet R, Wilder-Smith A, Larson H (2020) The pandemic of social media panic travels faster than the COVID-19 outbreak. J Travel Med 27:taaa031
Donovan J (2020) Social-media companies must flatten the curve of misinformation. Europe PMC. Nature, PMID: 32291410
Dorogovtsev SN, Mendes JFF (2002) Evolution of networks. Adv Phys 51:1079
Dorogovtsev SN, Mendes JFF (2003) Evolution of networks: from biological nets to the internet and WWW. Oxford University Press, Oxford
Fard AE, Verma T (2021) A comprehensive review on countering rumours in the age of online social media platforms. In: Qureshi I, Bhatt B, Gupta S, Tiwari AA (eds) Causes and symptoms of socio-cultural polarization: role of information and communication technologies. Springer
Flaherty DK (2011) The vaccine-autism connection: a public health crisis caused by unethical medical practices and fraudulent science. Ann Pharmacother 45(10):1302–1304
Fredrickson MM, Chen Y (2019) Permutation and randomization tests for network analysis. Soc Netw 59:171–183
Gaffney AM, Rast III, Hackett JD, Hogg MA (2013) Further to the right: uncertainty, political polarization and the American "tea party" movement. Soc Influ 9(4):272–288
Galam S, Gefen Y, Shapir Y (1982) Sociophysics: A new approach of sociological collective behaviour. I. mean-behaviour description of a strike. J Math Soc 9(1)
Garimella K, Gionis A, Parotsidis N, Tatti N (2017a) Balancing information exposure in social networks. In: Advances in neural information processing systems, pp 4663–4671
Garimella K, Morales GD, Gionis A, Mathioudakis M (2017b) Reducing controversy by connecting opposing views. In: WSDM'17: proceedings of the tenth ACM international conference on web search and data mining, pp 81–90
Glauber RJ (1963) Time-dependent statistics of the Ising model. J Math Phys 4:294
Godlee F, Smith J, Marcovitch H (2011) Wakefield's article linking MMR vaccine and autism was fraudulent. BMJ:64–66
Conover MD, Ratkiewicz J, Francisco M, Gonçalves B, Menczer F, Flammini A (2011) Political polarization on twitter. In: Fifth international AAAI conference on weblogs and social media. ICWSM, Barcelona
González-Padilla DA, Tortolero-Blanco L (2020) Social media influence in the COVID-19 pandemic. Int Braz J Urol 46:120–124
Gupta S, Deodhar S (2021) Understanding digitally enabled complex networks: a plural granulation based hybrid community detection approach. Inf Technol People
Gupta S, Kumar P (2021) A constrained agglomerative clustering approach for unipartite and bipartite networks with application to credit networks. Inf Sci 557:332–354
Gupta S, Kumar P (2016, August) Community detection in heterogenous networks using incremental seed expansion. In: 2016 international conference on data science and engineering (ICDSE). IEEE, pp 1–5
Gupta S, Kumar P (2020) An overlapping community detection algorithm based on rough clustering of links. Data Knowl Eng 125:101777
Gupta S, Jain G, Tiwari AA (2021) Investigating the dynamics of polarization in online discourse during COVID-19 pandemic. In: Conference on e-business, e-services and e-society. Springer, Cham, pp 704–709

Gupta S, Kumar P, Bhasker B (2016) A rough connectedness algorithm for mining communities in complex networks. In: International conference on big data analytics and knowledge discovery. Springer, Cham, pp 34–48
Hussain A, Ali S, Ahmed M, Hussain S (2018) The anti-vaccination movement: a regression in modern medicine. Cureus:1–8
Jin C, Li Y, Jin X (2017) Political opinion formation: initial opinion distribution and individual heterogeneity of tolerance. Physica A 467:257–266
Ju C, Wang J, Shi J (2020) The intelligent method of public opinion polarisation modelling and simulation analysis based on multi-dimensional and multi-level evaluation. Behav Inf Technol 1–13
Justwan F, Baumgaertner B, Carlisle JE, Clark AK, Clark M (2018) Social media echo chambers and satisfaction with democracy among democrats and Republicans in the aftermath of the 2016 US elections. J Elect Public Opin Parties:424–442
Khan S, Faslu Rahman CK, Haritha CV, Jose B, Tiwari R, Dhama K (2020) COVID-19 vaccine acceptance: beliefs and barriers associated with vaccination among the general population in India. J Exp Biol Agric Sci 8(Spl-1-SARS-CoV-2):210–218
Kligler-Vilenchik N, Baden C, Yarchi M (2020) Interpretative polarization across platforms: how political disagreement develops over time on Facebook, Twitter and WhatsApp. Social Media+Society 6(3)
Kozma B, Barrat A (2008) Consensus formation on adaptive networks. Physical Review E 77(1):016102
Krackhardt D (1988) Predicting with networks: nonparametric multiple regression analysis of dyadic data. Social Networks 10(4):359–381
Krapivsky PL, Redner S (2003) Dynamics of majority rule in two-state interacting spin systems. Phys Rev Lett 90:238701
Kumar P, Gupta S, Bhasker B (2017) An upper approximation based community detection algorithm for complex networks. Decis Support Syst 96:103–118
Laato S, Islam AKMN, Islam MN, Whelan E (2020) What drives unverified information sharing and cyberchondria during the COVID-19 pandemic? Eur J Inf Syst 29(3):288–305. https://doi.org/10.1080/0960085X.2020.1770632
Li HO, Bailey A, Huynh D, Chan J (2020) YouTube as a source of information on COVID-19: a pandemic of misinformation? BMJ Glob Health 5:e002604
Lin, Y., Hu, Z., Zhao, Q., Alias, H., Danaee, M., and Wong, L. (2020). Understanding COVID-19 vaccine demand and hesitancy: a nationwide online survey in China. PLOS Negl Trop Dis.
Müller P, Schemer C, Wettstein M, Schulz A, Wirz DS, Engesser S, Wirth W (2017) The polarizing impact of news coverage on populist attitudes in the public: evidence from a panel study in four European democracies. J Commun 67(6):968–992
Newman MEJ (2003) The structure and function of complex networks. SIAM Rev 45(2):167–256
Ortiz-Sánchez E, Velando-Soriano A, Pradas-Hernández L, Vargas-Román K, Gómez-Urquiza JL, Cañadas-De la Fuente GA, Albendín-García L (2020) Analysis of the anti-vaccine movement in social networks: a systematic review. Int J Environ Res Public Health 17(15):5394. https://doi.org/10.3390/ijerph17155394
Papakyriakopoulos O, Medina Serrano JC, Hegelich S (2020) The spread of COVID-19 conspiracy theories on social media and the effect of content moderation. The Harvard Kennedy School (HKS) Misinformation Review, 1, special issue on COVID-19 and misinformation. https://doi.org/10.37016/mr-2020-033
Pastor-Satorras R, Vespignani A (2004) Evolution and structure of the internet: a statistical physics approach. Cambridge University Press, Cambridge
Pepys MB (2007) Science and serendipity. Clin Med (London, England), 562–578
Phuong TT, Nguyen DC, Nguyen AT, Nguyen LH, Vu GT, Nguyen CT, Le HT (2020) Fake news affecting the adherence of national response measures during the COVID-19 lockdown period: the experience of Vietnam. Front Public Health.

Puri N, Coomes EA, Haghbayan H, Gunaratne K (2020) Social media and vaccine hesitancy: new updates for the era of COVID-19 and globalized infectious diseases. Hum Vaccines Immunother 16(11):2586–2593

Qureshi I, Bhatt B, Gupta S, Tiwari AA (2020) Causes, symptoms and consequences of social media induced polarization (SMIP). Inf Syst J. https://onlinelibrary.wiley.com/pb-assets/assets/13652575/ISJ_SMIP_CFP-1586861685850.pdf

Qureshi I, Bhatt B, Gupta S, Tiwari AA (2021) Introduction to the role of information and communication Technologies in Polarization. In: Qureshi I, Bhatt B, Gupta S, Tiwari AA (eds) Causes and symptoms of socio-cultural polarization: role of information and communication technologies. Springer

Qureshi I, Fang Y, Haggerty N, Compeau DR, Zhang X (2018) IT-mediated social interactions and knowledge sharing: role of competence-based trust and background heterogeneity. Inf Syst J 28(5):929–955

Robins G, Lewis JM, Wang P (2012) Statistical network analysis for analyzing policy networks. Pol Stud J 40(3):375–401

Romer D, Jamieson KH (2020) Conspiracy theories as barriers to controlling the spread of COVID-19 in the US. Soc Sci Med 263:113356

Ross DL (1968) Leicester and the anti-vaccination movement, 1853–1889. Trans Leicester Archaeol Hist Soc 43:35–44

Sasahara K, Chen W, Peng H, Ciampaglia GL, Flammini A, Menczer F (2020) Social influence and unfollowing accelerate the emergence of echo chambers. J Comput Soc Sci:1–3

Schmidt A, Zollo F, Scala A, Betsch C, Quattrociocchi W (2018) Polarization of the vaccination debate on Facebook. Elsevier 3606

Shahsavari S, Holur P, Wang T, Tangerine TR, Roychowdhury V (2020) Conspiracy in the time of corona: automatic detection of emerging COVID-19 conspiracy theories in social media and the news. J Comput Soc Sci 3:279–317

Simms KT, Hanley SJ, Smith MA, Keane A, Canfell K (2020) Impact of HPV vaccine hesitancy on cervical cancer in Japan. Lancet Public Health 5:223–224

Sood V, Redner S (2005) Voter model on heterogenous graphs. Phys Rev Lett 94:178701

Sunstein CR (2017) # republic. Princeton University Press, Princeton

Ulvi O, Lippincott N, Khan MH, Mehal P, Bass M, Lambert K, Haque U (2019) The role of social and mainstream media during storms. J Public Health Emerg 3:2–4

Wakefield AJ (1999) MMR vaccination and autism. Lancet 354. https://doi.org/10.1016/S0140-6736(05)75696-8

Wilson ME, Chen LH (2020) Travellers give wings to novel coronavirus (2019-nCoV). J Travel Med 27(2):taaa015. https://doi.org/10.1093/jtm/taaa015

Wojcieszak ME (2011) Computer-mediated false consensus: radical online groups, social networks and news media. Mass Commun Soc 14(4):527–546

Yardi S, Boyd D (2010) Dynamic debates: an analysis of group polarization over time on Twitter. Bull Sci Technol Soc 30(5):316–327

Investigating Dynamics of Polarization of YouTube True and Fake News Channels

Manideepto Das, Priya Singh, and Adrija Majumdar

Abstract In the era of the information age where information is easily accessible and shared over the internet it has become increasingly difficult for people to judge whether the news is authentic or fake. The concept of fake news is not new, it has been going on for decades in the context of religious figures, politicians, and celebrities involved in the spread of misinformation. However, with the advent of the concept of channels, the owners of social media channels have started posting fake or controversial topics to increase the subscribers and viewership. The video-sharing and viewing platform, YouTube has increased in popularity in recent years for entertainment and news purposes. Thus, it has become crucial for controlling the spread of fake information as people subscribed to a particular channel would see more polarization as increased notifications of that channel go to its subscribers which generally superimpose the viewpoints of the channel onto its subscribers and other viewers. In this chapter, we try to analyze the behavior of users in fake news channels. After epidemiological modeling of users in both fake news channel and authentic news channel we deduce the movement of users from viewers to subscribers in that channel using the transfer coefficient values calculated from our model. From our study we find that there is enhanced polarization of views in case of fake news, and the chances of a person subscribing to a fake news is quite high once exposed as compared to true news channel.

1 Introduction

Information sharing has changed and evolved drastically with the advent and popularity of the Internet. In the past 5 years, the internet penetration rate increased from 27% to 50%, owing to the various government initiatives under Digital

M. Das (✉) · P. Singh · A. Majumdar
Indian Institute of Management Ahmedabad, Ahmedabad, Gujarat, India
e-mail: p19manideepto@iima.ac.in; p19priyas@iima.ac.in; adrija@iima.ac.in

I. Qureshi et al. (eds.), *Causes and Symptoms of Socio-Cultural Polarization*,
https://doi.org/10.1007/978-981-16-5268-4_4

India campaign.[1] With increasing internet penetration and the affordability of smartphones, an increasingly larger proportion of the population have access to online platforms such as Facebook, Twitter, YouTube, etc. which are instrumental in transmitting news and information to a very wide audience. In earlier times, most of the information was shared and broadcasted using magazines, televisions, newspapers, and other media which had people controlling and checking what goes out as information or news.[2] Today, there are no checks, and anyone can use their social media accounts and handles to post anything on the platforms. News items spread like wild-fire due to direct connectivity between the producers and the consumers and the gap between these categories is diminishing (Törnberg 2018). While this phenomenon has made news and information accessible and quicker for the masses, this has also led to several issues like misinformation, fake news, biased narrative, mistrust and paranoia (Jain et al. 2021b; Fard and Verma 2021; Ghai et al. 2021). There has been a degradation in the quality and credibility of information available to the users (Törnberg 2018). Digital misinformation is a major threat to our society according to the World Economic Forum.[3]

The video-sharing and viewing platform, YouTube has increased in popularity in recent years (Jain et al. 2021a; Gupta et al. 2021). Youtube has more than 2 billion users who consume daily more than 1 billion hours of video (Ros-Gálvez et al. 2021). Additionally, among active social media users, YouTube accounts for the largest penetration, standing at 82 percent as of Q3 FY20.[4] People from all walks of life turn to YouTube for entertainment and news. Owing to the ease of data point collection and higher use vis-à-vis other social media platforms, YouTube seems most relevant for this research. Online mediums such as YouTube use various algorithms to decide what content to show to the users based on what they do on various platforms. They show the users extreme content that fringes their political views without them realizing it.[5] The spread of fake news on YouTube also has implications in leading to phenomena like echo chambers which leads to political polarization. Also, with the advent of YouTube channels, the subscribers of the channel get more and more notification about the content in the channels which forces a particular viewpoint of the channel onto the subscribers without even realizing it and the effect could be worse especially if the channel is disseminates fake news. This work is an attempt to study the impact of YouTube fake channels on the users. For studying the impact of YouTube fake channels, we have first categorized a YouTube channel into True and Fake based on the veracity of content they have uploaded in the last three months. Next, we study the epidemiological modeling of users in the channels. Using this we obtain rate of movement of users in the channel. We then perform a random network-theory based simulation to study

[1] https://www.statista.com/statistics/240960/share-of-indian-population-using-social-networks/

[2] https://www.weforum.org/agenda/2016/01/q-a-walter-quattrociocchi-digital-wildfires/

[3] https://www.weforum.org/agenda/2016/01/q-a-walter-quattrociocchi-digital-wildfires/

[4] https://www.statista.com/statistics/240960/share-of-indian-population-using-social-networks/

[5] https://www.nytimes.com/interactive/2019/06/08/technology/youtube-radical.html

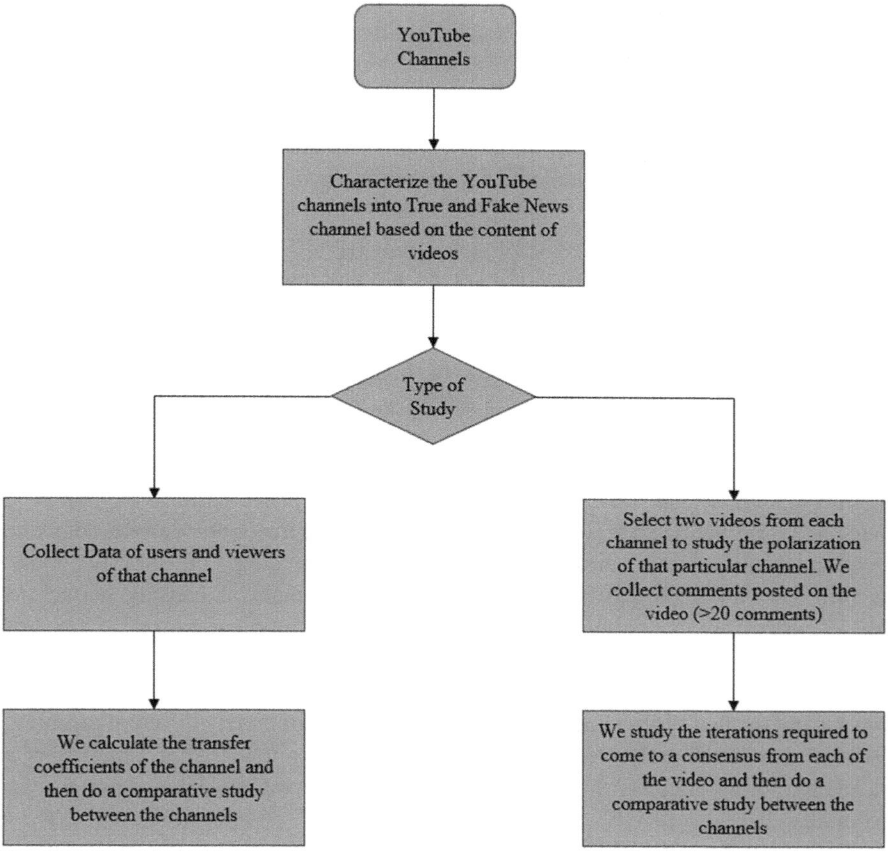

Fig. 1 Flow chart of our study of Fake news channels

the opinion formation in the comments posted on several YouTube videos across different areas from those channels. The flowchart of the study is provided in Fig. 1. From the study, we conclude that the users of fake YouTube channels took more time to come to a common consensus as compared to a user of authentic news channels. Also, it is observed that though the chances of a user to get exposed to a fake news channels are less but once exposed there is a high chance of him to subscribe to a fake YouTube channel.

2 Background

In this section, we discuss the fundamental literature that we are going to connect in solving the problem.

2.1 Fake News

Fake news, a relatively new term in the mainstream language, refers to the "stories that are fabricated that obtain little to no verifiable facts"[19]. The propagation of false information is almost identical to that of accurate information, with the possibility of going viral and influencing public opinion at large. The intent of fake news can be multi-fold ranging from news satire to propaganda (Allcott and Gentzkow 2017; Roozenbeek and Van Der Linden 2019) or just an attempt to create mass hysteria through deception. As per a survey conducted by Statista Research Department between December 2018 and January 2019, a whopping 88% of first-time voters agreed with fake news being a problem in India. Apart from elections, there have been many other instances of fake news propagation, for example, CAA 2019, Coronavirus pandemic, Kashmir issue etc. The false information that we receive can primarily classified into three categories, namely, misinformation, disinformation, mal information (Wardle and Derakhshan 2018). Misinformation is information, which is false, but it is not created to cause harm to anyone. The person disseminating such information believes it to be true (for example, someone posting an out-of-date article unknowingly). Disinformation, on the other hand, is information that is false and is created with the intent of causing harm to a person, organization, or country (for example, a competitor projecting false statistics of a company to discredit it in the eyes of the public. In this case, the person disseminating such information knows it to be false. Mal information is based on reality, but the news is twisted out of context to give a completely different meaning. This is also deliberately created to cause harm (for example, using a picture of a dead child or a refugee without any context to incite hatred against a community or a country).[6]

With the advent and increasing popularity of the internet, the spread of false information has become a growing issue worldwide, especially due to the ease with which information can be shared (Wang et al. 2018). Fake news refers to false or fabricated information disguised as authentic news which is similar to news content when looked at and read. There are various other definitions of false information that have been proposed in the literature (Tandoc Jr et al. 2018). Fake news and rumors are some of the most common terms of false information in the media. There are various types of categorizations of fake news and rumors. According to (Allcott and Gentzkow 2017) fake news is defined as "a news article that is intentionally and verifiably false". Rumors refer to information that has not been confirmed by official sources yet and is spread mostly by users on social media platforms (Bondielli and Marcelloni 2019). Apart from fake news and rumors, there are also other types of false content that have been studied, namely, social spammers, clickbait and fake reviews. So, as we can see that Fake news is very similar to malinformation part of

[6] http://www.mikekujawski.ca/2019/09/05/misinformation-vs-disinformation-vs-malinformation/

false information as the news is twisted to make it look authentic and hence ending up misguiding people.

During the 2016 US presidential elections, the term fake news became increasingly common in Google searches in the US. Since then, the term has remained quite popular and attracts a lot of attention from researchers (Allcott and Gentzkow 2017). Fake news not only creates a hurdle for people taking a decision but also, in some cases, brainwashes many people into believing things that are not good for society as a whole. Governments across the globe have recognized this risk. Steps need to be taken to curb the spread of fake news to avoid panic and disharmony in society.

Global health is also threatened by the spread of fake news on social media. COVID-19 outbreak in February 2020 which shook the whole world, according to WHO, also resulted in a massive 'infodemic', or a plethora of information.[7] Due to this untrusted and unverified plethora of information, it has been a concern for people in the pandemic, be it for health-related information, government policies, factual or casualty data, etc. Disinformation overload can lead to serious effects like uncertainty, anxiety, fear at a very large scale compared to past epidemics, which is harmful to the people. The use of social media for sharing false news and hate messages during the pandemic is an issue of concern. During the pandemic, people are mentally affected, and the spread of such news can have serious repercussions on people's mental health as well. (Ornell et al. 2020).

Polarization is related to misinformation via an inverted u-shape relationship. The case of the least misinformation, when individuals combine information from various sources to form a true opinion, is the ideal state with least polarization. Additionally, at the other end of spectrum, when there is maximal misinformation to the extent that public at large converge to an erroneous belief, is another case with minimal polarization. Finally, there is a state when public on average are acquainted with true facts, yet there are large masses of people lying on extremes of belief distribution, a case of intermediate misinformation leading to high polarization.

Researchers face various challenges in data collection to study false information. One of those is that false information is only a very small fraction of the total content available on the internet. Social media like Facebook have strict policies with respect to the analysis of data produced or published on them. Different types of misinformation require different types of studies and therefore very few data repositories are available publicly (Bondielli and Marcelloni 2019).

The most common source of fake news is malicious websites that aim to spread misinformation. This gives a way to collect articles that have a high probability of being fake news. People falling prey to such websites may not just be the result of their own ignorance; the websites may be masquerading reputed websites with minor, insignificant changes that tend to go unnoticed. One of the easiest methods to

---

[7] https://www.who.int/news-room/feature-stories/detail/immunizing-the-public-against-misinformation

identify potentially fake news is to identify its source. However, that does not mean that fake news cannot be found on verified sources (Bondielli and Marcelloni 2019).

There are certain organizations that are dedicated to busting fake news. Altnews is one such organization in India with a whopping 287 K followers on Twitter targeting fake news across all domains, be it political, criminal, etc. There are various other initiatives taken by other social media platforms like Facebook etc. in warning users over news content by giving a disclaimer below with the link of a trusted source.

In this research we study the behavior of users in the fake news channels and do a comparative study with the true news channels to see the rate at which users keep subscribing and moving in and out of the channels.

2.2 Polarization

Polarization can have a "state" definition as well as a "process" definition. Polarization as a state is one where an opinion has led to opposing opinions to a theoretical maximum. Polarization as a process is one where this opposition increases as time passes (DiMaggio et al. 1996). Various impacts of political polarization have been seen in the USA with respect to the impeachment of President Donald Trump. On the voting to advance the articles of impeachment to the floor of the House of Representatives, 23 members (all Democrats) voted "Yes" and 17 members (16 Republican and 1 Democrat) voted "No". Even during the discussion that followed, Democrats wanted Trump to be impeached for overstepping while Republicans defended him and called the allegation a sham.[8]

The way information is shared with users on the internet by using various algorithms that take into account the ideologies of the users is also believed to be contributing to polarization (Qureshi et al. 2020, 2021). Former US President Barack Obama in an interview talked about political polarization:

> If you are getting all your information off algorithms being sent through your phone and it's just reinforcing whatever biases you have, which is the pattern that develops, at a certain point, you just live in a bubble, and that's part of why our politics is so polarized right now. I think it's a solvable problem, but I think it's one we have to spend a lot of time thinking about. – Barack Obama, *January 2018*.[9]

Below are a few examples of news topics that have been quite notorious in creating polarizing views:

- The Ram Mandir case: The land near Ayodhya has been a matter of dispute for a long time now. Whether the land is to be allocated to the Babri Masjid or for

[8] https://www.i-com.it/en/2020/01/17/trump-impeachment-polarization/

[9] https://www.cnbc.com/2018/01/12/former-president-barack-obama-warns-on-polarizing-media-us-electoral-system.html

the Ram Mandir has created polarising views across India. People have been divided into two main polarized camps, the Hindutva Bhartiya view, according to which Ayodhya is a symbol of Indian civilizational values versus the secular view according to which Ayodhya is playing a role in the destruction of the constitutional Republican foundation of modern India. The intense passion with which ordinary Indians have heated up this issue has resulted in both sides evading responsibility for many other real challenges faced by the citizens.[10]
- Sushant Singh Rajput suicide case: This suicide of an Indian actor, in the midst of the COVID-19 pandemic gave some prime-time fodder to the Indian media that lasted for several months and became a topic for political debate. There were two important patterns found from data obtained from various sources such as Twitter, YouTube, etc. One, it was apparent from the retweet rates on Twitter that commentators profited from this discussion as it got higher engagement than other prevalent news at that time. Second, politicians in following their own agenda proved instrumental in bending the case to 'murder' rather than 'suicide'.[11]

Such instances of polarization hamper the smooth functioning of any society and may lead to instances of civil protests, violence, riots, etc. The most apt example of this would probably be the ongoing pandemic. During times like this, people need to act together to combat COVID-19. On the contrary, the existing polarised divides seem to have deepened placing even more undue strain on the functioning governmental bodies. In such events of unforeseen uncertainties, the primal human nature of passing the blame onto each other gets unleashed. This is not just limited to a small group of people, instead, even countries are blaming each other for the pandemic.

Social media has made interaction between individuals and information sharing extremely convenient and easy. Debates about whether social media is bringing diverse people together or leading to the formation of more closed communities is not a new one. Irrespective of the geographical distances, people can discuss all sorts of topics on such platforms with like-minded individuals or individuals with similar interests. These conversations can be on open forums or blogs, but also in closed groups such as private communities on various social media platforms (Barberá 2020; Kumar et al. 2016, 2017; Gupta and Kumar 2020, 2021; Gupta et al. 2016; Gupta and Deodhar 2021). Users interacting with other users of similar views might reinforce their own beliefs and viewpoints and notions while isolating themselves from the users having a different or opposite view. This phenomenon is called as the formation of echo chambers where users reinforce their own viewpoints while disregarding any information that might be different from or opposed to their opinions. Just like our own sound comes back to us during an echo, similarly our

---

[10] https://indianexpress.com/article/opinion/columns/ayodhya-ram-temple-construction-mahatma-gandhi-ramrajya-6582141/

[11] https://www.firstpost.com/india/anatomy-of-a-rumour-an-analysis-of-social-media-content-surrounding-sushant-singh-rajputs-death-8883751.html

own points and ideologies circle and come back to us in such a closed community which is why these are referred to as echo chambers. Echo chambers might result in political polarization which makes it difficult to resolve controversial issues due to a lack of fact-based debates (O'Hara and Stevens 2015; Garimella and Weber 2017). Spending a lot of time in a particular echo chamber leads to feelings of negativity and hostility towards the people of an opposite political ideology. Figure 2 provides comments highlighted for two videos with various viewpoints that lead to polarization.

2.3 Life-Threatening News

There are several types of news that users come across. Life-threatening news comprises of facts or opinions pertaining to events that might pose a risk to the life of individuals. While many news items have direct implications on users, others don't affect the consumers personally at all. Life-threatening news, true or fake regardless, might affect the users and provoke them to act accordingly. The reaction of users to life-threatening news might be different from their reaction to other news that does not have any relation to their life directly. The consumer of life-threatening news reacts differently from those of regular news, as the former affects their health & wellbeing on a personal level. For example, during 2020, the onset of COVID-19 resulted in a lot of news articles and videos surfacing on a daily basis many of which became viral on platforms like YouTube, Twitter, Facebook etc. These articles and videos had the ability to create panic and anxiety among the users as their life could be directly linked to these. On the other hand, news items like Sushant Singh Rajput's death, no matter how much ever talked about, did not pose any threat to the lives of the common users in general. In this research, we explore the life-threatening aspect of news in consensus formation as it would help us understand the polarization linked to life-threatening news.

2.4 Epidemiological Modelling of Fake News

A very interesting approach employed to study and model information spread is the application of epidemiological models. These models have been borrowed from the compartmental models used to understand the spread of infectious disease in a population. Kermack and McKendrick's model introduced in 1927 was one of the first compartmental models to be published which motivated other such models. This model divides the population into several compartments: S (Susceptible), I (Infectious) or R (Recovered). S(t), I(t), R(t) are the number of people in each of these compartments at a given time. People move between the compartments. The SIR system can be represented by a set of ordinary differential equations which can be solved to arrive at the solutions as functions of time. Several other models have

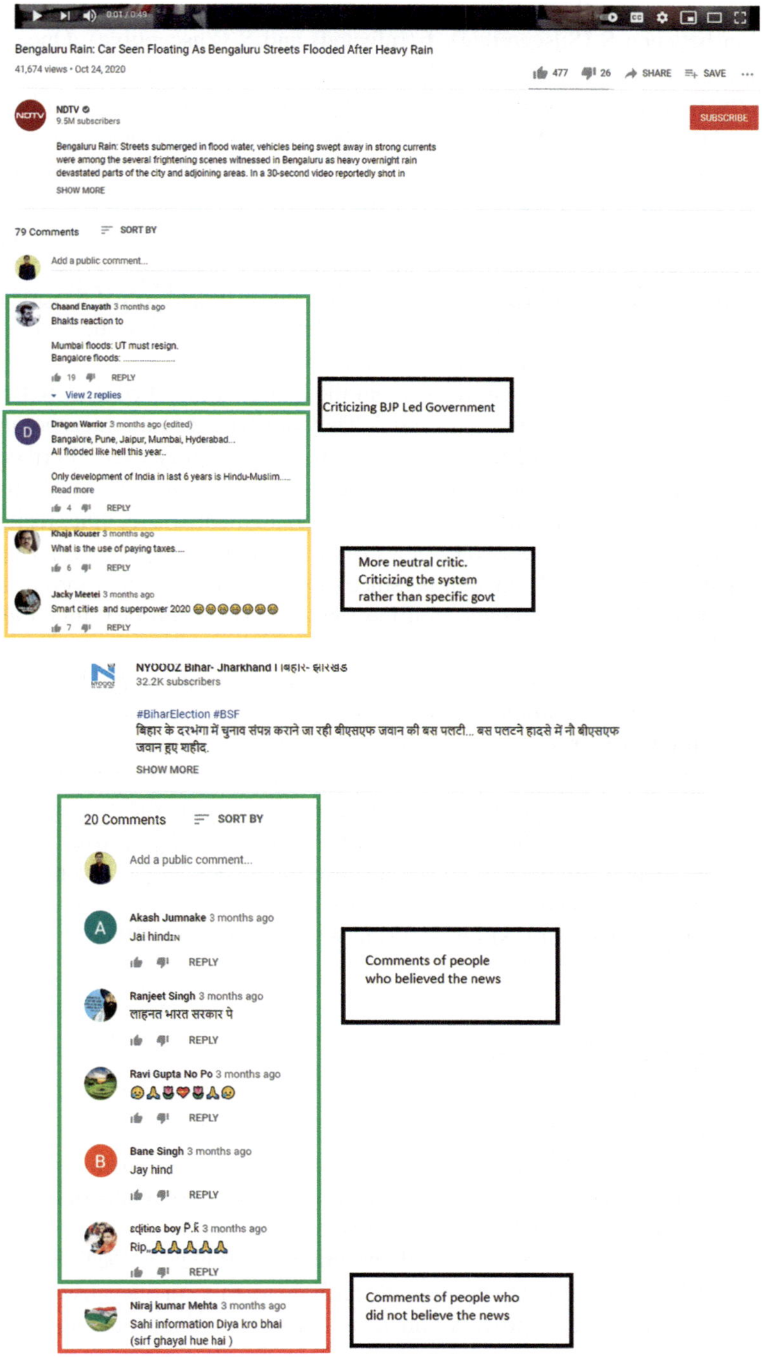

Fig. 2 Comments highlighted for two videos with various viewpoints that lead to polarization

been used to explain the spread of information, e.g., SIS. In an SIS model, users transition between S (Susceptible), I (Infected) and S (Susceptible). Once a user gets exposed to the news, they directly move to the infected compartment.

SEIZ was an adaptation of the SIR model to understand the adoption of Feynman diagrams (Bettencourt et al. 2006). SEIZ model has four compartments namely S (Susceptible), E (Exposed), I (Infected), Z (Sceptic). The major improvement in the SEIZ model is the incorporation of the delay which was missing in the SIS model. There have been a few attempts to apply epidemiological models to modeling fake news. Jin et al. (2013) tried to find the transition of the users between various compartments in SIS and SEIZ models. For this study, they selected 8 stories from various domains in an attempt to cover a wide range of topics such as politics, terrorism, entertainment, and crime from different parts of the world. They further argued using their mathematical results that the SEIZ model fitted the Twitter data much more accurately than the SIS model. They attribute it to the incorporation of the "delay" in the posting of news by the "Exposed" category users. Further, they also showed that the SEIZ model could be used successfully to distinguish rumours from true news on Twitter data. This can be further augmented with other techniques to accurately identify rumours / fake news from true news.

In our study we used SIS modelling since the parameters S, I are normalized by dividing susceptible and Infected with the total N respectively. By this, the scale of subscribers and views across channels are taken care of. Suppose a channel that has more exposure to users is normalized when the subscribers are divided by the number of views thus eliminating the factor of the scale of subscribers. Thus, a channel with fewer views and fewer subscribers becomes similar to a channel with more views and more subscribers. It helps us in understanding the rate of movement proportion of users rather than the number of users itself. Also, the two states signify that when a user unsubscribes from the channel, it means they move back to the susceptible state and still have a chance of subscribing back which is very much the case these days. Since recovery is possible, that is, a lost subscriber can return to the channel on further exposure, SIS model is preferred instead of SIR.

2.5 Consensus Formation

How people interact with each other, that is, their emerging social behaviour is strongly influenced by interaction with their neighbours (Kozma and Barrat 2008). The statistical physics approach tries to capture this using basic rules of opinion formation which is typically governed by herding behaviour. So, a group of interacting people tends to form their opinions through a local majority or by simply imitating their neighbours. According to this, in the absence of any external intervention, this process can result in one of three outcomes. One, a global consensus can be reached, in which all the people form the same opinion. Alternatively, these people can form two groups which have radically opposing views, commonly referred to as polarization. Lastly it can result in a fragmented opinion with many small groups holding their own individual opinion different from the other groups (Kozma and Barrat 2008). In such a case, the size of the population would be a major factor to determine the number of opinion fragments. In the simpler models, modelling consensus formation opinions are represented by a binary variable (which can assume two values, 0 or 1). However, these models do not capture realistic social interactions. Therefore, models incorporating features such as memory mimic the realistic situation more acutely. Further fine-tuning can be achieved by introducing the notion of bounded confidence wherein a person will only interact with another person if their opinions are close enough. A hyperparameter, tolerance, denotes the bounded confidence; different values of tolerance will lead to different states of polarization (Kozma and Barrat 2008). The Deffuant model can be used to model large number of coexisting opinions in contrast to the Voter model which can only take in two opinions.

We wish to study this epidemiological modelling of fake news. In our study, we would be using the Network simulation methodology to study the dynamics of polarization in the case of True news and Fake news channels based on two sample videos from each of the channels.

3 Methodology

3.1 Epidemiological Modelling to Understand the Dynamics of Users in True and Fake News

In this paper we try to understand the behavior of YouTube users across fake and True news channels. To study the behavior of users across channels we use the epidemiological modeling to understand the transfer dynamics of users in a channel.

The origin of epidemiological modeling dates to the times of pandemic where people modeled the spread of infectious disease using various models to understand the transfer dynamics of the diseases i.e., the movement across various categories like the susceptible category, infected category etc. (Hethcote 1989). For modeling, the population is divided into disjoint sets which change with time. For example, the sets infected remains the set of people infected which keeps on changing with time as people move to either death or recovered category. This model changes according to the disease and the requirement. For the diseases which offer no immunity, we use the SIS model, for the diseases which offer lifetime immunity we use the SIR model, for the diseases which offer partial immunity we use the SIRS model etc. (Fig. 3).

For modeling the behavior of YouTube users, we would be using the SIS model. We would be using this model as a user can only be in two states that are susceptible and infected. Infected is when he subscribes to the channel and susceptible is when he does not subscribe to the channel. It can be due to various factors like not feeling the channel relevant, not liking the channel content, channel content not intersecting

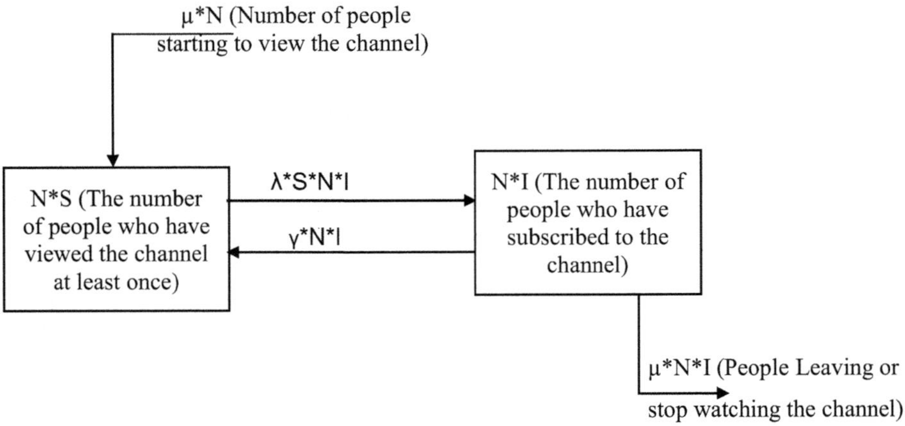

Fig. 3 SIS modelling. (Adapted from Hethcote 1989)

with a user's viewpoint or ideology etc. So as long as the channel is not able to convince a user to subscribe, we consider a user to be a susceptible user. A user can move into susceptible when he views the channel at least once. Next the user can move from susceptible to infected when he starts liking the content of the channel and ends up subscribing. A user can also move from infected to susceptible when he unsubscribes the channel. For the deaths in Fig. 3, we assume it to be a constant natural rate of leaving that might happen due to other external factors.

In this model, we have two states S(t), I(t)

N: Total Population for a channel (Total number of views for that channel)

S(t): Represents the proportion of people who are susceptible to being infected. In calculating this we subtract the number of subscribers from the number of views and then divide with N.

I(t): Represents the proportion of people out of population N to subscribe to a channel. In this, we divide the number of subscribers with N.

$S(t) + I(t) = 1$

λ = Coefficient of infection

γ = Coefficient of users leaving subscription and moving back to susceptible position

μ = Natural rate of people entering or leaving a channel

Equations

$$S'(t) = -\lambda * I * S + \gamma * I + \mu - \mu * S \quad (1)$$

$$I'(t) = \lambda * I * S - \gamma * I - \mu * I \quad (2)$$

$$I(t) = \left(e^{(\gamma+\mu)*(\sigma-1)*t}\right) / \left(\left(\sigma * \left(e^{(\gamma+\mu)*(\sigma-1)*t} - 1\right) / (\sigma - 1)\right) + 1/I_0\right) \quad (3)$$

$$S(t) = 1 - I(t) \tag{4}$$

Where $\sigma = \lambda / (\gamma + \mu)$, I_0 = Initial proportion of people subscribing to a channel.

Here σ is known as the contact rate. It is a measure of the rate of infection i.e., the rate at which people are getting infected or in our case the rate at which susceptible people are subscribing to a channel. γ represents the rate at which users are coming out of the subscription and moving back to susceptible and μ represents the natural rate of users entering or leaving the channel.

3.2 *Network Simulation Methodology to Investigate User Polarization in True and Fake News*

Once we understand the characteristics of users' movement across the true and fake channels, we try to understand the dynamics of polarization in these channels by picking up 2 videos from each of the channels and studying the comments. For that, we try to simulate a network of users who interact with each other to form an opinion with the help of graphs, where a YouTube user who has commented with a timestamp is represented by a unique node and the interaction between users are represented by an edge. The sentiment score of a user is used as an input to the simulation to create an opinion after having random encounters with another person that is in the network.

Various statistical models have been used in the past to study the social behavior of individuals such as culture adoption, spreading of linguistic conventions and the dynamics of opinion formation (Kozma and Barrat 2008) We use the work of this paper to model our network for user interaction to form a consensus. We use a tolerance level as a threshold to decide whether to select a user as to whether that user would influence the other user while interacting if the sentiment scores between the two users are less than the tolerance level. It is taken care that the tolerance level is not too large as being large would make all users come to a common consensus. If the tolerance level is too small then it would be too difficult for two users to come to a consensus. In our case, we take the tolerance level to be 0.3. So, if the sentiment scores of two users are less than 0.3 i.e., the tolerance level then the first user is expected to change his opinion based on the sentiment of the second user.

The initial graph formation is done using the Erdos-Renyi random network model. Initially if there are N users then N nodes are created. After that, the edges are created based on the random interaction of users. For simulating the initial random interaction of users, we fix a probability on the interaction of any two users. For example, if there are N users (N nodes), the total number of interactions possible would be ${}^{N}C_{2}$ interactions (N*(N–1)/2). Since each connection has a probability of p then the total number of connections would be ${}^{N}C_{2}$*p. Thus, each node would have a connection to N*p nodes on average. For example, if there are 100 nodes and the total number of edges in our graph would be 495. Thus, each node would have on an average 10 edges. Here we have assumed that the interaction between users happen randomly and is independent of attributes such as like mindedness, personality etc. This is the limitation of our work. We have also picked up this assumption and the probability of random interaction (i.e., $p = 0.1$) from the work of (Kozma and Barrat 2008).

In our algorithm, once the initial graph is formed, we take a random node (YouTube user) and then calculate the polarity scores (sentiment scores) of that user. We then take the polarity scores (sentiment scores) of all the neighbors in the graph and then select the neighbors who all fall within the tolerance level ($|s_1 - s_2| < TL$). Then the final polarity score s_1 of the initial user is updated based on the mean of all the neighbor polarity scores $s_1 = \mu*(s_1 + mean*(abs(s_1 - s_2)))$. This is done for all the nodes in the graph for an iteration. The same process is repeated for successive iterations. Based on the number of iterations required to reach a consensus we can comment on the polarity score. The higher iterations the higher the bias and difficulty to come to a consensus and the higher the polarization. By increasing the μ we can just impact the convergence times but not the dynamics as it would be relative. It has been observed from the paper (Kozma and Barrat 2008) that as the value of μ changes from 0.1 to 0.5 in intervals of 0.1 (while they tried to do sensitivity analysis), then only the convergence times or iterations to converge changes and not the dynamics of opinion formation.

For taking the value of Tolerance level (TL) we tried to do sensitivity analysis on the values of TL. By varying the values of TL in intervals of 0.1 from 0.1 to 0.7 we can see that for very low values of TL (0.1, 0.2) there is no convergence of opinion whereas for higher values (0.4, 0,5,0.6, 0.7) there was a broader consensus among users with no significant insights.

Below is a pseudo-code that depicts the working algorithm of the simulation.

Input A graph with N nodes (Number of YouTube users comment) and ${}^{N}C_2*p$ edges with each node has a polarity score s_i € {0,1}. The threshold level (TL) = 0.3, $\mu = 0.5$, max number of iterations ($i = 100$), $p = 0.1$ (probability of any two users interacting)

Algorithm:

```
For each iteration i from 0 to 100
    For each node j from 0 to N
        For all the neighbors nbr of j
            If(|Sj-Snbr| < TL) {nbr_list.add(Snbr)}
        End
        If(length(nbr_list)>0)
            { Sj = μ * (Sj+ mean[nbr_list] (|Sj -Snbr|) }
            empty(nbr_list)
        Else
            no change in value of Sj
    End
End
```

The output would be a network where all users would have a common opinion/consensus or there would be multiple clusters with a group of users in each cluster with each cluster representing a set of opinions.

4 Illustration of Examples

4.1 Illustration on YouTube Channel Depicting the Epidemiological Modelling

In order to depict the SIS modeling, we would be using the example of Zee News. So, we simulated our model in MATLAB. For the collection of data, we have used the subscribers and viewers data for a channel across a span of the last 30 days. We collected our data from the "noxinfluencer" site.

The time is represented in intervals of days like 1 to 30 with 1 being the first day from where we are collecting data to 30 being the 30th day. We have started capturing the data for channels after they gained maturity and established themselves for a long time. The S and I are calculated as depicted in Table 1. Once we have data as depicted in Table 1 we try to fit in the curve (Eq. 3) to the data points collected using lsqnonlin function of MATLAB. While fitting the curve on all the data points the corresponding coefficients (λ, γ, μ) are calculated. Then we later compare the coefficients across true news and fake news channels to bring in a few characteristics of fake news channels and true news channels (Table 5).

Below are the respective values got for Zee News (Table 2). The curve fit of the SIS model is provided in Fig. 4.

4.2 Illustration on YouTube Video Depicting the Model Used for Polarization of Users

In order to depict our model used in studying the polarization of users we use a video titled "PM Modi Celebrates Diwali With Armed Forces in Jaisalmer | Republic TV's

Table 1 Sample of data for epidemiological modeling

Time	No. of Views (N) In 000's	No. of Subscribers (X) In 000's	Susceptible (Y–X) In 000's	Infected(X) In 000's	S (N-X)/N	I (X/N)
1	5800	29.05	5770.95	29.05	0.994991379	0.00500862
2	5810	29.1	5780.9	29.1	0.994991394	0.00500861

Table 2 Transfer coefficient values of Zee News

Topic	Gamma	Lambda	Mu	Sigma
3.4946	6.3664	2.8721	0.999953	3.4946

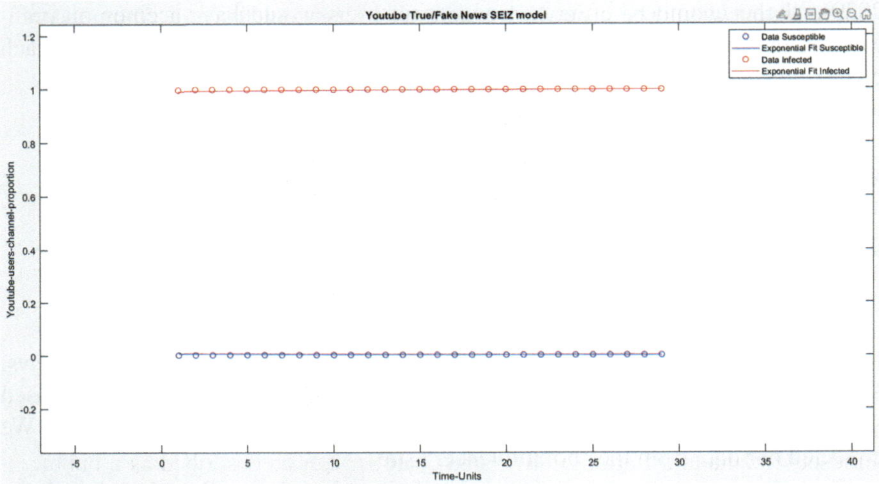

Fig. 4 Curve fit of the SIS model in MATLAB

Report". In this video which has been characterized as true news, we have collected the comments from the video using a comments extractor written in Python. After extraction of comments, we calculated the sentiment and the sentiment score using Azure Analysis Tool in Excel for the comments. The scores ranged from 0 to1 and the categories for a sentiment were positive, negative and neutral.

Once the data was prepared, we ran our experiment using the network simulation algorithm as mentioned in the 3.1 section. The network simulation algorithm was written in R language. We ran our algorithm for 100 iterations. At the end of each iteration, we plotted a density graph with the number of people with a consensus score on the Y-axis and the Consensus score on the X-axis. We could see that as the iterations increased mode and more people were converging to a consensus. In the initial iteration, we could see a kind of normal graph with the number of people across each polarity scores bin but as iterations progressed more and more people came closer to a single polarity score.

We can see that in the initial iteration for the YouTube video the density function is more spread out as it converges as the iterations increase. From Fig. 5 we can see that around the 50th iteration we have all users at a single polarity score.

5 Experiments and Results

5.1 Data Extraction, Cleaning & Experiment Setup

For SIS modeling we used noxinfluencer to collect the number of subscribers and viewers for a YouTube channel over a period of 30 days. We selected the channels

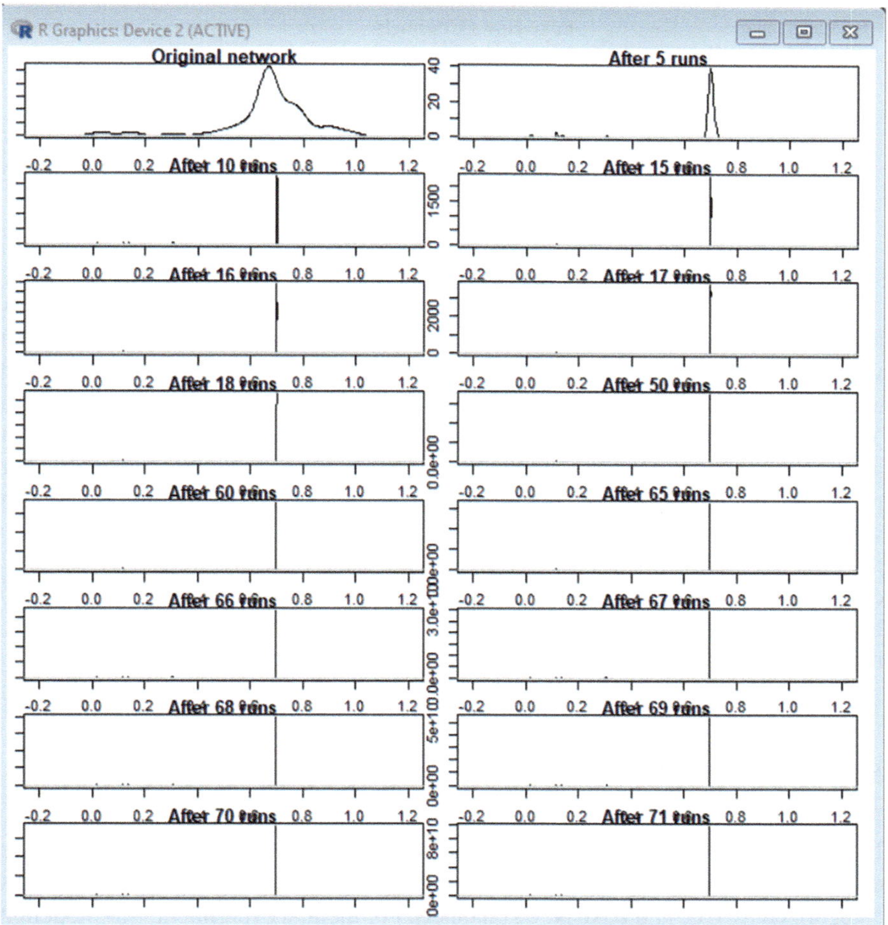

Fig. 5 COVID a distraction: Illustration of consensus formation with N = 100, p = 0.1, TL = 0.3

that were in the matured stage and have established themselves over a period of time. We categorized the channels as true or fake news channel based on the video content they had on their channels. We implemented our model in MATLAB to curve fit the SIS curve onto the datapoints got from our data. Once the curve is fitted in using the lsqnonlin function we try to compare the various coefficients (λ, γ, μ) across the two categories True and Fake news to understand the movement of users across different states Susceptible and Infected.

Fake News Channels
Study News
NYOOOZ Bihar- Jharkhand
True News Channels
Republic World
Zee News
NDTV

Next for the collection of data for investigating dynamics of polarization across the channels, we selected 2 news videos from the respective channels. Our selection was also in such a way that it could also be segregated into Life & Health-related and Non-Life & Health-related videos. First, we extracted the comments from YouTube using the YouTube APIs present in python. We used comments >20 so that a consensus is formed. Because it is observed that for videos with a smaller number of videos the data set is not large enough to form an opinion or consensus. Once we have the comments, we use Microsoft's Azure Text Analysis API to calculate the polarity scores (range between 0 and 1) of each of the comments and also to categorize the comments as positive, negative or neutral. We then used the found-out sentiment score of each comment into our Opinion based network simulation model as described in Sect. 3.1.

5.2 *Experimental Results*

In this section, we present the results we got from two experiments that we have conducted to understand the behavior of YouTube users across various channels categorized as True and Fake News channels. For the first experiment, SIS modeling was carried out on True News and Fake News. The second experiment was carried on Polarization and consensus formation across 1.) True News and Fake News and 2.) on Life & Health-Related and not Life & Health-Related.

For the epidemiological modeling (SIS modeling) we tried to find the transfer coefficients of fake news channels vs true news channels. The details of fake news channels and true news channels are given in Table 3 and the transfer coefficients for the respective channels are also given in Table 4.

It can be seen from the graph that both the values of γ, μ are less for fake news as compared to the true news. It can also be seen that the value of σ is more for the case of Fake News as compared to True News. Also, there is a kind of more variability seen for the values of σ (Table 5) in Fake News as compared to True News.

The results of our opinion formation experiment for Fake and news and True News are given in Table 6.

We can observe that as iterations increase the density function starts to converge. More and more people come under a small range until everything is converged and all people come to a common opinion and hence a spike around a single polarity

Table 3 News channels and their details

News Channels (YouTube)	Details
Republic World	Republic TV was launched in May 2017 by Arnab Goswami. It can majorly be categorized a true news channel due to the content shared by their channel in YouTube seemed to be facts.
Zee News	Zee news by Zee Media Corporation launched in 1999 can be classified as a news channel primarily due to majority of news content to be true.
NDTV	New Delhi Television Limited is Indian Media company launched in 1988. It is also categorized as a True News channel due to majority of news content to be true and containing facts.
Study News	Study News has a YouTube news channel which contains news items in a exaggerated way due to which we categorized it under Fake news channel.
NYOOOZ Bihar- Jharkhand	NYOOOZ Bihar- Jharkhand is a You Tube news channel which is categorized as a Fake News channel as it had various content exaggerated and few cooked up stories like Sushil Modi going to take place of Nitish Kumar etc.

Table 4 Transfer coefficients of each news channel

Topic	Type	Gamma	Lambda	Mu	Sigma
Republic World	TRUE	3.0726	5.7877	2.7163	0.999793
Zee News	TRUE	3.4946	6.3664	2.8721	0.999953
NDTV	TRUE	4.2206	7.9285	3.7077	1.000025
Study News	FAKE	0.0012	0.0066	0.00056	3.751364
NYOOOZ Bihar- Jharkhand	FAKE	1.9246	3.4682	1.5457	0.999395

Table 5 Average of coefficients of True News and Fake News in SIS modeling

True News	Gamma (γ)	Lambda (λ)	Mu (μ)	Sigma (σ)
Average	3.595933	6.6942	3.0987	0.999924
STDEV	0.58067	1.107405	0.533131	0.000119
Fake News	Gamma (γ)	Lambda (λ)	Mu (μ)	Sigma (σ)
Average	0.9629	1.7374	0.77313	2.375379
STDEV	1.360049	2.447721	1.092579	1.945936

score. It is observed that only one echo chamber is formed and not multiple spikes at the end from which we can conclude that with our parameters all the users have come to a common consensus or opinion for all the videos (Appendix A.1.1).

We have seen that there is no correlation between the number of comments with the number of iterations but on average fake news requires more iterations to form consensus than true news. Also, the standard deviation is large for fake news as it depends on the type of fake news for the speed of reaching a consensus (Fig. 6).

We have also analyzed the graphs in terms of Life & Health category. We have here too found that life and health-related news take more time i.e., a greater number of interactions or iterations to come to a consensus (Fig. 7).

Table 6 Experiment results of polarization and consensus formation experiment

Topic	No. of Iterations for Stabilizing	No. of Comments	True/fake	Life & health/non-life & health
Darbhanga Bus accident	25	20	FAKE	Life & Health
PM Modi Diwali Celebration with BSF	18	100	TRUE	Not Life & Health
Nitish Kumar oath	15	50	TRUE	Not Life & Health
Indian army Gilgit Baltistan	20	233	FAKE	Life & Health
COVID Tally	30	92	TRUE	Life & Health
Bengaluru Rain	25	90	TRUE	Life & Health
118 Chinese apps banned	28	255	TRUE	Not Life & Health
Farmers' Protest	15	136	TRUE	Not Life & Health
Nepal Attacks India	15	402	FAKE	Life & Health
India China War ahead	40	31	FAKE	Life & Health

6 Discussion and Inferences

In SIS-based modeling, we have taken proportion for values of S and I, to normalize the effect of having a large number of followers for one channel and a smaller number of followers or views for another channel. The rate of flow of people across each category that is from susceptible to infected or vice versa is quite high for true news as compared to fake news. So, it means that there is more flow of people in real news channels as compared to fake news. However, for the case of fake news channels, it can be seen the contact rate (**Sigma** (σ)) is high for fake news as compared to true news. It signifies that though there is less flow of people across categories once a person gets into a fake channel population (user who has viewed the fake channel) the chance that the user would move to the infected category is quite high. That means the user has more chance to subscribe to the channel once the user has entered the fake channel. We have also seen the values of γ and μ (Table 4) is more in case True news that suggests that there is more rate of people getting visibility of the true news channel and also a high rate of people naturally leaving this news channel.

For studying the dynamics of polarization, the selection of YouTube videos was based on diverse topics (Table 7). The news topics selected ranged from Politics, War, Health-related etc. This diverse range of topics was selected for each of the categories of True News and Fake News to nullify any effect of other factors that might influence or bias our results for studying the dynamics of polarization. We classified the selected YouTube videos into the categories of Life & Health-related and Not Life & Health-related to study the effect of the life threat factor.

We observe that on average (from Fig. 3) the average number of iterations and the standard deviation of Fake News is high. It can be attributed to the fact that in the case of fake news there is a balance of people from both sides, that is people who are critiquing the fake news as well as those people who are supporting the fake news.

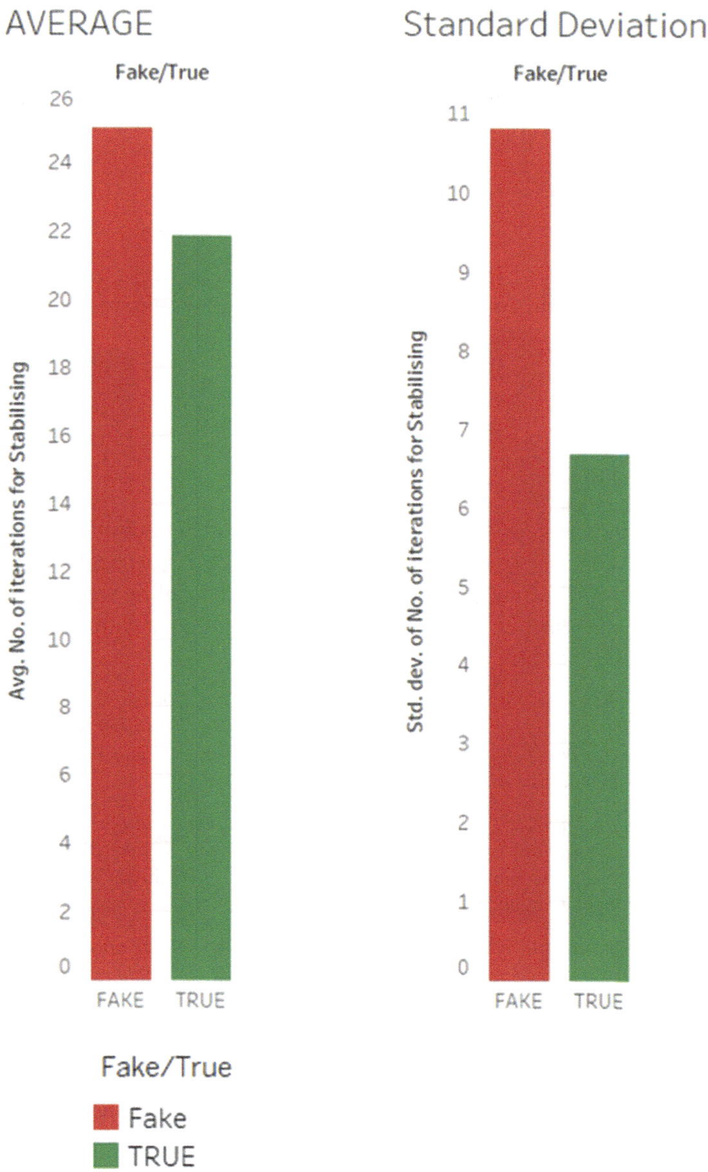

Fig. 6 Average and SD of true and fake news in number of iterations in polarization mode

This polarity in viewpoints of users of YouTube who are exposed to Fake News is why more time is taken to reach a consensus which can be validated from a greater number of iterations. The high standard deviation can also be attributed to the level of fakeness involved with fake and true news. Sometimes if the news is too trivial

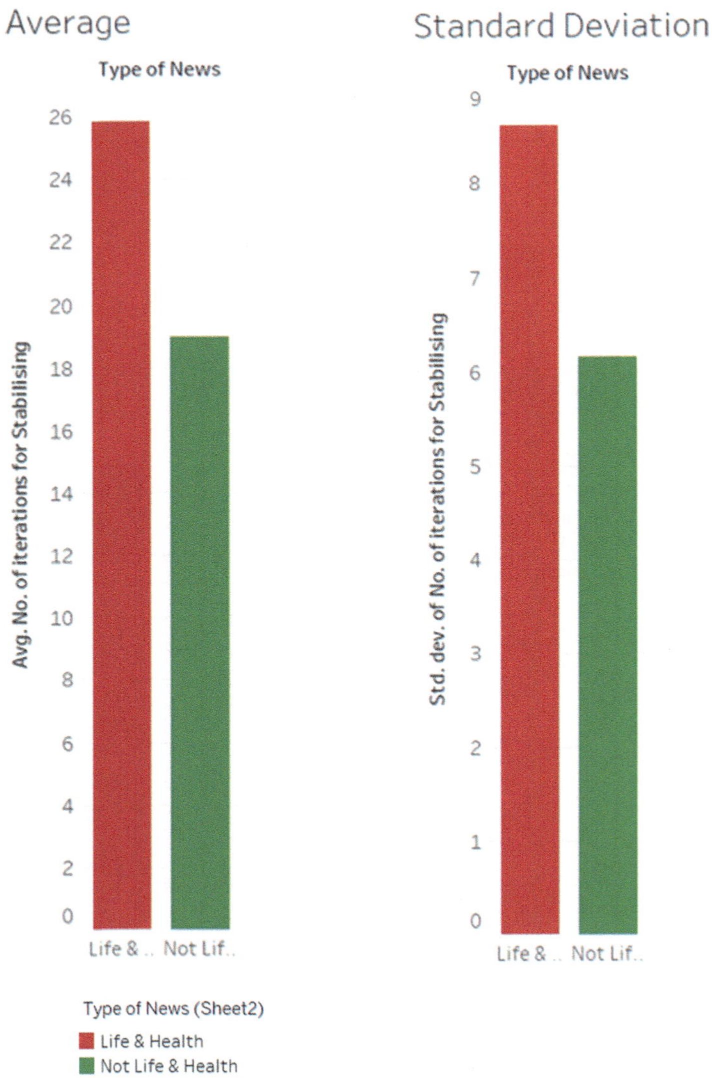

Fig. 7 Average and SD of life & health and non-life & health news in number of iterations in polarization mode

and fakeness is high like "Nepal blowing down India's plane and India attacking Nepal" people come to a very quick consensus.

Another observation that we observed in the case of Life and Health-related kind of news there is a greater number of iterations required to reach a consensus (Table 6). Also, the degree of variability in the number of iterations is high in the case of Life & Health-related kind of news (Table 6). This can be attributed to the fact that for Life & Health related kind of news on an average people look for more

Table 7 Selection of news topics for classification as true and fake news for use in experiments

Topic	YouTube channel (Video Link)	Description
Darbhanga Bus accident	NYOOOZ Bihar-Jharkhand (https://www.youtube.com/watch?v=xxwheXH9H18)	In this news item, it was claimed that the toppling of the bus claimed the lives of 9 BSF jawans and it was due to the bad road but the reality was that the bus toppled due to a mistake of the driver and the BSF was just injured and not dead. It was classified as fake news and health/life-related.
PM Modi Diwali Celebration with BSF	Republic World (https://www.youtube.com/watch?v=RcZOrYth7VA)	This news video by Republic World was related to PM Narendra Modi's visit to Jaisalmer to spend time with Jawans during Diwali. It was classified as True News and non-health/life threat-related news.
Nitish Kumar oath	Zee News (https://www.youtube.com/watch?v=ADW001QhmOM)	This news video by Zee News speaks about Nitish Kumar's oath after the NDA alliance won the Bihar elections of 2020. It was classified as True News and non-health/life threat-related news.
Indian army Gilgit Baltistan	Study-News (https://www.youtube.com/watch?v=zIPOjdgztU4)	In this news, the Indian army attacked Gilgit Baltistan and defeated the Pakistan army and now Gilgit Baltistan is under India. It was classified as Fake news and non-health/life threat-related news.
COVID Tally	NDTV (https://www.youtube.com/watch?v=z7G-SRTGFRk)	In this news video, the anchor is seen telling the daily numbers of COVID which was tallying with the other sources of COVID like https://www.covid19india.org/ etc. This news has been classified as True news and health/life threat-related news.
Bengaluru Rain	NDTV (https://www.youtube.com/watch?v=4Ukl83Pk3s8)	In this news the anchor was seen talking about the rains in Bengaluru and how it damaged public property giving an example of a car. This news has been classified as True news and health/life threat related news.
118 Chinese apps banned	Republic World (https://www.youtube.com/watch?v=wyyEQDKC8NM)	In this news video anchor is seen showing the government's decision of banning 118 chinese apps. This news has been classified as True news and non health/life threat related news.
Farmers' Protest	Zee News (https://www.youtube.com/watch?v=xQYjvun9FuA)	This news video gives details about Famer's protest and march towards Delhi and also talks about the Twitter war going on between various leaders. This news has been classified as True news and non-health/life threat related news.
Nepal Attacks India	Study-News (https://www.youtube.com/watch?v=8guEJ6NUIYA)	In this video the anchor is announcing the news that Nepal has attacked India and one of the Indian planes have been blown and it is time for India to attack Nepal now. This news has been classified as Fake news and health/life threat related news.
India China War ahead	Study-News (https://www.youtube.com/watch?v=0hLgOUG4Lp4)	In this video anchor talks about an inevitable war soon ahead between India and China and India has started preparing for the war and will attack anytime. This news has been classified as Fake news and health/life threat related news.

validation before coming to a consensus as there are more equal distribution of people with both for and against the viewpoint. The high standard deviation can also be attributed to the level of threat involved with the life & health-related kind of news. For example, in the case of COVID-19 tally, where the stakes were high there were people equally distributed on both sides where one section of people wanted to be cautious and did not want to take chance and another section of people who did not want their livelihoods to be affected due to increasing cases ended up taking more time in coming to a consensus. It can be validated with the fact that though there were large number of information campaigns across the world but still there were a good number of people who kept venturing out thus resulting in a surge of COVID-19 cases.

7 Conclusion

There is a growth of misinformation in the era of the Internet, and hence, it has become important to control the spread of fake news. The importance of it could be understood in the COVID-19 era where it was crucial to get the right information as the internet was filled with false news regarding government policies (Apuke and Omar 2021). In the case of fake channels, through our experiment, we have observed that, though the rate of entering or leaving the channels is not too high once a user gets exposed, then on average, the user has higher chances of subscribing to the fake channel as compared to TRUE news. But it has also been observed that the variability of a user subscribing to a fake channel is also very high which can happen to various other factors like the amount of fakeness a channel has.

We have also seen that there are some fake news channels where the chance for users to reach a common consensus does take a longer time (a greater number of iterations), which means that there are users who are going to believe the fake news for a longer time. It has a direct negative impact on the lives of people as they would be taking wrong decisions based on their belief in fake news.

Given the vulnerability of a user getting infected with the fake news following having a negative impact on himself and others around him, it is important to curb the spread of fake news. To curb the spread of fake news there have been demands on service/network providers from regulators. Social media have however taken steps by having a news-related authentic source attached to that particular video so as to give warning to users to not follow or believe the news before crosschecking the link provided below the video. One such instance could be seen that whenever there is COVID-19 related news, there is a suggestion box or link below with the link directing to the government site that contains genuine information. Social media could also come up with another feature that would classify news as prospective false news and give a warning to the user to be careful before believing the news. There are also videos which are by intent made false due to various reasons like parody, drama etc. So, the social media platforms could provide a tag for mentioning that it is for parody purposes.

We can extend our experiment to study the behavior of users across various other categories like Environment, Economy etc. along with exploring posts, videos on other social media platforms like Twitter, Facebook etc. which could provide interesting insights.

Another area of exploration would be to find the reaction and behavior of people in the news that is made by intent for entertainment purposes like a parody. We could explore the dynamics of polarization in those channels and how long does it take for a person to reach a consensus in those channels. We could see the rate of people entering or leaving the channels and the rate and at which they enter or leave. We can also use mathematical models like SEIZ to understand how many people believe the news in such channels whose intention is to make parody videos for entertainment purposes (Isea and Lonngren 2017). A future avenue of research could be to understand whether such channels are harmful or are the channels well taken and understood by the audience thus not adversely impacting the lives of people.

A.1 Appendixes

A.1.1 Appendix 1: Showing the Number of Iterations Required for Consensus or Opinion Formation for Each of the News Topics

Darbhanga Bus Incident

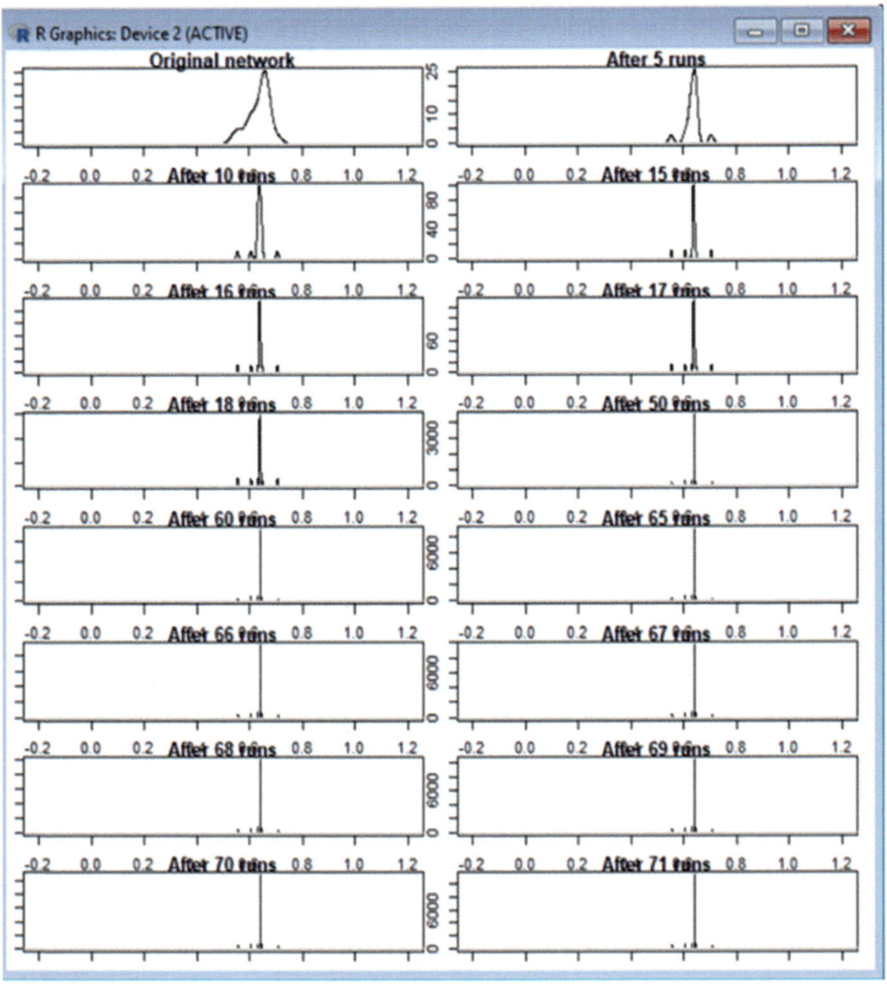

Baltistan Army

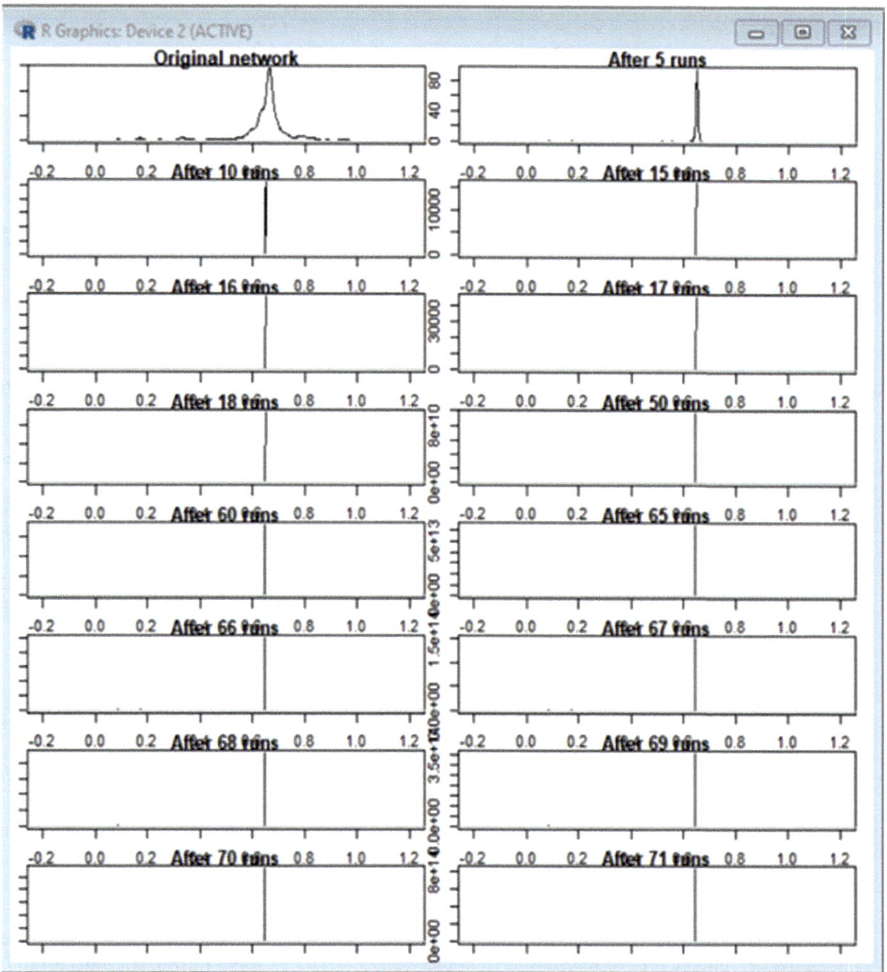

PM Modi Diwali Celebration with BSF

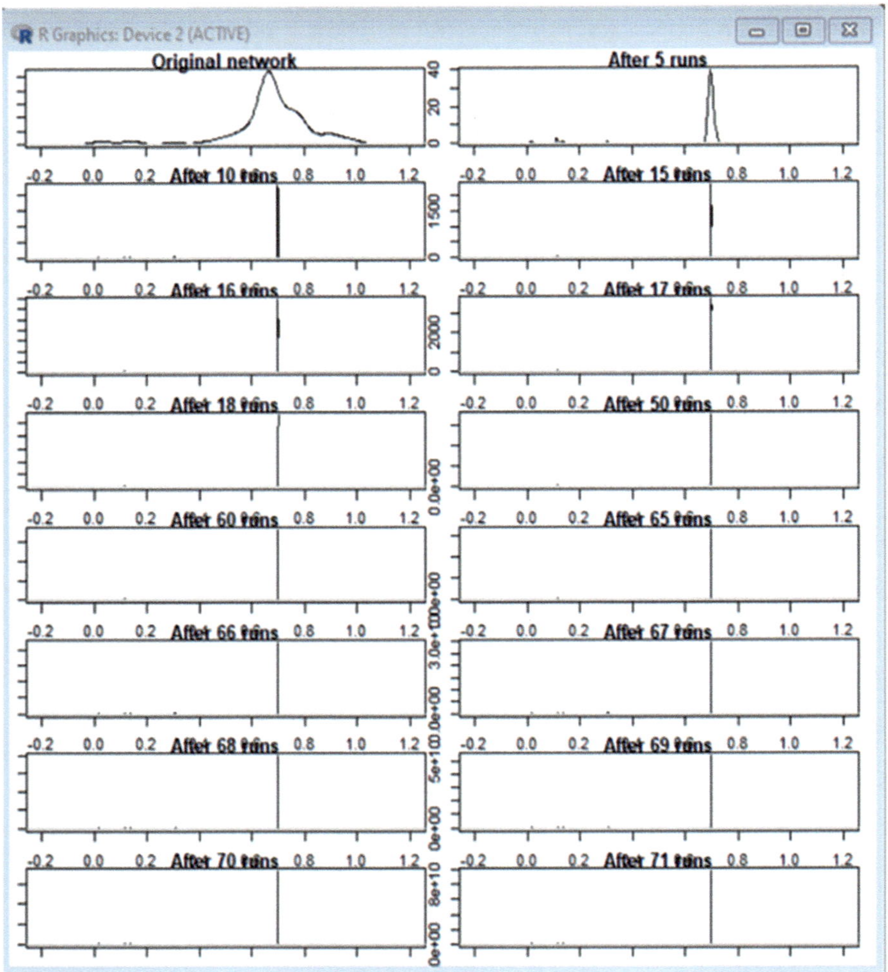

COVID Tally

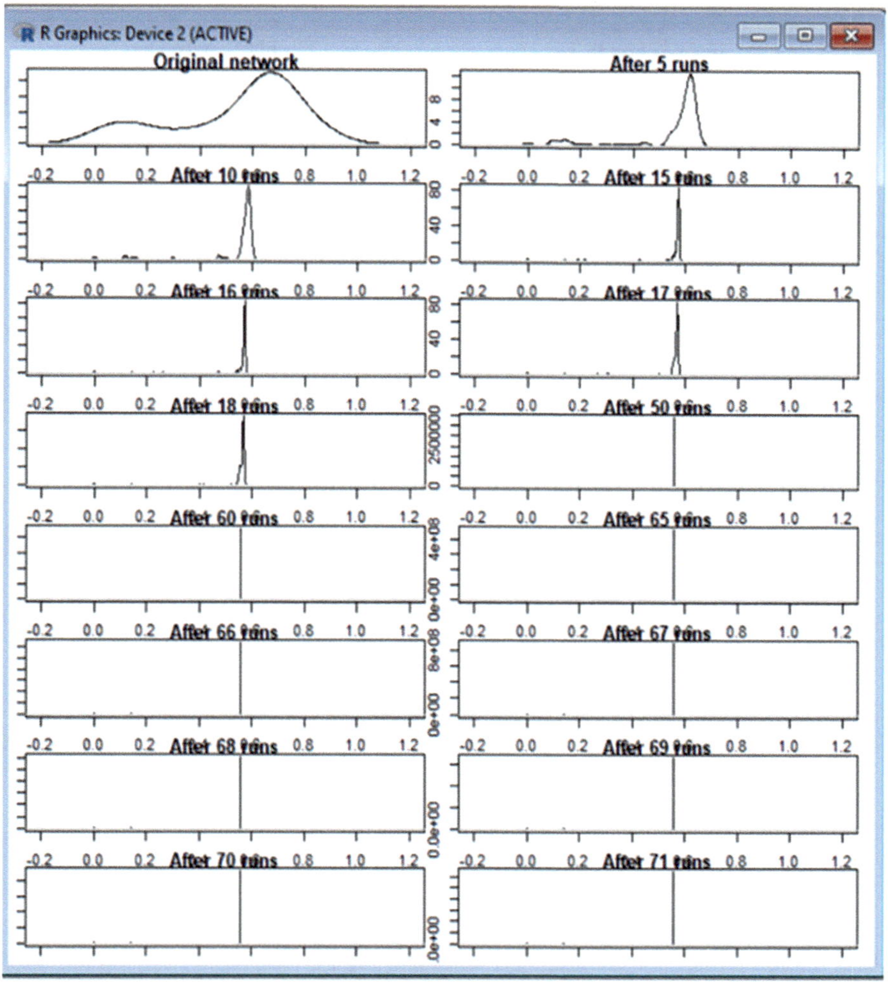
R Graphics: Device 2 (ACTIVE)
Original network
After 5 runs
After 10 runs
After 15 runs
After 16 runs
After 17 runs
After 18 runs
After 50 runs
After 60 runs
After 65 runs
After 66 runs
After 67 runs
After 68 runs
After 69 runs
After 70 runs
After 71 runs
-0.2 0.0 0.2 0.4 0.6 0.8 1.0 1.2

Nitish Kumar Oath

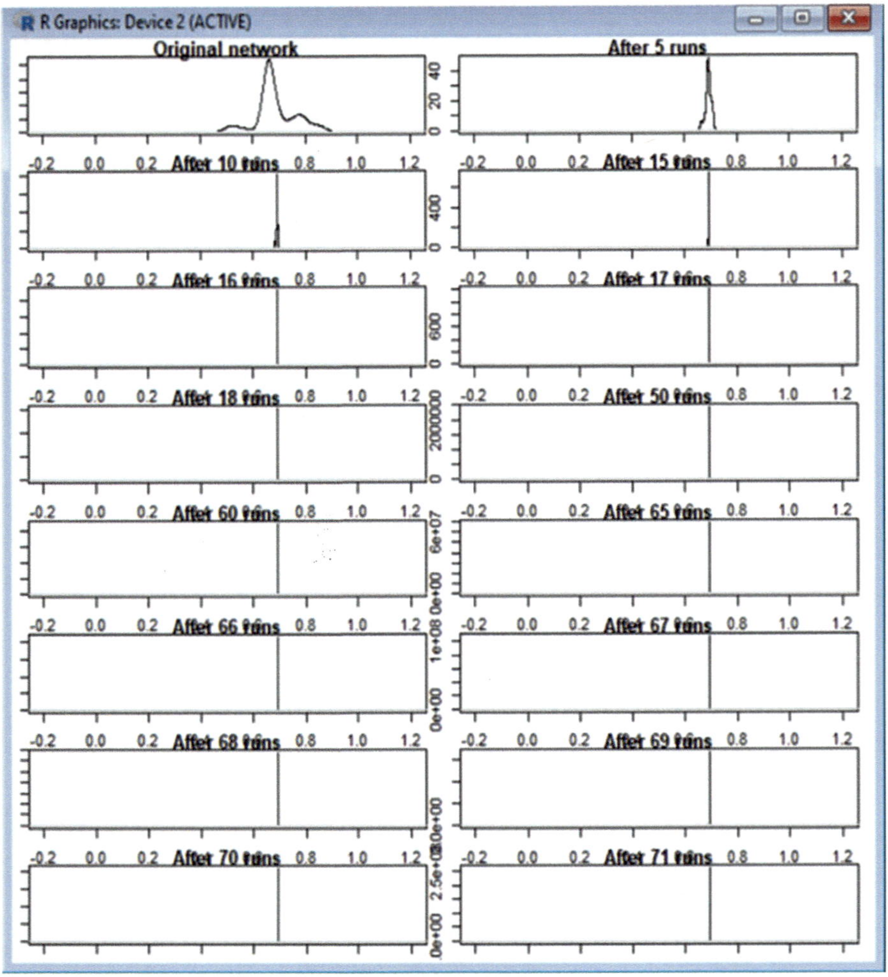

Bengaluru Rains

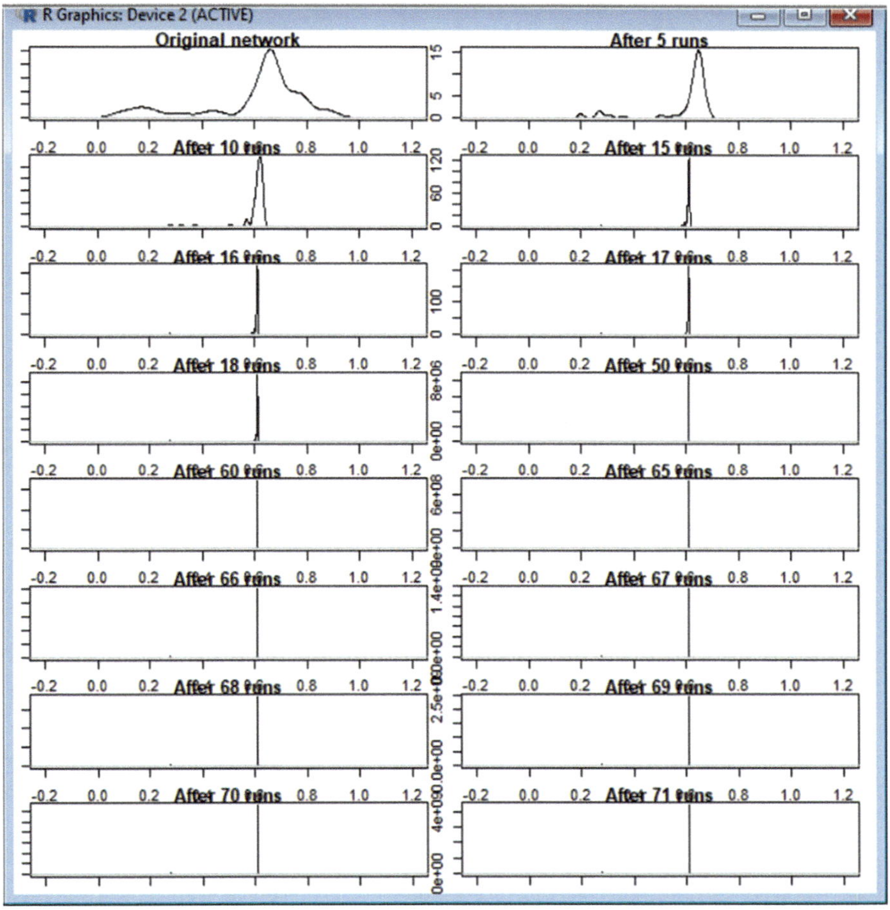

118 Chinese Apps Banned

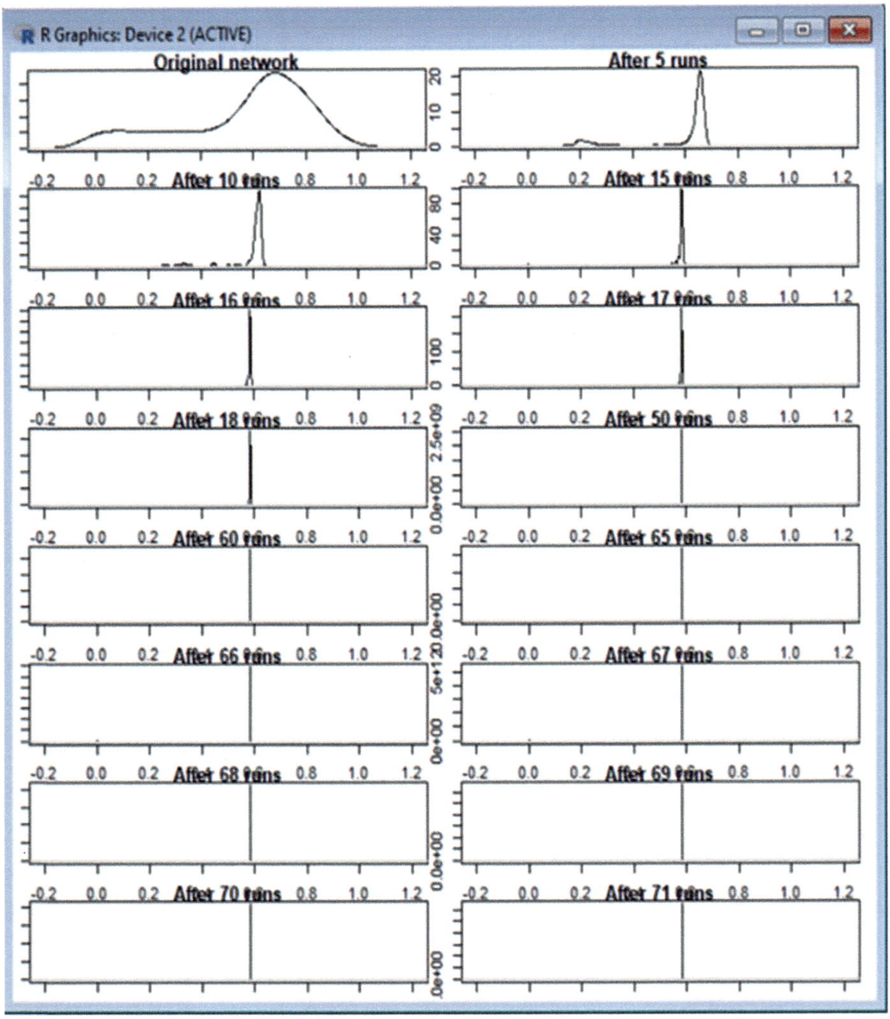

Farmers' Protest

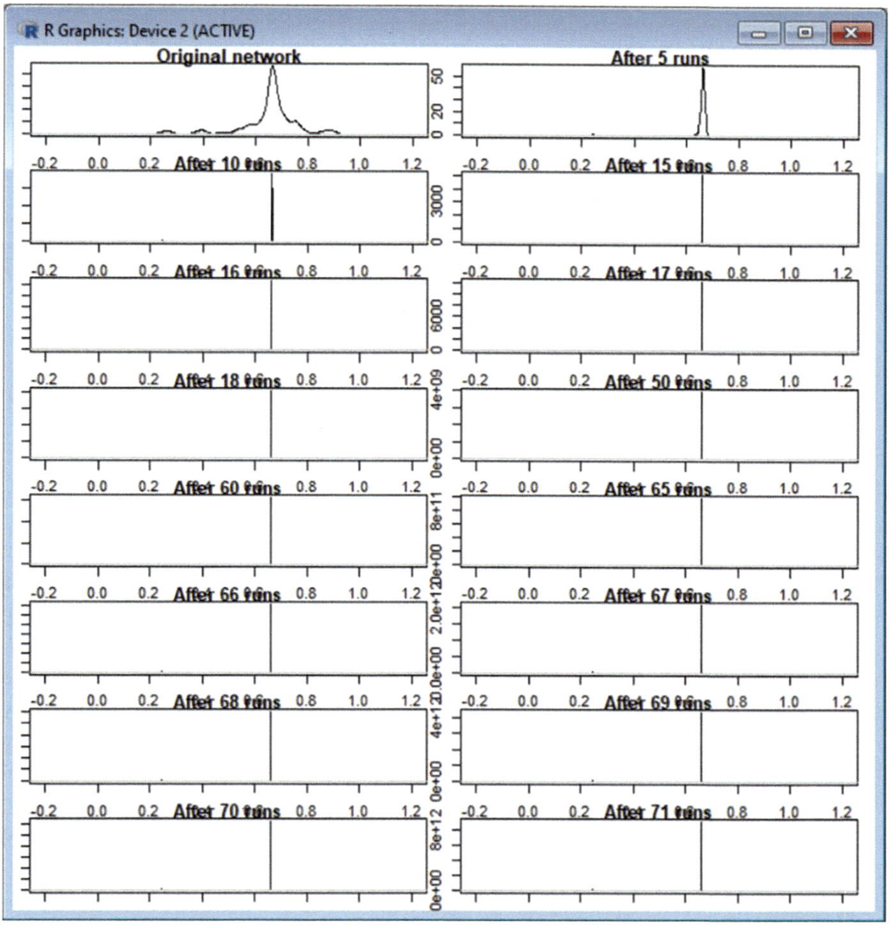

Nepal India

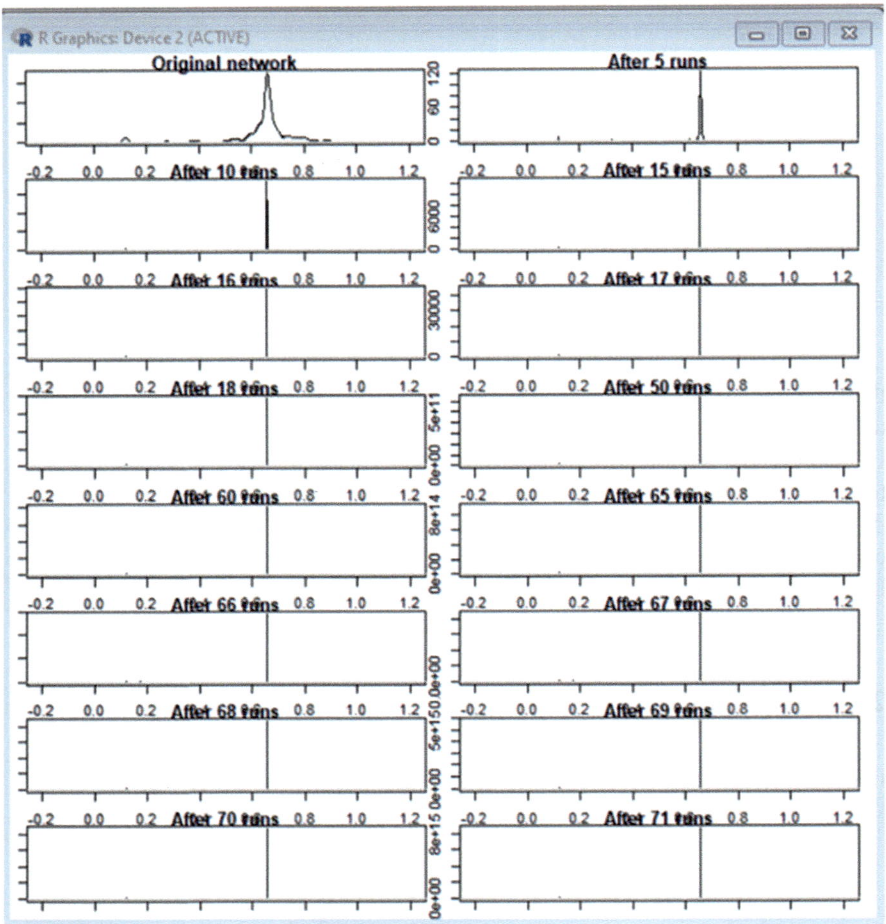
R Graphics: Device 2 (ACTIVE)
Original network
After 5 runs
After 10 runs
After 15 runs
After 16 runs
After 17 runs
After 18 runs
After 50 runs
After 60 runs
After 65 runs
After 66 runs
After 67 runs
After 68 runs
After 69 runs
After 70 runs
After 71 runs

India China

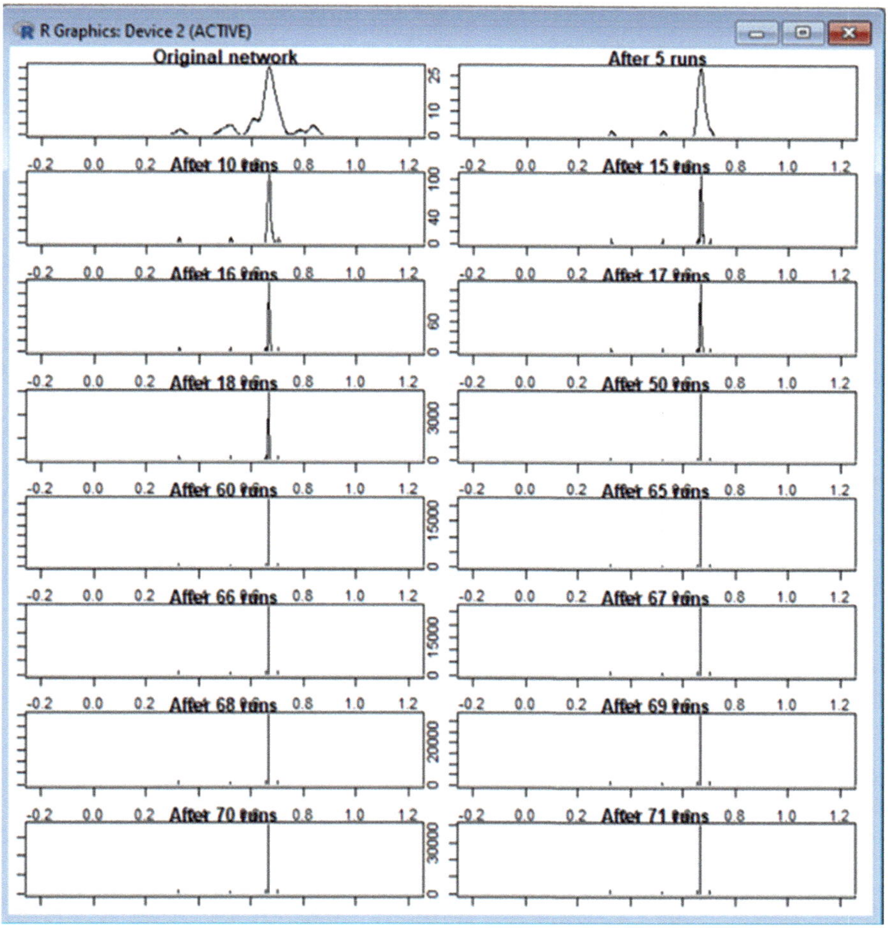

A.1.2 Appendix 2: Subscribers and Viewers Data as Got from Site https://www.noxinfluencer.com/

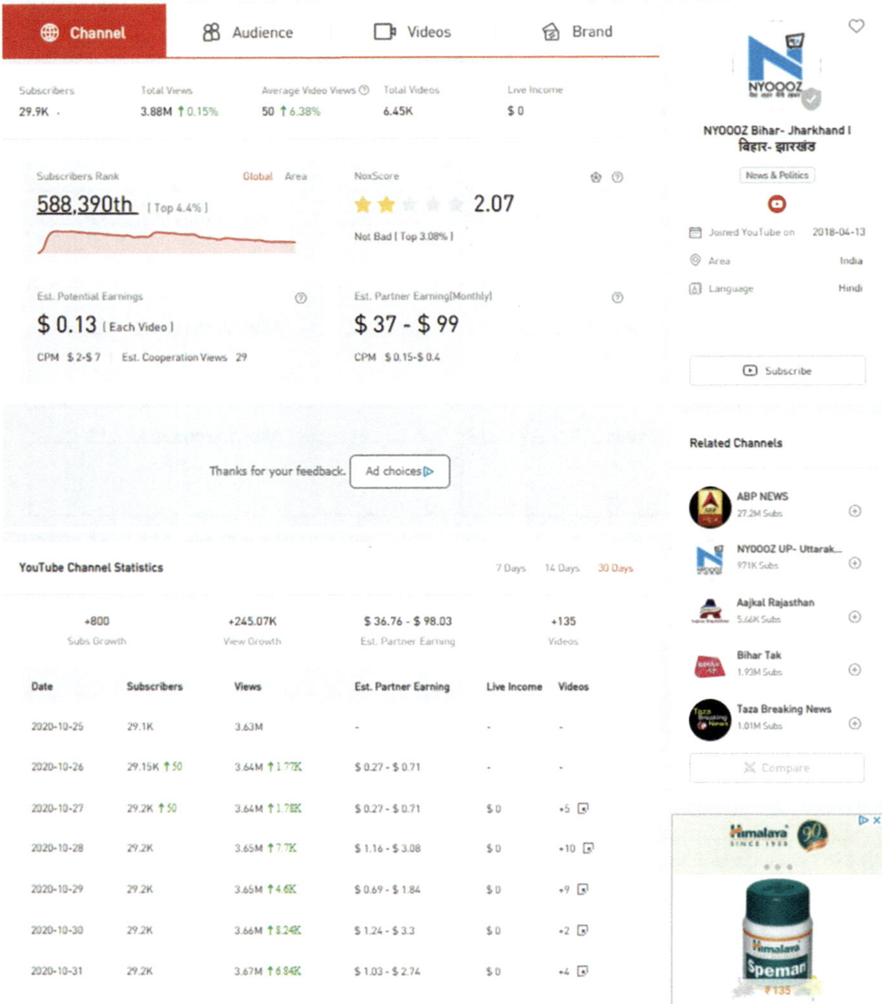

Views History Data (Recent Year)
Daily
Total
4M
3M
2M
2019-11-30
2020-01-10
2020-02-20
2020-04-01
2020-05-12
2020-06-22
2020-08-02
2020-09-12
2020-10-23
Views Data
7 Days
30 Days
Views for the Last 7 Days: 56,606
Views Compared to Previous Last 7 Days: 78,686
15K
12K
9K
6K
3K
11-17
11-18
11-19
11-20
11-21
11-22
11-23

A.1.3 Appendix 3: Average of Fake News vs True News for the Calculation of Sigma ($\sigma = \lambda / (\gamma + \mu)$)

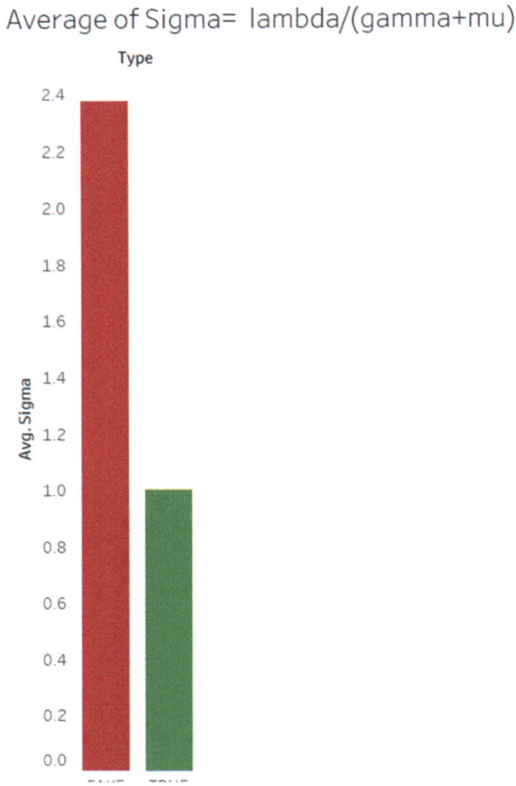

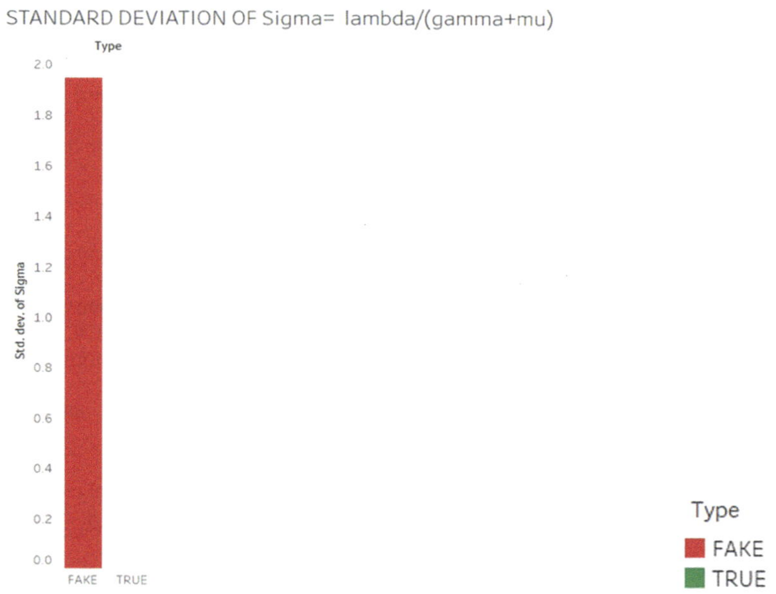

References

Allcott H, Gentzkow M (2017) Social media and fake news in the 2016 election. J Econ Perspect 31(2):211–236

Apuke OD, Omar B (2021) Fake news and COVID-19: modelling the predictors of fake news sharing among social media users. Telemat Inform 56:101475

Barberá P (2020) Social media, echo chambers, and political polarization. Social Media and Democracy: The State of the Field, Prospects for Reform, 34

Bettencourt LM, Cintrón-Arias A, Kaiser DI, Castillo-Chávez C (2006) The power of a good idea: quantitative modeling of the spread of ideas from epidemiological models. Physica A Stat Mech Appl 364:513–536

Bondielli A, Marcelloni F (2019) A survey on fake news and rumour detection techniques. Inf Sci 497:38–55

DiMaggio P, Evans J, Bryson B (1996) Have American's social attitudes become more polarized? Am J Sociol 102(3):690–755

Fard AE, Verma T (2021) A comprehensive review on countering rumours in the age of online social media platforms. In: Qureshi I, Bhatt B, Gupta S, Tiwari AA (eds) Causes and symptoms of socio-cultural polarization: role of information and communication technologies. Springer

Garimella VRK, Weber I (2017, May) A long-term analysis of polarization on Twitter. In: Proceedings of the international AAAI conference on web and social media, vol 11, no. 1

Ghai A, Kumar P, Gupta S (2021) A deep-learning-based image forgery detection framework for controlling the spread of misinformation. Inf Technol People.

Gupta S, Deodhar S (2021) Understanding digitally enabled complex networks: a plural granulation based hybrid community detection approach. Inf Technol People

Gupta S, Jain G, Tiwari AA (2021, September) Investigating the dynamics of polarization in online discourse during COVID-19 pandemic. In: Conference on e-Business, e-Services and e-Society. Springer, Cham, pp 704-709. September

Gupta S, Kumar P, Bhasker B (2016) A rough connectedness algorithm for mining communities in complex networks. In: International Conference on Big Data Analytics and Knowledge Discovery. Springer, Cham, pp 34–48. September

Gupta S, Kumar P (2020) An overlapping community detection algorithm based on rough clustering of links. Data Knowl Eng 125:101777

Gupta S, Kumar P (2021) A constrained agglomerative clustering approach for unipartite and bipartite networks with application to credit networks. Inf Sci 557:332–354

Hethcote HW (1989) Three basic epidemiological models. In: *Applied mathematical ecology*. Springer, Berlin/Heidelberg, pp 119–144

Isea R, Lonngren KE (2017) A new variant of the SEIZ model to describe the spreading of a rumor. Int J Data Sci Anal 3(4):28–33

Jain G, Sreenivas AB, Gupta S, Tiwari AA (2021a) The dynamics of online opinion formation: polarization around vaccine development for COVID-19. In: Qureshi I, Bhatt B, Gupta S, Tiwari AA (eds) Causes and symptoms of socio-cultural polarization: role of information and communication technologies. Springer

Jain G, Suman S, Gupta S, Tiwari AA (2021b) Media bias and Bollywood: an untold story. In: Qureshi I, Bhatt B, Gupta S, Tiwari AA (eds) Causes and symptoms of socio-cultural polarization: role of information and communication technologies. Springer

Jin F, Dougherty E, Saraf P, Cao Y, Ramakrishnan N (2013, August) Epidemiological modeling of news and rumors on twitter. In: Proceedings of the 7th workshop on social network mining and analysis, pp 1–9

Kermack WO, McKendrick AG (1927) A contribution to the mathematical theory of epidemics. In: Proceedings of the royal society of London. Series A, Containing papers of a mathematical and physical character, 115(772), 700–721

Kozma B, Barrat A (2008) Consensus formation on adaptive networks. Phys Rev E 77(1):016102

Kumar P, Gupta S, Bhasker B (2017) An upper approximation based community detection algorithm for complex networks. Decis Support Syst 96:103–118

O'Hara K, Stevens D (2015) Echo chambers and online radicalism: assessing the Internet's complicity in violent extremism. Policy Internet 7(4):401–422

Ornell F, Schuch JB, Sordi AO, Kessler FHP (2020) "Pandemic fear" and COVID-19: mental health burden and strategies. Braz J Psychiatry 42(3):232–235

Qureshi I, Bhatt B, Gupta S, Tiwari AA (2020) Call for papers: causes, symptoms and consequences of social media induced polarization (SMIP). Inf Syst J. https://onlinelibrary.wiley.com/pb-assets/assets/13652575/ISJ_SMIP_CFP-1586861685850.pdf

Qureshi I, Bhatt B, Gupta S, Tiwari AA (2021). Introduction to the role of information and communication Technologies in Polarization. In: Qureshi I, Bhatt B, Gupta S, Tiwari AA (eds) Causes and symptoms of socio-cultural polarization: role of information and communication technologies. Springer

Roozenbeek J, Van Der Linden S (2019) The fake news game: actively inoculating against the risk of misinformation. J Risk Res 22(5):570–580

Ros-Gálvez A, Meseguer-Martínez Á, López-Buenache G (2021) The dynamics of the university impact on YouTube: a comparative analysis. Soc Netw Anal Min 11(1):1–7

Tandoc EC Jr, Lim ZW, Ling R (2018) Defining "fake news" a typology of scholarly definitions. Digit Journal 6(2):137–153

Törnberg P (2018) Echo chambers and viral misinformation: Modeling fake news as complex contagion. PLoS One 13(9):e0203958

Wang Q, Yang X, Xi W (2018) Effects of group arguments on rumor belief and transmission in online communities: An information cascade and group polarization perspective. Inf Manag 55(4):441–449

Wardle C, Derakhshan H (2018) Thinking about 'information disorder': formats of misinformation, disinformation, and mal-information. Ireton, Cherilyn; Posetti, Julie. Journalism,'fake news'& disinformation. Unesco, Paris, pp 43–54

Part II
Social Aspects of Polarization

Political Polarization in Australia: A Case Study of Brushfires in Australia

Zhiwen Zheng and Babita Bhatt

Abstract The frequency and severity of bushfires have increased in the past decades across the globe. Despite the socio-economic and ecological devastation brought by the bushfires, there is a lack of serious actions preventing the risk of bushfire. We argue that this lack of action results from the political polarisation around the causes and mitigation strategies around the bushfire. Using the case study of 2019–2020 Australian bushfire, we specifically demonstrate the role of social media eco-chambers in reinforcing political affiliations and perpetuating extreme positions. Based on our analysis, we provide practical and theoretical insights on social media-induced political polarisation around climate change.

Keywords Political polarisation · Bushfire · Climate change · Social media · Social cohesion

1 Introduction

The year 2019 has seen several large and in some cases, unprecedented wildfires wreaking havoc across the world (WWF 2020). For example, California battled its worst fire season in the modern history; the Amazon faced its third-largest fire on record, while the parts of the Arctic and central Asia also experienced unusually severe blazes (Dunne 2020). Towards the end of 2019, Australia began to face its largest bushfires on record, which due to its disastrous impact on health, biodiversity and the economy, is considered Australia's costliest natural disaster to date (Deacon 2020).

While wildfire can be important for maintaining and restoring ecosystem processes and regenerating forests and grasslands area, as the above example shows, there is an increase in the frequency and severity of the fire. Additionally, the regions experiencing fire are also shifting, and more fires are occurring in the

Z. Zheng (✉) · B. Bhatt
Australian National University, Canberra, Australia
e-mail: zhiwen.zheng@anu.edu.au; babita.bhatt@anu.edu.au

I. Qureshi et al. (eds.), *Causes and Symptoms of Socio-Cultural Polarization*,
https://doi.org/10.1007/978-981-16-5268-4_5

ecosystems that are not adapted to wildfire. If the trend continues, a greater number of more intense fires will have lasting changes in vegetation structure and composition, release millions of extra tonnes of carbon in atmosphere, and have dire consequences for biodiversity, health, and the economy (WWF 2020; Dunne 2020). As such, understanding the causes of wildfire and how to prevent wildfire disaster need scholarly attention.

While there is a consensus on the disastrous consequences of wildfires, the causes and solutions to prevent the potential threat of wildfires are widely contested (Prior and Eriksen 2013). Many scientific studies find climate change and wildfires mutually reinforcing, however, there are also counterarguments linking wildfires to natural cycles, arson emergency and eco-terrorism (Weber et al. 2020). Social media echo-chamber has played a key role in reinforcing these positions resulting in polarised perspectives around the important issue.

This paper uses the 2019–2020 bushfire in Australia to illustrate polarisation around the causes and policy solutions to the bushfire. While the bushfire is a regular occurrence in Australia and has a devastating impact on the ecology and human life, there is no agreement over what causes these bushfires and what strategies need to be adopted to address the bushfire. Specifically, given the unprecedented nature of the bushfire in 2019–2020, it was expected that a consensus on managing bushfires would emerge and collective action will prevail. However, a systematic review of the statements of public figures in the media suggests a polarisation of viewpoints. Consequently, we study these polarised views and the role of social media in exacerbating these political divides.

Based on our systematic review of media sources, we divide these polarised views into two groups: (a) The Traditionalists groups and (b) the Environmentalists group.

The Traditionalists view seasonal bushfire as an inherent part of Australia's environment and explain the intensity of bushfire in some years as an arson emergency. However, the environmentalist finds the traditionalists' position completely wrong and misleading and claim that climate change is the underlying cause of the prolonged dry and hot conditions that have increased the risk of extreme fire conditions in Australia (Vardoulakis et al. 2020). This polar opposite view has resulted in a policy gridlock where no clear strategy to address the bushfire has been proposed.

Subsequently, the polarisation is increasingly seen along the party lines. For example, in a survey, 38 % of Liberal and Nationals, and only 9% of Labour, voters reported severe doubts on climate change (Bowe 2020). Almost 64% of Australian respondents supported the proposition that "Australia should be doing more to address climate change" in a slight growth from 62% two years ago and a sharp increase from 54% three years ago (Crowe 2020). The PwC's latest survey of community attitudes shows that 60% of Australians are now more concerned about climate change than before the 2019–2020 bushfire, and 51% of Australians believe that we need to put less emphasis on coal for domestic energy (Pwc 2020).

Additionally, the debates on bushfires tend to polarise the citizens on economic and environmental issues. We observed that the mutual dislike and divisions between Coalition (Liberal +National party) and Greens voters are increasing, which is likely fuelled by their irreconcilable attitudes towards climate change. In fact, it reflects the new political geography of the nation, which features the divide between the inner cities who express a strong link between climate change and the bushfires and the suburban who are more worried about power prices, coal mining, and manufacturing jobs (BBC News 2019). As a result, the issue of bushfire has become extremely polarised and politicised in Australia (Fuller 2020).

In this paper, we explained these polarised issues in detail. We first define polarisation and the role of social media. We then discuss the polarised view on Australian bushfires. Using a systematic review of social media websites, we identify two extreme positions on the bushfire in Australian policy space. We then discuss our findings which show the persistence of political identity in environmental politics (Wilson 2020). While climate change plays a role in escalating bushfire crisis, our research shows that political polarisation and politicking around the issue has taken the precedence. We believe it is happening because social media has enflamed political polarisation driven by political elites who set the tone for policy discourse and as a result, influence the public (Tucker et al. 2018). This polarisation around the causes of bushfire makes it difficult to resolve the crisis efficiently. Our research contributes to the literature on the causes and consequences of polarisation for policy and society.

2 Literature Review

Polarisation is a *systemic attribute of society in which a small number of groups are highly homogenised internally, but they are progressively different and opposed to external groups at the same time* (Lucas and Warman 2018, p. 988). These polarised coalitions are isolated, dominant, and opposing groups within a social discourse and the differentiation among groups are socially constructed around culture, polity, or responses to specific issues. Elite polarisation stimulates political polarisation by creating a public that is more reliant on party identification, rather than on critical thinking for political attitudes (Robison and Mullinix 2016). Research shows that citizens intuitively draw on from their affective attachments to the party to process the information and are persuaded by those whom they like and trust, instead of listening to arguments from those they distrust or dislike (Lucas et al. 2019). As a result, the motivated responders in a polarised context apply political frames to agree or disagree and usually rely on these frames with more active or negative beliefs (Zhou 2016).

In modern society, social media plays an important role to enhance polarisation, specifically around political identities (Qureshi et al. 2020). In the following paragraphs, we explain how social media can exacerbate political identities. First, social media can spread information to the public by reinforcing the broad parameters of elite debates (Boutyline and Willer 2017; Livingstone and Lunt 1994). The wide-ranging information shared on digital media can attract like-minded people where people seek out information that confirms and reinforce their existing beliefs (Flaxman et al. 2016). Thus, social media is often criticised for intensifying political polarisation by creating echo chambers, insulating people from opposing views (Jost and Amodio 2012). Echo chambers reinforce pre-existing political opinions within a homogeneous group and limit exposure to opposing political views (Kim and Kim 2019; Qureshi et al. 2020). Consequently, a lack of exposure to the opposing views can lead to polarised groups that are antagonistic towards external groups. It can also strengthen irrationality, mutual dislikes and hatred towards others when they are not in their echo chamber (Boutyline and Willer 2017).

Second, social media can be used by different parties to share misleading information with the public (Qureshi et al. 2020). During the 2019–2020 bushfire, social media played an important role in sharing and polarising information to mislead the public (Bauder 2020; Rannard 2020). For example, the Fox News made repeated suggestions of an arson epidemic or arson emergency (Bauder 2020). According to critics, by 'creating' an arson emergency, many social media outlets were aiming to systematically undermine any link between the 2019–2020 bushfires and climate change, to decrease trust in scientific expertise, and to delegitimise liberal democratic authority (Knaus 2020).

It is also important to note that the disinformation spread on social media is complex because it often has a "grain of truth". For example, in the case of arson emergency that was spread on social media, "*the motivation underlying this [fake news] often tends to be not changing people's opinions about the bushfire itself and how it's happening, but to sow discord and magnify already existing tensions in polarised political issues*." (Nguyen and Bogle 2020).

Additionally, politically polarised media posts that show a lack of care and interest in the core issues itself can result in an 'instrumental' public engagement in which the unconcern publics' interests match with the policies favoured by those in power (Kim and Kim 2019).

These discussions suggest that individuals' responses to critical issues such as bushfire, climate change are motivated primarily by what they value, and the narratives of their social group, not their acceptance of scientific fact (Lucas and Davison 2019). For example, in the case of politically polarised issues, individuals' political identity often overtakes actual issues prompting a partisan response. As such, polarisation originated through motivated reasoning is closely tied to political interest (Zhou 2016). Political polarisation has adverse consequences for any action as it fails in challenging the existing assumptions and arrangements and has no scope for reflexivity and inclusivity in knowledge, policy, and communication (Pepermans and Maeseele 2014). In the next section, we apply these theoretical discussions to analyse political polarisation on bushfire and their effect on policy and politics in Australia.

3 Bushfire in Australia

A review of recent documents suggests that seasonal bushfire is a widespread and regular occurrence in Australia. It has contributed considerably to shape Australia's geographical environment over millions of years (Deacon 2020). While bushfires play an important role in maintaining and restoring ecosystems (NASA 2020), the frequency and extent of bushfire can have dire consequences for biodiversity, health, and the economy (Schaben 2020). For example, the 2019–2020 fire season in Australia has been unprecedented and unparalleled in its intensity, scale, and socio-environmental cost. By 28 February 2020, more than 17 million hectares of the forests have been damaged, an area larger than that of the average European country and around five times the size of fires in the Amazon (Parliament of Australia 2020). By 8 January 2020, approximately one billion mammals have lost their lives, and many species are on the verge of extinction (The University of Sydney 2020). Economically, it is Australia's costliest natural disaster to the date (Duncombe 2020). In the following paragraphs, we discuss the environmental, social and economic cost of bushfire to Australia.

Firstly, air pollution and water pollution resulting from seasonal bushfires have adverse effects on citizens' health. The burning of the forests produces harmful smoke, and fine particle, resulting in air population (Maicd 2020). For example, during the period of the 2019–2020 seasonal bushfires across Australia, an estimated 600 million tons of carbon dioxide was released into the atmosphere, compared to the total releases of approximately 530 million tons from Australian human sources (WWF 2020). Additionally, bushfire ash can congest rivers and streams and threaten water quality (UNEP 2020; Water Quality Australia n.d.).

Secondly, 2019–2020 seasonal bushfires also had a negative impact on biodiversity. There is a fear that frequent seasonal bushfires may accelerate the extinction process for a range of animals and plants. Over the last 200 years, Australia has the highest extinction rate for animals globally (Kilvert 2020). As an illustration, in 2019–2020, one billion mammals and hundreds of billions of insects lost their lives (Fuller 2020).

Finally, the 2019–2020 bushfires have adverse effects on the Australian economy, including immediate cost and indirect cost. The immediate cost caused by bushfires is often impact on the areas of tourism, agricultural and retail income. As tourism and agriculture are the backbones of Australia's economy, the direct damage done by bushfires in these areas is obvious and instant. Meanwhile, the indirect cost is linked to decreased worker productivity, increased health spending, and post-disaster reconstruction (Duncombe 2020). Bushfires also negatively affect individual health and well-being. Further, with the risk of lives and damaged property, many people are forced to move from their original habitats, which also affect community cohesion and post-disaster reconstruction (Prior and Eriksen 2013). In short, these illustrations of the recurrence and the impact of bushfires in Australia provide the context of this research.

4 Methodology

We performed a systematic review of public domain information, news, and debates to understand various actors' positions on bushfire. This information was extracted from Factiva. To isolate the effect of COVID-19, we searched for articles from November 2019 to February 2020. We used the following keywords in our research: *bushfire, Australia, cohesion, climate change, polarisation, and social media.* Following Riaz et al. (2011), we decided to rely on quotes as the primary unit of analysis rather than the entire article, as quotes can be easily attributed to the actors and show their opinion on the causes and consequences of bushfire. We retrieved a total of 293 articles related to the topic. We read through each article and found 85 relevant quotes.

We used the following steps in our data analysis: First, we identified the actor in each quote and compiled these quotes by actor categories (Riaz et al. 2011). Second, we analysed the content of each quote and coded them in first order themes. Third, these first-order themes were collapsed into *three* second-order themes: causes, consequences and solutions of bushfire. Fourth, in this stage, we looked into the extant literature on political polarisation and bushfire in Australia and compared it with our data. The iteration between literature and data helped in collapsing the second level themes into two broad categories: The traditionalists and the Environmentalists.

In the following section, we examine the information received from the public domain and narrate the polarised views of these two different camps.

5 Findings

5.1 The Traditionalists

Traditionalists view seasonal bushfires as an inherent nature of Australia's environment. They argue that the 2019–2020 is a regular seasonal bushfire, and the intensity of the fire was due to the deliberately lighting in many remote areas. Many Australian native plants such as Eucalyptus forests depend on fire to release their seeds, so the fire is seen as essential for the natural ecosystem (Bond et al. 2004; Ogden et al. 1998; Wiser et al. 1997). Many politicians in Australia have framed the bushfire crisis through this logic.

> *Bushfires are natural disasters, and they wreak this sort of havoc when they affect our country, and they have for a very long time* (Scott Morrison, Australian prime minister as quoted by Tharoor 2020).

> *The sort of thing that we are always going to be prone to in a country such as ours - a land of droughts and flooding rains as the poet [Dorothea Mackellar] said all those years back.* (Tony Abbott, Former Australian prime minister as quoted by Knott 2020).

> *Climate change was 'a load of crap'... an idea pushed by city folk with 'no experience in the bush' and no understanding of Australia's punishing, cyclical climate* (McCole, as quoted by Lamb 2020a).

Although bushfire in Australia is a regular event, the intensity and scale of 2019–2020 bushfires were exceptional and uncontrollable. Therefore, the causes of bushfires were widely speculated on social media. One of the most shared speculations by the traditionalists was arson epidemic or arson emergency. On Twitter, hashtag #ArsonEmergency claiming that nearly 200 arsonists are behind the Australia fires went viral and was retweeted widely across the globe. The hashtag was even shared by the ex-President of the USA D. J Trump and Fox News opinion pundit S. Hannity (Irfan 2020; Trump (Jr.) 2020).

Although it was proved to be fake news, #ArsonEmergency had attracted people's attention across the globe. However, ABC News reports that only about 1% of bushfires in NSW were officially attributed to arson, and it is even less in Victoria (Nguyen et al. 2020).

5.1.1 Economic Logic

A closer look at the traditionalists' position highlights an underlying economic logic closely linked to Australia's political economy of exporting coal. Coal, as one of Australia's largest exports, has accounted for about 25% of Australia's resource exports in the last 10 years (Cunningham et al. 2019). In 2018, coal accounted for about 60% share of energy generation in Australia, and the value of coal exports was $67 billion (Cunningham et al. 2019). There is a great demand for Australian coal because of its higher energy content and relatively low content of toxic gases (Cunningham et al. 2019). Without coal, Australia's electricity supply will be affected, and Australia's lucrative iron ore exports will not be possible. Therefore, Australia's coal has a significant impact on Australia's GDP and export economy.

> *Australia's coal-based power is fundamental for energy competitiveness, the aluminium sector and thousands of industrial jobs, many in Queensland, the state that delivered Morrison his election victory* (Matt Canavan, Queensland LNP senator and Former Resources Minister, as quoted by Kelly 2019).

Based on the economic logic, many political elites believe that it is too risky to relate bushfire with the energy industry and climate change. In order to maintain a profit from the conventional energy industry, they argue that there is no evidence to show that the energy industry is releasing enough greenhouse gases to cause climate change.

> *Imagine if we tried to assess the practical and economic costs of Australia shifting to zero emissions within a decade and compared them with the environmental benefits. Clearly, the costs would be too immense and complex to quantify accurately, and the benefits would be too small to identify* (Greg Mullins, Former NSW fire commissioner as quoted in The Australia 2020a).

Climate change is a global phenomenon. And we are doing our bit as part of the response to climate change. But I think to suggest that with just 1.3 per cent of global emissions that Australia doing something differently, more or less, would have changed the fire outcome this season, I do not think that stands up to any credible scientific evidence at all (Scott Morrison, The Australian Prime Minister as quoted by Twomey 2019).

These discussions reflect an economic logic deeply rooted in the short-term time horizon (Parthiban et al. 2021; Qureshi et al. 2018a). The research from psychological and socio-cultural studies also support these views. Evidence suggests that a strong reliance on existing social systems for security, reassurance, and stability is especially important for people who identify as being ideologically on the Right (Konrad et al. 2017).

Further, a short-term time horizon prioritises immediate needs (Kistruck et al. 2013), which is often necessary during the crisis.

I firmly believe those of us in leadership positions must prioritise immediate needs (Albanese 2020).

However, in policymaking, a short-term horizon that aims to satisfy immediate needs can generate system-justifying tendencies linked to a lack of concern about climate change (Feygina et al. 2010).

If Australia adopted higher and more reckless emission reduction targets, there would be a trade-off and 'we wouldn't be having these fires – that is just not true', [and] of course, global changes in the environment and the climate have a broader impact on the world's weather systems. What we have always said, though, is you cannot link any individual single emissions reduction policy of a country -whether it is Australia or anyone else – to any specific fire event. I mean, that's just absurd and to suggest that that is the case would be simply wrong. (Scott Morrison, The Australian Prime Minister, as quoted by Twomey 2019).

The underlying economic logic is clear in the government's response to climate change.

The Nationals need to support new government-underwritten coal-fired power plants in order to be the party for workers ... workers in coal mines, workers in shipyards and workers in factories (Matt Canavan, The former resources minister, as quoted by Lamb 2020b).

Instead of taking any action on climate change or reducing the reliance on coal, traditionalists believe that bushfires can be addressed by removing flammable materials and building community resilience. Traditionalists seek support to their arguments by historical practices of Indigenous Australians, who have a tradition of using fire as a land management tool for clearing land to protect properties from uncontrolled fires (Baillie and Bayne 2019). It is known as hazard reduction burning. Prescribed burning in risk areas can reduce the load by creating fuel breaks, where fuel (such as tree and leaves) is removed to prevent the spread of a fire, to protect infrastructure. Regulations of hazard reduction burning put in place mean that the Australian government is now dependent on government agencies for carrying out controlled burns (Lamb 2020a). A recent report found that the Australian government had been taking a minimal approach to prescribed burning (Anderson et al. 2018). In recent years, the government has implemented an overhaul of fuel and land management practices, which is almost doubling the area of prescribed burning with covering 5% of public land every year (Anderson et al. 2018).

Realising the limitation of top-down policy measures in addressing bushfires, the traditionalists are also aiming to improve local coordination between police, fire agencies, and the local community (Prior and Eriksen 2013). These bottom-up, community-driven solutions aim to strengthen social capital and build community cohesion (Bhatt 2017). A series of disasters can challenge the socio-cultural elements of lives, such as community cohesion and belonging (Calo-Blanco et al. 2017). For example, in Whittlesea, citizens reported a change in their connections and belongings (i.e community cohesion) after the Black Saturday fires.

> *The newer people coming in, they are not invested like the older people are in the community.* (Lamb 2020a).

Reconstruction is the most important action after bushfires, and one of the most crucial recovery factors is rebuilding social cohesion (Prior and Eriksen 2013). It is suggested that the government should help communities to rebuild infrastructure with a sense of place, purpose, and belonging after a natural disaster (Prior and Eriksen 2013). However, the environmentalists argue that the traditionalists use community logic to advance their agenda of a 'minimalists' government' and to justify their inaction against climate change. In the next section, we discuss their position.

5.2 The Environmentalist

The environmentalists claim that the 2019–2020 bushfire is caused by climate change, which is directly affected by extreme weather events. They argue that climate change has exacerbated the hotter and drier weather conditions in Australia, increasing their frequency and size (Schaben 2020).

> *I think that Michael McCormack needs to read the science, and that is what I am going by, is the science… It is not a political thing! It is a scientific fact that we are going through climate change.* (Carol Sparks, Mayor of Glen Innes Carol, as quoted by Goloubeva and Haydar 2019).

> *Bushfires are a symptom of climate change.* (Neil Bibby, the former chief executive of Victoria's Country Fire Authority, as quoted in Osborne-Crowley 2019).

> *The RACGP's position on climate change is pretty clear, that we see there's a link between climate change and increasing drought as well as bushfires, and climate change is a public health issue.* (Dr Ashlea Broomfield, NSW ACT faculty council of the Royal Australian College of GPs, as quoted in Parise 2018).

The warming weather condition has been accompanied by heatwaves, with the increasing frequency of incidence, duration, and high temperature. The heat and drought factors are used as two indicators of extreme bushfire weather conditions (Vardoulakis et al. 2020). Geoscience Australia (n.d.) supports that the intensity and speed of a bushfire rely on ambient temperature, fuel moisture, and fuel load.

Ambient temperature and fuel moisture are closely related to climate change. Thus, the increasing frequency of uncontrolled bushfires can be expected in a warming world. Above 58% of Coalition voters believe that bushfire weather conditions are expected to increase in severity for many regions of Australia in the future (Geoscience Australia n.d.).

> *We don't have inner-city greens up here. It is the driest it's been for 130 years. The average river levels are the lowest they have ever been up here. This area is not a dry area historically [but] it is all changed over the last 10 to15 years.* (Claire Pontin, MidCoast Council deputy mayor, as quoted in Dye et al. 2019).

> *Drier weather and longer fire seasons have made fuel reduction burning really challenging because there is a narrower window of time for safe burning to take place and a lack of resources.* (Shane Fitzsimmons, the commissioner for New South Wales Rural Fire Services, as quoted in Farand 2020).

> *I think it is highly irresponsible to seek to shut down conversations about the impact of climate change when the nation is confronting a really serious bushfire threat in which climate is clearly a factor* (Mark Greenhill, Blue Mountains council mayor, as quoted in Judt 2020)

With long term human-induced changes in climate, the environmentalists argue that the nature of bushfires in Australia has changed (Climate Council 2019).

> *Climate change has supercharged the bushfire problem. Fires are literally off the scale on this warming planet.* (Greg Mullins, the former chief of NSW Fire and Rescue, as cited in Osborne-Crowley 2019).

Australia's scientific community has warned the government that they should develop a plan to acclimate to climate change in a long time (Smith 2016). The 2007 annual report written by the Intergovernmental Panel on Climate Change (IPCC) states that the occurrence of extreme fire danger days seems to increase from 4% to 25% by 2020 and from 15% to 70% by 2050 in south-east Australia (IPCC Fourth Assessment Report (AR4) 2013).

> *Scientists definitely work and do not simply rely on opinions. The relationship between CO2 and climate change has been understood since 1856 when the work of Eunice Newton Foote was published. We have known since 2011 that this theory was proved in their laboratories by scientists from Exxon in 1934. This work was repeated by Exxon in more detail in 1977. Closer to home, the CSIRO did similar work, building a physical, not theoretical, climate model to demonstrate exactly how CO2 caused climate change.* (Michael Asten, as quoted in The Australia 2020b).

1) format; 2) Australian government
However, these notices were ignored by the Australian government.

> *Scientists have been warning us for more than 30 years that this would happen, yet here we are, choked in smoke, caused by the biggest bushfires so large and intense that there will be extinctions of animal and plant communities. Bushfires caused by the worst drought in living memory. Bushfires caused by climate change. These fires have been anticipated by scientists, by parks and wildlife staff, and by the fire services. And their warnings have been steadfastly ignored by negligent governments, too busy chasing growth to see what is happening before their eyes* (Smhhol, as quoted in Dye et al. 2019).

5.2.1 Sustainability Logic

Given the mounting evidence of rising temperatures leading to bushfires, the environmentalists suggest that the bushfire is best handled by limiting human interference with natural ecosystems (Bowman et al. 2011; Murphy et al. 2011). Although controlled burning has been used by indigenous communities across Australia for thousands of years, the environmentalists suggest integrated approaches to adapt to climate change with limited human interventions (Anderson et al. 2018).

> *As settled Australians, we are now living, working and occupying areas that used to freely burn. We cannot light a burn and let it free run.* (Shane Fitzsimmons, as quoted in Dye et al. 2019).

> *My fire agency had planned to burn 246,396 hectares of the state's public land last year, but was 'unable to do so, because it would have been unsafe'* (Chris Hardman, the chief fire officer for Forest Fire Management Victoria, as quoted in Lamb 2020a).

> *As we have now found with the eastern states fires tragically don't stop the fires we are facing. This is actually a climate change issue. And by prescribed burning at those lower temperatures, what you do is you drive a more flammable system within those first five years. So, then it takes fire again and again, and then the loop is welded into the ecology. When you do those high-frequency fires, that is when you lose your diversity* (Dunne et al. 2020).

Instead of controlled burning, the environmentalists propose a long-term strategy for climate change mitigation and adaptation. The mitigation of climate change requires reducing greenhouse gas emissions and challenging the powerful coal mining industry, so these actions are difficult to implement due to polarised views.

> *Australia puts out less than 1.3% of global emissions, but we're also only 0.3% of the population... This is not an argument against Australian action. We need to act in order to have credibility to preach the gospel to other nations that aren't doing anything.* (Fitzgibbon, as quoted in McDonald 2019).

> *The deadly over the summer should send a very powerful warning that Australia was exceedingly vulnerable to climate change, that Australia cannot solve climate change on its own, that Australia depends on all other countries helping to solve climate change, and that there is no way that Australia can act in its own interest by asking other countries to help solve climate change if it does not do its part.* (The editor of financial review, James Fernyhough 2020).

The climate change mitigation and adaptation strategies proposed by environmentalists also rely on collaboration and coordination between different actors worldwide. As bushfire and climate change are mutually reinforcing, designing short-sighted policies is seen as limited in addressing the root of the problem (Zhou 2016).

In this context, some propose the global decarbonisation as an emerging trend for addressing global warming (Skarbek and Jotzo 2014). However, it requires a large global movement of technology and capital (Butler et al. 2020). The decarbonisation in Australia relies on importing technology by making and using hydrogen and exporting it to low-resource nations to decarbonise (Butler et al. 2020).

> *It [global decarbonisation] is a 'preferred option' with high-efficiency, lower-emissions coal technology combined with carbon capture and storage, ahead of a 'just transition' for*

coal workers and communities towards a modern nuclear power industry. (The CFMEU, as cited in Financial review 2020).

The cost to Australia of not getting to zero netemissions is $2.7 trillion. That is 20 times the cost of acting. We have the most to gain economically from being part of a global transition to a zero-emissions economy. CSIRO said last year that reducing emissions to net zero by 2050 will deliver stronger economic growth, higher wages, lower energy bills-that's not from the Labor Party but from CSIRO. (Professor Garnaut, Melbourne University, as quoted by Mazengarb 2020).

6 Discussion and Conclusion

The above discussion on bushfire shows a polarised opinion about the causes and mitigation strategy of bushfire. While discussing these polarised perspectives, we find that these two perspectives are different on three dimensions: The dominant logic used for framing the crisis, the time horizon, and the mitigation strategies. While the traditionalists overtly argue that bushfire is naturally occurring, an analysis of their position shows that the crisis is framed around the dominant economic logic. Due to the party inclinations, the traditionalist adheres to the policies that are short-term, growth-oriented, and meet the economic needs of people. They proposed solutions that are inspired by the indigenous culture and focus on community resilience; however, critics link it to their ideology of minimalist government. On the opposite extreme are environmentalists who frame the crisis through sustainability logic. They take a long-term perspective and support policies that are around climate change mitigation and adaptation.

We also observe a mutual dislike among the supporter of each position, and this rigid stand often results in policy gridlock. We argue that this polarisation has a damaging consequence for the Australian economy and society. Instead of these two extremes, we propose a hybrid logic that balances economic and sustainability logic (Bhatt et al. 2019; Shalini et al. 2021). A hybrid logic can create an inclusive narrative by showing concern for the environment (climate change) while also meeting individuals' economic needs (Parthiban et al. 2020). It can be particularly useful for social organisation when negotiating with the government, especially when government action is required to make the necessary change (Qureshi et al. 2016).

A hybrid logic can also help in addressing elite political polarisation. When elites achieve a consensus and leave echo chambers, it is assumed that their supporters could also reach a consensus on critical questions such as climate change, inclusive growth (Seo 2020). However, it is not always in the interests of political parties to disrupt polarisation or to interrupt ruts (Lucas and Warman 2018). Therefore, we support the view that the initiation of sub-political negotiation may come from outside of institutions of traditional authority such as an academic field or NGO or social movements.

Meanwhile, the hybrid logic can reframe climate change action around human dignity, human rights, and poverty alleviation (Qureshi et al. 2018a). This can address distrust that is epidemic among voters. For example, The Australian National University's recent Australian election survey shows distrust of politicians rose from an already high 63% in 2014 to 76% in 2016 (McAllister 2019). Data also reveals that too many voters feel neither being heard nor their needs being met. Understanding their concern can create significant improvements in legitimising democracy.

Additionally, changing the discourse on the usage of social media is also needed to address polarisation. As social media allows citizens to easily post, comment and distribute news and political content to their online social networks, it should be based on the principles of inclusivity, responsibility, transparency, and accountability. Governments and social media platforms have recently started to pay more attention to these principles and have taken various actions to control the spread of misinformation. For example, the Australian Electoral Commission has launched a program, "stop and consider", on social media platforms including Facebook, Twitter and Instagram on 15 April 2019 (Buckmaster and Wils n.d.). This program is an essential media literacy campaign against fake news by encouraging voters to check and consider the source of electoral communication carefully.

Furthermore, research also shows the potential of social media in managing heterogeneity and in bridging geographical divides (Qureshi et al. 2018b). IT-mediated social interactions and knowledge sharing are important. For example, during the bushfire crisis, while some used social media for spreading fake news, others used it as 'a force for good' (Sokolov 2020). The photos and videos of bushfire shared on social media brought lots of attention to the issue. Millions of people from different parts of the world donated money for bushfire relief and recovery activities (Sokolov 2020). Policymakers need to introduce policies, such as point based reward system, to encourage good behaviour on social media platforms. Likewise, bad behaviour, such as spread of fake news and social flaming, needs to be discouraged through penalties and social media sanctions.

To conclude, our research shows the dire consequence of polarisation for society and the economy. We recommend a move towards hybrid logic and inclusive framing to address polarisation resulting from political identities that are aggravated by social media echo chamber. We argue that a hybrid logic can address polarisation by integrating the economic and environmental concerns rooted in the traditionalists' and environmentalists' positions. We encourage future researchers to explore these issues through empirical studies of social media echo chamber. As social media is a 'double-edged sword', understanding the conditions, features and regulations that facilitate positive social interactions and reduce polarisation would also be worth exploring (Qureshi et al. 2020).

References

Albanese A (2020) Adversity brings out the best in us, The Sydney Morning Herald. Retrieved from https://www.smh.com.au/politics/federal/adversity-brings-out-the-best-in-us-20200123-p53u4r.html

Anderson D, Chubb P, Djerf-Pierre M (2018) Fanning the blame: media accountability, climate and crisis on the Australian "fire continent". Environ Commun 12(7):928–941

Baillie BR, Bayne KM (2019) The historical use of fire as a land management tool in New Zealand and the challenges for its continued use. Landsc Ecol 34(10):2229–2244

Bauder D (2020) Cable news ratings up 72 percent over 2019. ABC News. Retrieved from https://abcnews.go.com/Business/wireStory/cable-news-ratings-72-percent-2019-73595804

BBC News (2019) Is climate change to blame for Australia's bushfires? Retrieved from https://www.bbc.com/news/world-australia-50341210

Bhatt B (2017) The role of social enterprises in building inclusive social capital: evidences from multi-case, qualitative field study. Doctoral dissertation, Carleton University

Bhatt B, Qureshi I, Riaz S (2019) Social entrepreneurship in non-munificent institutional environments and implications for institutional work: insights from China. J Bus Ethics 154(3):605–630

Bond WJ, Dickinson KJM, Mark AF (2004) What limits the spread of fire-dependent vegetation? Evidence from geographic variation of serotiny in a New Zealand shrub. Glob Ecol Biogeogr 13:115–127

Boutyline A, Willer R (2017) The social structure of political echo chambers: variation in ideological homophily in online networks. Polit Psychol 38(3):551–569

Bowe W (2020) All the fun of the fair. Retrieved from https://www.pollbludger.net/2020/02/04/all-the-fun-of-the-fair/comment-page-10/

Bowman DM, Balch J, Artaxo P, Bond WJ, Cochrane MA, D'Antonio CM, Defries R, Johnston FH, Keeley JE, Krawchuk MA, Kull CA, Mack M, Moritz MA, Pyne S, Roos CI, Scott AC, Sodhi NS, Swetnam TW, Whittaker R (2011) The human dimension of fire regimes on Earth. J Biogeogr 38(12):2223–2236. https://doi.org/10.1111/j.1365-2699.2011.02595.x

Buckmaster L, Wils T (n.d.) Responding to fake news. Parliament of Australia. https://www.aph.gov.au/About_Parliament/Parliamentary_Departments/Parliamentary_Library/pubs/BriefingBook46p/FakeNews

Butler C, Denis-Ryan A, Kelly R, Stewart I, Yankos T (2020) Decarbonisation futures: solutions, actions and benchmarks for a net zero emissions Australia. ClimateWorks Australia. Retrieved from https://www.climateworksaustralia.org/resource/decarbonisation-futures-solutions-actions-and-benchmarks-for-a-net-zero-emissions-australia/

Calo-Blanco A, Kovářík J, Mengel F, Romero JG (2017) Natural disasters and indicators of social cohesion. PLoS One 12(6):e0176885. https://doi.org/10.1371/journal.pone.0176885

Climate Council (2019) The facts about bushfires and climate change. Retrieved from https://www.climatecouncil.org.au/not-normal-climate-change-bushfire-web/

Crowe D (2020) Australians back climate change action while science divides along party lines. The Sydney Morning Herald. Retrieved from https://headtopics.com/au/australians-back-climate-change-action-while-science-divides-along-party-lines-11072089

Cunningham M, Uffelen V, Chambers M (2019) The changing global market for Australian coal. Reserve Bank of Australia. Retrieved from https://www.rba.gov.au/publications/bulletin/2019/sep/the-changing-global-market-for-australian-coal.html

Deacon B (2020) Californian fires are mirroring Australia's Black Summer, experts say, driven by record drought and heat. ABC News. Retrieved from https://www.abc.net.au/news/2020-09-18/record-drought-heat-driving-us-wildfires-mirroring-black-summer/12673376

Duncombe J (2020) Five environmental consequences of Australia's fires. Retrieved July 2, 2020, from https://eos.org/articles/five-environmental-consequences-of-australias-fires

Dunne D (2020) Explainer: how climate change is affecting wildfires around the world. CarbonBrief. Retrieved from https://www.carbonbrief.org/explainer-how-climate-change-is-affecting-wildfires-around-the-world. Accessed 29 Jan 2021

Dunne D, Gabbatiss J, Mcsweeney R (2020) Media reaction: Australia's bushfires and climate change. Retrieved from https://www.carbonbrief.org/media-reaction-australias-bushfires-and-climate-change

Dye J, Noyes J, Pitt H, Cormack L, Aubusson K, Clun R, Patty A (2019) 'Don't ... bring the politics into the fire': what people in the thick of the bushfires are saying about climate change. The Sydney Morning Herald. Retrieved from https://www.smh.com.au/politics/federal/don-t-bring-the-politics-into-the-fire-what-people-in-the-thick-of-the-bushfires-are-saying-about-climate-change-20191111-p539iu.html

Farand C (2020) Australia's climate change polarisation hampers long-term bushfire fixes. Retrieved July 4, 2020, from https://www.climatechangenews.com/2020/01/17/australias-climate-change-splits-hamper-long-term-bushfire-fixes/

Fernyhough J (2020) Australia 'cheating' on Paris, says former UN climate chief. Retrieved from https://www.afr.com/policy/energy-and-climate/australia-cheating-on-paris-says-former-un-climate-chief-20200308-p547yf

Feygina I, Jost JT, Goldsmith RE (2010) System justification, the denial of global warming, and the possibility of "System-sanctioned change". Personal Soc Psychol Bull 36(3):326–338. https://doi.org/10.1177/0146167209351435

Financial review (2020) Breaking of the drought will dampen climate flare-ups. Retrieved from https://www.afr.com/politics/federal/breaking-of-the-drought-will-dampen-climate-flare-ups-20200210-p53zap

Flaxman S, Goel S, Rao JM (2016) Filter bubbles, echo chambers, and online news consumption. Public Opin Q 80(S1):298–320

Fuller K (2020) Have more than a billion animals perished nationwide this bushfire season? Here are the facts. ABC News. Retrieved from https://www.abc.net.au/news/2020-01-31/fact-check-have-bushfires-killed-more-than-a-billion-animals/11912538

Geoscience Australia (n.d.) Bushfire. Retrieved from https://www.ga.gov.au/scientific-topics/community-safety/bushfire

Goloubeva J, Haydar N (2019) Regional mayors criticise politicians for failing to link climate change and deadly bushfires. ABC News. Retrieved from https://www.abc.net.au/news/2019-11-11/carol-sparks-climate-change-federal-government-clairepontin/11691444?fbclid=IwAR3GVlJy8UgwxUzF4YtEYm0RiJKnPe9An9vTWGRJ529UrBC_uXjs2nEqxBg

IPCC Fourth Assessment Report (AR4) (2013) Retrieved July 4, 2020, from https://archive.ipcc.ch/publications_and_data/publications_ipcc_fourth_assessment_report_wg2_report_impacts_adaptation_and_vulnerability.htm

Irfan U (2020) The viral false claim that nearly 200 arsonists are behind the Australia fires, explained. Vox. Retrieved July 4, 2020, from https://www.vox.com/2020/1/9/21058332/australia-fires-arson-lightning-explained

Jost JT, Amodio DM (2012) Political ideology as motivated social cognition: behavioral and neuroscientific evidence. Motiv Emot 36(1):55–64. https://doi.org/10.1007/s11031-011-9260-7

Judt D (2020) Australia's devastating wildfires were not inevitable. The Nation. Retrieved from https://www.thenation.com/article/environment/australia-katoomba-pyrocb-wildfire/

Kelly P (2019) Politics of climate change fan the flames of deepening division. The Australian. Retrieved from https://www.theaustralian.com.au/inquirer/politics-of-climate-change-fan-the-flames-of-deepening-division/news-story/330999af14285944da0fc32f8d6b2ce5

Kilvert N (2020) Think Australia's bushfires killed a lot of animals? Weak environmental laws threaten the lives of more. ABC News. Retrieved from https://www.abc.net.au/news/science/2020-02-16/bushfire-wildlife-extinction-offsets/9622980

Kim Y, Kim Y (2019) Incivility on Facebook and political polarization: the mediating role of seeking further comments and negative emotion. Comput Hum Behav 99:219–227

Kistruck GM, Beamish PW, Qureshi I, Sutter CJ (2013) Social intermediation in base-of-the-pyramid markets. J Manag Stud 50(1):31–66

Knaus C (2020) Bots and trolls spread false arson claims in Australian fires 'disinformation campaign'. Retrieved from https://www.theguardian.com/australia-news/2020/jan/08/twitter-bots-trolls-australian-bushfires-social-media-disinformation-campaign-false-claims

Knott M (2020) 'Almost a religious aspect': Tony Abbott downplays link between bushfires and climate change. The Sydney Morning Herald. Retrieved July 4, 2020, from https://www.smh.com.au/world/north-america/almost-a-religious-aspect-tony-abbott-downplays-link-between-bushfires-and-climate-change-20200122-p53tj7.html

Konrad AM, Seidel MDL, Lo E, Bhardwaj A, Qureshi I (2017) Variety, dissimilarity, and status centrality in MBA networks: is the minority or the majority more likely to network across diversity? Acad Manag Learn Educ 16(3):349–372

Lamb K (2020a) In fire-hit rural Australia, climate debate burns deep. Retrieved from https://fr.reuters.com/article/uk-climate-change-australia-rural-idUKKBN2050F0

Lamb K (2020b) Australia's fires have fuelled a heated climate change debate. Retrieved from https://www.irishexaminer.com/opinion/commentanalysis/arid-30981354.html

Livingstone S, Lunt P (1994) Talk on television audience participation and public debate (edition.). Routledge, London

Lucas CH, Davison A (2019) Not 'getting on the bandwagon': when climate change is a matter of unconcern. Environ Plan Nature Space 2(1):129–149. https://doi.org/10.1177/2514848618818763

Lucas C, Warman R (2018) Disrupting polarized discourses: can we get out of the ruts of environmental conflicts? Environ Plan Politics Space 36(6):987–1005

Lucas C, Corner A, Davison A, Leith P (2019) Not everyone cares about climate change, but reproach won't change their minds. The Conversation. The Conversation Media Group Ltd, Australia

Maicd M (2020) The ongoing impact of bushfires on the Australian economy. Retrieved July 02, 2020, from http://aicd.companydirectors.com.au/membership/company-director-magazine/2020-back-editions/march/the-ongoing-impact-of-bushfires-on-the-australian-economy

Mazengarb M (2020) Australia faces $3.4 trillion economic bill for failure to act on climate change. Retrieved from https://reneweconomy.com.au/australia-faces-3-4-trillion-economic-bill-for-failure-to-act-on-climate-change-41179/

McAllister L (2019) Trust in government hits all-time low. Retrieved from https://www.anu.edu.au/news/all-news/trust-in-government-hits-all-time-low

McDonald M (2019) How to answer the argument that Australia's emissions are too small to make a difference. The Conversation. Retrieved from https://theconversation.com/how-to-answer-the-argument-that-australias-emissions-are-too-small-to-make-a-difference-118825

Murphy BP, Williamson GJ, Bowman DM (2011) Did central Australian megafaunal extinction coincide with abrupt ecosystem collapse or gradual climate change? Glob Ecol Biogeogr 21(2):142–151. https://doi.org/10.1111/j.1466-8238.2011.00668.x

NASA (2020) Fire, the USA. Retrieved from https://earthobservatory.nasa.gov/global-maps/MOD14A1_M_FIRE

Nguyen K, Bogle A (2020) Fires misinformation being spread through social media. ABC News. Retrieved from https://www.abc.net.au/news/2020-01-08/fires-misinformation-being-spread-through-social-media/11846434

Nguyen K, Brunero T, Thomas S, Keans D, Mills N (2020) The truth about Australia's fires – arsonists aren't responsible for many this season. ABC News. Retrieved July 4, 2020, from https://www.abc.net.au/news/2020-01-11/australias-fires-reveal-arson-not-a-major-cause/11855022

Ogden J, Basher LR, McGlone MS (1998) Fire, forest regeneration and links with early human habitation: evidence from New Zealand. Ann Bot 81:687–696

Osborne-Crowley L (2019) As Australia burns, why is the government refusing to talk about climate change? Retrieved July 4, 2020, from https://www.gq.com.au/success/opinions/as-australia-burns-why-is-the-government-refusing-to-talk-about-climate-change/news-story/4b4b656efd61d090cfb3c3e560484431

Parise I (2018) A brief review of global climate change and the public health consequences. Aust J Gen Pract 47(7):451–456. https://doi.org/10.31128/AJGP-11-17-4412

Parliament of Australia (2020) 2019–20 Australian bushfires—frequently asked questions: a quick guide. Retrieved from https://www.aph.gov.au/About_Parliament/Parliamentary_Departments/Parliamentary_Library/pubs/rp/rp1920/Quick_Guides/AustralianBushfires

Parthiban R, Qureshi I, Bandyopadhyay S, Bhatt B, Jaikumar S (2020) Leveraging ICT to overcome complementary institutional voids: insights from institutional work by a social enterprise to help marginalized. Inf Syst Front:1–21

Parthiban R, Qureshi I, Bandyopadhyay S, Jaikumar S (2021) Digitally mediated value creation for non-commodity base of the pyramid producers. Int J Inf Manag 56:102256

Pepermans Y, Maeseele P (2014) Democratic debate and mediated discourses on climate change: from consensus to de/politicisation. Environ Commun 8(2):216–232. https://doi.org/10.1080/17524032.2014.906482

Prior T, Eriksen C (2013) Wildfire preparedness, community cohesion and social–ecological systems. Glob Environ Chang 23(6):1575–1586

Pwc (2020) Aussie CEOs all doom and gloom on economy with climate change concerns rising. Retrieved from https://www.pwc.com.au/press-room/2020/pwc-ceo-survey-climate-change-concerns-rising.html

Qureshi I, Kistruck GM, Bhatt B (2016) The enabling and constraining effects of social ties in the process of institutional entrepreneurship. Organ Stud 37(3):425–447. https://doi.org/10.1177/0170840615613372

Qureshi I, Sutter C, Bhatt B (2018a) The transformative power of knowledge sharing in settings of poverty and social inequality. Organ Stud 39(11):1575–1599. https://doi.org/10.1177/0170840617727777

Qureshi I, Fang Y, Haggerty N, Compeau DR, Zhang X (2018b) IT-mediated social interactions and knowledge sharing: role of competence-based trust and background heterogeneity. Inf Syst J 28(5):929–955

Qureshi I, Bhatt B, Gupta S Tiwari AA (2020) Call for papers: causes, symptoms and consequences of Social Media Induced Polarization (SMIP). Inf Syst J. https://onlinelibrary.wiley.com/pb-assets/assets/13652575/ISJ_SMIP_CFP%20(002).pdf

Rannard R (2020) Australia fires: misleading maps and pictures go viral. BBC News. Retrieved from https://www.bbc.com/news/blogs-trending-51020564

Riaz S, Buchanan S, Bapuji H (2011) Institutional work amidst the financial crisis: emerging positions of elite actors. Organization 18(2):187–214

Robison J, Mullinix K (2016) Elite polarisation and public opinion: how polarization is communicated and its effects. Polit Commun 33(2):61–282. https://doi.org/10.1080/10584609.2015.1055526

Schaben P (2020) Wildfires have spread dramatically-and some forests may not recover. National Geographic. Retrieved from https://www.nationalgeographic.com/science/2020/01/extreme-wildfires-reshaping-forests-worldwide-recovery-australia-climate/#close

Seo B (2020) Why the climate wars are set to get worse. Financ Rev. Retrieved from https://www.afr.com/politics/federal/why-the-climate-wars-are-set-to-get-worse-20200205-p53xx8

Shalini, Manoharan, B, Parthiban R, Qureshi I, Bhatt B, Rakshit K (2021) Digital technology-enabled transformative consumer responsibilisation: a case study. Eur J Market

Skarbek A, Jotzo F (2014) Australia can get to zero carbon emissions and grow the economy. The Conversation. Retrieved from https://theconversation.com/australia-can-get-to-zero-carbon-emissions-and-grow-the-economy-32015. Accessed 30 Oct 2020

Smith MS (2016) History of climate adaptation research. Retrieved July 4, 2020, from https://research.csiro.au/climate/introduction/history-of-climate-adaptation-research-in-csiro/

Sokolov M (2020) Social media as a force for good: the case of Australian bushfires. Retrieved from https://www.thedrum.com/opinion/2020/02/17/social-media-force-good-the-case-australian-bushfires. Accessed 30 Oct 2020

Tharoor I (2020) Australia wildfires: Scott Morrison continues to deny climate threat despite 'apocalyptic' blazes. Retrieved July 4, 2020, from https://www.independent.co.uk/news/world/australasia/australia-wildfires-scott-morrison-climate-change-kangaroos-koalas-a9275231.html
The Australia (2020a) Bushfire politicking latest trick in Green New Squeal. Retrieved from https://www.theaustralian.com.au/subscribe/news/1/?sourceCode=TAWEB_WRE170_a_GGL&dest
The Australia (2020b) All pain and no gain in achieving emissions targets. Retrieved from https://www.theaustralian.com.au/subscribe/news/1/?sourceCode=TAWEB_WRE170_a_GGL&dest
The university of Sydney (2020) More than one billion animals killed in Australian bushfires. Retrieved from https://www.sydney.edu.au/news-opinion/news/2020/01/08/australian-bushfires-more-than-one-billion-animals-impacted.html
Trump (Jr.), D. [Donald Trump Jr.] (2020) #ArsonEmergency claiming that nearly 200 arsonists are behind the Australia fires went viral and was retweeted widely across the globe including by the President of the USA and Fox News opinion pundit Hannity. Retrieved July 4, 2020, from https://twitter.com/DonaldJTrumpJr/status/1214565369697845249
Tucker J, Guess A, Barbera P, Vaccari C, Siegel A, Sanovich S, Stukal D, Nyhan B (2018) Social media, political polarization, and political disinformation: a review of the scientific literature. SSRN. Retrieved from https://doi.org/10.2139/ssrn.3144139
Twomey D (2019) PM Morrison: no evidence links Australia's carbon emissions to bushfires. Eco News. Retrieved July 4, 2020, from http://econews.com.au/62936/pm-morrison-no-evidence-links-australias-carbon-emissions-to-bushfires/
UNEP (2020) Ten impacts of the Australian bushfires. Retrieved from https://www.unenvironment.org/news-and-stories/story/ten-impacts-australian-bushfires
Vardoulakis S, Marks G, Abramson MJ (2020) Lessons learned from the Australian bushfires. JAMA Intern Med 180(5):635. https://doi.org/10.1001/jamainternmed.2020.0703
Water Quality Australia (n.d.) Bushfires and water quality. Retrieved from https://www.waterquality.gov.au/issues/bushfires
Weber D, Nasim M, Falzon L, Mitchell L (2020) # ArsonEmergency and Australia's "Black Summer": polarisation and misinformation on social media. In: Multidisciplinary international symposium on disinformation in open online media. Springer, Cham, pp 159–173
Wilson S (2020) Hotter and drier: environmental disasters in Australia. Retrieved from https://www.foreignbrief.com/natural-disasters/hotter-and-drier-environmental-disasters-in-australia/
Wiser SK, Allen RB, Platt KH (1997) Mountain beech forest succession after a fire at Mount Thomas Forest, Canterbury, New Zealand. N Z J Bot 35:505–515
WWF (2020) The hidden cost of Australia's bushfire crisis could be billions. Retrieved from https://www.wwf.org.au/news/news/2020/the-hidden-cost-of-australia-s-bushfire-crisis-could-be-billions#gs.mo68si
Zhou J (2016) Boomerangs versus javelins: how polarization constrains communication on climate change. Environ Politics 25(5):788–811. https://doi.org/10.1080/09644016.2016.1166602

(De)polarizing ICT Debates of Reservations and Affirmative Action Policy: A Plea for Reparations in India and the U.S.

Kofi-Charu Nat Turner, Nagaraju Gundemeda, and Sabiha Sultana

Abstract This paper explores the role of information and communication technologies (ICT) in exacerbating social polarization in India and the United States. The paper aims to examine the role of ICT in shaping public opinion and group convictions about the reservation policy in India and the policy of affirmative action in the U.S. The proliferation of ICT platforms has meant the widening of spaces of social articulation across gender, race, religion, and castes whereby supporters and critics of these policies represent their claims and contestations. This widening creates concomitant insulation in "echo chambers" where exposure to content consistent with individual and group opinions reinforces existing beliefs, attitudes, and the resulting behavior. In both India and the U.S., the ideological systems and social values of dominant races and castes tend to dominate the multiple ICT platforms sowing further (mis)trust in the state-sponsored development policies aimed at educating and empowering subjugated groups such as Blacks in the U.S. and Dalits (ex-untouchables) in India. The paper argues that ICT mediated ideas of equality and justice fail to recognize centuries of racial and caste oppression and based on the content analysis of the data, a reparations policy in both nations that works towards the democratization of virtual spaces to represent the voices of the voiceless is one of the best remedies.

Keywords Reservation policy · Affirmative action · Oppression · Information and communication technology · Discrimination

---

K.-C. N. Turner (✉)
Department of Teacher Education and Curriculum Studies, College of Education, University of Massachusetts, Amherst, MA, USA
e-mail: nturner@umass.edu

N. Gundemeda
Department of Sociology, School of Social Sciences, University of Hyderabad, Hyderabad, India

S. Sultana
Directorate of Secondary and Higher Education, Ministry of Education, Dhaka, Bangladesh

I. Qureshi et al. (eds.), *Causes and Symptoms of Socio-Cultural Polarization*,
https://doi.org/10.1007/978-981-16-5268-4_6

1 U.S. Racial Policy from Affirmative Action to Reparations: An Introduction

It was never more evident than on January 6, 2021, Trump insurrection at the U.S. Capitol, how dangerous false/(mis)information could be once circulated millions of times online in "echo chambers" using multiple ICT platforms. From 24-hour cable news channels FOX News, OAN (One American News Network), social media Twitter and Facebook, far-right websites Breitbart.com, messaging apps Telegram and message boards Parler, white supremacist lies can now be amplified in ways previously inconceivable. The mob of white supremacist insurrectionists, who laid siege to the U.S. capital, killing five people and injuring many more, had been fed a high-tech soup of lies and inaccurate information regarding a host of subjects. Most notably the domestic terrorists that stormed the Capital cited following @realDonaldTrump's baseless Tweets of fraud during the 2020 U.S. presidential election. These followers for years had been whipped into a frenzy with disproved and discredited conspiracy theories from Obama's citizenship, a violent invasion of Central American asylum seekers and Qanon, to name a few.

The lie of white supremacy and the ensuing cults following white supremacist ideologies is not new in the United States. In fact, like India, the United States has had a tortured relationship with a segment of its non-White citizenry for the past three centuries. But unlike the hierarchical system in India based on *caste* (Bhardwaj et al. 2021; Bhatt et al. 2022; Sutter et al. 2022), the European settler colonialists in the United States invented a hierarchical system based on *race* that Menakem (2017) refers to as *white body supremacy*. In order to implement *white body supremacy* fact denial and a white-washing of the history of the attempted genocide and theft of Native American land and simultaneous kidnapping, enslavement and torture of Africans in America, what Winbush (2018) refers to as the *Maafa na Maangamizi* has been the *modus operandi* in the United States. Therefore, the resulting U.S. culture of a racialized hierarchy with white bodies firmly planted on top remains largely intact. Omi and Winant (1994) pointed out decades ago that although the series of racial categories in the U.S. are socially created, transformed and destroyed through time, the experience of racial minorities such as African Americans, Latinx Americans, Native Americans, and Asian Americans (blacks, browns, reds, and yellows) with race-based slavery and segregation, have tended them to favor a racial identity which demanded group rights.

In her groundbreaking book Caste, Wilkerson (2020) writes about caste systems as artificial rankings of human value based on ancestry designed by the dominant caste and notes,

> Throughout human history, three caste systems have stood out. The tragically accelerated, chilling, and officially vanquished caste system of Nazi Germany. The lingering, millennia-long caste system of India. And the shape-shifting, unspoken, race-based caste pyramid in the United States. (p.17).

While Wilkerson, leaves out the horrific system of apartheid in South Africa, Nelson Mandela helped to dismantle in the early 1990s, the two surviving systems of caste in India and the United States she does mention are taken up in this chapter in relationship to each other and how ICTs continue to perpetuate them through echo-chambers online.

2 Affirmative Action

Facing the facts, on and offline, is a starting point to producing a more equitable society. Acknowledging that local, state and federal legislation in the U.S. have been instrumental in anti-Black discrimination and has produced race-based inequality is the first step toward ending it. Affirmative Action is a policy first introduced in the United States to do just that. Introduced as a response to the social uprisings in the early 1960s against Jim Crow laws in the Southern states and the second class citizenship status afforded to African American descendants of enslaved Africans nationwide, Affirmative action attempted to prohibit discrimination in employment based on race, color, religion, sex or national origin. Title VII of the Civil Rights Act of 1964 was signed into law by President Lyndon Johnson and included a provision that stated if employers were found guilty of this type of discrimination "affirmative action ... or any other equitable relief as the court deems appropriate"[1] could be instituted.

While Kurtulus (2012) found the share of minorities and women in high-paying skilled occupations grew during the 1970s and early 1980's unfortunately these advances due to affirmative action disproportionately benefited white women. In fact,

> Women are now more likely to graduate with bachelor's degrees and attend graduate school than men are and outnumber men on many college campuses [but] those benefits are more likely to accrue to white women than they are to women of color, and that imbalance has very real effects on employment and earnings later in life. In other words: affirmative action works, and it works way better for white women than it does for all the other women in America. [2]

So while originally intended to address historical discrimination against Blacks and other racialized minorities in the U.S. the main beneficiaries were white women.

---

[1] U.S. Equal Employment Opportunity Commission, Title VII of the Civil Rights Act of 1964, accessed November 17, 2020 https://www.eeoc.gov/statutes/title-vii-civil-rights-act-1964

[2] IM Diversity, "Affirmative Action is Great for White Women. So Why Do They Hate It?," accessed November 17, 2020 https://imdiversity.com/diversity-news/affirmative-action-is-great-for-white-women-so-why-do-they-hate-it/

3 Affirmative Action in the Media

During the 1980s under the Reagan administration promoted in the media the concepts of "welfare queens" (undeserving Black women receiving welfare) as well as a "war on drugs" (a war on Black people) primarily aimed at denigrating Black people. This media campaign led to a white backlash against not only Black people but the small gains Black Americans and other racialized minorities made under Affirmative Action. White women lead this backlash serving as the primary plaintiffs in the major Supreme Court affirmative action cases even though they had been the main beneficiaries (for example *Hopwood v. Texas* in 1996. Cheryl Hopwood, *Grutter v. Bollinger*, Barbara Grutter, *Gratz v. Bollinger*, Jennifer Gratz, 2003 *Fisher v. the University of Texas* in 2016, Abigail Noel Fisher and Rachel Multer Michalewicz.

Collectively these cases weakened public support for Affirmative Action to the point that even Justice Lewis Powell ruled in the 1978 case *Regents of the University of California v. Bakke* that attaining a diverse student body was the only real interest that survived legal scrutiny. Powell emphasized that the.

> nation's future depends upon leaders trained through wide exposure' to the ideas and mores of students as diverse as this Nation of many peoples, [suggesting] that the point of affirmative action was to foster a more varied classroom environment for "leaders," thus shifting the intended beneficiary of the program from the historically discriminated against to the nation that had discriminated against them. (Reyes 2018).

The point here is that the mass media including liberals and conservatives is controlled by the dominant race in the U.S.—whites.

4 Introducing Reparations

Reparations is not a new concept in the history of the United States or the world for that matter. Jewish survivors of the Holocaust, the state of Israel and their descendants in the U.S. benefited from reparations paid by Germany and its corporations in 1952 of more than 3.5 billion marks (more than 2 billion dollars). In 1988, President Reagan apologized for the internment of Japanese Americans and authorized a payment of $20,000 (equivalent to $43,000 today) to each former internee eventually disbursing more than the equivalent today of 3.4 billion dollars. Regarding Black Reparations for Slavery, the formerly enslaved Africans began demanding reparations from the U.S. government with the Freedmen's Bureau immediately upon their release from bondage, and special field order No.15 proclaimed by General Sherman during the American Civil war ordered plots of land no larger than 40 acres (16 ha) and mules to the newly freed African families.

Perhaps the best-known activist, organizer and proponent in favor of Black Reparations was Queen Mother Moore who was a member of Marcus Garvey's organization the UNIA and a founder of the Republic of New Afrika which all demanded self-determination, land and reparations. In 1989 Rep. John Conyers, Jr. of Michigan introduced the Congressional Bill H.R. 40 and joined the movement for Black Reparations by calling for the creation of a commission to study and submit a formal report to Congress with its findings and remedies for reparations.

Radical and progressive Black people took up this call for Black Reparations and began national campaigns and formed organizations like N'COBRA (National Coalition of Blacks for Reparations in America) as the policy of Affirmative Action was further weakened by Proposition 209 passed in 1996 in California. The bill dropped enrollments of Blacks at the University of California Berkeley and UCLA by more than 60 percent and renewed nationwide calls for Black reparations.[3] These effects were so staggering that in that year after Prop 209, Berkeley Law School had only one new black student. The U.S. experiment with Affirmative Action had failed and the justification for keeping it now resided in the compelling interest of universities for a diverse student body. Reyes (2018) argues for an epistemological shift in our collective understanding of affirmative action saying "Affirmative action should be about reparations and leveling a playing field that was legally imbalanced for hundreds of years and not about the re-centering of whiteness while, yet again, demanding free (intellectual) labor from the historically disenfranchised."

Ladson-Billings (2006) in the American Education Research Association presidential address, building on her earlier work in culturally relevant pedagogy and critical race theory (Ladson-Billings 1995), is largely credited for attempting to disrupt the pattern of conquest and marginalization in education and reframes the so-called "achievement gap" as an education debt. The address lays out clearly how four debts—historical, economic, sociopolitical, and moral—is owed to historically marginalized communities and students in school because of hundreds of years of prohibition on teaching and learning an indigenous language, literacy, and cultural practices. Ladson-Billings (2006) creates a space in the educational research community for a long-overdue conversation about reparations in education for all historically marginalized communities and the need to "develop schools and curricula that met the unique needs of [African Americans] a population only a few generations out of chattel slavery" (p. 6). Perhaps in one of the most clearly defined treatise articulating a plan for reparations in education, Nzingha (2003) calls for a $155 billion budget (as adjusted for inflation) as a part of a program of reparations for slavery in the field of education.

[3] Zachary Bleeme, "The impact of Proposition209 and access-oriented UC admissions policies on underrepresented UC applications, enrollment, and long-run student outcomes" accessed November 17, 2020 https://www.ucop.edu/institutional-research-academic-planning/_files/uc-affirmative-action.pdf

5 The Case of Caste and Reservations in India

Caste is a South Asian phenomenon. Though caste is popularly associated with Hinduism, the impact of caste ideologies could be observed among the non-Hindu religious groups such as Christians, Muslims and Sikhs. Dalits (the ex-untouchables) are the victims of the caste system. They are subjected to multiple forms of discrimination and deprivation because of their social rank in the caste hierarchy (Bhardwaj et al. 2021; Bhatt et al. 2022; Sutter et al. 2022). Dalits are reduced to a second-class citizens in India. The caste system in Indian society needs to be approached from the orthodox and heterodox traditions both in the pre-modern era and the modern era. Diverse Indological discourses highlight the sub-human position of Dalits throughout the ages even in the twenty-first century. The everyday forms of humiliation, discrimination and atrocities against Dalits across the states in Indian society demonstrates caste as the ruler in India (Ghurye 2016; Gundemeda 2020; Ratnamala 2012; Khumbhar 2018).

6 Reservation Policy as Social Engineering Strategy

The progress of the nation is measured by the human development indicators and inclusive policies and practices of the state and civil society. Though most of the Western nations transformed into modern democracies and advocate for the right to equality, still most of these so-called modern nations including the UK and USA fail to institutionalize the spirit of egalitarian values and morals of social justice in dealing with diverse racial minorities and ethnic communities. Reservation policy in India was introduced by the colonial state based on the social categories such as caste, tribe and religion. Shah (1996) argues that reservation policies were designed to serve the colonial interests as part of the divide and rule policy. However, the reservation policy in post-independent India was a brainchild of Dr. B.R Ambedkar, the champion of social justice theory and chief architect of the Indian constitution. The scope of reservations varies from one social group to the other. The Indian constitution extends reservations for Scheduled Castes (SCs) and Scheduled Tribes (STs) in education, employment and political spheres whereas the other backward classes (OBCs) are entitled to reservations only in education and employment (Jaffrelot 2006).

The debates around reservation policies in India can be classified into four types; first, caste-based group reservation, second, class-based group reservation, third, class in the caste-based reservation, and fourth, no reservation. Those who support caste-based group reservations believe that the caste system is responsible for the exclusion of marginal castes in general and Dalits in particular for thousands of years so they should be compensated by fixing quotas as per their population in education, employment and political spheres. They argue that it should be continued as long as the caste system exists. However, the class-based group reservation

Table 1 Analyzed literature against affirmative action

Against Affirmative Action (AAA)	Title	Publication	Year
Stanley Fish	The Nifty Nine Arguments against Affirmative Action in Higher Education	*The Journal of Blacks in Higher Education*	2000
Frisancho, V., Krishna, K.	Affirmative action in higher education in India: targeting, catch up, and mismatch.	*Higher Education*	2016
Bagde, S., Epple, D., & Taylor, L.	Does affirmative action work? Caste, gender, college quality, and academic success in India.	*American Economic Review*, *106*(6), 1495–1521.	2016
Bertrand, M., Hanna, R., & Mullainathan, S	Affirmative action in education: Evidence from engineering college admissions in India.	*Journal of Public Economics*, *94*(1–2), 16–29.	2010
Krishna, K., & Tarasov, A.	Affirmative action: One size does not fit all.	*American Economic Journal: Microeconomics*, *8*(2), 215–52.	2016
MN Srinivas	Caste and 21st Avatar	Orient black swan	2000

believes in the decline of the caste system and its ideological foundations of discrimination. They argue for the use of an economic class as the main criterion for the classification of beneficiaries of reservation. They highlight the poor among the upper castes and ignore the social roots of discrimination. To cater to the aspirations of the poor, the government of India invented a new reservation policy for Economically Weaker Sections (EWS) of the society.

Class in the caste-based reservation believes in the selective application of reservation policy. According to it, the upper and middle class among the reserved categories should be eliminated from the reservation. They argue that because of their inclusion, the needy among the reserved categories are not able to benefit from the reservation policy. No reservation group strongly advocates for the merit argument. They highlight the right to equality and underscore the right to equality of opportunities and conditions (Tables 1 and 2).

An attempt has been made to review some of the social science debates on the social conditions of Dalits in India the critical significance of reservations for social upliftment of the marginal sections of Indian society. The Indian state since the independence times visualized group reservation as a means of economic mobility and social development. That's why; it is common to find reservations for women, Muslims and the disabled in some of the states in India. Though the state policy of reservations for SC and ST was met with social disgust, it is the Mandal

Table 2 Analyzed literature in defense of affirmative action policy

In defense of Affirmative action policy			
Gupta, Asha	Affirmative Action in Higher Education in India and the US: A Study in Contrasts	UC Berkeley Research and Occasional Papers Series	2006
Sujit m. Raman	Caste in Stone: Consequences of India's Affirmative Action Policies	Harvard International Review Vol. 21, No. 4	1999
Sukhadeo Thorat and Katherine S. Newman	Caste and Economic Discrimination: Causes, Consequences and Remedies	Economic and Political Weekly Vol. 42, No.	2007
Peter H. Schuck	Affirmative Action: Past, Present, and Future	Yale Law & Policy Review Vol. 20.	2002
Vivek Prahladan	Emergence of the Indian Constitution: Affirmative Action and Cultural Fault Lines	Economic and Political Weekly Vol. 47, No. 7	2012
Prakash Louis	Affirmative Action in Private Sector	Economic and Political Weekly Vol. 39, No. 33	2004
Rochana Bajpai	Rhetoric as Argument: Social Justice and Affirmative Action in India, 1990	Modern Asian Studies Vol. 44, No. 4	2010
C. Basavaraju	Reservation Under The Constitution Of India: Issues And Perspectives	journal of the Indian Law Institute Vol. 51, No. 2	2009
Pradeep Kumar	Reservations within Reservations: Real Dalit-Bahujans	Economic and Political Weekly Vol. 36, No. 37	2001
Sonalde Desai and Veena Kulkarni	Changing Educational Inequalities in India in the Context of Affirmative Action	Demography Vol. 45, No.	2008
Orhan Aygün and Bertan Turhan	Large-Scale Affirmative Action in School Choice: Admissions to IITs in India	The American Economic Review	2017
Aswini Deshpande Rajesh Ramachandram	10% Quota- Is Caste Still an Indicator of Backwardness?	EPW	2019
Wankhede, G. G.	Accessing higher education: Affirmative action and structured inequality – The Indian experience.	*Social Change*, *38*(1), 31–51.	2008
Chalam, K. S	Caste-based reservations and human development in India.	SAGE Publications India.	2007

Commission[4] recommendation of 27 percent reservation for OBCs that led to public outrage and the anti-reservation movement across the states in India in general and in the north India in particular. It was led by anti-reservation groups hailing from the upper castes. Public spaces and the higher education institutions across India became the spaces of anti-reservation protests.

The classical debates around the reservation policy and its practices engage on universal principles such as equality of opportunity, social justice, secularism, individual liberty, equality, merit, competence, efficiency, nation-building, and national integration (Galanter 1984; Anthonyraj and Gundemeda 2015). The pro-reservation groups justify the reservation as a means for a compensatory mechanism for age-old discrimination, deprivation, exclusion and social stigma.

Reservation sponsored development cultivated a sense of *dignity for Dalits across the states in India.* BB Malik (2019) claims that access to land enabled Dalits to overcome the roots of economic discrimination embodied in the caste system. He examines the relationship between caste and land ownership in Indian society. Modern occupations helped Dalits live with a sense of achievement, not merely a source of livelihood, but also a means of achieving a sense of dignity. There are several studies that deal with the implementation of *Reservation Policy in India. Scholars from diverse branches of the social sciences* question the impact of reservation policies in education, employment and political representation. They argued that though reservation policy cultivates a sense of hope among the marginalized categories, empirical data reveals that the state and its agencies never fully implemented the policy in educational institutions or the public sector at all levels since its inception. They argue that the reservation policy is being implemented only in class-IV jobs, not class-I jobs. Thus the marginal representation of SC/ST in the positions of power reveals the covert forms of discriminatory policies followed by the state agencies. (Thorat and Senapati 2006).

Some of the leading scholars on reservations claim that the Impact *of Reservation on Admissions to Education in India* enabled millions of students from SC and ST to complete their schooling and university education. They argue that these categories of students would not have been able to reach the universities without the reservation policy because of poverty and a persistent lack of access to cultural and social capital. However, it is also important to understand the post-university life of these students regarding their eventual career pathways (Weisskopf 2004). Jaffrelot (2006) one of the leading scholars in the field of the political economy of the reservation policy in India argues that the impact of reservations for SC/ST is limited. His view is that the reservation policy hasn't changed the lives of Dalits and Adivasi substantially. A series of socio-political movements, along with the implementation of the Mandal[4] commission report has led to the rise of OBCs in North India. It has been the autonomous OBCs politics that has been one of the

[4] B.P. Mandal, the chairmanship of backward class commission recommended for 27% reservations for OBC in education and employment in India. OBC comes under the shudra varna who have deprived of economic, educational and employment opportunities for ages.

lasting outcomes of the OBC reservation policy in education and employment in the Northern states of India.

The foregoing studies present the empirical facts related to the meanings of reservations for the marginalized and their continued political deprivation while implementing reservations. The life of Dalits (Channa and Mencher 2013) in Indian society is manifested in diverse forms of exclusion in access to the economic capital and discrimination in cultural and social spheres. At this juncture, it is pertinent to explore how ICTs mediate public opinion on reservation debates in social media in India.

7 Re-presentation of Reservation Policy in India

At this juncture, it is important to examine how the media and its means of ideological state apparatuses such as ICTs shape public opinion on reservation policy in education, employment and political spheres (Althusser 1971). Several media platforms such as movies, multimedia, Facebook, Whatsapp and others are complicit in shaping public opinion on reservation policy. It is also important to explore the nature of public response on the champions of reservations such as B.R. Ambedkar. The supporters of reservations strive hard to protect reservation policy by floating diverse associations on online and offline modes. Though the offline battles in favor or against were very common in the pre-liberalization, privatization and globalization (LPG) era, the emergence of ICTs changed the nature and direction of public engagement on the state policies and reservation debates in India. The scope and scale of ICTs enabled the advocates of diverse ideologies to articulate their agenda. Hence, the role of ICTs in shaping public opinion on any public issue has far-reaching implications. Social media is considered a source of information collection and dissemination of critical information for shaping public debates and opinions. Social media forums act as democratic and un-democratic spaces to change public opinion on social and cultural values associated with castes and reservation policies. However, the question is how far-reaching ICTs as mediating technologies act in democratic spaces whether or not they promote the voices of the historically marginalized communities across the country remains a big question. It is also important to acknowledge ICTs role in responding to the ideas and images of Dr. B.R. Ambedkar, the champion of democracy and social justice in India.

Social media is a powerful tool that has gained critical significance and so it is important to analyze how the reservation policy and its advocates are covered and judged on social media. It is assumed that private beliefs and values determine public opinions. The opinions towards the historically excluded and marginalized tend to be determined by the political ideologies, socio-cultural background, exposure to diverse ideologies, and access to media technologies. People's perceptions irrespective of if they defend or oppose reservations demonstrate the nuances and intricacies in dealing with reservation policy in the Indian public sphere.

8 Caste and Media: Re-presentation of Reservation Policy in India

What is the role of media in shaping the debate on the reservation policy in India? This is an important sociological question. Most of the critical scholars argued that the media presents biased views against the Dalits and other historically marginalized groups in India who have been deprived of the material, cultural and spiritual resources they are entitled to as human beings. B. R. Ambedkar realizing the significant role of media in presenting the voice of the oppressed Dalits started a newspaper titled Mooknayak during the colonial era. Despite the growing participation of Dalits in higher education since the 1970s, it is extremely difficult to find Dalits as media heads and in charge of editorials and reportage. As Dalits feel the sense of discrimination in the mainstream media both print and electronic, they always explore alternative media channels to present their views and voices (Balasubramaniam 2011). The most heinous crimes and atrocities against the Dalits have never been given due coverage in the mainstream media. Thus the current generation of Dalits believes strongly in the potential role of ICTs to articulate voices once unheard in digital media.

8.1 Dalit Media and Counter Public Space

Dilip Mandal (2020) articulates the significance of Dalit Media for the Dalits. He reminds us of the vision of Dr. B.R Ambedkar regarding the power of media for Dalit upliftment and to represent the counter voices of the oppressed order. Mandal in his paper titled, "What Mooknayak was for Ambedkar, YouTube is for Dalits Today" argues the power of Dalit YouTube. Millions of subscribers to these Dalit YouTube channels demonstrate the Dalit sense of owning the word and redefining the world. He celebrates it as a great move towards diversity in media ownership in the era of media social segregation in India. Thakur (2019) in *New Media and the Dalit Counter-public Sphere* discusses the new trends in Dalit articulations in diverse technology-mediated media forums. What is the meaning of new media for Dalit activism? What are the lessons Dalits learned from the #BlackLivesMatter movement? Thakur shows the positive relationship between the rise of online media platforms and the surge in Dalit mobilization on the diverse issues of regional and national significance. He claims that most of the digital Dalits use internet-mediated media as means of countering the public sphere. It enables them to represent their issues and set the agenda on their own terms. Dalit narratives, to a certain extent, counter the dominant narratives on the issues of public policy sponsored by the state.

9 Discussion

When the Japanese made their case for reparations, the U.S. general population was largely unaware of the concentration camps that had been established for Japanese Americans (Tateishi 2020). Today the Indian and U.S. general populations remain largely unaware of the centuries-long length and sheer brutality of caste and race-based chattel slavery on its respective citizenry. Like Tateishi (2020) who knew that concessions from Congress would only come with a mass media education campaign about the government's civil rights violations an even greater scale social media and ICT campaign will be required to shift public opinion in favor of Reparations for Dalit, SCs, STs, OBCs and African Americans.

To transform the Reservations and Affirmative Action Policy in India and the U.S. into a consciousness shift in favor of Reparations, educational campaigns must include explicit critical media literacy instruction along with multimodal media production (MMP) in the curriculum in these countries (Turner 2011). (Re)organizing instruction around this type of critical media literacy has two-fold implications. First, these instructions address important social issues that are needed for public consciousness. Second, students need to develop critical media literacies for making an effective MMP with successful semiotic presentations. Hence, an MMP is an effective tool to address social justice issues as well as a hands-on pedagogy. Students can reflect on their oppression, communicate biases, and claim what they deserve. Finally, these literacies would help students to become active agents of social transformation in the U.S. and India.

As the idea of multimodal texts emerges, accessing information in today's world goes beyond the traditional idea of only accessing and making meaning of printed texts. Multimodal texts including audio-visuals have a broader impact than what only one mode of language can achieve (Gee 2003). Based on the idea of multimodal texts, the traditional idea of literacy thus advances into media literacy. Critical media literacy further discusses the ability to read and produce multimodal texts that address social justice issues (Turner 2005). According to Goodman (2003), critical literacy is.

> the ability to analyze, evaluate, and produce print, aural, and visual forms of communication. Critical literacy empowers low-income, urban teenagers to understand how media is made to convey particular messages and how they can use electronic and print technologies themselves to document and publicly voice their ideas and concerns regarding the most important issues in their lives. (p. 3)

Gee (2003) views critical media literacy as empowering people to identify and produce meaning in a *semiotic domain* (pp. 18–19). Critical media literacy is the skill to identify, analyze, and produce multimodal texts intended for addressing social inequality. For instance, while creating her media, Sultana got an opportunity to build her critical media literacy that enabled her to look beyond language and to understand the complex combination of multimodal communication. It also trained her to critically deconstruct this combination in a way that revealed the power and patriarchal structures responsible for women's oppression in her society. Once she was able to do that, she could raise her critical voice and position herself as an active agent of social transformation (Sultana and Turner 2019). The role of literacy has shifted from consuming information to creating information (Beers 2007). Apart from becoming an integral part of our lives, media and technology are significant for being "the major contemporary means of cultural expression and communication" (Buckingham 2003, p. 5). Even though social networking, watching a video on YouTube or playing video games might seem like mere entertainment, such activities have been proven to construct social illusion, develop biases, preserve stereotypes, and communicate identities.

As information creates people's perception about a system or policy and disseminates blind biases over time, people can hardly erase that perception. Therefore, our political discourse is shaped by the information we get and the media we encounter. Social stereotypes regarding Policies of Reservations and Affirmative Action are created by the information people immerse themselves in. According to Pager and Shepherd (2008), "Although great progress has been made since the early 1960s, the problem of racial discrimination remains an important factor in shaping contemporary patterns of social and economic inequality." For instance, caste or racial discrimination exists in employment, wages, housing, credit, and the consumer market. Ito (2009) in his empirical paper shows caste-based discrimination in rural North India's labor market by analyzing the household data. His analysis provides evidence of discrimination against backward classes regarding their access to regular employment (cf. Qureshi et al. 2018). His results suggest that up to now the achievements of India's reservation policy have been inadequate. However, the question is whether policies and actions can change the social mindset. Coate and Loury (1993) in their study regarding the joint determination of employer beliefs and worker productivity show that affirmative action can make employers believe that the identified groups are not equally productive even though they are.

As we all become technologically savvy in our daily communication, it is obvious that our social actions and policies also need to integrate the effective use of technology, media production, and multiliteracies to ensure the masses' active participation in social reforms. "The Multiliteracies approach suggests a pedagogy for active citizenship, centered on learners as agents in their own knowledge processes, capable of contributing their own as well as negotiating the differences between one community and the next" (Cope and Kalantzis 2009, p. 72). Along with becoming efficient high-tech users, this active agency can help people become critical thinkers to be engaged in issues of social justice worldwide.

There are signs that a campaign for reparations is breaking through to mainstream media as evidenced by the 2020 Democratic Party presidential primary where reparations were discussed and affirmed alongside the racial reckoning occurring in the United States after the years #BlackLivesMatter protests against police/white vigilante murders of Trayvon Martin, Eric Gardner, Walter Scott, Tamir Rice, Sandra Bland, Ahmaud Arbury, Breonna Taylor, George Floyd, and the COVID-19 pandemic which all disproportionately killed Black Americans. We hope that a consciousness shift, of the Reservations and Affirmative Action Policy in India and the U.S., to a program of Reparations is an idea whose time has come. We encourage educators, activists, community members and governments to use the tools of ICTs and social media to promote nationwide conversations of healing that a Reparations policy will bring everyone.

10 Conclusion

Caste and Race are two important social institutions that guide the everyday life of Indians and Americans. The public sphere and diverse political, economic and educational institutions are guided by the overt and covert forms of discrimination against the socially stigmatized categories such as Dalits and African Americans. The core agenda of discrimination in the sense of superiority is shared by the upper castes of Indian society and the whites of American society. Despite the reservation policy in India and affirmative action policy in America, it is unfortunate to witness the need for Black lives Matter and Dalit lives Matter struggles even now two decades in the twenty-first century in the U.S. and India. The sociological writings of W.E.B. Du Bois on critical race theory and B.R Ambedkar's study on the origin of untouchability set the political sociological agenda for Blacks and Dalits to represent their voices and demand full human dignity.

It is unfortunate to note that despite a hundred years of democracy, Dalits and Blacks continue to struggle for social democracy in the public sphere and institutions. Their selves are humiliated on an everyday basis. This sense of deprivation leaves them vulnerable and suffering in multiple ways. Based on the empirical studies on the politics of representation in the reservation and affirmative policies the paper argues that there is a need to go beyond the affirmation of reservation policy. The demand for reparations as an alternative policy is advanced to correct the historical injustice and legitimization of the sub-humanization. A reparation policy should include not only the economic and political positions but the right to dignity and self-respect in the truest form.

Thus the paper submits that the debates on the reservation and affirmative policies primarily inform the sense of loss by the socially privileged races and castes and sense of deprivation by the marginal races and castes in the US and India. Though the implementation of affirmative action policy and reservation policy for these marginal sections led to their limited inclusion in informal institutions and seats of power and authority, a critical review of the studies on the representation of affirmative policy debates shows that only a class of minorities from the historically underprivileged groups got into modern institutions whereas the majority still struggle to secure meaningful livelihoods and dignified lives. However, most of the privileged races and caste shares antagonistic views on the ICT platforms and social media on the laws of positive discrimination and principle and philosophy of social justice.

Thus the paper argues that the ICT mediated social media platforms instead of bridging the social walls rather contributing towards the polarization of social groups on the racial and caste issues in India and the USA.

References

Althusser L (1971) Lenin and philosophy, trans. B. Brewster. Monthly Review Press, New York

Anthonyraj P, Gundemeda N (2015) The idea of social justice: a sociological analysis of the university students' reflections on the reservation policy in India. J Sociol Soc Anthropol 6(1):125–135

Balasubramaniam J (2011) Dalits and a lack of diversity in the newsroom. Econ Polit Wkly 46(11)

Beers K (2007) The measure of our success. In: Beers K, Probst RE, Rief L (eds) Adolescent literacy: turning promise into practice. Heinemann, Portsmouth, pp 1–13

Bhardwaj A, Kumar Mishra S, Qureshi I, Kamal Kumar K, Konrad AM, Seidel MDL, Bhatt B (2021) Bridging caste divides: middle-status ambivalence, elite closure, and lower-status social withdrawal. J Manag Stud 58(8):2111–2136

Bhatt B, Qureshi I, Sutter C (2022) How do intermediaries build inclusive markets? The role of the social context. J Manag Stud

Buckingham D (2003) Media education: literacy, learning and contemporary culture. Polity Press, Cambridge

Channa SM, Mencher JP (2013) The life of Dalits: views from the bottom on caste in India. Sage, New Delhi

Coate S, Loury G (1993) Will affirmative-action policies eliminate negative stereotypes? Am Econ Rev 83(5):1220–1240. Retrieved November 16, 2020, from http://www.jstor.org/stable/2117558

Cope B, Kalantzis M (2009) "Multiliteracies": new literacies, new learning. Pedagogies Int J 4(3):164–195. https://doi.org/10.1080/15544800903076044

Galanter M (1984) Competing equalities: law and the backward classes in India. University of California Press, Berkeley

Gee JP (2003) What video games have to teach us about learning and literacy. Palgrave Macmillan, New York

Ghurye GS (2016) Caste and race in India. Sage, New Delhi

Goodman S (2003) Teaching youth media: a critical guide to literacy, video production, and social change. Teachers College Press, New York

Gundemeda N (2020) Caste in the twenty-first century India: sociological reflections on university students perceptions in south India. Asian Afr Stud 29(1):89

Ito T (2009) Caste discrimination and transaction costs in the labor market: evidence from rural North India. J Dev Econ 88(2):292–300

Jaffrelot C (2006) The impact of affirmative action in India: more political than socioeconomic. India Rev 5(2):173–189

Khumbhar Y (2018) Identity and resistance: a study of Dalit assertion in Odisha. M. Phil Dissertation submitted to the Department of Sociology-University of Hyderabad-India

Kurtulus FA (2012) Affirmative action and the occupational advancement of minorities and women during 1973–2003. Ind Relat, 51(2): 213–246. https://doi-org.silk.library.umass.edu/10.1111/j.1468-232X.2012.00675.x

Ladson-Billings G (1995) Toward a theory of culturally relevant pedagogy. Am Edu Res J 32:465–491

Ladson-Billings G (2006) From the achievement gap to the education debt: understanding achievement in U.S. schools. Educ Res 35(7):3–12

Malik BB (2019) Poverty of social construction and landlessness: dignity for Dalits in eastern Uttar Pradesh. Contemporary Voice of Dalit 11(2):150–171

Mandal D (2020) What Mooknayak was for Ambedkar, YouTube is for Dalits today. ThePrint.5/2/2020. https://theprint.in/opinion/what-mooknayak-was-for-ambedkar-youtube-is-for-dalits-today/359196/

Menakem R (2017) My grandmother's hands: racialized trauma and the pathway to mending our hearts and bodies. Central Recovery Press, Las Vegas

Nzingha Y (2003) Reparations + education = the pass to freedom. In: Winbush RA (ed) Should America pay? Slavery and the raging debate on reparations. Harper Collins, New York
Omi M, Winant H (1994) Racial formation in the United States: from the 1960's to the 1990's, 2nd edn. Routledge, New York
Pager D, Shepherd H (2008) The sociology of discrimination: racial discrimination in employment, housing, credit, and consumer markets. Annu Rev Sociol 34:181–209
Qureshi I, Sutter C, Bhatt B (2018) The transformative power of knowledge sharing in settings of poverty and social inequality. Organ Stud 39(11):1575–1599
Ratnamala V (2012) Media on violence against Dalits. Contemporary Voice of Dalit 5(2):183–192
Reyes K (2018) Affirmative action shouldn't be about diversity. Available at https://www.theatlantic.com/ideas/archive/2018/12/affirmative-action-about-reparations-not-diversity/578005/
Shah AM (1996) The judicial and sociological view of other backward classes. In: Srinivas MN (ed) Caste: its twentieth century avatar. Penguin Books, New Delhi
Sultana S, Turner KCN (2019) Social dispositions against women: using critical media literacy to promote social justice. In: Mikulec EA, Bhatawadekar S, McGivern CT (eds) Readings in language studies, Volume 7: Intersections of peace and language studies. ISLS, Laguna Beach, pp 133–150
Sutter C, Bhatt B, Qureshi I (2022). What Makes Resource Provision an Effective Means of Poverty Alleviation? A Resourcing Perspective. Organ Sci. https://doi.org/10.1287/orsc.2021.1570
Tateishi J (2020) Redress: the inside story of the successful campaign for Japanese American reparations. Heyday Books, Berkeley
Thakur AK (2019) New Media and the Dalit counter-public sphere. Telev News Media 21(4):360–375
Thorat S, Senapati C (2006) Reservation policy in India -Dimensions and issues (Working Paper Series-Indian Institute of Dalit Studies-New Delhi)
Turner KCN (2005) Critical media literacy: a tool for transforming inequalities in society. Unpublished manuscript, University of California, Berkeley
Turner KCN (2011) Rap universal: using multimodal media production to develop ICT literacies. J Adolesc Adult Lit 54(8):613–623
Weisskopf TE (2004) Impact of reservation on admissions to higher education in India. Econ Polit Wkly 39(39):4339–4349
Wilkerson I (2020) Caste: the origins of our discontents. Random House, New York
Winbush R (2018) The warrior method: a parents' guide to rearing healthy black boys. Amistad, New York

Part III
Cultural Aspects of Polarization

Impact of ICT on Literary Censorship: A Study of Selected Controversial Texts in Contemporary India

Fujeena Abdul Kader and Upender Gundala

Abstract The study investigates cyber-attacks on three literary texts and their authors to follow contemporary India's latest censorship trends. While this is a global trend, the chapter emphasizes the current Indian situation referring to the three critical cyber-attacks on literary texts and authors—Perumal Murugan, Hansda Sowvendra Shekhar, S. Hareesh, who saw a violent side of social media, concerning their literary productions. To understand the phenomenon of social media vilification, the study engages with two terms; Post-Truth and Echo Chambers. A reading of three texts, *One Part Woman* (2014), *The Adivasi Will Not Dance* (2017), and *Meesha* (2018) with their respective contexts, the chapter tries to explore the role of Social Media and various Information and Communication Technologies (ICTs) in the changing trends of censorship in contemporary India. It is observed that diverse political and religious sections control censorship, affecting polarization in society. Using social media as a platform, lurking under the comfort of the echo chambers, chiefly stimulated by religion, politics, and socio-cultural aspects, polarization is uncomplicated to trigger violence against the authors.

Keywords Censorship · Indian literature · Social media · Post-truth · Echo chambers · Polarization

1 Introduction

Since time immemorial, literary books have been censored, banned, and suppressed due to socio-political, religious, cultural and sexual grounds, chiefly based on the beliefs and views of various people of different backgrounds. In India, numerous books have been banned over the decades due to several reasons mentioned above. Though there are far-ranging reasons for the ban, some are particularly sensitive such as the 'defamation' of dominant ideologies and beliefs.

F. A. Kader (✉) · U. Gundala
National Institute of Technology Rourkela, Rourkela, Odisha, India
e-mail: gundalau@nitrkl.ac.in

I. Qureshi et al. (eds.), *Causes and Symptoms of Socio-Cultural Polarization*,
https://doi.org/10.1007/978-981-16-5268-4_7

This chapter focuses on specific cyber-attacks on literary texts and authors to follow up on the latest censorship trends in contemporary India. While literary censorship restraints books, one can observe that Social Media and Information and Communication Technologies (ICTs) provide the masses with easy access to literary books/articles, even if they are banned. Once a book is published, the writers can receive instant feedback from the readers through various ICT based platforms. However, the recent social media vilification occurrences on the writers such as Perumal Murugan, Hansda Sowvendra Shekhar, and S. Hareesh expose the unfavourable side of ICT.

A piece of literary writing and its author's background offers readers considerable information, significantly about the socio-cultural context of the particular period it is written. When a reader goes through this book and the chapter—which reflects the specific age—they also will be taking a glimpse of this period. All literary texts have time, place, and therefore the socio-cultural aspects involved with them. Considering the aspects above of censorship in contemporary India, the chapter attempts to analyze the selected texts viz., *One Part Woman* (2014) by Perumal Murugan, *The Adivasi Will Not Dance* (2017) by Hansda Sowvendra Shekhar, and *Meesha* (2020) by S. Hareesh.

When a book is published in contemporary India, the writer gets instant responses (also from people who have not read the book) through various social media platforms. Open intimidation and malicious misrepresentation, and provocation to violence through social media can be observed as a common strategy devised against the writers demanding their books to be banned. Moreover, the recent occurrences of social media slander happening inside the echo chambers targets a writer, silencing them, resulting in the authors' literary death. This paper analyses the role of ICT in establishing the link between the censorship of literary texts and the polarization of opinions. The study attempts to explore the selected three texts, which were once banned/controversial, from the perspective of echo chambers, socio-cultural polarization, and post-truth. These texts present distinct themes such as 'highlighting the unusual practice of a childless couple of *Gounder*[1] community of Tiruchengode (Tamil Nadu) in the late 1930s, emphasizing the saga of *Santhal*[2] lives in Jharkhand and recounting the story of a *Pulayan*[3] man who challenges the upper castes in the first half of the twentieth century Kerala, respectively. The study explores the selected texts from various perspectives of post-truth, chiefly to trace the banned texts in the mainstream by analyzing the writers and their humiliations in the different platforms of social media. All these works present the lives of ordinary people of different periods and have triggered controversy among the Indian citizens of this decade. Hence, provide insights into the very recent approaches to censorship concerning the role of Social Media and ICTs in India.

[1] A title used by various communities originating in the Indian state of Tamil Nadu.

[2] Santhal tribes are the largest ethnic groups in Central India.

[3] A previously untouchable caste among Kerala Hindus.

Remarkably, the controversial or banned texts put forth several questions about the social, cultural, and political prospects influencing books' context. Such texts raise several queries on truth; any society's truth concept depends on ideologies, beliefs, faith, culture, and emotions. In India, numerous books have been banned over the decades for several reasons, ranging from defamation of ideas and ideologies of a community, culture, religion to nationalist or secularist politics. Censorship or other forms of restraint have been the government's response to 'popular' demand (Chandran 2018). In other words, the citizens' request is accepted by the nation-state to protect public morality or the sovereignty to avoid conflict or polarization. The discursive censorship by mobs happening in broad daylight is far worse as it tends to create pressure on writers, who then become over-cautious in their writing. The "unofficial ban" (Bhattacharya and Arka 2016) by mobs is visible in the form of book burning, threatening of writers and publishers, obstruction of sale, and attacking the writers verbally and physically. However, the issue of whether the censorship in India help in avoiding polarization remains inexplicable. At present, the "unofficial ban" has taken a different path—social media vilification of the writers and their books. Therefore, using a part new historical approach and part hermeneutic approach, the study explores the selected texts, predominantly to trace the role of ICT in polarization, practically in the light of literature in India and its censorship.

Polarization is not a new phenomenon. Since printing technology initiation in the late fifteenth century, humans have faced polarization due to the published content.

> As the Gutenberg typography filled the world, the human voice closed down. People began to read silently and passively as consumers. Architecture and sculpture dried up too. In literature, only people from backward oral areas had any resonance to inject into the language—the Yeats, the Synges, the Joyces, Faulkners, and Dylan Thomases. (McLuhan 1962).

The books hinted dangerous were burnt—"the simplest and most natural execution of censorship" (Hilgers 1908). Even though printing allowed the Bible's translation into native languages, the countries where Protestantism triumphed did not experience the heyday of civilized values or free speech (Cohen 2012). The censorial inspection of books significantly increased, and the Lateran Council of 1515 proclaimed that no book should be printed without a prior examination by ecclesiastical authority (Chadwick 1991). That was possibly a method to avoid liberal thinking in the first place or polarization among the people. Hence, we can observe that the relationship between polarization and censorship had already been established throughout history.

> In Oliver Cromwell's England and John Calvin's Geneva, Protestants were as censorious as the Catholic monarchies in France and Spain, and equally determined to persecute heretics, witches and dissenters (Cohen 2012).

Technologies developed from Gutenberg to electronic and to the digital. We live in an age where both print and digital culture go hand in hand. Those technologies are meant to educate and connect people. The contemporary research shows strong evidence that digital culture increases polarization in society, spread fake news, and enflames violent hate crimes (Allcott and Gentzkow 2017). Digital technology would contribute to retribalization, predicted by the Canadian philosopher Marshall McLuhan far back in 1962.

In the nineteenth century, information communication was possible through newspapers and the press, then radio and television became dominant in the twentieth century. In the early 2000s, the digital or online platforms helped us expose and interpret excess, diverse views and opinions. Then in the social media came the advent of echo chambers and filter bubbles[4]—groups of like-minded citizens—where they are shielded from opposing perspectives (Pariser 2011). Social media, or, in other words, the participatory web, is fluid, changeable, and circular so that users (knowingly or unknowingly) are producers, consumers, and distributors of the content at the same time (Khosravinik 2017).

New internet technologies and digitalization that were supposed to aid the possibility of tightening the bonds between humans instead seem to have led to a tattering of our social fabric. We are torn into social groups with separate world-views (Tornberg 2018). Inside the echo chambers, people would be cloistered from contrary views and meaningful exchanges with people of different beliefs. The algorithms and methods used in constructing fake news effectively manipulate people; hence, affecting social and ideological polarization (Flaxman et al. 2016). In conclusion, echo chambers in social media play a substantial role in niche politics and non-mainstream representations and exclusionary nationalist discourses, and engrained undemocratic rhetoric (Copsey 2003).

2 Background

"In today's age of the Internet and artificial intelligence, we have struck an equally dangerous bargain: we have allowed algorithms to invade our privacy, excavate our minds and manipulate our deepest thoughts" (Kulkarni 2020). Internet and artificial intelligence will learn a great deal about the users, even know their emotions, better and be able to mimic emotions on their own (Sunstein 2017). Emotions and beliefs getting more significance than facts is the most dangerous phase of post-truth phenomena. In this upturned world, "where politicians tell lies of such mind-boggling magnitude that altogether new terms have to be invented to do them justice, while literary authors make desperate attempts to find some semblance of reality" (Reinhoud 2019). It is high time to take a closer look at the wilderness of

[4] "Echo chamber" is a tightly connected set of nodes more inclined to share a common view on a given narrative. "Filter bubble" is a situation in which someone only hears or sees news and information that supports what they already believe and like, especially a situation created on the internet as a result of algorithms (= sets of rules) that choose the results of someone's searches. For understanding the relationship between echo chambers and misinformation, see, Törnberg, Petter. 2018. "Echo Chambers and Viral Misinformation: Modeling Fake News as Complex Contagion". PLOS ONE 13 (9): e0203958. doi:10.1371/journal.pone.0203958.

post-truths, as they are shared through the ICTs, which in turn perhaps causes socio-cultural polarization. Possibly, literature and literary studies should take a vital role in its inspection, as these are the establishments most closely involved with the task of representations of reality and the imagination alike (Reinhoud 2019).

In his work, *Passions: 'An Oblique Offering'* (1992), Derrida comments on literature and democracy,

> No democracy without literature; no literature without democracy... each time that a literary work is censured, democracy is in danger, as everyone agrees. The possibility of literature, the legitimation that a society gives it, the allaying of suspicion or terror with regard to it, all that goes together—politically—with the unlimited right to ask any question, to suspect all dogmatism, to analyse any presupposition, even those of the ethics or the politics of responsibility.

India being a huge democratic country, had seen censorship in moral, political, and religious aspects. There are governing bodies that enforce censorship. The Constitution of India guarantees freedom of speech, but certain restrictions have been placed on maintaining communal and religious harmony. Within the government or outside, there are certain competing groups (political or religious) for the exercise of power, and they often inflict restrictions on some practices of caste-based or religion-based habits or rituals or even threaten individuals and groups if it is against their political interests (Bhardwaj et al. 2021; Bhatt et al. 2022; Bhattacharya and Arka 2016).

As literature is associated with politics and different aspects of the culture connected with the people and their being, writers have a great responsibility for what they express through their texts. Derrida states that the license to say everything under the pretext of fiction makes literature a "powerful political weapon" (Derrida and Attridge 1992).

In the US presidential elections and the Brexit referendum, the Oxford English Dictionary selected Post-truth as the word of the year 2016. The ICT platform has a significant role in making post-truth the most researched term since then. Echo chambers can lead people to believe in lies, and it is not easy to correct them even if the truths are presented with facts subsequently. Several commentators have suggested that Donald Trump will not be the president if it were not for the influence of fake news (Allcott and Gentzkow 2017). Trump's response After the 2020 US election, without any factual basis, Trump and his Republican allies claimed that electoral fraud was rampant (The Guardian 2021). This engagement with truth and politics has become too significant. It does not need something to be 'true' for citizens to be convinced, but their commitment to certain beliefs make them believe in something.

With the aid of the Internet and Social media, post-truth displays its immense reach; falsehoods can go viral in a matter of seconds. Consequently, it becomes nearly impossible to decide facts from fake news. According to the Israeli public intellectual, historian and professor, Yuval Noah Harari, post-truth has always been around, and Homo sapiens is a post-truth species—"So if you blame Facebook, Trump or Putin for ushering in a new and frightening era of post-truth, remind yourself that centuries ago millions of Christians locked themselves inside a self-reinforcing mythological bubble, never daring to question the factual veracity of the Bible, while millions of Muslims put their unquestioning faith in the Quran" (Harari 2018).

In Marshall McLuhan[5]'s words, "we begin to react in depth to the challenges of the global village, we all become reactionaries" (Playboy Magazine 1969). Of course, the global village is a space where people worldwide connect instantly and continuously. Presently, people use Facebook or Instagram and see what they want to see, which subsequently affects their understanding of the world. The users see what their friends share, and like them, and if they follow something distinctive, and that is what they see the most. What displays in their feed is their choice and not anyone else's. Twitter, Facebook, and especially Google, with the algorithm's power, do some curating by learning about individuals and even know their emotions (Sunstein 2017). The effects of the algorithmic filtering, internet users are likely to be provided with material that conforms to their standing interests and, in effect, is isolated from differing viewpoints (Pariser 2011). They know a person's political convictions and can even categorize them, ranging from "very conservative, conservative, moderate, liberal, and very liberal" (Sunstein 2017). Many confirm their interests, both out of choice and chance, to various distinctive groups by sharing what they share to go after with the flow, forgetting to make our actual assessments. So, people are just trying to be a part of the majority by choosing conformity over truth, and it is a simple, engaging activity that many do, which does not sound so simple. "Conformity is little more than a desire to be polite or to fit in – but arguably it can even in its own right be dangerous" (Ball 2017). It is noticed that people follow or imitate the trend without an accurate assessment of the subject.

An individual can share his/her thought about a book on social media and get feedback from numerous users instantly and form opinions based on an open exchange of information. According to James Ball, the practice of sharing the posts, saying or writing things without measuring the value of truth, and the consequences, is a signalling behaviour that the internet users display (Ball 2017). Ball comes up with the term 'virtue signalling,' a signalling behaviour "such as disliking political correctness, supporting free speech or attacking metropolitan elites working as signalling devices of the political right" (Ball 2017). Therefore, while social media lets people make more informed decisions about controversial books, it also "allows those seeking to ban materials to better organize their campaigns and present their arguments in a more focused and forceful manner" (Narayanaswamy and Weaver 2015).

---

[5] Marshall McLuhan Interview from Playboy, 1969. McLuhan explains to the interviewer Eric Norden that his definition of media is "all media, from the phonetic alphabet to the computer, are extensions of man that cause deep and lasting changes in him and transform his environment." Luhan's "definition of media is broad; it includes any technology whatever that creates extensions of the human body and senses, from clothing to the computer."

3 Literature Review

Indeed, there was censorship before the advent of Social Media and ICTs. They were triggered by causes such as religion, politics, or other ideological issues. Presently, technology makes possible an incredible speed of information movement, where people use it to pour their ideas—post, share, and comment—often without thinking. The rise in intolerance threatens the freedom of speech, thus forcing the writers into silence due to the 'unofficial' censorship adopted by the intolerant groups by different means. Mini Chandran opines that the present scenario of censorship in *The Democratisation of Censorship: Books and the Indian Public* (2010) as:

> The alarming trend in India today is censorship by the mob, or in other words, the true democratization of censorship, where it has ceased to be a punitive measure wielded by the government.

From pre-independent India to the present, literary censorship's trajectory shows that the authors who are critical in dealing with the existing life matters in Indian society have struggled for free expression, mainly due to various groups' restraint. The themes of religion, caste, community, ritual practices, and popular beliefs, are more susceptible to controversies (cf. Qureshi et al. 2018; Riaz & Qureshi 2017; Sutter et al. 2022). The emergence of publication industries troubled and complicated the political life of the British officials. In the nineteenth century, the British were doubtful about whether and how to control the movement of ideas within Indian society (Barrier 1974).

> Caught between a tradition that favored a free press and anxiety overall but the most innocuous criticism, the British swung back and forth from strict controls to virtual freedom of expression (Barrier 1974).

The British perspective towards India had become more stringent after the 1857 Sepoy Mutiny. The isolated and sporadic mutinies of the dissatisfied people showed unity after the Mutiny. With the Licensing Act of 1857, also called the 'Gagging Act,' the British intensified the control over the press. More rigid laws were implemented for surveillance; the Press and Registration of Books Act of 1867 (Act 25) was one among such laws enacted by them. The Indian Press Bill Act, 1910, is one of the significant acts which had the provision to remove publications from circulation. It only provided a provision through appeal to a special bench of high court judges and could decide the publication's fate.

The British used censorship law to create everlasting religious tensions and endorse conservative groups in each religion (Mahaprashasta and Ramakrishnan 2015). *Rangila Rasul*, an Urdu booklet critical of Prophet Muhammad's sexual affairs, was published by an Arya Samaj member, Raj Pal, in 1923. The British tried to stir up communal tensions between Hindus and Muslims, acquitting Raj Pal of deliberately offending Muslim sentiments (Mahaprashasta and Ramakrishnan 2015). Due to extensive evidence and appeals, his trial dragged for almost three years. This case[6] "stimulated controversy and a secondary set of "exposes" on Muslim and Hindu saints" (Barrier 1974).

Another text, *Angaaray,* an Urdu collection of short stories published in 1932 written by the progressive writers of the time—Sajjad Zaheer, Ahmed Ali, Rashid Jahan, and Mahmud-uz-Zafar—was proscribed by the British raj in 1933 as per the demand of the Central Standing Committee of the All-India Conference, Lucknow (Shingavi 2014). The book condemned the religious orthodoxies among Muslims and the inequalities and economic troubles due to British rule. In 1996, Shabana Mahmud stated this book acted as a powerful catalyst, introduced significant changes in Urdu literature, and helped establish the most influential literary movement of the twentieth century, the Progressive Writers Association (Mahmud 1996). "The early decades of the twentieth century also witnessed the completely political writer through the Progressive Writers Movement" (Chandran 2017). Writers who looked upon writing as a tool for social change threatened the existence of the British raj. In the early 1920s, the 'Khilafat Movement' united the Muslims and Hindus on a political platform to stand against the British. Threatened by this move, the British began to appease religious leaders to their benefit by imposing bans on print media to start with (R Menon 2006). Perhaps, censorship practised in British India was propaganda devised by the British to create a rift between the Hindu and the Muslim communities and mute the influential voices of writers.

The British also proscribed books which they alleged were sexually explicit. Books with such content were thought offensive by flag-bearers of both Victorian morality and Indian traditions. Some of the texts of such category are, The *Land of the Lingam* (1937) by Arthur Miles, *Mysterious India* (1940) by Moki Singh, and *The Scented Garden: Anthropology of the Sex Life in the Levant* (1945) by Bernhard Stern.

After independence, most of the administrative, bureaucratic, and legal systems were adopted by the Indian Government from the British. The Indian Penal Code (IPC), which is still in India, was initially drafted by Macaulay and entered in 1860. Therefore, the law governing censorship in India is still having its roots in the British period. India is a country of several religions, traditions, customs, cultures, and practices; hence, censorship laws or rules are implemented to prevent conflicts among diverse religious communities/castes to maintain unity in diversity (Goyal and Agarwal 2018).

Sovereign India witnessed the banning of several books such as Aubrey Menon's *Rama Retold* (1956), a secular retelling of the Hindu epic raged a group of Hindu priests; consequently, Prime Minister Jawaharlal Nehru took steps to ban the book (Chandran 2017). In 1988, Salman Rushdie's *The Satanic Verses* was banned in

---

[6] Raj Pal was found guilty and sentenced to eighteen months of rigorous imprisonment. However, on May 4, 1927, Justice Dalip Singh of the Lahore High Court declared that the booklet did not fall under 152 A and freed the publisher. This surprise verdict left Hindus and Muslims stunned and leading Muslims to wider protests. To read further see Barrier, Norman Gerald. 1974. *Banned Controversial Literature and Political Control in British India, 1907-1947*. Columbia, MO: University of Missouri Press.

India before any other country (Dhavan 2008). The Rajiv Gandhi government's banning of Rushdie's book is vital in the history of the ban in India. After India, countries with majority Muslim populations such as Pakistan, Egypt, Saudi Arabia, Somalia, Bangladesh, Sudan, Malaysia, Indonesia, and Qatar also banned the book (Karolides et al. 2011). *Jinnah: India, Partition, Independence* by Jaswant Singh was prohibited by the BJP-ruled Gujarat state government in 2009. Asserted that it contained derogatory references to Sardar Vallabhbhai Patel (Shourie 2009). Jaswant Singh saw his relations with BJP turning sour after his book exposed a benign view of Jinnah (Iwanek 2020). The ban on Singh's book was lifted when the Gujarat High court declared the ban curtails fundamental rights (Bhan 2009)

Observing the banning of literary texts in India, it is not just the mobs of religious nationalists acting the leading role in the "democratization of censorship" (Chandran 2010). Censored by the Communist government in West Bengal for writing the controversial book *Lajja* (1993), Taslima Nasreen was attacked in the southern Indian city of Hyderabad by members of the state legislative assembly (BBC News Online 2007). In 2003, Nasreen's autobiography *Dwikhondito* (2003) was banned in the Indian state of West Bengal on the charges of hurting religious sentiments. Calcutta High Court lifted the ban in 2005 after editing the objectionable portions (Sujato Bhadra vs State of West Bengal 2005). One year after the vast success and translation of her novel *The God of Small Things* (1997) into Indian region languages, Arundhati Roy faced a legal case demanding censorship of her book allegedly for hurting public morality (Popham 1997). These books and controversies show how literary works creates a polarization of opinions.

This study mainly focuses on the writers and their books that are controversial on online platforms. After four years, in 2017, writer, poet, and former BJP MLA Vishnu Surya Wagh's anthology of poems in colloquial Konkani, *Sudirsukt – Hymns of a Shudra* (2013), has run into controversy in Goa (The Wire 2017). On 15th August 2017, the book was selected as the winner of the Goa Konkani Academy (GKA) Award in the poetry category. However, a social media campaign circulated some of its verses and shared them "out of context" (Nair 2021). Wagh's book stirred a volatile debate for "the description of the Gaud Saraswat Brahmin (GSB) community as exploiters, use of "abusive" words to describe caste elite women and the usage of a local language throughout the book, unlike the unadulterated Konkani language endorsed by the caste elite in the state" (Khan 2017). As an FIR was filed against the author, numerous literary figures came out in support of Wagh. The book published four years ago and released by the chief minister, Manohar Parrikar himself, a GSB, created such a commotion. Though the answer lies deep in Goa's history and caste dynamics, the controversy was ignited when some of its content was shared online. Foerstel and Knox find that as ICT has become widespread, the objections to challenged books become more specific (Foerstel 2002; Knox 2015).

Bloomsbury India withdrew the controversial book *Delhi Riots 2020: The Untold Story* (2020) due to the online uproar by the writers, publishers, and the so-called liberals. The book aims to authenticate the claim that the Delhi riots happened over six days in February 2020 were premeditated and executed by Urban-Naxal-Jihadi elements (Garuda Books 2020). The claim is contradicted by Amnesty International,

Human Rights Watch, and the Delhi Minorites Commission[7]. The virtual launch was then done on Facebook and YouTube channel by Garuda publishing house on September 20, 2020. Amid the Covid-19 pandemic, the virtual and online publications prove the deep sense of responsibility that the writers and publishers have towards society. Monika Arora, one of the book's writers, who had protested against Wendy Doniger's *The Hindus* (2009), tweeted, "we will work together against Intellectual fascism, throttling of voices and threats to freedom of expression by the issuance of DIGITAL FATWAS by international left lobbies. We have a right to speak and right to write . . . " (Arora 2020).

For the writer and journalist Rana Ayyub, author of the award-winning book *Gujarat Files: Anatomy of a Cover Up* (2016), which focuses on the organized violence against Muslims in Gujarat 2002, Social Media slander was not less challenging. Ayyub had been trolled and was disturbed seeing her face morphed and photoshopped onto different images in her Facebook inbox and via Twitter (PEN International 2018). She was threatened by gang rape to leave journalism. Ayyub received solidarity from the American non-profit Committee to Protect Journalists (CPJ) and PEN International.

Written a book, *Why Women are Blamed for Everything* (2020), about why women are blamed for crimes committed against them, a British academic, Dr. Jessica Taylor, had been subjected to coordinated online attacks and trolls along with laptop hacking (Flood 2020). The British novelist, Zadie Smith, has made it clear that staying away from social media helps her write without fearing other people's reactions (The Guardian 2017). Simultaneously, Salman Rushdie quit Twitter in 2017, saying, "This kind of snarky, discourteous, increasingly aggressive tone of voice. I just thought, 'I don't like this.' These people would not speak like this if they were sitting in a room with you" (The Guardian 2017).

Lady Chatterley's Lover by D.H Lawrence, originally published in Italy in 1928, was immediately banned by governments worldwide for its obscenity content (Charles 2019). "In India, bookseller Ranjit Udeshi was prosecuted for selling an unexpurgated copy in 1964" (Puranik 2018). Alexander Campbell's book *The Heart of India* (1958) got banned in March 1959 on "grounds of being 'repulsive'" (Suroor 2012). Does every book stay forbid forever? Nilanjana Roy says that a taboo is not absolute, and it varies with time and geography; hence, a text cannot stay restricted ever (Roy 2012). In her search for the banned books, she found that in the 1960s, Lady Chatterley's Lover's uncensored copies were being published in Britain and the US; she also found the whole text of *The Heart of India* on a website (Roy 2012). It elucidates that technology provides the masses with easy access to literary books.

[7] See Amnesty International India New Delhi/Bengaluru 28 August 2020 Investigative Briefing. Available online at https://www.amnestyusa.org/wp-content/uploads/2020/08/Investigative-Briefing.pdf. See "Shoot the Traitors" Discrimination Against Muslims under India's New Citizenship Policy. Available at: https://www.hrw.org/sites/default/files/report_pdf/india0420_web_0.pdf. Also see Northeast Delhi violence: Police biased, didn't stop riots, says Delhi Minority Panel. Available at: https://economictimes.indiatimes.com/news/politics-and-nation/police-biased-didnt-stop-riots-delhi-minority-panel/articleshow/77007065.cms Last Accessed on October 4, 2020

Therefore, the unexpurgated versions of banned texts can be accessed from any part of the world through the internet.

Henceforth, when comprehending literary censorship trends in India, censorship law was probably British Raj's weapon to divide different communities in pre-independent India. The same has been a weapon for the politicians to garner the votes in post-independent India. As discussed earlier regarding the recent cases, the Supreme Court acted as a saviour for the book and its writer in contemporary India. Possibly, this also explains why there have been relatively few cases of censorship on literary works in India recently. It can also be perceived as a result of the instant communication in ICTs—intervening, copying, linking, and recommending (Cohen 2012)—between the reader and the writer.

Nowadays, communication is taking place online much than in public spheres. Social media have become a platform for the expression of populist and ideological rhetoric. Studies have shown that social media can lead to increased polarization firming up partisan political and ideological attitudes (Hong and Kim 2016; Sunstein 2017). Even though the Internet, in its early days, seemed 'free and open,' it is now estranged and "closed off behind protective barriers" (Darnton 2014).

Scholars are ever more concerned about the adverse impact of populist or ideological rhetoric articulated on the Internet (Baum and Groeling 2008; Hong 2013; Hong and Nadler 2016; Levendusky 2013; Webster and Ksiazek 2012). In the 1977 interview on TV Ontario's *The Education of Mike McManus*, Marshall McLuhan explains the future of information and communication technologies. In the early fifties, Marshall McLuhan (1911–1980), the Canadian philosopher, coined the term global village[8]—one world interconnected by the digital nervous system. As he predicted, the world has become a global village, and we observe retribalization signs. "Retribalization is the process by which our electronically reawakened nervous systems and our intense, real-time, and simultaneous participation via electronic media put us back in touch with ourselves and with each other in a state of decentralized tribal existence" (Gahr 2011). When we observe the several online campaigns and cyberattacks by the extremist agents on writers, we tend to believe in the happening of retribalization—where people get more and more savage and impatient (McLuhan 1977, 0.42). The mobs threaten the writers to withdraw their books. If the writers hesitate, their families receive rape threats. Ritual of book burning is another method carried out by violent protestors.

[8] McLuhan expounded it further in his texts The Gutenberg Galaxy: The Making of Typographic Man (1962) and Understanding Media: The Extensions of Man (1964). He predicted the global village, one world interconnected by an electronic nervous system, making it part of our popular culture even before it happened.

4 Case Discussions/ Descriptions:

4.1 One Part Woman (2014)

When *Maadhurobaagan*'s (2010) translation was published, the Tamil fiction writer and essayist Perumal Murugan confronted issues that the original text had not ever met from the caste-Hindu right-wing groups (Geetha, 2015). In 2014, the novel was translated from Tamil to English as *One Part Woman* by Aniruddhan Vasudevan. In his book, the author depicts an age-old custom followed by the childless women at the premises of a temple in Thirichengodu. Although the writer had a bitter experience regarding the translation, it won the Sahitya Akademi award in 2016 for the text's English translation.

The trend of censorship has been shifting and, more evidently, with the advent of people's consummation of news from the web and social media. People who acquire information from Facebook or other social media platforms are less likely to receive evidence or attempt to search for the truth but rather believe in the false story (Allcott and Gentzkow 2017). Certain portions of *One Part Woman* (2014) discuss the historical temple chariot festival at Tiruchengode, an ancient temple. One night, the rules of sexual conduct are relaxed, consenting men and women to engage in sexual activity regardless of their marital norms. To the couple Kali and Ponna of Murugan's book, this custom is recommended. They have been confronting the struggles of childlessness and the consequent social stigma. Without Kali's consent, Ponna is taken to the festival, and she consents to have sex with a man. The root of agitations against the novel was "sexual permissiveness," which was stared as misleadingly representing the community's history. Eventually, melodramatically the book failed the test of obscenity. The Madras High Court declared that obscenity should be taken based on how it is perceived by society at large (S. Tamilselvan vs The Government of Tamil Nadu 2016).

Murugan issued an unconditional apology out of concern for his family's well-being. The Court noted that the novel did not intend to the prurient interests of persons but defined a childless couple's emotional toils. The Court declared those objecting might choose not to read the book as banning a book merely because it hurt certain people's sensitivity is not a solution (S. Tamilselvan vs The Government of Tamil Nadu 2016).

The difference between a historical work and literature based on folklore—capturing human emotions—became a debatable issue, which sought the court's attention. Murugan asserted that the novel fits in the latter category and did not propose representing the practice (at the temple festival) as historical truth. At all times, tangled in myths and fictions, not every believer questions the facts behind the myths. All cultures create and communicate through stories, and myth-making is a significant human creative activity. Storytellers, writers, poets, and thinkers create and use symbols to form, interpret and deconstruct experience, produce works of beauty and importance—whether religious or secular—and bring into play the human imagination in a rich diversity of ways. Widely held cultural or religious festivals in India are celebrated reminiscing the myths[9] or legends[10]. They all form an essential part of the socio-cultural life—that is, when the 'truth' begins to form. A similar kind of festival was the chariot festival of the androgynous god *Ardhanarishvara*. On the fourteenth night, societal taboo relating to extramarital sex relaxes. Men are considered gods where women may choose their 'god' to sleep together to accomplish their wish of motherhood.

When it comes to the different festivals celebrated in India, the stories behind them may or may not be true, or, sometimes, people do not want to know the truth to celebrate the festivals. Whether such festivals are based on folklore or historical facts, become secondary. The beliefs and rituals are already imprinted as truths in the people of different communities and cultures. The concept of "carnival" is deeply rooted in the human psyche on both the collective and individual levels (Bakhtin 1984). In carnival, ensuring reunification of the unlikeliest people and unacceptable behaviour is welcomed and accepted. Kali's mother persuades him to allow Ponna to be sent to the chariot festival,

> Why don't we give it a try? If you accept it, it will all work out. A lot of women go this and that way. Who knows about these things? Even if people know, they ignore it. They say nothing is wrong as long as it is done in secret... All men who set their foot in Karattur on the eighteenth day are gods. It is god who is giving this. It is not a problem if we keep our mind on god. Who knows which god comes with what face? It is the nature of gods not to reveal their faces. (Murugan 2014).

In Kerala, the Kodungalloor *Bharani* festival[11], the devotees who attend or celebrate are predominantly lower caste, though it features *Nairs* and royal family members (Radhakrishnan 2014). Men and women sing famous for the t*heripaatu*[12] songs composed of expletives, innuendos, and explicit sexual references to dedicate to the Goddess they worship. There are numerous histories, narratives, and myths intersecting in the background of this festival of 'lewd songs.' Moreover, people participating in it by engaging with their beloved deity deeply engage with their culture. In the festival space, they celebrate their subcultural identity, forgetting the divisions and hierarchies in the real world. The ideas of profane, sanctity and devotion are interlinked in a vitalizing manner, indicating the liberation from all authority and sacred symbols. In other words, a subversion of the power is visible. Hence, there has been a movement to censor the *theripaatu* and ban the festival (Radhakrishnan 2014). There are always movements to silence the opposition of hegemony. In Murugan's fictional novel, a subversion of power is evident when a

[9] According to Oxford dictionary, myth is something that many people believe but that does not exist or is false. https://www.oxfordlearnersdictionaries.com/definition/english/myth?q=myths

[10] Legends - A story from ancient times about people and events, that may or may not be true; this type of story. https://www.oxfordlearnersdictionaries.com/definition/english/legend?q=legend

[11] Bharani festival is a month-long festival which takes place annually in March in Kodungalloor Sree Kurumba Bhagavathi Temple. It is dedicated to the goddess Bhadrakali, a form of Maha Kali or Parashakthi worshipped in Kerala.

[12] Songs of expletives

temple festival sanctions a sexual permissive night. Moreover, a woman who wants to conceive takes the lead of this night adds to the novel's subversion elements.

Murugan faced threatening phone calls, vulgar and violent abuses in social media for several weeks. The declaration of his death as a writer was made through the same platform when he could not accept the sudden changes that happened to his life. Social media is a platform where people could put up their thoughts or bring people's attention to a particular issue. Still, it has another side, too—people could form clusters and attack people in words and go beyond limits.

He used the same platform (Facebook) to announce his literary death on January 13, 2015:

> Author Perumal Murugan has died. He is no god, so he is not going to resurrect himself. Nor does he believe in reincarnation. From now on, Perumal Murugan will survive merely as a teacher, as he has been (Murugan 2017). (a part of the note translated by Leonard M. and Vellaisamy).

Though only a small section of society involved in this act of terrorization, somehow silence of the government on the matter of his safety, when he was facing intimidations of all sorts combined with his people's belligerence, made him believe that the writer in him was no more alive.

> The printing press, the advent of mass publications and publicity, the intrusive effects of propaganda, technological innovations including radio, television and the internet, and various other changes, have resulted in an information revolution which is controlled by the influential-simultaneously encouraging both information monopolies as well as restricted plurality of voices in a market place of information and ideas. (Dhavan 2008, p. 48)

The television media and channels run by different political parties, less conspicuously extremists are knitting their ideologies through images, vocabularies, and icons into people's everyday lives; affirming, how a woman should be, the ways to be patriotic, and so on. The debates between the extremists and the self-fashioned 'liberals' on social networking sites, mainly Facebook, WhatsApp, and Twitter, have been expanded even to rural India. The attempts to spread the ideologies and beliefs facilitate affordable smartphones, through which people can handle anonymous accounts in social media and dash against the social activists and writers. With the advent of social media, censorship of writings has taken a different path, such as mass attacks, abuses, and violent comments.

Through online posts, several intellectuals and the liberals supported Murugan during the crisis and opposed the ban. Possibly, intellectual life is shaped according to what is available online. Many people support the freedom of speech, but to put this freedom into practice, sometimes, is a dangerous task, mainly if the subject is unique and far different from the majority. Dismissing the case against Perumal Murugan, the Madras High Court said, "If you do not like a book, throw it away. There is no compulsion to read a book. Literary tastes may vary—what is right and acceptable to one may not be so to others. Yet, the right to write is unhindered" (S. Tamilselvan vs The Government of Tamil Nadu 2016).

After his return to the writing, Murugan said,

> A censor is seated inside me now. He is testing every word that is born within me. His constant caution that a word may be misunderstood so, or it may be interpreted thus, is a real bother. But I'm unable to shake him off. If this is wrong, let the Indian intellectual world forgive me, (Naskar 2016)

The translation of *One Part Woman* and the outbreak of protests led to his' artistic suicide'. The role of Social Media and other ICTs is significantly predictable. It facilitates the spontaneous and fast flow of information leads to many kinds of opinions and ideologies, both healthy and abusive. However, in this case, the progressive nature of social media and online development of intellectual life has not helped the writer escape from the clutches of censorship.

4.2 *The Adivasi will not Dance (2017)*

The Jharkhand based writer Hansda Sowvendra Shekhar, who is the author of *The Adivasi will not Dance* (2017), narrated the careful and sensitive treatment of Jharkhand life, in all its harshness, violence, and beauty, which has earned him a truthful literary readership and also criticism, particularly from the people of his community and region. They regarded his book as 'pornographic' and depressing, mainly concerning the portrayals of Santhal women, which led to its banning in Jharkhand. However, *The Adivasi will not Dance* features Adivasis' adversities, chiefly caused due to modernity and capitalism, and their marginalization.

The short story "*They Eat Meat!*" from Shekhar's collection *The Adivasi will not Dance* (2017) is about a Santhal family shifted to Vadodara, Gujarat, with all the crucial and distinguishing features of its culture from Jharkhand, a state-recognized for its diversity of tribal groups. By their separation from their people, the moral anxiety in Biram Kumang and Panmuni-jhi intensifies when they quit eating meat, not to upset their neighbours' caste purity and sentiments. They are even asked to hide the fact that they are tribal. When the Godhra riots hit, they too locked themselves up at home like the rest of their neighbours. A mob of Hindu rioters attacks the only Muslim family in their area. In a positive turn of events, the women in the neighbourhood come together to protect the Muslim women alone at home. From the rooftops, the women throw utensils at the mob to dissuade them. "The same utensils that are used to cook 'pure' vegetarian food, thereby reinforcing a caste hierarchy, are now weaponised to protect the 'outsiders.'" (Minj 2018)

When her husband gets a transfer to Ranchi, Pamuni-jhi felt at home and says, "No one minds what we eat here... And we don't mind what others eat" (Shekhar 2017). The interweaving of caste, food practices, and communal tension offers an observation on how minority communities in India have to conform to be accepted in different parts of the country. Santhals are very fond of eating meat, including beef and pork, and therefore, they cannot acculturate themselves into any popular culture, neither Hindu nor Muslim. They meet varied socio-political and cultural issues working in marginalising their cultural practices, and discovering themselves insecure and uncertain in the mass of people belonging to different races. Since their cultural preferences are distinct, they are most often discriminated against, degraded, and abused. The intolerance and bigotry towards tribal communities like Santhals can be related to recent mob lynchings, which victimized and tortured several Muslims for consuming beef, and tribals are no exception in this case (Tudu 2019).

Among the short stories of Shekhar's, the most controversial was "*November is the month of migrations*". It describes a poor Santhal family travelling from Jharkhand to West Bengal as part of the seasonal migration for work. While they wait for the train, one of the daughters engages in prostitution for fifty rupees and two cold bread pakoras with a non-Santhal police officer. Shekhar, a Santhal himself, intends to portray the hard and harsh lives of ordinary people. Shekhar's stories are powerful narratives of violence towards Adivasis. The dispossession of Adivasis from land and their helplessness against mining firms' power and politicians' cruelties. In the last short story, "*The Adivasi will not Dance*", the author portrays the treatment of Adivasis as heritage-toys who perform for tourists to brag about the 'rich' diversity of India but are destined to forever stay as gallery exhibits, powerless to access good education and health.

Accused of portraying Santhal women in a bad light, he was harassed online and offline; his effigy and copies of the book were burnt. Santhal academics and writers were among the majority of the protestors. The book was banned. Shekhar, a medical practitioner, working for the Jharkhand government, was suspended from the service.

By citing Shekhar's example, several eminent Indian writers and artists stated the collective attacks on authors on social media,

> Writer Hansda Sowvendra Shekhar has been attacked on Facebook over a period of time, with accusations that his work is "pornographic", and that it makes use of Adivasis, in "English language writing", for the writer's gain. Shekar's "critics" have set up a Facebook page called Pornocopeia to defame him as a writer of pornography, and posted pictures of others in the writing community as "friends of a pornographer". In addition to this defamation, and the loss of privacy of the writer and his friends, the critics who have been trolling Shekar have taken their persecution of the writer to the next level. (The Wire 2017)

The online abusing of the writer and provoking the Adivasis to burn his effigy and copies of his books shows how a part of society can be incited and stimulated through social media campaigning against the authors. Notwithstanding entering into the digital culture, it is also observed where an increase in fake news and widespread misinformation are acknowledged, persistently rather than truth. The technology grows and offers the users aberrant and abundant access to information and different ways to express their opinions without restraint. However, how the same is used to silence authors may lead to the death of their creativity.

4.3 *Moustache (2020)*

S. Hareesh's novel *Moustache* (2020)—*Meesha* (2019) is a Malayalam novel translated by Jayasree Kalathil—in which the hero, Vavachan (aka Moustache), is a *Pulayan* converted to Christianity. The story set in *Kuttanad*[13] in the first half of the twentieth century gives readers a picture of the *Pulayan* community who were predominantly agricultural workers, and some were engaged in fishing. The upper caste landowners treated them as property and exchanged them along with the land. To this polarized region, the missionaries come into force to lure such communities into Christianity.

Vavachan gets to play the role of a policeman with a 'big' moustache in a drama. Though he does not have any dialogue, his mere appearance shudders the audience. Vavachan refuses to shave off his moustache even after the show ends. The lower castes are banned from wearing a moustache. His powerful performance with his moustache, frighten the typically upper-caste audience, stimulating in them recollections of characters of Dalit power. Besides that, the moustache had given him regular meals. Even though he was accustomed to not having anything for days, regular food availability during the drama days had changed his metabolism. To get food regularly, he sets out to Malabar in search of Ezhuthachan, the play director.

Nevertheless, soon, Moustache becomes a figure of power and the terror of the upper-castes. The folks spread the rumours of the superpower of Moustache. It shows how a small village spread big stories without the prey's knowledge; even in the absence of Information and Communication Technology, the canards spread in seconds, turning him into a figure of mythic proportions! There form groups to attack him, and no one able to touch him. Infinite stories come up and reinvent the legend of his magic moustache in which birds perch, lets its owner appear instantaneously in different places, and vanish. The moustache grows till it touches the sky, as thick as rain clouds. Even though the story takes place nearly seventy years ago in the background of Kerala's social life, the internet generation can still relate to the caste and gender rift prevailing in the country.

The thought-provoking novel led to controversy after being serially published three chapters in *Mathrubhumi*, a Malayalam weekly. In the book, two characters discuss why young women are dressing prettier when going to temples. One character says, "They're subconsciously giving the signal that they are available for mating," and the priests "traditionally been the experts in these things." (Hareesh, 2020). This particular part of the book was taken out of context and circulated on social media, offended many alleging that it shows the Hindu women in a bad light. Hareesh announced the novel's withdrawal due to the threats against him and his family in social media, explaining, "I am too weak" (The Wire 2018).

He was forced to deactivate his Facebook account. The effect of polarization in social media is evident when certain "fringe groups misusing specific content of the novel to market unethical ideas" (The Hindu 2018). In his letter to S. Hareesh, Perumal Murugan says he "should wait till the hatred ebbs" (Murugan 2018). Several scholars and writers voiced against the fanatics and mobs and expressed solidarity with Hareesh.

[13] Kuttanad is region that spreads across the three districts—Alappuzha, Kottayam and Pathanamthitta—in the southern state of Kerala, India.

Poet K. Satchidanandan comments,

> There is an attempt to divide our society, which is a part of a larger political project. This was a deliberately stoked controversy because we have already had a lot of writing of this kind, including by writers and intellectuals who established the Yogakshema Sabha, which was a Namboothiri reform platform. (Sengupta, The Hindu 2018)

McLuhan said that only artists could illuminate the present, while the bulk of society was glancing backwards. According to McLuhan,

> ... inherent in the artist's creative inspiration is the process of subliminally sniffing out environmental change. It has always been the artist who perceives the alterations in man caused by a new medium, who recognizes that the future is the present, and uses his work to prepare the ground for it. But most people, from truck drivers to the literary Brahmins, are still blissfully ignorant of what the media do to them (Norden and Rogaway 1969).

Perhaps, the book written by a writer is like a ledger in *Kaalan's*[14] hands, as the narrator said in *Moustache* (2020) by S. Hareesh. Moustache snatches away the ledger from *Kaalan*. After reading it, his moustache bows in reverence. Unable to bear the heaviness of the knowledge he had attained; he lay down on the bare earth and dozes off under the night sky. "Did the ledger talk about Moustache running away with *Kaalan*'s book?' Of course. And that we're talking about it?" It contains "all the information about all creatures, from worms to human beings, who have lived since the beginning of the world, and about those yet to be born" (Hareesh 2020).

The social media vilification of writers through 'fake news' or prop up dubious narratives has a distressing effect on free speech and opinion. Sitting inside a cosy online bubble, cyberbullying, spreading misinformation, or countering threats is not what people anticipated in the early days of the internet—expected everyone could freely exchange fresh ideas and contemplate others' points of view.

Meesha (2019), being abundant of Magical realism elements, did not face the fate of Salman Rushdie's *The Satanic Verses* (1988), chiefly due to the Supreme Court's apt verdict, disapproving the culture of banning books as it directly obstructed the free flow of ideas. The court heard a PIL filed by a Delhi resident, N Radhakrishnan, demanding removing specific excerpts from the novel, claiming that it was showing Hindu women in a bad light. On behalf of the bench of three judges, Chief Justice of India Dipak Misra authored the judgment. The Court declared a book cannot be banned—"language used in the dialogue cannot remotely be thought of as obscene, and the concept of defamation does not arise" (N. Radhakrishnan v. Union of India 2018). The bench further said, "You are giving undue importance to this kind of stuff. In the age of the internet, you are making this an issue. It is best forgotten," (The New Indian Express 2018).

[14] The God of Death

5 Discussion

No writer wants the world to end because of their book. As the words of the Prophet of Modernism, Stephane Mallarme (1842–1898) echoes, they want "Everything in the world exists to end up as a book" (Mallarme 1957; translated by Gorelick). The online campaigns and wild protests against writers create fear in their minds, not only about their survival but the anxiety of inciting large-scale conflicts in the society (Chandran 2018).

When conservatives of their respective community threatened the writers Murugan and Shekhar, they lost their job for a while. The religious fundamentalists threatened Hareesh that his hands would be chopped off if he does not withdraw his writings. The attacks on the three writers may prove McLuhan's predictions that humankind reverts to an oral society or show immature behaviours. According to him, the artist has the power and courage of the seer to see the digital world's dangerous trends and grasp the outer world's language and relate it to the inner world (McLuhan, cited in Norden 1969).

Social Media allows supreme control of news consumption as people can filter and pick content rendering to their tastes and predispositions and live in an echo chamber. The echo chambers cut off their connections of communication to the world and change whom they trust. The expectation that social media would provide space to marginalized groups and develop democratic discussions seems to be leading to more toxic debates. These unhealthy debates inside brutally affect the writers and artists outside as it challenges their freedom of expression and, more often, their freedom to life. Ignorance is rarely appreciated, as they always lock themselves inside an echo chamber of like-minded friends and self-confirming newsfeeds, which make their beliefs constantly reinforced and seldom challenged (Pariser 2011). Consequently, the polarized mobs take weapons, behave savagely, even by attacking writers on the streets. The role of extremist agents further adds to the polarization.

Justice Markanedy Katju says that India is an open field of polarization from the post-independent era and shows an exponential upsurge in religious polarization in recent years.[15]

> Communalism was artificially created after suppressing the 1857 Mutiny (in which Hindus and Muslims fought together against the British) by the British rulers as part of their divide and rule policy, and this was continued even after Independence, but now it has increased exponentially (Katju 2019).

The online abuses and harasses of writers can be seen as examples of how the retribalization process is happening in the present scenario. McLuhan's insight into the global village made him identify the retribalization process. There are groups of

---

[15] Justice Markandey Katju expresses his views on communal polarization happening in India. See The religious polarization of India. Available at: https://indicanews.com/2019/11/22/the-religious-polarization-of-india Last Accessed on: September 26, 2020.

people bending their heads in front of social media and taking orders unsightly. The online campaigns against the writers through virtual groups and anonymous profiles on Facebook, Instagram, and other social media sites may lead to the emergence of different intolerant groups in the society attacking writers and thinkers. This global village (with arduous interfaces and abrasive situations) is turning into tribal; humans are going back into the bicameral mind, which is tribal collective, without any individual consciousness and their main kind of sport butchering each other (McLuhan 1977). He further remarks, "Once we have surrendered our sense and nervous systems to the private manipulation of those who would try to benefit from taking a lease on our eyes and ears and nerves, we don't really have any rights left" (McLuhan 1964). The intolerant groups or fanatics[16] in India have surrendered their senses act violently, which gives the readers a horrid picture of a society that is intolerant, dogmatic, and regressive towards the writers.

The pressure exerted by the mob is harmful to creativity as it leads the writers to go through self-censorship. One cannot assess a writer's motives without knowing his early development or more over his subject matter is dependent on the age he lives in (Orwell 1946). Whenever they initiate such writings, the fear of consequences may shut the writers' creativity forever; not everyone may resurrect like Perumal Murugan after confronting the risk of his life.

6 Conclusion

India seems to be polarized by socio-political views and religious-cultural beliefs. It is not easy for such people to imbibe or be tolerant after reading a piece of work beyond their understanding. This is where the censorship law plays its most significant role. It appears that the censorship in India is gradually discharging from the hands of the administrative machinery to the masses of different political and religious sections. Stimulated by religion, politics, or other ideologies, in the contemporary situation, lurking under the echo chamber's comfort, it is easy to trigger violence against anybody, mainly using social media and various other ICT platforms. Hence, it is witnessed that the rise in intolerance threatens the freedom of speech and therefore forces the writers into silence by the "unofficial" censorship adopted by the aforesaid prejudiced groups. It can be noticed that there are specific competing groups of various political parties, which often inflict restrictions on writers and their writings, predominantly using social media. As a result, the writers fear being targeted and politically vigilant; they practise self-censorship and avoid unsafe ideas or thoughts ensuing "a sanitized but mediocre literature" (Chandran 2017).

[16] "The fanatic is commonly defined, 'normed,' as a person excessively or abnormally religious; s/he needs to be controlled." (Ansari 2003, p. 38)

In pre-independent India, printing technology contributed to the polarization of Indians in many ways. In other words, the British used the censorship of books to divide and control the united people in the 1857 Sepoy Mutiny. The rebellious literature and far-reaching political literature of Indians terrified them. Today, one can observe echo chambers based on various religiopolitical ideologies, hence hardly blame the internet. Conceivably, following the history of banning books, one cannot just blame any particular political group; all, the right, left, and the secular wings have stood against a book if it harms their political interests. It is perceived that in the present era of social media, every political group locks their respective masses in partisan narratives and locks out conflicting evidence and information.

The tribal echo-chambers with their own beliefs potentially contribute to the polarization of public opinions. As misleading information could go viral in seconds, and as the same media provides reliable information, it becomes virtually impossible to distinguish between facts and fake news. This becomes the best platform to play with the emotions of the users. As discussed earlier, the post-truth gives more importance to emotions than facts. In the short stories of Shekhar, the descriptions about poverty, oppression, and the helplessness of Adivasis due to industrialization are ignored by the online abusers but alleges the writer as a porn writer, claiming that he represented the Santhal women in a bad light to trigger the controversy. In the case of Hareesh, a particular excerpt of his book *Meesha* was circulated out of context to persuade the bubble-mates. It is also observed that online users are losing the ability to differentiate information from opinion when they see repeated posts and comments through online media. Considering people's existence in the digitally progressive world, many people believe that all have absolute freedom and wide possibility to exchange new ideas and consider other points of view. However, what is happening in this post-truth world is Cyberbalkanization, which "is the segregation of the Internet into smaller groups with similar interests, to a degree that they show a narrow-minded approach to outsiders or those with contradictory views." (Technopedia 2013). It is significant to make sure that the online information should be made navigable rather than curated or restricted to evade the danger of the Internet turning into bigoted clusters and ensure a healthy exchange of information.

Consequently, the study focused on the Indian writers facing unofficial censorship and how the echo-chambers with their specific ideologies possibly contribute to the polarization of public opinion. Further, to show how the catastrophe of post-truth intensifies, animates, or twists, the study also tried to explore how print and digital technologies contribute to the contemporary Indian scenario's polarisation. It is also witnessed that the authors whose works are controversial online or offline are opening a broad platform for such controversial texts to publish using various digital technologies. Thus, the availability of banned books on the internet reaches a more general audience across the globe.

References

'Meesha' row: Supreme Court decries practice of banning books (2018) The New Indian Express, August 3. https://www.newindianexpress.com/nation/2018/aug/03/meesha-row-supreme-court-decries-practice-of-banning-books-1852562.html

Allcott H, Gentzkow M (2017) Social media and fake news in the 2016 election. J Econ Perspect 31(2):211–236. https://doi.org/10.1257/jep.31.2.211

Ansari MT (2003) Refiguring the fanatic: Malabar 1836–1922. In: Marayam S, Pandian MSS, Ajay S (eds) Subaltern Studies XII, Muslims, Dalits, and the fabrications of history. Permanent Black and Ravi Dayal Publisher, New Delhi, pp 36–77

Arora M (2020) Ishkaran, we will work together against Intellectual fascism, throttling of voices and threats to freedom of expression by issuance of DIGITAL FATWAS by international left lobbies. We have a right to speak and right to write. Is it too much to ask for in this New India? Twitter, April 7, 2020. https://twitter.com/advmonikaarora/status/1297776238057013250

Bakhtin M (1984) Rabelais and his world. Trans. Helene Iswolsky. Indiana University Press, Bloomington

Ball J (2017) Post-truth: how bullshit conquered the world, 1st edn. Biteback Publishing, London

Barrier NG (1974) Banned controversial literature and political control in British India, 1907–1947. University of Missouri Press, Columbia

Baum MK, Groeling T (2008) New media and the polarization of American political discourse. Polit Commun 25:345–1365. https://doi.org/10.1080/10584600802426965

Bhan R (2009) Blow for Modi as HC lifts ban on Jaswant's Book. NDTV.Com. https://www.ndtv.com/india-news/blow-for-modi-as-hc-lifts-ban-on-jaswants-book-400877

Bhardwaj A, Kumar Mishra S, Qureshi I, Kamal Kumar K, Konrad AM, Seidel MDL, Bhatt B (2021) Bridging caste divides: middle-status ambivalence, elite closure, and lower-status social withdrawal. J Manag Stud 58(8):2111–2136

Bhatt B, Qureshi I, Sutter C (2022) How do intermediaries build inclusive markets? The role of the social context. J Manag Stud

Bhattacharya S, Arka (2016) Censorship and literature: introductory responses. Sanglap J Lit Cult Inq 2(2):1. https://www.academia.edu/14952406/Sanglap_CFP_Literature_and_Censorship_Vol_2_I

Chadwick H (1991) Decrees of The Ecumenical Councils. Edited by Norman P. Tanner. 2 Vols. Pp. Xxvi+2473. London: Sheed & Ward; Washington DC: Georgetown University Press, 1990. 145.00. J Theol Stud 42(2):737–738. https://doi.org/10.1093/jts/42.2.737

Chandran M (2010) The democratisation of censorship: books and the Indian public. Econ Pol Wkly 45(40):27–31. https://www.jstor.org/stable/25742141

Chandran M (2017) The writer, the reader and the state: literary censorship in India. Sage, Thousand Oaks

Chandran M (2018) "Dr. Mini Chandran: on literary censorship in India" interview by Sanskriti Nagar, Of Books & Bookworms, December 11, 2018. https://ofbnbmagazine.com/2018/12/11/dr-mini-chandran-on-literary-censorship-in-india/

Charles R (2019) 'Lady Chatterley's Lover' was banned 90 years ago. Now we're—Yawn—bored by obscenity. The Washington Post. https://www.washingtonpost.com/entertainment/books/lady-chatterleys-lover-was-banned-90-years-ago-now-were%2D%2Dyawn%2D%2Dbored-by-obscenity/2019/12/16/dcf6bc86-1f79-11ea-86f3-3b5019d451db_story.html

Cohen N (2012) You can't read this book: censorship in an age of freedom. Fourth Estate, London

Copsey N (2003) Extremism on the net: the extreme right and the value of the Internet. In: Political parties and the Internet: net gain? Routledge, London, pp 218–233

Darnton R (2014) Censors at work: how states shaped literature. The British Library, London

Derrida J (1992) Passions: 'an oblique offering'. In: Wood D (ed) Derrida: a critical reader. T.J Press Ltd., London, pp 5–35

Derrida J, Attridge D (1992) Acts of literature. Routledge

Dhavan R (2008) Publish and be damned: censorship and intolerance in India. Tulika Books, New Delhi

Flaxman S, Goel S, Rao JM (2016) Filter bubbles, echo chambers, and online news consumption. Public Opin Q 80(S1):298–320. https://doi.org/10.1093/poq/nfw006

Flood A (2017) Zadie Smith says using social media would threaten her writing. The Guardian. https://www.theguardian.com/books/2017/sep/21/zadie-smith-says-using-social-media-would-threaten-her-writing

Flood A (2020) Author of book about victim blaming bombarded with misogynist abuse. The Guardian. https://www.theguardian.com/books/2020/apr/24/author-book-victim-blaming-misogynist-abuse-jessica-taylor

Foerstel HN (2002) Banned in the U.S.A.: a reference guide to book censorship in schools and public libraries. Revised and Expanded Edition. Greenwood Publishing Group, Inc.

Gahr T (2011) McLuhan's retribalization and the end of individualism, nationalism, and privacy. Academia.edu. https://www.academia.edu/8159155/McLuhan_s_Retribalization_and_the_End_of_Individualism_Nationalism_and_Privacy

Garuda Books (2020) Delhi Riots 2020: the untold story. https://www.garudabooks.com/delhi-riots-2020-the-untold-story

Geetha V (2015) Notes on a literary death. Econ Polit Wkly 50(3). https://www.epw.in/journal/2015/3/web-exclusives/notes-literary-death.html

Goyal K, Agrawal G (2018) A critical analysis on book censorship in India. Supremo Amicus 4. https://supremoamicus.org/wp-content/uploads/2018/06/v4g23.pdf

Harari YN (2018) 21 lessons for the 21st century. Jonathan Cape, London

Hareesh S (2020) Moustache. Trans. Jayasree Kalathil. Harper Perennial, New Delhi

Hilgers J (1908) CATHOLIC ENCYCLOPEDIA: censorship of books. Newadvent.Org. https://www.newadvent.org/cathen/03519d.htm

Hong S (2013) Who benefits from Twitter? Social media and political competition in the U.S. House of Representatives. Gov Inf Q 30(4):464–472. https://doi.org/10.1016/j.giq.2013.05.009

Hong S, Kim SH (2016) Political polarization on twitter: implications for the use of social media in digital governments. Gov Inf Q 33(4):777–782. https://doi.org/10.1016/j.giq.2016.04.007

Hong S, Nadler D (2016) The unheavenly chorus: political voices of organized interests on social media. Policy Internet 8(1):91–106. https://doi.org/10.1002/poi3.110

Iwanek K (2020) Judged by the cover: Remembering the controversy around Jaswant Singh's book on Jinnah". Thediplomat.Com. https://thediplomat.com/2020/10/judged-by-the-cover-remembering-the-controversy-around-jaswant-singhs-book-on-jinnah/

Karolides NJ, Bald M, Sova DB (2011) 120 banned books, 2nd edn. Checkmark Books, New York

Khan N (2017) Former BJP MLA'S book on caste rocks Goa politics". Hindustan Times. https://www.hindustantimes.com/india-news/former-bjp-mla-s-book-on-caste-rocks-goa-politics/story-vdRdbTPnE9uXvaXsq8qAZK.html

Khosravinik M (2017) Right Wing populism in the west: social media discourse and echo chambers. Insight Turkey 19(3):53–68. https://doi.org/10.25253/99.2017193.04

Knox EJM (2015) Book Banning in 21st-century America. Rowman & Littlefield, Lanham

Kulkarni V (2020) By using Google, Facebook, Amazon, are we giving up our 'freedom'? The quint. https://www.thequint.com/voices/opinion/artificial-intelligence-machine-learning-algorithms-facebook-google-amazon-profiling-influencing-opinions#read-more#read-more

Levendusky MS (2013) Why do partisan media polarize viewers? Am J Polit Sci 57(3):611–623. https://doi.org/10.1111/ajps.12008

Mahaprashasta AA, Ramakrishnan, V (2015) Politics of ban. Frontline. https://frontline.thehindu.com/cover-story/politics-of-ban/article7002952.ece

Mallarme S (2021) The book Stephane Mallarme. Trans. Sylvia Gorelick. Exact Change, New York

Mahmud S (1996) Angāre and the Founding of the Progressive Writers' Association. Modern Asian Studies 30(2):447–467. https://www.jstor.org/stable/313015

McLuhan M (1962) The Gutenberg galaxy: the making of typographic man. University of Toronto Press, Toronto

McLuhan M (1977) Violence as a quest for identity. Interview by Mike McManus. Video, 6.46. https://www.youtube.com/watch?v=ULI3x8WIxus&t=45s
Minj N (2018) The adivasi will not dance: "why should the truth be whitewashed?". Feminism in India. https://feminisminindia.com/2018/04/17/book-review-the-adivasi-will-not-dance
Murugan P (2014) One part woman. Trans. Aniruddhan Vasudevan. Penguin Books, Chennai
Murugan P (2017) "Literature and Censorship". Trans. Leonard, M. Dickens and Vellaisamy, P. Women Philos J 4–5:125. https://en.unesco.org/themes/social-transformations/womenphilosophersjournal
Murugan P (2018) Perumal Murugan's letter to S. Hareesh: and it will subside.... The Hindu, July 29. https://www.thehindu.com/opinion/op-ed/and-it-will-subside/article24534808.ece
N Radhakrishnan v Union of India (2018) SCC OnLine SC 1499. https://globalfreedomofexpression.columbia.edu/cases/n-radhakrishnan-v-union-india/
Nair S (2021) Awarded, then trashed: Goa Poet hounded for questioning Brahmins. The Indian Express. https://indianexpress.com/article/india/goa-former-bjp-mla-vishnu-surya-wagh-poet-hounded-for-questioning-brahmins-4896000/
Narayanaswamy R, Weaver KD (2015) The impact of information and communication technologies on book challenge trends in the United States: an analysis. Webology 12(2). http://www.webology.org/2015/v12n2/a137.pdf
Naskar S (2016) Murugan's Tamil poems translated into English. Sunday Guardian Live, August 27. https://www.sundayguardianlive.com/culture/6201-murugan-s-tamil-poems-translated-english
Norden E, Rogaway P (1969) Marshall McLuhan interview from playboy, 1969 Eric Norden Interview by. In person. Toronto.
Orwell G (1946) Politics and the English language. Libcom. https://libcom.org/ files/Politics%20and%20the%20English%20Language%20-%20George%20Orwell.pdf
Pariser E (2011) The Filter bubble: how the new personalized web is changing what we read and how we think. Penguin Books, New York
Popham P (1997) Under fire, but India is in my blood. The Independent, September 21. https://www.independent.co.uk/news/world/under-fire-but-india-is-in-my-blood-1240454.html
Puranik A (2018) Here Are some interesting facts about the formerly banned and censored novel, 'Lady Chatterley'S Lover'. The Economic Times. https://economictimes.indiatimes.com/magazines/panache/here-are-some-interesting-facts-about-the-formerly-banned-and-censored-novel-lady-chatterleys-lover/articleshow/62845961.cms
Qureshi I, Sutter C, Bhatt B (2018) The transformative power of knowledge sharing in settings of poverty and social inequality. Organ Stud 39(11):1575–1599
R Menon, Nandagopal and Katakam Anupama 2006. Politics of ban. Frontline, February 24. https://frontline.thehindu.com/the-nation/article30208459.ece
Radhakrishnan S (2014) Sanitising the profane. SubVersions 1:202–234. http://subversions.tiss.edu/?p=124
Ramachandran R (2018) Kerala gets its own Perumal Murugan, Thanks (Again) to the Sangh Parivar. TheWire, July 8. https://thewire.in/books/kerala-author-s-harish-withdraws-book-dueto-sang-parivar-threat
Reinhoud EL (2019) The post-truth era: crises of truth in (post-)postmodern literature. Utrecht University Repository. https://dspace.library.uu.nl/handle/1874/384022
Riaz S, Qureshi I (2017) Emergence of a new institutional logic: shaping the institutionally complex field of community radio in India. In: Seidel SL, Greve HR (eds) Emergence: research in the sociology of organizations, pp 383–418
Roy N (2012) Banned books week: Ashok Malik on unbanning the banned. Nilanjana Roy, October 24. https://nilanjanaroy.com/2012/09/30/banned-books-week-ashok-malik-on-unbanningthe-banned/
S. Tamilselvan v. Government of Tamil Nadu (2016) SCC OnLine Mad 5960. https://indiankanoon.org/doc/142445245/

Sengupta S (2018) For India's offence-happy brigade, 'Meesha' is the latest fodder. The Hindu, August 5. https://www.thehindu.com/books/on-malayalam-author-s-hareeshs-novel-meesha-controversy/article24591794.ece
Shekhar HS (2017) The adivasi will not dance. Speaking Tiger, New Delhi
Shingavi S (2014) Angaaray, 1st edn. Penguin Books, New Delhi
Shourie A (2009) The ban and the law – Indian Express. Archive.Indianexpress.Com. http://archive.indianexpress.com/news/the-ban-and-the-law/507016/
Sujato Bhadra vs State Of West Bengal (2005) (4) CHN 601, 2005 CriLJ 368. https://indiankanoon.org/doc/79421/
Sunstein CR (2017) #Republic: divided democracy in the age of social media. Princeton University Press, Princeton
Suroor H (2012) You can't read this book. The Hindu. https://www.thehindu.com/books/you-cant-read-this-book/article2953626.ece
Sutter C, Bhatt B, Qureshi I (2022) What makes resource provision an effective means of poverty alleviation? A resourcing perspective. Organ Sci. https://doi.org/10.1287/orsc.2021.1570
Taslima Nasreen: Controversy's Child (2007) BBC News Online, November 23. http://news.bbc.co.uk/2/hi/south_asia/7108880.stm
Technopedia (2013) Definition – what does Cyberbalkanization mean? February 11, 2013. https://www.techopedia.com/definition/28087/cyberbalkanization
Törnberg P (2018) Echo chambers and viral misinformation: modeling fake news as complex contagion. PLoS One 13(9):e0203958. https://doi.org/10.1371/journal.pone.0203958
Tudu T (2019) "They eat meat!": a study of tribal culture in non-tribal vicinity. Res J English Lang Literat 7(3):144–147. https://doi.org/10.33329/rjelal.73.144
University of California Davis database (1969) The playboy interview: Marshall McLuhan. Playboy Magazine:1–23. https://web.cs.ucdavis.edu/~rogaway/classes/188/spring07/mcluhan.pdf
Webster JG, Ksiazek TB (2012) The dynamics of audience fragmentation: public attention in an age of digital media. J Commun 62(1):39–56. https://doi.org/10.1111/j.1460-2466.2011.01616.x
Writers Condemn Online Harassment, Effigy Burning of Author Hansda Sowvendra Shekhar (2017) The Wire, August 3. https://thewire.in/politics/writers-condemn-online-harassment-effigy-burning-author-hansda-sowvendra-shekhar

Investigating Social Media Induced Polarization on National Education Policy 2020

Bhavna Sharma and Kirti Vasuja

Abstract Social media is the platform where individual person can share their opinions on any event through various social networking sites and this shows the diversity in beliefs of different persons belonging to different cultures which lead to the formation of echo chambers. Social media is playing a crucial role in increasing the polarization by creating echo chambers about current events. The main aim of the study was to assess the social media induced polarization and to study the opinion of social media users toward attitudinal change about National Education Policy (NEP) 2020. The study was conducted using both primary and secondary information. Descriptive and content analysis were used to analyse the data. The findings of the study revealed that maximum number of phrases included in the posts of twitter about NEP 2020 gives out the meaning for acceptance of NEP 2020 and the maximum number of social media users has an opinion that there is an attitudinal change about NEP 2020 due to the use of social media. Further research could be conducted using several social media platforms to determine the polarization of government policies.

Keywords National Education Policy 2020 · Social media · Polarization · Attitudinal change

1 Introduction

The rapid evolution of the Web has transformed the way to connect people through social media during the five stages from Web 1.0 to Web 5.0. Although affections, feelings and emotions have been gaining relevance in society and scientific thought for more than a decade now, in the future, we will be dealing with a sensory emotive Web (Web 5.0) (Benito-Osorio et al. 2013).

B. Sharma (✉) · K. Vasuja
Department of Commerce, BPS Women University, Sonipat, Haryana, India
e-mail: dr.bhavnasharma@bpswomenuniversity.ac.in

I. Qureshi et al. (eds.), *Causes and Symptoms of Socio-Cultural Polarization*,
https://doi.org/10.1007/978-981-16-5268-4_8

A huge amount of data has been produced by the millions of social media users on daily basis are effectively exploited to get the information providing details about human behaviour and dynamics. Such data is commonly known as Big Data, which provides information about users' interests, behaviour, likes and preferences which can be used in a large set of applications (Belcastro et al. 2019a, b).

Various social networking sites have been developed like Facebook, Google+, Instagram and microblogging services such as twitter, blogs, wikis which allow users to connect, communicate and interact with each other across the world. Virtual media is featured by user generated content, relational networking and online identity creation (Magro et al. 2012). Due to change in way of communication, social media affected every individual without considering their status and become a significant part of everyday life (AlAlwan et al. 2017; Dwivedi et al. 2016; Kapoor et al. 2018). The exchange of information on social media through ICT can also lead to the formation of public spheres due to diversity in public opinion belonging to different cultures. The concept of content creation and consumption is enhanced by ICT induced platforms (Qureshi et al. 2021). Social media becomes a perfect platform for people across the world to communicate about common topics such as sports, politics and entertainment. On social media around 33% of social media users were engaged in commenting, discussing, posting about politics (Hossain et al. 2018).

Social media usage is one of the most crowd-pleasing online activities which is used by over 3.6 billion people all over the world in 2020 and is expected to be increased to 4.41 billion by 2025. On average 144 minutes per day were spent by internet users on social media and messaging apps. (https://www.statista.com/statistics/278414/number-of-worldwide-social-network-users/). The number of internet users has been growing since 2010 and almost 86% of adults of age 18–29 years use social media and 72% of adults and 87% of teens were involved in text messaging at that time (Madden 2010; Lenhart 2010).

Social interaction defines social media as it is collaborative and participative in nature. Moreover, social media empowers users to speak using its various platforms. Social media users can publish immediately in near real time with the help of social media technologies (Bertot et al. 2012). This leads to requests about the influence of social media services in terms of their ability to facilitate information. The wide range of interaction on twitter may promote positive social outcomes and like-minded people of the same group have varied opinions which lead to debates and diversity of views within a group (Yardi and Boyd 2010). In various research fields polarization has been found. Marazzo and Bessi (2018) considered the hashtags in tweets that were labeled as positive and calculated the polarization score for each faction. Chin et al. (2016) determined the sentiment involved in emojis contained in posts.

Culture is the significant variable which influences the communication pattern among different group of people, organizations etc. and leads to the formation of communication groups. The socio-cultural differences tend to create echo chambers toward a specific topic having a great impact in shaping our society which is essential for the development of the country like healthcare, climate change, education, warfare etc. Yeo et al. (2018) found that faith-based, distrust of local authority, and humanitarian assistance were prominent cultural indicators in the flood response communication among all the cultures. Moreover, it was also revealed that partisan divisions were extended to cultural tastes and lifestyle preferences (Shi et al. 2017). Social connectedness from the cognitive and motivational processes found to be more influential for social media usage (Netto and Macada 2019).

Over the course of the twentieth century, polarization can be defined as a trend of contemporary political life in many democracies. In India, political polarization has its roots from in colonial period and has brought to a dangerous level today due to divisions of India's national identity. The main drivers of increasing political polarization are India's ongoing economic transformation, changes in traditional and social media, and the rise of competitive caste politics (Bhardwaj et al. 2021; Bhatt et al. 2022; Qureshi et al. 2018; Sahoo 2020; Sutter et al. 2022). Taka, 2015 said that political polarization is a danger to the functioning of democracy. Twitter is playing a significant role in political polarization as well as in real politics. To diffuse information and the persons rallying to movement during Arab Spring, twitter was proved to be an efficient tool (Sunstein 2018). Furthermore, echo chambers were created on social media regarding COVID-19 vaccination and political polarization around climate change (Jain et al. 2021; Zheng and Bhatt 2021).

Universities are free spaces. They can be considered as a catalyst of scientific and economic change, as well as a medium of equalization of chances and democratization of society by making possible equal opportunities for people—contributing not only to economic growth but also to social equality or, at least, lesser inequality. The Union Education Minister Sh. Ramesh Pokhriyal Nishank encouraged students to read the National Education Policy (NEP) 2020, while answering queries on it on social media on October 1, 2020. He was answering questions on his official Twitter handle @DrRPNishank. Pokhriyal had tweeted on September 28, 2020 inviting questions from students on NEP 2020 under the hashtag #NEPTransformingIndia. From technical education and sports studies, Pokhriyal dwelt on a range of topics. (https://www.abpeducation.com/news/education-minister-answers-questions-on-nep-on-social-media/cid/1204437). Thus after this communication by Education Minister, discussion on NEP 2020 started on Twitter.

Education is one of the fundamental aspects of life for developing human potential and achieving a just and equitable standard of life. The gap between the current state of education and the required state of learning must be filled with the help of reforms and NEP 2020 is one of those reforms. The NEP2020 proposes the revision in education structure including its regulation and governance to achieve the aspirational goals of education. But the different opinions of people created controversies about the NEP 2020 and resulted in the formation of echo chambers on social media.

Furthermore, social media interaction takes active participation in showing interest towards government policies and helps policymakers to consider citizen's preferences in the formulation phase of public policy and monitor public opinion during the implementation phase of policies (Ceron and Negri 2016).

Similarly, social media analytics is being used to monitor and control the government policies according to the public involvement and it was revealed that social media analytics can be used when tested for GST and Demonetization (Joseph et al. 2017; Singh et al. 2018, 2020). Social media has the potential to transform the relationship between politicians, bureaucrats and citizens focusing on the concept of e-government (Carter and Belanger 2005; Clarke and Margetts 2014; Margetts 2009). The previous studies related to social media analytics provokes to research more about the social media response towards government policies like NEP2020.

The paper is structured further into seven sections. The second section discusses brief literature regarding polarization through social media in politics and various determinants resulting to attitude polarization. Moreover, it also includes studies monitoring and controlling government policies through social media and its use in E-Government. The third section includes a brief description of the proposed research methodology. Following that the fourth section presents analysis and interpretation of the analysis. Section five discusses the study. The sixth section describes the practical implication and the seventh section includes limitations and future direction of study. In the last section conclusion of the study is described.

2 Review of Literature

Various researches have used social media to measure political polarization, the effect of social media during different events, attitude polarization and group polarization on different specific topics. Research papers included in the study are from the year 1989–2019 published in various reputed journals. Research papers were downloaded from various databases such as Google Scholar, Researchgate, JSTOR, Emerald Insight, Springer etc. Those research papers were collected which were related to the terms polarization and selected based on social media induced polarization. With the help of meta-theoretical analysis of existing literature has been reviewed.

This section covers meta-theoretical analysis of existing literature, theoretical framework and research gap. The first section describes the meta-theoretical analysis of existing literature related to social media induced polarization categorized on the basis of various research fields. The second section provides a theoretical framework which explains the theories and processes related to polarization. While, the third section gives information about the limitation of previous studies based on which research gap has been found.

2.1 Meta-Theoretical Analysis of Existing Literature About Polarization Through Social Media (Table 1)

2.2 Theoretical Framework of Study

Several theories have been developed to understand the concept of polarization in the fields of sociology, psychology and communication research. El-Shinnawy and Vinze (1998) usedSocial Comparison Theory (SCT) and Persuasive Argument Theory (PAT) for process based group polarization where the decision of group polarization was based upon the comparison decision at an individual level, face to face group setting and Group Support System (GSS) literature. Chitra and Musco (2019) modified the Friedkien- Johnson opinion dynamic model by adding one more factor to the model i.e. network administrator and he also developed a mathematical framework for studying the effect of filter bubble on the social network where it was confirmed that with the slight change in respect of network administrator created echo chamber and increased the effect of polarization. Another conceptual model was also framed to know the effect of filter bubbles and echo chambers on information technology identity construction by adding cognitive and motivational processes in it (Netto and Macada 2019). Similarly, various theories have been framed which are used to determine polarization using different factors in different research fields (Fig. 1).

2.3 Research Gap

The existing literature focuses on social media induced polarization only in some specific fields such as political issues. Various authors analysed the polarization through social media in different aspects like attitude polarization, political polarization, group polarization etc. but the role of social media in polarizing public opinion toward government policies has not been explained yet. Although social media has been used in various studies to monitor and control governmental policies but polarization effect has not beenstudied.

Table 1 Meta-theoretical analysis of existing literature about polarization through social media

Author Name/Year	Objective	Findings	Critical discussion on methodology used
Smith (1989)	To examine the effect of involvement subject to restaurant schemas on attitude polarization.	It was found from the study that when the situational involvement is high evaluation by the customers was stable and conductive to attitude polarization.	• Conduct selective literature review • Data collected from undergraduate students of business
McCann (1995)	To assess the attitudinal effect of campaign participation and partisan fragmentation during the 1988 nomination politics resulting to ideological polarization.	It was found that ideological polarization can be possible due to campaign participation and the behaviour of political involvement influences the participant's beliefs in number of ways.	• A database of Active Minority study was taken into consideration • ordinary least square regression with assumption of unidirectional causality was used • Conduct selective literature review
El-Shinnawy and Vinze (1998)	To examine the group polarization by focusing on communication medium, task characteristics, group composition from both outcome and process based perspectives.	The results of analyses revealed that task characteristics and communication medium had a signification effect on both group polarization and persuasive arguments but group composition had no significant interaction with group polarization, persuasive arguments and medium of communication.	• Social Comparison Theory (SCT) and Persuasive Argument Theory (PAT) were used • Consider narrow sample of literature
Mouw and Sobel (2001)	To developed an appropriate method to study the attitude polarization about abortion in ordinal variable and ascertained the change in polarization over time which assessed the validity of cultural wars.	The results of the study did not suggest any increase in polarization over 25 years and the model was not found appropriate to analyse GSS data. Furthermore, latent variable in the study was assumed as normally distributed and used the ordinal scale to analyse the data.	• A cumulative probit model with heteroscedasticity and variable cutpoints was computed on ordinal scale. • Focuses on attitude polarization

(continued)

Table 1 (continued)

Author Name/Year	Objective	Findings	Critical discussion on methodology used
Yardi and Boyd (2010)	To examine the effect of twitter conversation about a specific case of shooting and subsequent death of Dr. George Tiller who was famous for late term abortion in United States on group polarization and extremism.	The findings of the study stated that wide range of interaction on twitter may promote positive social outcomes and like-minded people of the same group have varied opinions which lead to debates and diversity of views within group. Further, individual tweets were not found to be significant to determine the levels of anger or emotion.	• More than 30000 tweets were captured over next 60 days from the time of death • Focuses on group behaviour and polarization
Conover et al. (2011)	To determine in what way social media shape the networked public sphere and allows communication with different political orientations between different communities.	The findings of the study revealed that content of political discourse remain highly partisan on twitter.	• Cluster analysis was employed using networked clustering algorithms to determine two highly segregated communities of users
Jones (2013)	To examine the effect on opinion change working in partisan environment organization than less partisan environment organization.	The result showed that partisan workplace environment effects opinion and increase polarization among republicans more as compare to democrats.	• Focuses on the environment in which partisan working • Consider lesser literature review
Guerra et al. (2013)	To perform a systematic comparison of social media networks emerging from polarization and non-polarization by collecting data from social networking sites such as twitter, facebook and blogs.	The results of the study revealed that polarized networks shows a low concentration of high degree nodes in the boundary between two communities.	• Modularity was employed to analyse the opinions of individuals on twitter about gun control issues in United States. • Focuses on comparison of social networks

(continued)

Table 1 (continued)

Author Name/Year	Objective	Findings	Critical discussion on methodology used
Abascal-Mena et al. (2015)	To examine the political and social movement in twitter with the help of quantitative analysis by applying graph theory and social network analysis to explore sociosemantic information.	The communities of more than 10% focuses on the important concepts which gave more semantic information from tweets than the tweets that include hastags in it. Therefore, it is important to be focused on retrieving main themes of concepts.	• The concepts of graph theory and social network analysis were used for the analysis of tweets using Gephi software to understand the social behaviour. • Focuses on movement in twitter
Yang et al. (2016)	To examine the association between traditional or online media use and perceived polarization.	The data showed that media use was related with the perceived polarization but not with attitude polarization. The another finding showed that those who were more liberal had more perceived polarization towards political party	• The data was gathered from ten countries • Focuses on assessing relation between different media use
Lee (2016)	To determine the significance of immediate political context towards opinion polarization through digital media communication in the case of the Umbrella Movement in Hong Kong in late 2014.	The findings revealed that political communication through social media had significant positive effect on the individual's attitude toward the movement.	• Data was collected from publically available polls and from two surveys conducted by the Centre for Communication and Public Opinion Survey at the Chinese University of Hong Kong.
Bessi et al. (2016)	To determine the behaviour of users of the same contents on different platforms – youtube and facebook.	The findings of the study showed that conflicting narratives results to the aggregation of users in homogeneous echo chambers and algorithms of content promotion found to be a major determinant of polarization effect from the online social media.	• Through qualitative analysis dataset of 12 million users was measured and consumption pattern of videos supporting science and conspiracy on facebook and youtube was compared.

(continued)

Table 1 (continued)

Author Name/Year	Objective	Findings	Critical discussion on methodology used
Yeo et al. (2018)	To determine the cultural nuances in from the 2016 Louisiana flood response by focusing on social media communications.	It was found that faith-based, distrust of local authority, and humanitarian assistance were prominent cultural indicators in the flood response communication among all the cultures.	• Data was collected using NodeXL from the twitter. • Network analysis and cluster analysis using Clauset–Newman–Moore cluster algorithm were employed.
Shi et al. (2017)	To examine the deep partisan divisions in the U.S. in politics this extended to culture, lifestyle choices and consumer preferences.	The findings revealed that partisan divisions extended to cultural tastes and lifestyle preferences.	• Consider narrow sample of culture related literature review • Focuses on variables like cultural preferences
Marozzo and Bessi (2018)	To analyse the polarization of social network users' behaviour and how the new sites were used by the rivalry during political campaigns.	The analysis showed that some new sites had polarization toward yes, some other sites had polarization toward no and polarization remains same of the new sites in the preceding weeks.	• Metadata of tweet was analysed by employing temporal analysis by using probability density function and complementary cumulative distribution function (CCDF).
Bail et al. (2018)	To examine the influence of disrupting selective exposure of partisan information toward political attitudes of the twitter users.	The study findings revealed that republicans were become conservative after following the twitter bot as comparison to democrats. As democrats exhibits slight change in their attitude and which was also found as insignificant.	• Focuses on exposure of information on twitter • Focuses on selective concerned research area
(Belcastro et al. 2019a, b)	To develop a new methodology form social media data analysis.	The result of both were found almost similar validates the new method.	• Proposed the new method based on the feed forward neural networks method for estimating

(continued)

Table 1 (continued)

Author Name/Year	Objective	Findings	Critical discussion on methodology used
Chitra and Musco (2019)	To modify the Friedkien- Johnson opinion dynamic model by adding one more factor to the model i.e. network administrator.	The findings of the experiment showed that with the introduction of network administrator twitter and reddit effect of polarization increased in both. Moreover, with the slight change in respect of network administrator created echo chamber and increased the effect of polarization.	• The researchers also developed mathematical framework for studying the effect of filter bubble on social network • Focuses on framing a dynamic model
Netto and Macada (2019)	To propose the conceptual model about the use of social media to know the influence of filter bubbles and echo chambers on Information Technology (IT) Identity construction.	Social connectedness from the cognitive and motivational processes found to be more influencing for social media usage.	• Focuses on cognitive and motivational process self-concept, self-disclosure, self-monitoring, self-presentation, self-awareness, self-enhancement, self-verification, sense of belonging and social connectedness for IT identity construction
Bryson (2019)	To examine the opinion polarization of political information among the excluded counterparts on the internet.	Significant difference was not found in opinion on the basis of demographic characteristics of the respondents. It was found that all the groups were polarized into the political sphere when they get access to online information about politics.	• The independent variable was survey cheating which means the accessibility of political information online and dependent variable was polarization as ideological consistency

(continued)

Table 1 (continued)

Author Name/Year	Objective	Findings	Critical discussion on methodology used
Jin and Ye (2019)	To compare the difference between Weibo and Zhihu in context of the media nature, audience structure, recommendation algorithm, degree of behaviour constrain, and information filter to know the relationship of difference of social media platforms with attitude polarization.	It was found that Weibo had significant positive relationship with the attitude polarization but Zhihu had no relationship with attitude polarization. Further, weakening effect of legal knowledge was found on attitude polarization.	• Multiple and hierarchical regression analysis was used to conduct the study • Focuses on Attitude polarization taken as dependent variable, legal knowledge and three independent questions were taken as independent variable
Singh et al. (2019)	To monitor and control the public policies cloud computing and social media analytic capabilities were combined.	The results of study revealed that GST had a strong support initially but after its implementation public's opinion changed into negative response. After considering hardship of people government took various steps to resolve the confusion and negative opinions and due to preventive measures public opinion again changed into positive toward GST.	• Amazon EC2 cloud with RStudio server was used • Focuses on cloud computing to monitor public policies

- The least number of studies have been conducted on the government policies through social media analysis.
- The Literature reviewed suggests that the polarization effect of government policies through social media can be determined.
- Considering the existing literature it is explored that all the studies were conducted only based on social media opinions. Based on literature reviewed it was found that no study had been conducted yet on the opinions of people about the change in attitude due to the use of social networking sites.

So, based on above existing literature research gap can be fulfilled by doing research on polarization about NEP 2020 through social media and analysed through social media text analytic techniques. Moreover, opinions toward attitudinal change due to use of social media can be determined by collecting data from primary sources.

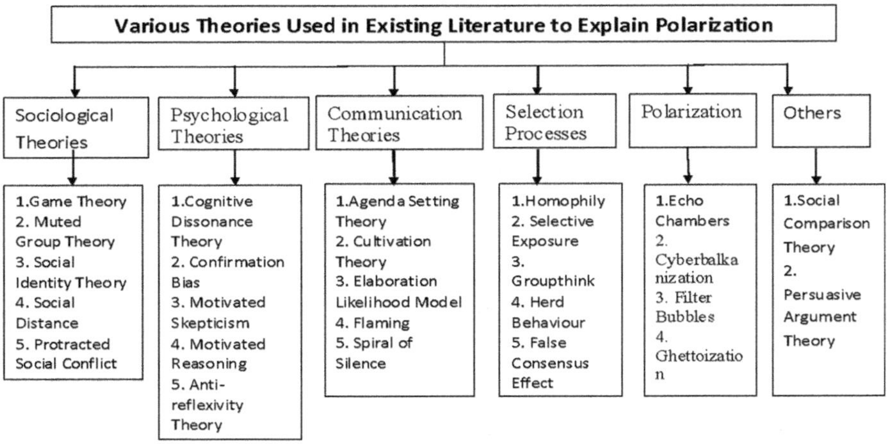

Source: Flow chart drafted on the basis of compiled literature reviewed

Fig. 1 Theoretical framework based on existing literature. (Source: Flow chart drafted on the basis of compiled literature reviewed)

3 Research Methodology

To assess the social media induced polarization about NEP 2020 and to investigate about the social media induced polarization towards the NEP 2020. To accomplish the aforementioned objectives, some sub-objectives are defined as follows:

- To study the extent of social media induced polarization NEP 2020.
- To discuss about the opinions of social media users toward attitudinal change for NEP 2020 by using social media.

The existing literature is reviewed through meta-theoretical analysis. Mix methodology is used and the study is of both qualitative and quantitative in nature. The first objective is about the analysis of polarization through social media data related to NEP 2020. To analyse the social media induced polarization the twitter data is extracted on different point of times in the month of August 2020 and November 2020. The proposed research methodology to achieve this objective consists of two parts (a) Data acquisition and (b) Data monitoring. The detail of each part is explained in the below sections:

(a) Data acquisition: First step in the research methodology was to acquire data for analysis. The study involves collection of data from social networking site twitter. In this study the twitter data streams to investigate the communication as the system supports millions of users' information shared about any topic at any moment was used. Twitter data streams helped to know about the ideas, opinions of the people which have been going in their mind. Twitter is a social media platform which is registered under the category social networking and micro blogging and it allows communicating and publishing them which are known as tweets (Abascal-Mena et al. 2015). Honeycutt and Herring (2009) revealed that twitter is a platform which allows the two persons to communicate in both directions. Data has been extracted from twitter in an unstructured format and converted into excel format by identifying the search terms on the basis of which data has been collected from the twitter.

(b) Data monitoring: Data has been monitored using various social media analytics techniques for extracting important information about the polarization towards NEP 2020 (Stieglitz and Dang-Xuan 2013). Social media analytics was classified into four categories: descriptive analysis, content analysis, network analysis and geospatial analysis (Singh et al. 2018). Descriptive analysis has been employed to gather the information about number of tweets, retweets, user id etc. After that, content analysis has been employed on collected data and frequency of phrases is classified into three categories namely positive, negative and neutral on the basis of observation as tweets includes some specific keywords giving out meaning to categorize them.

The data has been extracted using QDA Minor 6 and Wordstat 8 software. Twitter provides authorized APIs (Application Programming Interface) with the help of which data was fetched in an authenticated manner. To fetch the data from twitter, some important keywords were identified. Through the QDA Minor and Wordstat software all the tweets were downloaded using different hashtags like #NEP2020, #Nationaleducationpolicy2020, #rejectnep2020, #neptransformingindia etc. The tweets were not collected in real time but were downloaded after their publication. The total number of tweets collected were 4935 which also included retweets in it. In each collected post these specific hashtags were included along with the other keywords which were useful for understanding the argument used to determine the intentions of users in against and for the NEP 2020. Specifically, collected data includes user, text, timestamp, keywords, URL.

The second objective was to determine the opinions about the attitudinal change for NEP 2020 by using social media. To accomplish the objective well structured questionnaire has been prepared about the usage of social media and opinions of respondents towards attitudinal change for NEP 2020 due to use of social media.

Data has been collected through primary sources using Whatsapp a social media platform. Snowball sampling method was used to collect the data from social media users. A sample of 418 respondents has been taken from the all over the world as target population. The data has been collected through well-structured questionnaire using social media itself.

The data has been analysed using the Statistical Package for the social Science (IBM-SPSS) software (version 22) and descriptive statistical techniques by computing the frequency and percentage of responses as per the needs of objective and pie charts is also prepare wherever necessary. To support and confirm the first objective of study, the opinion of social media users toward attitudinal change about NEP 2020 due to use of social media is determined.

4 Analysis and Interpretation of Data

In this section of the study, the objectives formulated above are analysed and results are interpreted into two subsections:

- Extent of social media induced polarization towards NEP 2020.
- Opinion of respondents regarding attitudinal change about Indian NEP 2020 by using social media.

4.1 Social Media Induced Polarization About NEP 2020

To determine the social media induced polarization affect towards Indian NEP 2020 study includes two main concepts: (a) Collection of data from social media platform, (b) to know about the extent the polarization based on tweets shared by the twitter users (public) about NEP 2020 by monitoring the data. Data has been acquired from twitter database to investigate the conversation of social media users about NEP 2020. Data was extracted using application programming interface (APIs) with the help of keywords (searching terms). Some of the keywords were used such as #NEP2020, #Nationaleducationpolicy2020, #rejectnep2020, #neptransformingindia etc. to investigate about extent of polarization. The total numbers of tweets extracted from twitter were 4935 after their publication. Every post contained specific hashtag on the basis of which intention of the user has been determined in against and for of NEP2020. The classification of tweets was based on the positive, negative and neutral responses on the basis of observation. The data was collected using QDA Minor software and Wordstat 8 software and the content analysis as well as descriptive analysis were employed on collected tweets.

Descriptive analysis was computed about the characteristics of the twitter users in relation with the objective of the study. With the help of descriptive analysis based on frequency and percentage of the different phrases included in the tweets about NEP 2020 was classified into three categories namely, positive negative and neutral. Using content analysis different phrases has been obtained on the basis of which categorization was made. After getting frequency of phrases, all the phrases were critically examined and segregated into three categories having positive response (acceptance of NEP), neutral and negative responses (Rejection of NEP). These phrases included the some useful keywords which enable us to understand the acceptance or rejection of users toward NEP 2020. After categorization, the total of frequencies was determined and graphically presented.

Table 2 depicts the main hashtags which are used to find the tweets about NEP 2020. These hashtags includes #NEPtransformingindia, #NEP2020, #nationaleducationpolicy2020, #educationpolicy, #rejectnep2020, #resistnep2020 which are divided into three categories of positive, negative and neutral to know the responses of users toward NEP 2020.

Table 2 Key hashtags related to positive, neutral and negative tweets

Category	Hashtags
Positive	#NEPtransformingindia
Neutral	#NEP2020, #nationaleducationpolicy2020,#educationpolicy
Negative	#rejectnep2020, #resistnep2020

Source: Extracted from analysis by researcher

Table 3 Key phrases related to positive, neutral and negative tweets

Category	Phrases
Positive	Improved education excellence in education, Empower new India with the knowledge, Core equity and inclusion, Inclusion at its core, Comprehensive and holistic, Dedicated towards quality
Neutral	Education system, Digital literacy in India
Negative	Fault to be a student, NEP is undemocratic, Reject NEP today, Disagree with NEP

Source: Extracted from analysis by researcher

Table 4 Frequency of phrases showing polarization about NEP 2020

Phrases	Frequency	%frequency
Positive Phrases	1853	65.338
Neutral	842	29.689
Negative Phrases	141	4.9717
Total	2836	100

Source: Extracted from analysis by researcher

Table 3 shows the phrases used to classify the tweets into categories showing acceptance and rejection of NEP 2020 by the users. Improved education excellence in education, Empower new India with the knowledge, Core equity and inclusion, Inclusion at its core, Comprehensive and holistic, Dedicated towards quality were the various phrases which were considered as positive responses depicting acceptance toward NEP 2020. Some phrases have been taken as neutral which didn't include useful keywords supporting acceptance or rejection like Education system, Digital literacy in India. Fault to be a student, NEP is undemocratic, Reject NEP today, Disagree with NEP was the phrases considered as rejection of users for the NEP 2020 and considered in the negative responses.

Table 4 depicts the frequency of phrases which were categorized into positive, neutral and negative phrases representing the acceptance or rejection of users towards NEP 2020 and results shows that 65.338% of phrases extracted from content analysis includes specific keywords supporting the NEP 2020 and 4.91% of phrases of content analysis represented rejection towards NEP 2020 while 29.68% phrases didn't include specific keywords showing acceptance or rejection towards NEP 2020 (Fig. 2).

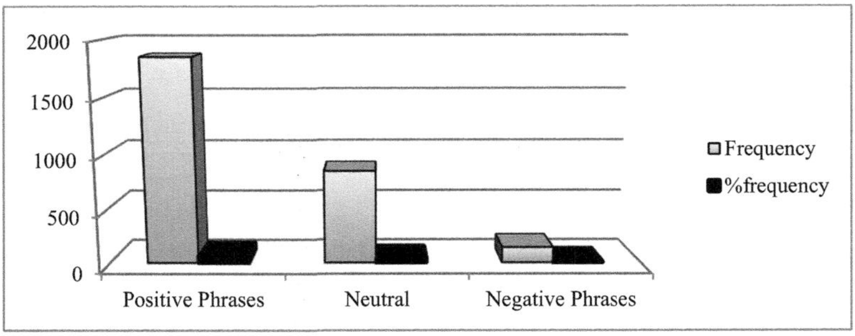

Fig. 2 Frequency of phrases showing polarization about NEP 2020

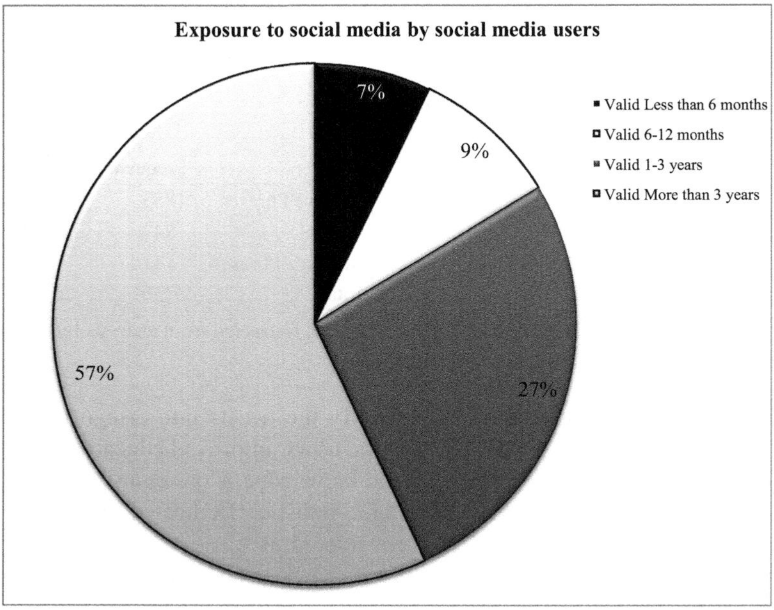

Fig. 3 Exposure to social media by social media users

4.2 Opinion of Respondents Toward Attitudinal Change About NEP 2020 by Using Social Media

The opinion of respondent about the attitudinal change for NEP 2020 has been determined on the basis of demographic factors (Gender, Age, Occupation) using descriptive analysis. Along with altitudinal change exposure to social media by respondents was also analysed.

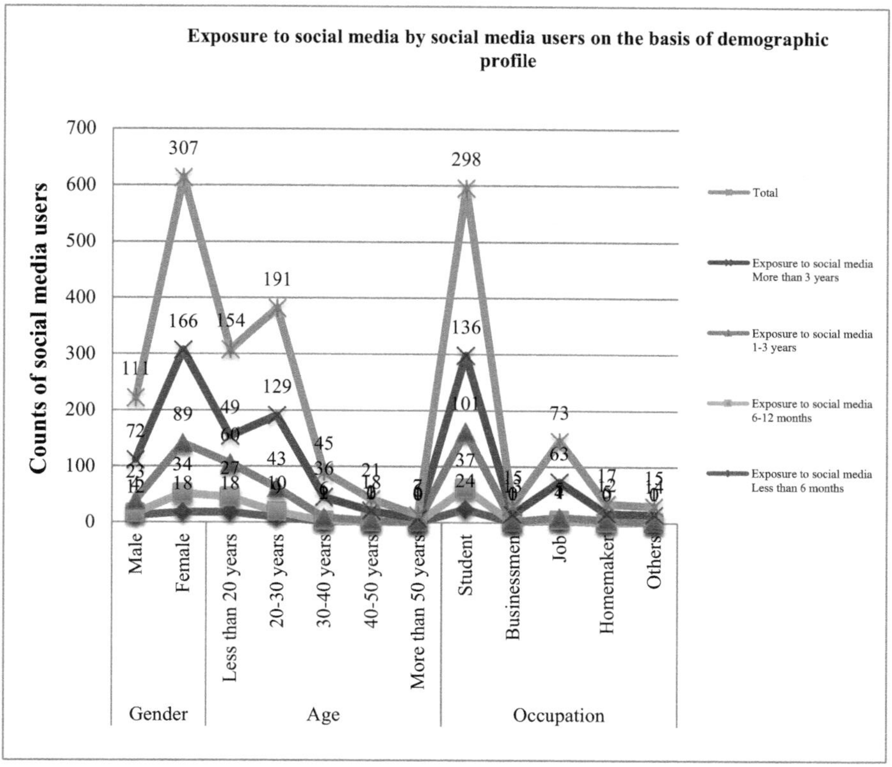

Fig. 4 Exposure to social media by social media users on the basis of demographic profile

4.2.1 Exposure to Social Media on the Basis of Demographic Profile

On the basis of demographic profile of respondents from how long social media is being used was determined. As the Fig. 3 summarizes maximum respondents were using social media from more than 3 years. 56.94% of respondents were using social media from more than 3 years. The least number of respondents that is 7.18% were using social media from past less than 6 months and 26.79% respondents were using social media from last 1–3 years (Table 5).

On the basis of gender, age and occupation from how long respondents are using social media was analysed. On the basis of gender, it has been revealed that out of total respondents 166 were the female respondents and 72 were male respondents who have been using social media from more than 3 years. On the basis of age respondents of 20–30 years were more involved in spending time on social media who were maximum number of students. On the basis of occupation 298 respondents out of total respondents were students who spent most of their time on social media from more than 3 years (Fig. 4).

Table 5 Exposure to social media by social media users on the basis of demographic profile

		Exposure to social media by social media users on the basis of demographic profile				Total
		Less than 6 months	6–12 months	1–3 years	More than 3 years	
Gender	**Male**	12	4	23	72	111
	Female	18	34	89	166	307
Total		30	38	112	238	418
Age	**Less than 20 years**	18	27	60	49	154
	20–30 years	9	10	43	129	191
	30–40 years	2	1	6	36	45
	40–50 years	1	0	2	18	21
	More than 50 years	0	0	1	6	7
Total		30	38	112	238	418
Occupation	**Student**	24	37	101	136	298
	Businessmen	1	0	1	13	15
	Job	4	1	5	63	73
	Homemaker	0	0	5	12	17
	Others	1	0	0	14	15
Total		30	38	112	238	418

Source: Extracted from analysis by researcher

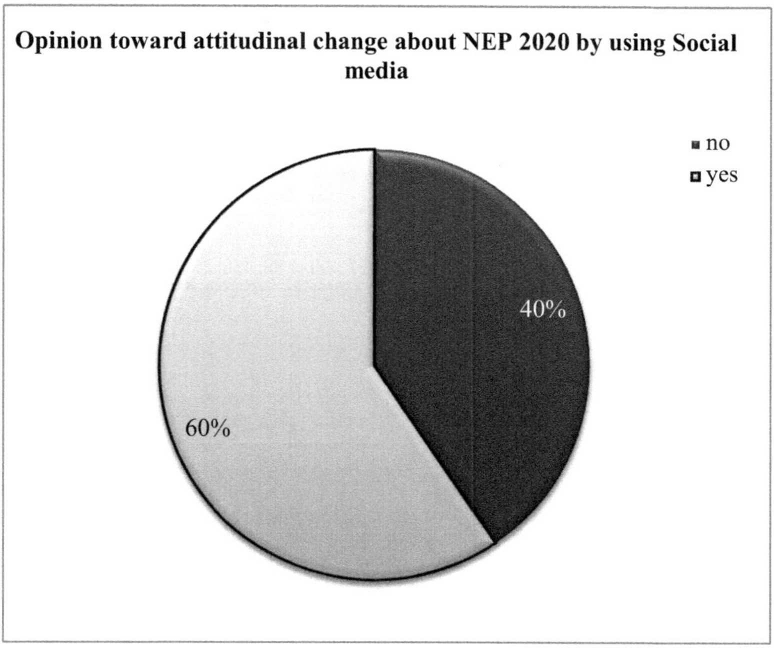

Fig. 5 Opinion toward attitudinal change about NEP 2020 by using Social media

4.2.2 Opinions Toward Attitudinal Change About NEP 2020 by Using Social Media

Opinions of the respondents regarding change in attitude about NEP 2020 after using social media on the basis of demographic profile were investigated.

As the Fig. 5 summarizes that maximum number of the respondents that is 59.57% has opinion that the usage of social media results to the change in attitude about NEP 2020 and on the other hand 40.43% disagrees for the change in attitude about NEP 2020 due to use of social media (Table 6).

On the basis of gender, age and occupation, opinions of the respondents about change in attitude toward NEP 2020 due to use of social media was determined. On the basis of gender 188 female respondents out of 307 female respondents agreed to the attitudinal change about NEP 2020 by using of social media occurs and 50 male respondents out of 111 male respondents disagreed about change in attitude about NEP 2020 due to use of social media (Fig. 6).

On the basis of age, it was analysed that 127 respondents out of 191 respondents belonged to the age group of 20–30 years who agreed for the change in attitude about NEP 2020 due to use of social media. It has been also observed from the analysis that majority of the respondents (182 students) are of the opinion that there has been an attitudinal change about NEP 2020 by using social media.

Table 6 Opinion toward attitudinal change about NEP 2020 by using social media on the basis of demographic profile

		Opinion toward attitudinal change about NEP 2020 by using social media on the basis of demographic profile		Total
		No	Yes	
Gender	**Male**	50	61	111
	Female	119	188	307
Total		169	249	418
Age	**Less than 20 years**	70	84	154
	20–30 years	64	127	191
	30–40 years	19	26	45
	40–50 years	12	9	21
	More than 50 years	4	3	7
Total		169	249	418
Occupation	**Student**	116	182	298
	Businessmen	6	9	15
	Job	33	40	73
	Homemaker	9	8	17
	Others	5	10	15
Total		169	249	418

Source: Extracted from analysis by researcher

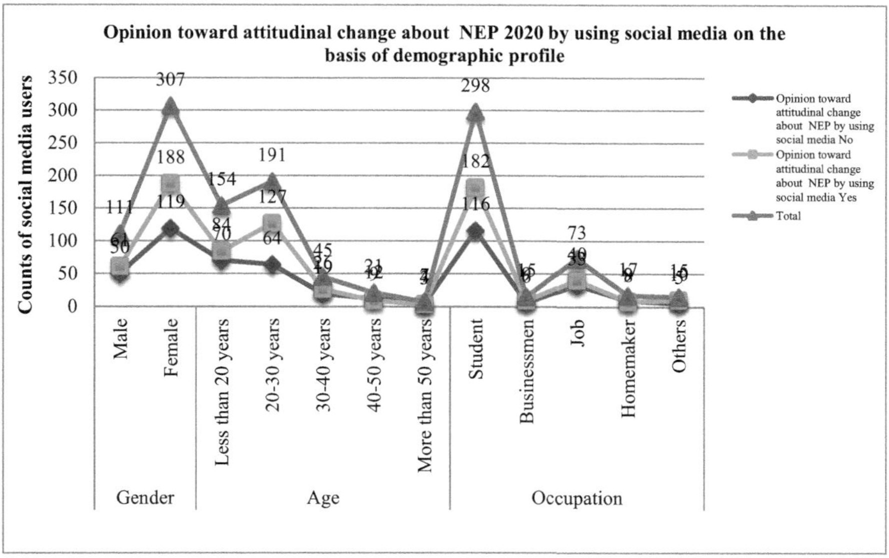

Fig. 6 Opinion toward attitudinal change about NEP 2020 by using social media on the basis of demographic profile

5 Discussion of the Study

Social media is playing a fostering role in transparency and making the interaction strong between citizens and public administrations (Christensen et al. 2015; Clarke and Margetts 2014; Margetts 2009). According to measure the public opinion use of social media becomes the hot topic for social network research. Interaction on digital media through networking sites tends to the formation of groups of like-minded peers as all the individuals like to move toward the opinions which are similar to their own opinions.

The main purpose of this study is to investigate the social media induced polarization about NEP2020. To achieve the main purpose polarization of social network users toward NEP 2020 and opinion of respondents toward attitudinal change NEP 2020 by using social media qualitative and quantitative methodology is used. Polarization about NEP 2020 through social media is measured by extracting public opinions shared on social media (twitter) about NEP 2020 on which descriptive analysis and content analysis employed. Content analysis helped in extracting phrases from the tweets of public on the basis of which categorization of responses is made possible by observation containing words which help to know response in favor or against of NEP 2020 and polarization through social media abut NEP 2020 is determined. Frequency of categorized phrases is calculated and results are analysed. Opinion of respondents toward attitudinal change about NEP 2020 is examined by collecting opinions through well structured questionnaire and descriptive analysis is employed using SPSS software. As the existing literature review does not include any kind of study showing the polarization for government policy through social media, to support and confirm the first objective of the study opinions of respondent through primary source of information is collected to confirm the results of content analysis. Questionnaire includes demographic profile (gender, age, occupation) of respondents, time period from which social media is being used and opinion toward attitudinal change about NEP 2020 due to use of social media. Data was collected using primary source of information which is distributed via social media all over the world.

The findings of the first objective are that public opinion about NEP 2020 on social media creates echo chamber as the most number of social media users are inclined in favor of NEP 2020. The results of analysis shows that most of the phrases included in tweets are positive representing the acceptance of NEP 2020. "Improved education excellence in education, Empower new India with the knowledge, Core equity and inclusion, Inclusion at its core, Comprehensive and holistic, Dedicated towards quality" are some specific keywords which are included in the tweets of public showing their positive inclination for NEP 2020. There are some words which do not show any kind of inclination in favor or against of NEP 2020 which are as follows: Education system, Digital literacy in India. "Fault to be a student, NEP is undemocratic, Reject NEP today, Disagree with NEP" are some phrases showing negative inclination for NEP 2020. The frequency of these phrases in each category is calculated and concluded that 65.338% of phrases are positively inclined, 4.971% of total phrases are negatively inclined to NEP 2020. Whereas, 29.689% of total phrases represents neutral responses showing no inclination toward negative or positive phrases.

Another finding of the study reveals the opinion of respondents toward attitudinal change about NEP 2020 by using social media. It also shows how long social media users are using social networking sites and opinion for the change in attitude. In this study on the basis of gender, age, occupation time period from which social media is being used by respondents and opinions toward attitudinal change is determined. It is measured to support and confirm the first objective to know the social media induced polarization about NEP 2020. It is concluded that maximum numbers of students of age group of 20–30 years are using social media from more than 3 years. Furthermore, it reveals that maximum number of female student respondents of age group of 20–30 years gives opinion in favor that there is an attitudinal change about NEP 2020 after using social networking sites.

In summary, this study presents the methodology of analyzing the polarization through social media about NEP 2020 opinions of social media users about attitudinal change about NEP 2020. Unlike the works in literature reviewed in which social media analytics techniques were used to analyse the text to know the public opinions shared on social media about specific topics , this study employed the descriptive and content analysis to extract the phrases giving out the opinions in favor and against of Government policy NEP 2020. As in the literature reviewed no study has been found in which polarization was determined for any government policy through social media. While social media was used in various studies to monitor and control the government policy on the basis of public opinions shared on the social media but polarization for any government policy is not found in the literature reviewed.

This study enhances the understanding of socio-cultural polarization as it discusses the polarization about the government policy of NEP 2020. This is one of the most crucial topics which is related to the persons belonging from different cultures and society. NEP 2020 comprises the policies for higher education, teacher education, professional education and private institutions which plays a significant role for each person who belongs to different society and for the development of nation. NEP 2020 is a new innovative solution which can completely transform the higher education system.

This is the only study in which polarization about NEP 2020 through social media is analysed as well as the results of study are confirmed through primary source of information for opinions toward the attitudinal change about NEP 2020. The study contributes to know the polarization effect for NEP 2020 on the basis of which decisions can be taken by the policy makers. In future research, importance can be given to many government policies which are framed in context of socio-cultural differences and many initiatives may be taken by considering the polarization effect. Further research studies may be conducted by considering large number of public opinions from different social media platforms and the government policies can be proposed for revision if required. Moreover, in this study limited numbers of questions are asked from the social media users to know their opinion about attitudinal change. So, in depth study may be made to know their opinions about the attitudinal change due to use of social media and to reduce or avoid the polarization effect.

6 Practical Implications of the Study

The practical implications for this study can be divided in two sub sections namely implications for society and implications for government. These sub sections are discussed as follows:

(a) Implications for society: Extensive implication of social media has been enabled by the interaction, global proliferation and increasing interpenetration of society. In developing countries, mobile technology has become the cheapest and latest communication method with the help of which social media get the opportunity to get expanded globally. Social media is now being used in every corner of the country and it affects every part of society, cultures differently (Hochwald 2013). So, it becomes significant to study the social media interaction and public opinions which creates echo chambers due to differences in cultures and societies on social media platforms. General public living in different societies belonging to different cultures is the main stakeholders of the system. Public are the one who rule the system with their opinions and with their actions and in today's era this is shown through social media.

As revealed from the results of our study, maximum number of social media users participated in research survey are student belonging to the age group of 20-30 years are using social media from more than three years and majority of the respondents have opinion in favor of attitudinal change about NEP 2020 due to use of social media. This finding shows that there is need to do further research work in the field of socio-cultural polarization through social media. Moreover, another finding of the study revealed that interaction on the twitter about NEP 2020 includes several positively inclined phrases which give the results in favor of this government policy. This acceptance of NEP 2020 is shown by the posts shared by the social media users on social media platform twitter which attracts other users to create echo chambers on social media platforms.

So, discussions on the social media platform polarize the public opinion without understanding the merits as well as demerits of government policies. They further share their concern and suggests recommendations as per their polarize group toward which they are inclined.

(b) Implications for government: Government is another main stakeholder of the system. Government is the one who formulates and impose policies on the general public of system. Due to increasing use of social media public interaction has been increasing tremendously about the government polices which results to the proliferation on social media platform. So, government should take initiatives to spread awareness before the implementation of policies and monitor the social media induced polarization. There is a need to monitor and control the polarization on social media due to increased public interaction for the effective implementation of policies and government should consider the recommendations suggested by social media users. With the help of this study various remedial measures may be taken by the government to spread the understanding about specific policy and enable them to understand the policies in better way by taking significant initiatives.

For the better implementation of government policies, government should use the social media platform to spread awareness about policies and increase the understanding level among public so that there is less chances of social media induced polarization and social media platforms can be used for better purposes. The findings of the study may be proposed to government for formulation of policy matters to avoid polarization among various social media platforms.

As in this research study, all the posts which include negative words showing rejection of NEP 2020 may be used to take initiatives to work on the recommended suggestions.

7 Limitations and Future Directions

The main purpose of the study is to investigate the social media induced polarization and also provided some interesting results for the stakeholders. Along with the findings of the studies some limitations are faced on which there is need to be work on in future. Firstly, the data was collected from the twitter and whatsapp only. Secondly, tweets extracted are in small numbers and collected in limited time period. Thirdly, tweets are extracted after their publication not in the real time and also it includes both tweets and retweets, separate study on both may be considered in future research. Another limitation of this study is that only descriptive and content analyses were employed. Further, various social media analytics techniques, multivariate analysis techniques may be used on different variables to get better results in future. Moreover, in depth study of the opinions about attitudinal change about NEP 2020 using social media may be conducted in future by considering more variable while collecting data through other research tools like focus group discussion, case study and experience survey etc.

8 Conclusion

The advancement of Information and communication technology (ICT) brings a rapid pace of change around the world. People can communicate, interact, and exchange information with the use of ICT through technologies such as text messaging, video conferencing with other people in different regions of the world. Public interaction on social media allows sharing opinion about different government policies resulting to creation of echo chambers and social media induced polarization. To bring down the gap between the perception of government and general public several efforts are being made. However, all the studies conducted till date were related to polarization about specific topics through social media but these studies did not cover the research area of social media induced polarization about government policies. We started our research work by to be focused on to determine polarization about NEP 2020 through social media. This study aimed to investigate the social media induced polarization about NEP 2020 and to determine the opinion of social media users toward attitudinal change about NEP 2020 after using social media. To achieve the objective data was collected from primary as well as secondary sources. To extract the data twitter platform was used and specific keywords (search terms) were used such as #NEP2020, #Nationaleducationpolicy2020, #rejectnep2020, #neptransformingindia etc. Furthermore, primary source of information was used to know the opinions of social media users. Well structured questionnaire was prepared to collect the information about the change in attitude due to use of social media from social media users through social media platforms and snowball sampling method was employed. To determine the opinion toward attitudinal change about NEP 2020 by using social media, data was collected about the demographic profile of social media users, from how long they are using social media and their opinion towards the attitudinal change about NEP 2020 using social media. Frequency of time period from which they are using social media and opinion toward attitudinal change is determined individually. Along with individual frequency, frequency of time period from which they are using social media and opinion toward attitudinal change was analysed on the basis of demographic profile (Gender, Age, and Occupation) is also determined. The finding of the study revealed that 65.338% of total phrases social media users are positively inclined toward NEP 2020 showing the acceptance of policy by using positive terms in their posts on twitter. Out of total 2836 phrases 29.68% of total phrases represented the neutral responses towards NEP 2020 and the remaining phrases depicted the negative inclination towards NEP 2020. On the other side, the results of data collected through questionnaire concluded that maximum number of the respondents that is 59.57% was of opinion that the usage of social media results to the change in attitude about NEP 2020. While 40.43% disagreed for the change in attitude about NEP 2020 due to use of social media. No doubt social networking is beneficial for both society and government in different ways but polarization is not good for society as it creates echo chambers on social media and results to attitudinal change in social media users without understanding merits as well as demerits of government policies. There are few limitations like only twitter social media platform is used and tweets, retweets are not analysed separately. Furthermore, in depth information is not collected through primary sources about the attitudinal change due to use of social media. In future, research can be accomplished to know the polarization in different government policies by using different social media analytics techniques.

A.1 Appendix

Questionnaire prepared to know the opinion of social media users towards attitudinal change about NEP 2020 due to use of social media.

Section A: Demographic Profile

1. Gender:	☐	Male	☐	Female
2. Age:	☐	Less than 20 years	☐	20-30 years
	☐	30-40 years	☐	40-50 years
	☐	More than 50 years		
3. Occupation:	☐	Student	☐	Businessmen
	☐	Employee	☐	Homemaker
	☐	Others		

A.1

Section B: Opinions of Social Media Users

1. How long you have been using Social media?
   - Less than six month
   - 6–12 months
   - 1–3 years
   - More than 3 years
2. Do you feel any changes in your attitudes about NEP 2020 because of using social media?
   - Yes
   - No

Phrases extracted from the posts on twitter through Content analysis
Phrases extracted from Content analysis

Positive Phrases	Frequency
Dedicated towards quality	354
Dedicated towards quality improvement	232
Make education an exclusive	168
Alternative schooling in a phased	71
Ashramshalas in tribal dominated areas	71
Adult education will be executed	57
NEP strong innovative government initiatives	57
Quality education	48
Acknowledge our janasenas ideas	42
Shaping of the NEP	42
Current policy speak is quality education	41
Discussions concentrated	41
Improved education excellence in education	41
Develop key standard century skills	36
TET teachers are indeed essential	34
Ficci for startups training with part time	30
NEP gives us an opportunity	30
End the policy of reservations	29
Atmanirbhara bharata	21
Efforts will be focused	19
Empower new India with the knowledge	19
Paving way for atmanirbhar	17
Development through education	15
Faculty development	14
Insightful session	14
Valedictory function of atmanirbhara bharata	14
Core equity and inclusion	11
Inclusion at its core	11
Individual regardless of disparity	10
Calls upon higher education institutions	9
Forward to working	9
Make India a thriving	9
Snatching of state autonomy	9
Development of century skills	8
Faculty development programme	14
Careful designing of syllabi	8
Long awaited NEP	7
Online learning	7
Encouragingly provisioned for real time	7
Evaluation systems a consultative monitoring	7
Mother tongue	7
Eminent scientist and member	6
Esteemed panel of speakers	6
Transforming India	6

(continued)

Positive Phrases	**Frequency**
Highlighting the importance of NEP	6
Jump to fulsome praise	6
Potential to transform India	6
Trailer of nep looks interesting	6
NEP transforming India https	6
Education of the future	5
Giving them flexibility	5
Global education agenda that seeks	5
India a global knowledge superpower	5
Pointing out the strengths	5
NEP accomplish the stated goal	5
Sense of the Indian education	5
Augment the role of science	4
Benefit of school students	4
Comprehensive and holistic	4
Ensure quality	4
Era of teaching and learning	4
Evolution of technology	4
Exclusive interview with techconnect	4
Flexibility in making	4
Foundational learning NEP	4
Greater investments on adolescents	4
Implementation of India's national education policy	4
India has been taken steps	4
Interesting discussion on the evolution	4
Make education accessible	4
Efforts will be focused	3
Emerging disruptive technologies to transform	3
Empower new India with the knowledge	3
Focused on emerging disruptive technologies	3
Nep will empower new India	3
NEP transforming India Narendra Modi	3
Technologies to transform the education	3
Transform the education system	3
Neutral Phrases	**Frequency**
NEP but what about teqipiii	358
National education policy	98
Speak on national educational policy	62
Education NEP	23
Views about multifaceted education	21
National education policy	20
Education system	18
Higher education	15
Education system	15

(continued)

Positive Phrases	Frequency
Make India	13
Education policy NEP	12
Indian education	12
Economy's money supply	11
India s national education policy	10
Dream of an aatmanirbhar bharat	9
Implementation of the policy	9
Invite for your esteemed presence	8
National research foundation	8
Education policy	8
After days of intensive training	7
Designed keeping in mind	7
Digital literacy in India	7
Government will work on strategic	7
NEP aims	7
NEP conference	7
Indian education system	7
Foreign universities setting up shop	6
School education	6
Secrets of working memory https	6
Speaking in a webinar organised	6
Education sector	5
Vocational education	5
Based on western universalism	5
Indian education system	5
NEP pertaining to higher education	5
Part of the NEP pertaining	5
Pertaining to higher education https	5
Education for the youth	4
Negative Phrases	**Frequency**
Fault to be a student	21
Reject NEP https	18
Reject NEP today	14
Reject NEP aid	12
Reject NEP stop privatisation	11
Creation of money to fund	10
Disabled in educational institutions	9
Constraints and the nep digital literacy	7
Campaign against nep aid so submitted	7
Farms bill reject NEP stop privatisation strike november	7
Reject NEP aid so delhi https	7
Poor from getting quality education	5
Disagree that ashoka or NEP	5
Reject NEP aid so https	5
NEP is undemocratic	3

References

Abascal-Mena R, Lema R, Sèdes F (2015) Detecting sociosemantic communities by applying social network analysis in tweets. Soc Netw Anal Min 5(1):1–17

Alalwan AA, Rana NP, Dwivedi YK, Algharabat R (2017) Social media in marketing: a review and analysis of the existing literature. Telematics Inform 34(7):1177–1190

Bail CA, Argyle LP, Brown TW, Bumpus JP, Chen H, Hunzaker MF et al (2018) Exposure to opposing views on social media can increase political polarization. Proc Natl Acad Sci 115(37):9216–9221

Belcastro L, Cantini R, Marozzo F, Talia D, Trunfio P (2019a) Discovering political polarization on social media: a case study. In: 2019 15th international conference on semantics, knowledge and grids (SKG). IEEE, pp 182–189

Belcastro L, Marozzo F, Talia D (2019b) Programming models and systems for big data analysis. Int J Parallel Emerg Distrib Syst 34(6):632–652

Benito-Osorio D, Peris-Ortiz M, Armengot CR, Colino A (2013) Web 5.0: the future of emotional competences in higher education. Glob Business Persp 1(3):274–287

Bertot JC, Jaeger PT, Hansen D (2012) The impact of polices on government social media usage: issues, challenges, and recommendations. Gov Inf Q 29(1):30–40

Bessi A, Zollo F, Del Vicario M, Puliga M, Scala A, Caldarelli G et al (2016) Users polarization on Facebook and Youtube. PLoS One 11(8):e0159641

Bhardwaj A, Kumar Mishra S, Qureshi I, Kamal Kumar K, Konrad AM, Seidel MDL, Bhatt B (2021) Bridging caste divides: middle-status ambivalence, elite closure, and lower-status social withdrawal. J Manag Stud 58(8):2111–2136

Bhatt B, Qureshi I, Sutter C (2022) How do intermediaries build inclusive markets? The role of the social context. J Manag Stud

Bryson BP (2019) Polarizing the middle: internet exposure and public opinion. Int J Sociol Soc Policy

Carter L, Bélanger F (2005) The utilization of e-government services: citizen trust, innovation and acceptance factors. Inf Syst J 15(1):5–25

Ceron A, Negri F (2016) The "social side" of public policy: monitoring online public opinion and its mobilization during the policy cycle. Policy Internet 8(2):131–147

Chin D, Zappone A, Zhao J (2016) Analyzing twitter sentiment of the 2016 presidential candidates. Am J Sci Res

Chitra U, Musco C (2019) Understanding filter bubbles and polarization in social networks. arXiv preprint arXiv:1906.08772

Christensen HS, Karjalainen M, Nurminen L (2015) Does crowdsourcing legislation increase political legitimacy? The case of AvoinMinisteriö in Finland. Policy Internet 7(1):25–45

Clarke A, Margetts H (2014) Governments and citizens getting to know each other? Open, closed, and big data in public management reform. Policy Internet 6(4):393–417

Conover MD, Ratkiewicz J, Francisco M, Gonçalves B, Menczer F, Flammini A (2011) Political polarization on twitter. In: Fifth international AAAI conference on weblogs and social media.

Dwivedi YK, Shareef MA, Simintiras AC, Lal B, Weerakkody V (2016) A generalised adoption model for services: a cross-country comparison of mobile health (m-health). Gov Inf Q 33(1):174–187

El-Shinnawy M, Vinze AS (1998) Polarization and persuasive argumentation: a study of decision making in group settings. MIS Q:165–198

Guerra PC, Meira Jr W, Cardie C, Kleinberg R (2013) A measure of polarization on social media networks based on community boundaries. In: Seventh international AAAI conference on weblogs and social media

Hochwald T (2013) How do social media affect intra-state conflicts other than war? Connections 12(3):9–38

Honey C, Herring SC (2009) Beyond microblogging: conversation and collaboration via Twitter. In: 2009 42nd Hawaii international conference on system sciences. IEEE, pp 1–10

Hossain MA, Dwivedi YK, Chan C, Standing C, Olanrewaju AS (2018) Sharing political content in online social media: a planned and unplanned behaviour approach. Inf Syst Front 20(3):485–501

Jain G, Sreenivas AB, Gupta S, Tiwari AA (2021) The dynamics of Online opinion formation: polarization around vaccine development for COVID-19. In: Qureshi I, Bhatt B, Gupta S, Tiwari AA (eds) Causes and symptoms of socio-cultural polarization: role of information and communication technologies, Springer

Jin X, Ye QY (2019) Impact of different social media context on attitude polarization of hot topic online. In: 2018 Ph. D Student New Media conference

Jones DA (2013) The polarizing effect of a partisan workplace. PS Polit Sci Polit 46(1):67

Joseph N, Grover P, Rao PK, Ilavarasan PV (2017) Deep analyzing public conversations: insights from Twitter analytics for policy makers. In: Conference on e-business, e-services and e-society. Springer, Cham, pp 239–250

Kapoor KK, Tamilmani K, Rana NP, Patil P, Dwivedi YK, Nerur S (2018) Advances in social media research: past, present and future. Inf Syst Front 20(3):531–558

Lee FL (2016) Impact of social media on opinion polarization in varying times. Commun Public 1(1):56–71

Lenhart A (2010) Cell phones and American adults. Pew Research Center, Washington, DC

Madden M (2010) Older adults and social media. Pew Internet and American Life Project, Washington, DC

Magro MJ (2012) A review of social media use in e-government. Admin Sci 2(2):148–161

Margetts HZ (2009) The Internet and public policy. Policy Internet 1(1):1–21

Marozzo F, Bessi A (2018) Analyzing polarization of social media users and news sites during political campaigns. Soc Netw Anal Min 8(1):1–13

McCann JA (1995) Nomination politics and ideological polarization: assessing the attitudinal effects of campaign involvement. J Polit 57(1):101–120

Mouw T, Sobel ME (2001) Culture wars and opinion polarization: the case of abortion. Am J Sociol 106(4):913–943

Netto YC, Maçada ACG (2019) The influence of social media filter bubbles and echo chambers on it identity construction. Cephalalgia 90010:460

Qureshi I, Bhatt B, Gupta S, Tiwari AA (2021) Introduction to the role of information and communication technologies in polarization. In: Qureshi I, Gupta BB, Tiwari AA (eds) Causes and symptoms of socio-cultural polarization: role of information and communication technologies, Springer

Qureshi I, Sutter C, Bhatt B (2018) The transformative power of knowledge sharing in settings of poverty and social inequality. Organ Stud 39(11):1575–1599

Sahoo N (2020) Mounting majoritarianism and political polarization in India

Shi Y, Mast K, Weber I, Kellum A, Macy M (2017) Cultural fault lines and political polarization. In: Proceedings of the 2017 ACM on web science conference, pp 213–217.

Singh P, Dwivedi YK, Kahlon KS, Sawhney RS (2018) Intelligent monitoring and controlling of public policies using social media and cloud computing. In: International working conference on transfer and diffusion of IT. Springer, Cham, pp 143–154

Singh P, Dwivedi YK, Kahlon KS, Sawhney RS, Alalwan AA, Rana NP (2020) Smart monitoring and controlling of government policies using social media and cloud computing. Inf Syst Front 22(2):315–337

Singh P, Sawhney RS, Kahlon KS (2019) Twitter based sentiment analysis of GST implementation by Indian government. In: Digital business. Springer, Cham, pp 409–427

Smith RA (1989) The role of situational involvement in consumers' attitude polarization. J Bus Psychol 3(4):439–447

Stieglitz S, Dang-Xuan L (2013) Emotions and information diffusion in social media—sentiment of microblogs and sharing behavior. J Manag Inf Syst 29(4):217–248

Sutter C, Bhatt B, Qureshi I (2022) What makes resource provision an effective means of poverty alleviation? A resourcing perspective. Organ Sci. https://doi.org/10.1287/orsc.2021.1570

Sunstein CR (2018) # Republic: divided democracy in the age of social media. Princeton University Press.

Yang J, Rojas H, Wojcieszak M, Aalberg T, Coen S, Curran J et al (2016) Why are "others" so polarized? Perceived political polarization and media use in 10 countries. J Comput-Mediat Commun 21(5):349–367

Yardi S, Boyd D (2010) Dynamic debates: an analysis of group polarization over time on twitter. Bull Sci Technol Soc 30(5):316–327

Yeo J, Knox CC, Jung K (2018) Unveiling cultures in emergency response communication networks on social media: following the 2016 Louisiana floods. Qual Quant 52(2):519–535

Zheng Z, Bhatt B (2021) Political polarisation in australia: a case study of bushfires. In: Qureshi I, Bhatt B, Gupta S, Tiwari AA (eds) Causes and symptoms of socio-cultural polarization: role of information and communication technologies, Springer

Websites

https://www.statista.com/statistics/278414/number-of-worldwide-social-network-users/

https://onlinelibrary.wiley.com/pb-assets/assets/13652575/ISJ_SMIP_CFP-1586861685850.pdf

https://www.abpeducation.com/news/education-minister-answers-questions-on-nep-on-social-media/cid/1204437

Media Bias and Bollywood: An Untold Story

Gaurav Jain, Snehanshu Suman, Samrat Gupta, and Amit Anand Tiwari

Abstract It may not be hyperbole that the news media can create or destroy a celebrity in today's world. Media bias can influence public opinion and perception towards topics that are critical to our society. When such issues or controversies are related to celebrities followed by millions of people, any distortion of facts to suit a particular agenda engenders a bitter debate on social media, making the society further polarized. Our study identifies media bias in the key Indian news outlets, based on the online articles published on their portals on major controversies in the entertainment domain, particularly Bollywood (Bollywood is the common name given to the Indian Hindi film industry, primarily based out of Mumbai, India). Further, we segment these media outlets based on the sentiments exhibited across these articles to identify ideological similarities between the prominent media houses. Our findings suggest that while a few media outlets don't display a consistent bias, two distinct clusters of media outlets that have consistently opposing biases emerge. Our observation is essential for the users to understand and consume their news from media houses that display contrasting biases while reporting on Bollywood celebrities' controversies. Our work helps in understanding that if users follow only the channels exhibiting similar bias; they are likely to unknowingly adopt the same prejudice, making them further polarized towards or against the celebrity.

Keywords Media bias · Polarization · Bollywood · Celebrities · Controversies

1 Introduction

The film industry in India is a creative and overwhelming medium (Gupta et al. 2016). Bollywood actor's posters and paintings adorn various hoardings and

---

G. Jain · S. Suman · S. Gupta (✉) · A. A. Tiwari
Indian Institute of Management Ahmedabad, Ahmedabad, Gujarat, India
e-mail: ep19gauravj@iima.ac.in; ep19snehanshus@iima.ac.in; samratg@iima.ac.in; amit.tiwari@iimrohtak.ac.in

I. Qureshi et al. (eds.), *Causes and Symptoms of Socio-Cultural Polarization*,
https://doi.org/10.1007/978-981-16-5268-4_9

small shops. Bollywood music reverberates in buses, taxis, and auto-rickshaws, and roadside newspaper stalls are filled with gossip magazines about actors and actresses from Bollywood (Jaikumar 2003). Filmmakers and actors have calibrated most of the Indians' lives for decades, with a variety of fashions, lyrics, and dialogues portrayed in the films (Jaikumar 2003). This social appeal has resulted in the Indian film industry becoming an INR 183 billion market by value in 2020[1]. All this fanfare comes with a fair share of controversies surrounding Bollywood. Artists' bizarre and outrageous behaviors, defined as a conduct, an expression, or a statement, that is out of norms with that of the general public has become a significant aspect of any entertainment industry (Wood et al. 2016). Economic theories of human behavior, that study the phenomenon of minimizing the transaction and learning cost and maximizing the expected utility, show that these artists' bizarre behaviors could well be a carefully thought-out strategy to promote their work (Koku 1995). Nonetheless, controversies provide an artist a fair amount of publicity, either good or bad.

Controversies have been an integral part of any entertainment industry and more so when it comes to Bollywood. For example, many Bollywood personalities' names were dragged in the ongoing drug probe triggered after a Bollywood actor, Sushant Singh Rajput's unfortunate death. These Bollywood personalities are normally not accessible to the masses. Hence, any information that the public gathers about them is either through the social media posts put up by these personalities or through the news channels or media houses' reporting. Thus, news media could be considered as an interface between Bollywood and the masses. The narrative created by the media and the reactions of fans and consumers around that narrative related to a personality also contributes to that person's celebrity status, apart from just being well-known for their work (Lunardo et al. 2015). Therefore, it is an important research question to investigate if the news media is free of any bias or prejudice while reporting any incident related to Bollywood. In our study, while we investigate any media bias in the entertainment news reporting, we intend to focus on online news reporting as it has become one of the important ways of news consumption in today's world.

The Internet has transformed the way people consume news. Newspapers and news bulletins on radio or television was the only form of news consumption in the earlier days. Today's users get "instant helping" of the latest critical news of their choice on the platform they choose, be it email, mobile phones or social media platforms (Stassen 2010). To cater to this changing need of news consumption of the users, the mantra adopted by the modern-day news organizations is to be 'anytime, anywhere and on any platform.'[2]. This greater flow of information, both from the news providers to the consumers and vice versa in the form of user comments on the news articles in social media, is a paradigm of the concept of "information societies" within the information and communication technology (ICT) framework (Kader and Gundala 2021; Stassen 2010; Webster 2006). One of the central points of

[1] https://www.statista.com/statistics/235837/value-of-the-film-industry-in-india/

[2] https://niemanreports.org/articles/blogs-tweets-social-media-and-the-news-business/

the information societies theories is the association and the interconnectedness that it offers to its users at a global level through a greater degree of interactivity and personalization as compared to the earlier forms of media that was mostly offline (Stassen 2010). It has also been observed that as the individuals tend to scan through the news, they usually build their perception based on the peripheral information processing rather than the central thinking mechanism, thus basing their opinions and choices on the social media news (Ribeiro et al. 2018). Usually, users have a fixed set of news portals or apps from where they consume their daily news and have their own internal biases (Eveland and Shah 2003). Users may experience *echo chambers* if the news portals they refer to show a similar bias that reinforces their opinions, thus making them more polarized (Hamborg et al. 2018). Therefore, it has become even more important for today's news agencies to report only the facts of any topic without introducing any kind of bias while reporting so that the people engage with each other on the facts rather than on the perceptions of the news agency from where they are sourcing the news.

Our study intends to identify media bias by analyzing the sentiments exhibited by the news articles covering Bollywood incidents and thus identifying if there is an ideological similarity between the news portals publishing those articles. We investigated the online articles published on various India media websites reporting the major controversies in Bollywood. These controversies are related to different Bollywood personalities during the years 2017–2020. We didn't restrict ourselves to controversies around a single personality as it may not give us an accurate assessment of media bias because of the possibility of an inclination of specific news channels towards individual Bollywood personalities. We computed an overall sentiment exhibited by the news articles and assigned a sentiment score to each of the articles. Further, for each article, we distinguish the percentage of words that exhibit a positive or a negative sentiment. Using the articles' overall sentiment score and the percentages of positive and negative sentiment words, we identify the clusters of news channels/portals that demonstrate similar sentiments for each of the articles and thus display a similar bias.

People admire these public figures and try to imitate their good and bad behaviors (Koordeman et al. 2011). Therefore, understanding the existence of media reporting bias around Bollywood celebrities is important because media is the only source of information for the public about these personalities. Any events happening around film personalities tend to create polarization among the masses who follow these personalities (Park et al. 2015). For example, when Narcotics Control Bureau of India started investigating the nexus between Bollywood personalities and drug mafia after the death of Bollywood actor Sushant Singh Rajput, there was an increased polarization observed between the people who supported the drug probe and the ones who claimed it to be a vendetta against some Bollywood personalities[3]. When today's youth, who try to copy the lifestyles of their favorite Bollywood

[3] https://www.washingtonpost.com/world/asia_pacific/india-bollywood-republic-tv-times-now/2020/11/06/e2b27256-1ab3-11eb-8bda-814ca56e138b_story.html

personalities, are led to believe that their icons consume drugs, they may try to follow the same, leading to disastrous consequences for their families and society (McCutcheon et al. 2002). Therefore, if the users are aware of the media houses' leanings with respect to the domain of the news, they could consume the news with a pinch of salt without getting further polarized (Gentzkow and Shapiro 2006).

2 Literature Review

2.1 Media Bias, Its Forms and the Impact on Society

Independent press is essential to society's well-being as it is an information mechanism for the public to make individual and collective decisions (Baron 2005; Ellman and Germano 2009). Media organizations act as gatekeepers of information by regulating the news consumed by the common people and therefore play a significant role in socio-cultural evolution (Ribeiro et al. 2018; Shoemaker et al. 2009). Media is considered as one of the four pillars of democracy (Keane 1992). Due to this powerful role played by the media in our society, there is a worry among researchers that a deregulated and ideologically partisan media could have a high impact on the political outcomes and on the society (Chiang and Knight 2011; Groseclose and Milyo 2005; Ribeiro et al. 2018). Therefore, the question arises as to what media bias is. There are several definitions of media bias. A classical definition of media bias describes it as both intentional, i.e., it must be a conscious choice, and sustained, i.e., it should not be an isolated incident but a systematic tendency (Hamborg et al. 2018; WIlliams 1975). One of the other definitions describe media bias as a preference to a certain political or social ideology and not something to do with inaccurate or dishonest information dissemination (Groseclose and Milyo 2005). Yet another definition of media bias talks about three types of biases: gatekeeping, statement and coverage (D'Alessio and Allen 2000; Hamborg et al. 2018). Gatekeeping or selection/agenda bias relates to the stories that a media organization selects or rejects for reporting. Statement or presentation bias is about the slant in which the articles are written to make a certain point. Coverage bias relates to the visibility given to certain topics or entities in the media coverage.

There could be various causes of media biases. Media biases could be introduced due to the lack of balance between the two sides of the stories, resulting in one side receiving undue attention. There could be journalists' personal preferences, resulting in their stories being biased towards their individualistic beliefs. Bias may result from the fabrication of information, distorted or hidden facts by journalists or their sources, or the partisan views of the owners, editors, or journalists (Baron 2005). Several studies have investigated the media bias by evaluating the content produced based on its correctness, balance, and fairness (Ribeiro et al. 2018). Today's news media is widely viewed as biased, and individuals perceive this bias' direction to be opposed to their own inclinations (Baron 2005; Eveland and Shah

2003). Results of the studies on media bias perceptions on the two events, 1980 US presidential elections and 1982 Beirut massacre, suggested that the perceived bias was more likely to be seen as bias against one's own position (Vallone et al. 1985). However, the degree of these media bias perceptions may be associated with the personal factors such as the extent of the political involvement or the strength of the partisanship (Eveland and Shah 2003). Although the past research has examined the effects of the personal factors on media bias perceptions, little attention has been paid to the interpersonal factors such as the difference within personal communication networks or ideological similarities leading to homophily (Eveland Jr and Shah 2003). Users are likely to adopt biased views if the reporting of a news outlet is biased (Hamborg et al. 2018). These biased views are intensified through homophilic structures in the digitally enabled social networks due to mechanisms such as media framing and selective exposure homophily effect (Arceneaux et al. 2013; Bhardwaj et al. 2016; De Vreese 2005; Qureshi et al. 2018; Wojcieszak and Garrett 2018). Thus, users commonly experience echo chambers that reinforce their internal biases (Hamborg et al. 2018). Moreover, due to specific interests, language barriers or to avoid an information overload, most people only consult a subset of the news outlets that report on a particular topic (Hamborg et al. 2018; Newman et al. 2015). The creation of echo chambers caused by the media bias leads to the polarization of public opinion (Das et al. 2021; Sunstein 2002). Some researchers have been led to believe that media bias poses a challenge to the pillars of our democracy[4] (Kahneman and Tversky 1984; Zaller 1992). Media bias is a well-established phenomenon which has gained the attention of researchers and practitioners across the globe (Gentzkow and Shapiro 2006). Some of the past examples of biased reporting that have led to a polarized debate within our society, either offline or on social media, are-

1. A very famous 1959 Indian court case of Naval Commander K. M. Nanavati vs. State of Maharashtra where Commander Nanavati was tried for the murder of Prem Ahuja, his wife's lover. Commander Nanavati was a well-known personality with links to many high profile people in politics and media. Despite being established that Commander Nanavati committed the murder, a popular investigative weekly *Blitz* unleashed a propoganda of sympathy towards the Commander and made him a victim of the justice system. Due to this media bias, he got a lot of public support. *Blitz* played a crucial role in raising public opinion in favor of Nanavati and in keeping the issue alive until a pardon was granted after 3 years of life imprisonment.[5]
2. In January 2021, when the President of India unveiled Netaji Subhas Chandra Bose's portrait to commemorate his 125th birth anniversary, there were claims in the media that the portrait was of a film actor Prosenjit Chatterjee rather than of Netaji SC Bose. The event triggered an uproar on social media, especially

[4] https://www.news18.com/news/opinion/biased-mainstream-media-carries-grave-consequences-for-indian-democracy-2541333.html

[5] https://en.wikipedia.org/wiki/K._M._Nanavati_v._State_of_Maharashtra

Twitter, with some people started ridiculing the President and the government while others came in defense. The claim was later found to be false.[6]

3. In 2016, when a famous Bollywood couple Saif Ali Khan and Kareena Kapoor named their son *Taimur*, it opened a pandora's box as social media users and news outlets started claiming that he was named after the barbaric Mongol invader "Taimur" who conquered many parts of Persia and central Asia during the fourteenth century. Sections of social media users and news outlets started spewing lessons on why this is a good choice or not and created polarization around the use of this name[7].

In summary, there could be detrimental effects of media bias, more so when the users are unaware of the bias and assume that the information being presented to them is accurate and verified.

2.2 Celebrities and Controversies

The word celebrity is not just a noun but an adjective that implies that someone can draw attention (Furedi 2010). There are various definitions of a celebrity. One of them describes a celebrity as a human pseudo-event, or a person known for his or her "well-knownness" (Meyer and Gamson 1995; Monaco 1978). Alternatively, celebrity is also defined as someone "whose name has attention-getting, interest-riveting and profit generating value" (Archer et al. 2020; Rein et al. 1997). Another definition describes a celebrity as a "powerless elite", a group having a privileged social position that doesn't derive its status from institutionally granted social power, but from public attention (Alberoni 2007). However, there are several instances when the social power derived from public attention has led to institutional power (Alberoni 2007). For instance, Bollywood actors such as Anupam Kher and Paresh Rawal have held leadership positions with renowned institutions such as the Film and Television Institute of India and National School of Drama respectively. In essence, a core feature of celebrities could be the ability to capture attention (Archer et al. 2020). In modern contemporary societies, celebrities mostly come from a cultural realm- predominantly from films, television, music, sports, theatre and art fields and are mostly differentiated by their autonomy from the state institutions (Meyer and Gamson 1995).

Celebrities have been known to possess and exercise their epistemic power, an ability to influence what others know, think or believe (Archer et al. 2020). Most human beings possess varying degrees of epistemic power. There could be various sources of this epistemic power: a person having in-depth knowledge in a particular

[6] https://www.ndtv.com/india-news/netaji-subhash-chandra-bose-or-actor-prosenjit-chatterjee-who-played-him-president-ram-nath-kovind-house-portrait-stirs-new-row-2357746

[7] https://www.ndtv.com/entertainment/kareena-kapoors-son-taimur-already-twitter-star-for-controversial-name-foreign-media-1640151

area may be able to influence and convince others by providing relevant arguments, a person holding an institutional position and by virtue of it possesses epistemic power to influence others or a person having high perceived credibility may be able to exert their epistemic power (Archer et al. 2020). Although institutional sources of epistemic power should only be granted to deserving people, that may not always be the case. It is a cause of worry when someone's expertise in one area allows them to make unvalidated expert statements about a completely different area while having little or no knowledge of that matter. For example, when a well-known chemistry professor uses his position to make a public statement about how to treat cancer that is unrelated to his area of expertise, it's a case of that professor exerting his epistemic power into something that is not his area of expertise (Ballantyne 2019; Vukov et al. 2020). In general, celebrities tend to possess a higher perceived credibility than a normal person and this is somewhat evident in the long-running use of celebrities in political campaigning (Archer et al. 2020; Pornpitakpan 2008). A study on Oprah Winfrey's endorsement of Obama in the 2008 US presidential elections estimated that Winfrey was responsible for over 1 million votes for Obama (Garthwaite and Moore 2012). However, people accept celebrity endorsements not just in trivial matters. In another study, 24% parents were found to give some credibility, and 2% a lot of credibility, to what celebrities had to say on the safety of vaccinations for children (Archer et al. 2020; Freed et al. 2011). This observation shows that people are willing to trust what celebrities endorse even in matters concerning their children's health.

Controversies may arise when there is an assumption that an actor who possesses good acting skills is also an expert in other domains. News outlets that have a positive impression orientation towards this actor will highlight positive stories of his/her knowledge in other domains, and others will criticize his/her lack of knowledge in that domain. It is commonplace to have controversies around celebrities and more so when we talk about celebrities in Bollywood. A few examples of controversies that rocked Bollywood in the past few years are-

1. Days before the release of her film *Chhapaak*, Deepika Padukone visited Jawaharlal Nehru University (JNU) to meet the allegedly assaulted students for taking part in a protest. Amidst the frenzied situation, Deepika's visit to the university caused a huge polarization in the public with some people admiring her for supporting the students while others asking to boycott her movie because she stood by the students who were protesting for an unreasonable cause.[8]
2. The unfortunate death of Bollywood actor Sushant Singh Rajput in 2020 triggered a huge controversy when few media outlets claimed it to be a suicide while others contested that claim. This media divide resulted in polarization

[8] https://www.bollywoodhungama.com/news/features/2020recap-bollywoods-biggest-shocking-controversies-2020/

among Bollywood celebrities as well as their fans who supported the point of view that aligned with their own[9].

3. Actor Sushant's death controversy triggered a drug probe in Bollywood due to the speculation that his death could be a result of a drug overdose. A few celebrities were questioned by the drug probe agencies for their connection with the drug mafia and a couple of celebrities were arrested too. Their arrests created a huge divide among the industry and the public[10].

Controversies could manifest in multiple ways such as a court case on a soon to be released movie, gossip about a personal crisis of the star-cast, rumors about being romantically linked with a co-star or the lead star-cast taking a position on a present-day political or social issue. A credulous media further misrepresents the facts by planting fabricated stories around the controversies (Marwick and Lewis 2017). Although prior studies suggest that consumer behavior, to maximize the derived utility in entertainment consumption, has something to do with the celebrities' controversial activities and positions, there are a few unanswered questions such as: How does the propagation of misinformation in the media around celebrities lead to polarization and affect our society? In today's digitally interconnected world, what steps could be taken to minimize the consequences of social media induced polarization (SMIP) due to fake news and media bias (Bailey 2007; Fard and Verma 2021; Fong and Wyer 2012; Ogunsiji 2012; Qureshi et al. 2020; Qureshi et al. 2021).

3 Data and Methodology

We modeled the media bias in the channels covering Bollywood controversies using a sentiment analysis technique to identify leading news reporting channels' polarization. The channels were further grouped based on the polarization and the inter-group bias on the coverage of the issues was examined. The news articles related to major controversies in Bollywood were considered, and every news channel article's sentiment was computed. The news channel's sentiment and the distribution of positive and negative words published in the article were taken as the three variables. These variables were used to divide the channels in a number of groups such that the coverage of the articles by the channels within the groups were more similar than those in the other groups. The data pertaining to eleven prominent English news agencies reporting about eight major controversies on their websites was collected. One article each from the eleven news outlets was selected for each of the eight controversies to obtain a dataset of 88 news articles. Figure 1 lists the channels and the length of the article published for each of the articles.

[9] https://www.news18.com/news/movies/press-club-of-india-supports-boycott-of-kangana-ranaut-by-entertainment-journalists-guild-2229619.html

[10] https://www.hindustantimes.com/bollywood/bollywood-drug-probe-deepens-is-this-the-hindi-film-industry-s-worst-phase-ever/story-TFm2J0ekvvNmoQ7c9IlZrL.html

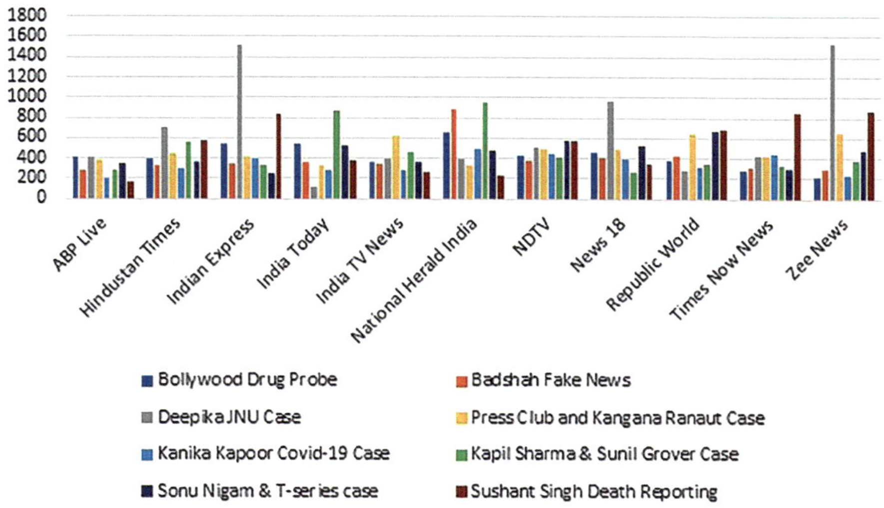

Fig. 1 The articles published by major Indian media channels and their length

To assess the media bias in the entertainment industry, we used lexicon sentiment analysis technique (Liu 2012). We then grouped the media agencies into different segments based on the sentiment data collected using K-means hierarchical clustering, a technique used to partition the observations (media agencies) into clusters and to minimize the variations, i.e. the squared Euclidean distances within the cluster (Hartigan and Wong 1979). Clustering, an unsupervised machine learning method of grouping similar objects in a dataset, has been proven helpful in solving various complex problems in the digital era (Gupta and Deodhar 2021; Gupta and Kumar 2020; Gupta and Kumar 2021; Gupta and Tiwari 2021; Gupta et al. 2016; Kumar et al. 2017). The channels were selected based on the coverage of the issue and the length of the articles published. Moreover, we only selected those articles, which reported the facts and rejected the opinion-based articles or the editorials.

The selected articles were cleaned by removing special characters and unrelated links to ensure data integrity. We divided the article's text into individual tokens and removed the stop words, i.e. common words that don't mean anything such as 'the', 'an', 'of' etc., We arrived at the sentiment score s_{ni}, where n denotes the article number and i denotes the article's news channels (Liu 2012). This lexicon technique allows our system to handle context dependent opinion words and also has a function to deal with conflicting opinion words in a sentence (Ding et al. 2008). We used the term frequency - inverse document frequency (TF-IDF) weighting scheme to identify the importance of a word in a news article compared to other articles (Aizawa 2003).

$$TF(t,n) = \frac{Number\ of\ times\ a\ term\ (t)\ occurs\ in\ a\ news\ article}{Total\ Number\ of\ terms\ in\ the\ article\ n} \tag{1}$$

$$IDF(t) = Log_{10}\left(\frac{Total\ number\ of\ news\ articles}{Number\ of\ articles\ without\ a\ term\ (t) in\ it}\right) \quad (2)$$

$$TF - IDF\ (t, n) = TF\ (t, n) * IDF(t) \quad (3)$$

We then looked at the distribution of positive, negative and neutral words in the article as an alternate approach and calculated p_{ni} and n_{in} as the percentage of positive and negative words for each news channel article. Since we had to identify the clusters within the media channels, we used a standardized scaling technique so that the three feature variables (s_{ni}, p_{ni}, and n_{ni}) contribute equally to the result. In this technique, the values are centred around the mean with a unit standard deviation (Milligan and Cooper 1988).

$$s'_{ni} = \frac{(s_{ni} - \mu)}{\sigma} \quad (4)$$

$$p'_{ni} = \frac{(p_{ni} - \mu)}{\sigma} \quad (5)$$

$$n'_{ni} = \frac{(n_{ni} - \mu)}{\sigma} \quad (6)$$

where, μ is the mean, σ is the standard deviation of the feature values, and s'_{ni}, p'_{ni} , and n'_{ni} are scaled values of s_{ni}, p_{ni} , and n_{ni}respectively.

By applying K-means clustering, an unsupervised segmentation approach, we grouped the channels that had similar sentiments into different categories. This approach was useful in our experiment since we didn't have labeled data (Steinley 2006). Based on the groups formed for all the eight articles, we created different combinations of the news channels that were part of the same cluster and grouped them to identify the channel's sentimental leaning. Pseudo code of the experiment is as below:

1. ***for*** *each news_item* ***n do***
2. ***for*** *each news_channel* ***i do***
3. *Determine the sentiment score* s_{ni}, p_{ni}, *and* n_{ni}
4. *Scale the values of* s_{ni}, p_{ni}, *and* n_{ni} *to determine* s'_{ni}, p'_{ni}, *and* n'_{ni}
5. ***end for***
6. *Group the news channels into k clusters based on* s_{ni}, p_{ni}, *and* n_{ni}
7. *Count the number of intra-group combinations formed*
8. ***end for***
9. *Identify the news channels that fall in the same cluster based on the intragroup combinations of the news items*

4 Experiment and Results

The text of the news articles were subjected to the sentiment analysis process. The graphical results pertaining to the sentiment analysis and clustering of the news outlets are shown in Figs. 2, 3 and 4 for the Bollywood drug probe controversy. The graph in Fig. 2 shows the sentiments exhibited by articles from each of the news agencies. We observe that almost all media houses, except National Herald India, displayed a negative sentiment on the drug controversy.

Along with the sentiment scores for each of the articles, the distribution of positive, neutral and negative words was obtained as shown in the graph in Fig. 3. While most of the words are neutral, this distribution gives us a more detailed view of these articles' positive vs negative sentiment words. A higher percentage of negative words makes the articles' overall sentiment negative, which is also corroborated by the sentiment scores in Fig. 2.

Based on the Eqs. 1, 2 and 3, we calculated the TF and IDF scores to identify the most characteristic words in the articles by assigning a numeric value to the words. A benefit of using the TF-IDF approach is that it ignores the words that are common to every article. For example, the word 'bollywood' is not very descriptive since all the articles are about Bollywood drug probe cases. As observed from the graph in Fig. 4, an experiment conducted using a two cluster solution shows the groupings of the media houses according to their sentiment score and the percentage of positive and negative sentiment words displayed for the Bollywood drug probe articles for the respective media outlets. A similar clustering was done on the articles' sentiment analysis for the rest of the seven controversies.

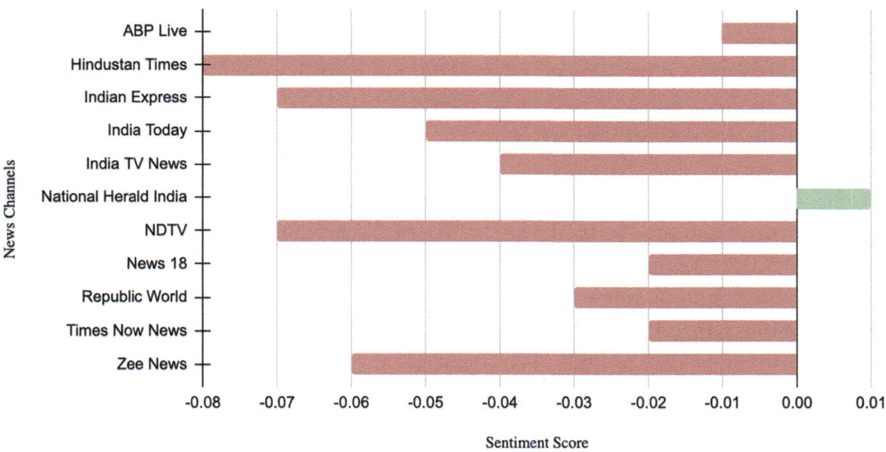

Fig. 2 Sentiment analysis score of the eleven news articles on Bollywood Drug Probe published in the news outlets' web portals.

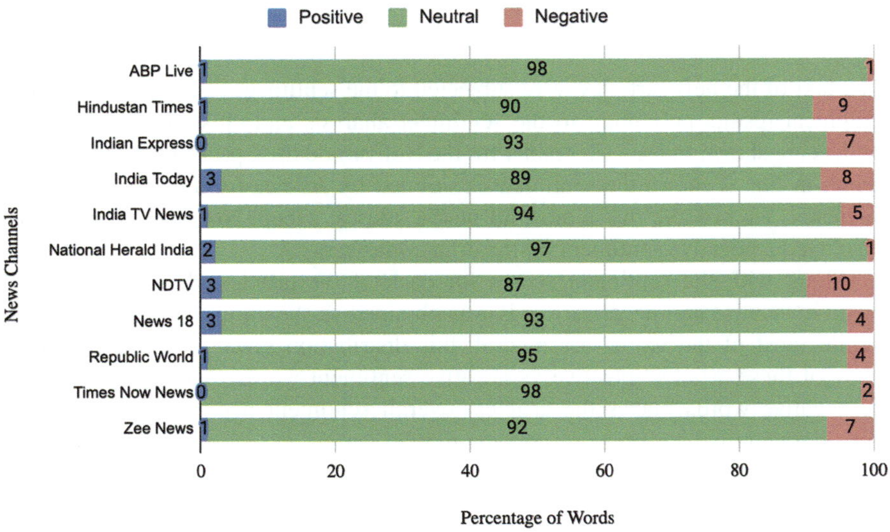

Fig. 3 %age distribution of the positive, neutral, and negative sentiment words of the eleven news articles on Bollywood Drug Probe published in the news outlets' web portals

On the basis of the clustering output of the eight articles, we created a two dimensional matrix of the news channels as shown in Table 1. The first row and column represents the news channels in the study and each cell represents the number of times the combination of the news channels were found in the same cluster for the eight articles. For example, ABP Live and India TV News were identified to be in the same cluster for seven news articles out of the eight articles. Similarly, we created a three and four dimensional matrix to identify the number of channels in the same cluster. Channels falling in the same cluster displays the similarity in their bias with respect to the news articles.

By analyzing the clustering outputs, we found that "NDTV", "Zee News", "Indian Express" and "Hindustan Times" were grouped in a single cluster, while "India TV", "ABP Live" and "National Herald" were grouped into another cluster. The four news outlets "India Today", "Times Now News", "Republic World" and "News 18" were found to be overlapping across the two clusters as shown in Fig. 5.

This observation is important because few news channels are shown in the same cluster in Fig. 5 that don't exhibit similar sentiments while reporting on news related to other domains like politics. For example, there is a vox-populi, supported by few studies, that Zee News and NDTV are usually not aligned in their sentiments while reporting on political news (Qayyum et al. 2018). However, our results

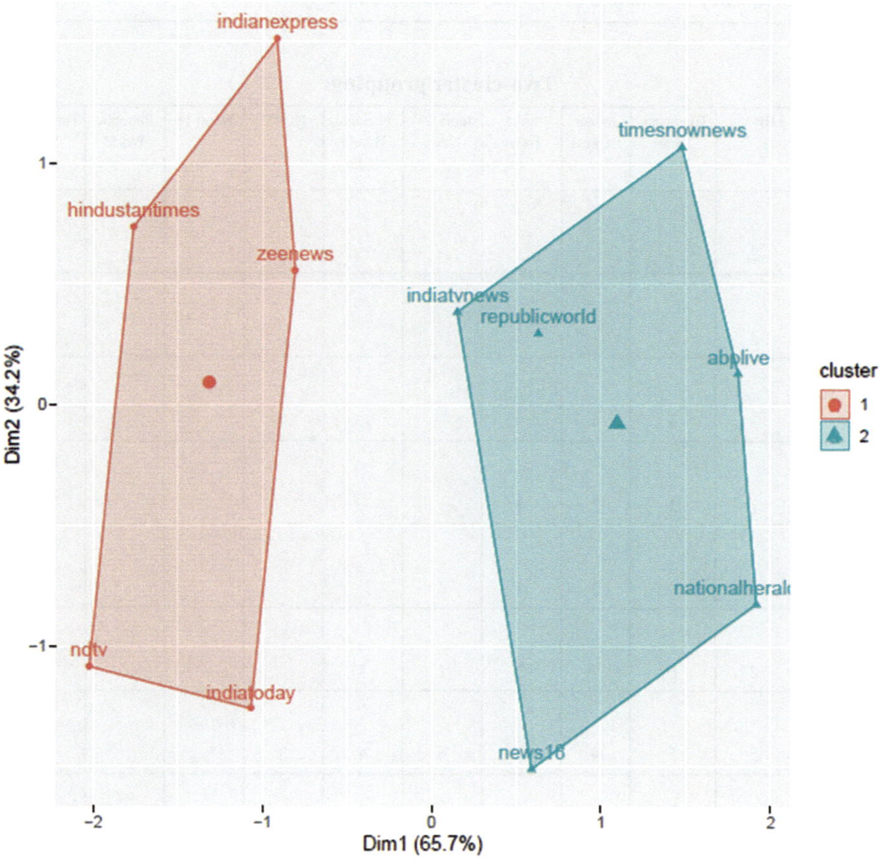

Fig. 4 Clustering output of the news outlets based on the Bollywood drug probe news coverage

show that while reporting on news related to Bollywood, Zee News and NDTV exhibit a similar sentiment across the controversies selected for this study. Thus, entertainment newsreaders, who like to read the news from Zee News and NDTV and have a common perception that these two media outlets don't have similar bias, may think they are looking at opposing perspectives of the same news. However, they are actually consuming news having similar bias thus becoming vulnerable to further polarization.

Table 1 Frequency distribution of two-way clustering output

Two-cluster groupings										
	ABP Live	Hindustan Times	Indian Express	India Today	India TV News	National Herald India	NDTV	News 18	Republic World	Times Now News
Hindustan Times	2									
Indian Express	3	5								
India Today	3	3	4							
India TV News	7	3	2	4						
National Herald India	5	3	2	4	6					
NDTV	2	6	7	3	1	3				
News 18	5	5	4	2	6	4	3			
Republic World	5	5	2	2	6	6	3	6		
Times Now News	3	5	2	2	4	4	3	6	6	
Zee News	1	7	4	4	2	2	5	4	4	6

5 Discussion and Conclusion

As the public opinion is formed based on the type of news they consume, users must view objective facts and different perspectives of the same topic (Hamborg et al. 2018). Absence of unbiased information may lead to uninformed decision making in crucial events such as elections (Hamborg et al. 2017; Mullainathan and Shleifer 2005). These days, when our society is becoming increasingly polarized, media bias detection is of high societal relevance (Hamborg et al. 2018). It helps the users become aware by not falling prey to the views of only a specific section of the media. Moreover, the use of social media and websites for news reporting

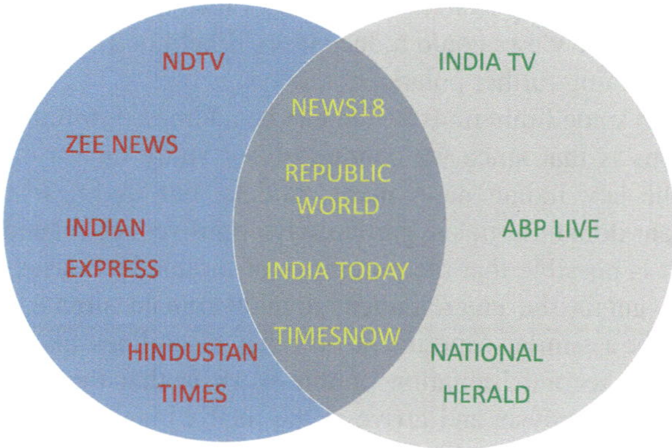

Fig. 5 Final segmentation of news outlets based on their biases reported for the controversies

facilitates the users' involvement as the user feedback is instant in comments and online discussion around the news topic. This constant interaction and feedback potentially result in a richer news experience for the users than traditional one-way news communication.

Our results show a clear existence of bias in the online news reporting related to our chosen topics in the entertainment domain. While a few news media outlets don't display a consistent bias for all the chosen topics, most of the media outlets in our study form a bipolar division based on the bias they exhibit while reporting on these topics. Our findings reveal that "Zee News," "Indian Express," "NDTV," and "Hindustan Times" fall into one category and display a similar bias. On the other hand, "India TV News," "ABP Live," and "National Herald India" fall into another category showing a similar bias but different to that of the first category of media outlets. This bipolar division indicates that these news outlets' users have a high propensity to get polarized if they choose to consume their news only from the outlets falling into the same category. For example, suppose a user is looking at the news articles on Zee News and Indian Express related to a specific event. In such a case, these articles will reinforce a particular bias, and the user will create a view according to that bias. Alternatively, if a user consumes news from Zee News and ABP Live, they are more likely to get both sides of the story to arrive at a more objective conclusion.

Bias in news media affects both the news coverage and how the individuals treat it. Individual news treatment pertains to the beliefs of the individuals (Baron 2005). Individuals usually transform their opinions based on their anticipation of the media bias as they understand that a reported story has a probability of being biased (Baron 2005). However, users don't necessarily understand if the bias shown by different news sources is similar or not to avoid consuming news from the media houses displaying a similar bias; thus, becoming more polarized by being a part of an echo chamber. Therefore, our observation is essential for the users to understand the category of media houses that are either unbiased or have contrasting biases so they can refer to the articles from a diverse set of media outlets. Consequently, this exposure to alternative views could reduce users' likelihood of getting into an echo chamber and becoming further polarized.

This study has some limitations which can be addressed in future research. One of the limitations is that since we conducted our study on various news reports published in the key Indian news media outlets, our findings are restricted to the entertainment domain articles, particularly controversies related to Bollywood personalities. It is possible that the groupings of the media houses, based on their biases, that we get in the entertainment domain remain similar or may change when we conduct a similar experiment on other disciplines like political, social, or economic. The second limitation of this work is that the methodology used to do the sentiment analysis and arrive at the media bias is not validated against any alternative methods. The third limitation is that the dataset we have used is relatively smaller in size. The study could be extended to include more news items and controversies in the entertainment domain and not just restricted to Bollywood.

Moreover, in future, this study could be extended to detect fake news reporting among the group of media houses displaying a similar bias. This fake news identification coupled with the extent of bias shown by the media outlets could provide interesting insights around the mechanisms that these outlets use to influence public opinion on the topics that have far-reaching implications on our society.

References

Aizawa A (2003) An information-theoretic perspective of tf–idf measures. Inf Process Manag 39(1):45–65

Alberoni F (2007) The powerless 'elite': theory and sociological research on the phenomenon of the stars. In: Stardom and celebrity: a reader, pp 65–77

Arceneaux K, Johnson M, Cryderman J (2013) Communication, persuasion, and the conditioning value of selective exposure: like minds may unite and divide but they mostly tune out. Polit Commun 30(2):213–231

Archer A, Cawston A, Matheson B, Geuskens M (2020) Celebrity, democracy, and epistemic power. Persp Polit 18(1):27–42

Bailey AA (2007) Public information and consumer skepticism effects on celebrity endorsements: studies among young consumers. J Mark Commun 13(2):85–107

Ballantyne N (2019) Epistemic trespassing. Mind 128(510):367–395

Baron DP (2005) Persistent media bias. J Public Econ 90:1–36

Bhardwaj A, Qureshi I, Konrad AM, Lee SH (2016) A two-wave study of self-monitoring personality, social network churn, and in-degree centrality in close friendship and general socializing networks. Group Org Manag 41(4):526–559

Chiang C-F, Knight B (2011) Media bias and influence: evidence from newspaper endorsements. Rev Econ Stud 78(3):795–820

D'Alessio D, Allen M (2000) Media bias in presidential elections: a meta-analysis. J Commun 50:133–156

Das M, Singh P, Mazumdar A (2021) Investigating dynamics of polarization of Youtube true and fake news channels. In: Qureshi I, Bhatt B, Gupta S, Tiwari AA (eds) Causes and symptoms of socio-cultural polarization: role of information and communication technologies. Springer

De Vreese CH (2005) News framing: theory and typology. Inf Design J Doc Design 13(1)
Ding X, Liu B, Yu PS (2008) A holistic lexicon-based approach to opinion mining. In: Proceedings of the 2008 international conference on web search and data mining, pp 231–240
Ellman M, Germano F (2009) What do papers sell? A model of advertising and media bias. Econ J 119(537):680–704
Eveland Jr WP, Shah D (2003) The impact of individual and interpersonal factors on perceived news media bias. Polit Psychol 24(1)
Fard AE, Verma T (2021) A comprehensive review on countering rumours in the age of online social media platforms. In: Qureshi I, Bhatt B, Gupta S, Tiwari AA (eds) Causes and symptoms of socio-cultural polarization: role of information and communication technologies. Springer
Fong CPS, Wyer RS Jr (2012) Consumers' reactions to a celebrity endorser scandal. Psychol Mark 29(11):885–896
Freed GL, Clark SJ, Butchart AT, Singer DC, Davis MM (2011) Sources and perceived credibility of vaccine-safety information for parents. Pediatr Suppl 1:107–112
Furedi F (2010) Celebrity culture. Society 47:493–497
Garthwaite C, Moore TJ (2012) Can celebrity endorsements affect political outcomes? Evidence from the 2008 US Democratic Presidential Primary. J Law Econ Organiz 29(2):355–384
Gentzkow M, Shapiro JM (2006) Media bias and reputation. J Polit Econ 114(2)
Groseclose T, Milyo J (2005) A measure of media bias. Q J Econ 120
Gupta S, Kumar P, Bhasker B (2016) A rough connectedness algorithm for mining communities in complex networks. In International Conference on Big Data Analytics and Knowledge Discovery. Springer, Cham, pp 34–48, September
Gupta S, Kumar S, Kumar P (2016) Evaluating the predictive power of an ensemble model for economic success of Indian movies. J Predict Markets 10(1)
Gupta S, Kumar P (2020) An overlapping community detection algorithm based on rough clustering of links. Data Knowl Eng 125:101777
Gupta S, Deodhar S (2021) Understanding digitally enabled complex networks: a plural granulation based hybrid community detection approach. Inf Technol People
Gupta S, Kumar P (2021) A constrained agglomerative clustering approach for unipartite and bipartite networks with application to credit networks. Inf Sci 557:332–354
Gupta S, Tiwari AA (2021) A design-based pedagogical framework for developing computational thinking skills. J Decis Syst:1–18
Hamborg F, Meuschke N, Aizawa A, Gipp B (2017) Identification and analysis of media bias in news articles. Humboldt-Universität zu Berlin
Hamborg F, Donnay K, Gipp B (2018) Automated identification of media bias in news articles: an interdisciplinary literature review. Int J Digit Libr 20:391–415
Hartigan JA, Wong MA (1979) AK-means clustering algorithm. J R Stat Soc: Ser C: Appl Stat 28(1):100–108
Jaikumar P (2003) Bollywood spectaculars. World Literature Today 77(3/4):24–29
Kader FA, Gundala U (2021) Impact of ICT on literary censorship: a study of selected controversial texts in contemporary India. In: Qureshi I, Bhatt B, Gupta S, Tiwari AA (eds) Causes and symptoms of socio-cultural polarization: role of information and communication technologies. Springer
Kahneman D, Tversky A (1984) Choices, values, and frames. Am Psychol 39(4):341–350
Keane J (1992) Democracy and the media—without foundations. Polit Stud 40(1_suppl):116–129
Koku PS (1995) On bizarreness in the entertainment industry. J Serv Mark 9(4):19–30
Koordeman R, Kuntsche E, Anschutz DJ, van Baaren RB, Engels RCME (2011) Do we act upon what we see? Direct effects of alcohol cues in movies on young adults' alcohol drinking. Alcohol Alcohol 46(4):393–398
Kumar P, Gupta S, Bhasker B (2017) An upper approximation based community detection algorithm for complex networks. Decis Support Syst 96:103–118
Liu B (2012) Sentiment analysis and opinion mining. Synth Lectures Human Lang Technol 5(1):1–167

Lunardo R, Livat F, Gergaud O (2015) Celebrities as human brands: an investigation of the effects of personality and time on celebrities' appeal. J Mark Manag 31(5–6):685–712
Marwick A, Lewis R (2017) Media manipulation and disinformation online. Data & Society Research Institute, New York
McCutcheon LE, Lange R, Houran J (2002) Conceptualization and measurement of celebrity worship. Br J Psychol 93:67–87
Meyer DS, Gamson J (1995) The challenge of cultural elites: celebrities and social movements. Sociol Inq 65(2):181–206
Milligan GW, Cooper MC (1988) A study of standardization of variables in cluster analysis. J Classif 5(2):181–204
Monaco J (1978) Celebrity: the media as image makers. Dell Publishers, New York
Mullainathan S, Shleifer A (2005) The market for news. Am Econ Rev 95(4):1031–1053
Newman N, Fletcher R, Levy D, Nielsen RK (2015) The Reuters Institute digital news report 2016. Reuters Institute for the Study of Journalism
Ogunsiji AS (2012) The impact of celebrity endorsement on strategic brand management. Int J Bus Soc Sci 3(6):141–145
Park S, Lee J, Ryu S, Hahn KS (2015) The network of celebrity politics: political implications of celebrity following on Twitter. Ann Am Acad Polit Social Sci 659(1):246–258
Pornpitakpan C (2008) The effect of celebrity endorsers' perceived credibility on product purchase intention. J Int Consum Mark 16(2):55–74
Qayyum A, Gilani Z, Latif S, Qadir J (2018) Exploring media bias and toxicity in South Asian Political discourse. In: 2018 12th international conference on open source systems and technologies (ICOSST), pp 1–8, IEEE
Qureshi I, Fang Y, Haggerty N, Compeau DR, Zhang X (2018) IT-mediated social interactions and knowledge sharing: role of competence-based trust and background heterogeneity. Inf Syst J 28(5):929–955
Qureshi I, Bhatt B, Gupta S, Tiwari AA (2020) Call for papers: causes, symptoms and consequences of social media induced polarization (SMIP). Inf Syst J
Qureshi I, Bhatt B, Gupta S, Tiwari AA (2021) Introduction to the role of information and communication Technologies in Polarization. In: Qureshi I, Bhatt B, Gupta S, Tiwari AA (eds) Causes and symptoms of socio-cultural polarization: role of information and communication technologies. Springer
Rein IJ, Kotler P, Soller MR (1997) High visibility: the making and marketing of professionals into celebrities. NTC Publishing Group, Lincolnwood
Ribeiro FN, Henrique L, Benevenuto F, Chakraborty A, Kulshrestha J, Babaei M, Gummadi KP (2018). Media bias monitor: quantifying biases of social media news outlets at large-scale. In: Proceedings of the twelfth international AAAI conference on web and social media (ICWSM 2018)
Shoemaker PJ, Vos TP, Reese SD (2009) Journalists as gatekeepers. In: The handbook of journalism studies
Stassen W (2010) Your news in 140 characters: exploring the role of social media in journalism. Glob Media J Afr Ed 4(1)
Steinley D (2006) K-means clustering: a half-century synthesis. Br J Math Stat Psychol 59:1–34
Sunstein CR (2002) The law of group polarization. J Polit Philos 10(2):175–195
Vallone RP, Ross L, Lepper MR (1985) The hostile media phenomenon: biased perceptions and perception of media bias in coverage of the Beirut massacre. J Pers Soc Psychol 49:577–585
Vukov JM, Rempala K, Klug M, Hornewer M (2020) From epistemic trespassing to transdisciplinary cooperation: the role of expertise in the identification of usual care. Am J Bioeth 20(1):52–54
Webster F (2006) Theories of the information society. Taylor and Francis Group, Routledge
Williams A (1975) Unbiased study of television news bias. J Commun 25(4):190–199

Wojcieszak M, Garrett RK (2018) Social identity, selective exposure, and affective polarization: how priming national identity shapes attitudes toward immigrants via news selection. Hum Commun Res 44(3):247–273

Wood M, Corbett J, Flinders M (2016) Just like us: everyday celebrity politicians and the pursuit of popularity in an age of anti-politics. Br J Polit Int Rel 18(3)

Zaller J (1992) The nature and origins of mass opinion. Cambridge University Press, Cambridge

Part IV
Consequences and Outcomes of Polarization: Trends and Future Research Directions

Polarisation in Information Ethics: The Debates Between Privacy and Common Goods in the Chinese Social Credit System

Zhiwen Zheng and Babita Bhatt

Abstract This paper explores polarisation in information ethics through the case study of China's Social Credit System (SCS), a data-powered, national reputation system which that aims to monitor, assess, and shape the behaviour of Chinese citizens and enterprises. Information ethics provides a normative framework to evaluate the role of technology in the development of a good society. However, the advent of big data has created polarisation on the ethical principles that should guide the storage, monitoring and tracking of big data. We situate this polarised debate in two ethical approaches: the common good approach and the individual liberty approach and apply the insights from these two approaches to SCS. The common good perspective views SCS as an important approach for cultivating good citizenship behaviour and promoting common good such as social stability and good governance. In contrast, the individual liberty perspective views SCS as a hindrance to individual autonomy and liberties. We discuss the implications of these findings using the 'contextual integrity' framework developed by Nissenbaum (Wash Law Rev 119(121):154–155, 2004; Privacy in context: technology, policy, and the integrity of social life. Stanford University Press, 2009) and suggest avenues for future research.

Keywords Information ethics · Polarization · Privacy · Common good · Big data

1 Introduction

Big data is a term commonly used for the large size and complexity of digital data—both structured and unstructured—that is generated from a variety of sources such as people, machines, or sensors (Kim et al. 2014). The creation and consumption of data continue to grow with 2.5 quintillion bytes of data added each day (Zhu et

Z. Zheng (✉) · B. Bhatt
Australian National University, Canberra, Australia
e-mail: zhiwen.zheng@anu.edu.au; babita.bhatt@anu.edu.au

I. Qureshi et al. (eds.), *Causes and Symptoms of Socio-Cultural Polarization*,
https://doi.org/10.1007/978-981-16-5268-4_10

al. 2015). Enabled in part by the proliferation of cheap sensors and data-storing devices, ICT based big data analytics has created an unprecedented opportunity to capture and process real-time information cost-effectively (Hsu et al. 2017). Evidence suggests that businesses and governments can derive value from this massive amounts of information and transform how they make decisions, track performance and measure outcomes. For example, in a survey on the business practices and information technology investments of 179 large publicly traded firms, Brynjolfsson et al. (2011) find that firms that adopt data-driven decision making can have a 5–6% increase in output and productivity. Similarly, McKinsey estimates that the use of big data analytics by EU European Union can reduce administrative costs by 15–20% and create the equivalent of at least US$223–446 billion in the new value (Manyika et al. 2011). Furthermore, many academic articles and policy reports have also proposed how government can use big data to address common good such as financial inclusion, public safety and fairness (Andrejevic and Gates 2014; Hatton 2015).

However, the increasing economic and political significance of big data has created a fear of surveillance capitalism (Zuboff 2015, 2019) and has raised ethical concerns around data privacy and individual liberties (Haggerty and Ericson 2000; Van-Dijck 2014). Researchers show that increasing datafication of social lives can promote extensive social surveillance and supervision (King et al. 2014; Schneier 2015), and lead to privacy intrusion (Zeng 2016; Schneider 2018). For example, in a survey conducted by Auxier and Rainie (2019), the majority of Americans have expressed concern about how much data is collected about them by the companies (79%) and the government (64%). Similarly, civil rights groups have also highlighted the worrying trend of the increasing surveillance power of the state. According to Silkie Carlo, senior advocacy officer with Liberty, a UK-based human rights watchdog group, *"under the guise of counter-terrorism, the state has acquired totalitarian-style surveillance powers and this is the most intrusive system of any democracy in history"*. In addition to these concerns for privacy and liberties, various reports have also warned how big data can perpetuate, exacerbate, or mask harmful discrimination (Munoz et al. 2016). For example, in various countries, a system technology used for profiling and scoring systems has been found to discriminate against minority groups or people with lower incomes (O'Neil 2016).

These empirical discussions and debates around the intention and the use of big data have revived an old age debate in political philosophy. At the heart of this debate lies the ethical concern about the nature of society and whether progress can be made by scarifying for the common good or protecting individual liberty and freedom. Nowhere is this debate is as polarised as in the context of the social credit system (SCS) that is being implemented by the government of China.

The SCS is a data-powered, national reputation system that aims to monitor, assess, and shape the behaviour of Chinese citizens and enterprises. Since the release of *the Planning Outline for the Construction of a Social Credit System* by the government of China in 2014, many cities and provinces have been trailing their own version to implement the project (Ahmed 2017b). The first stage of SCS is expected to be completed by the end of 2020, and there are polar opposite views from different groups on its impact on Chinese society. In this paper, we examine SCS as an institution to understand the polarised debates around information ethics. We first define information ethics and discuss two theoretical approaches: the ethical approach to common good and ethical approach to individual liberty. We then introduce the SCS and analyse the polarised perspectives on the intentions and outcome of implementing SCS. Through a systematic investigation of the polarisation around the SCS, our research contributes to the emerging field of information ethics and provides a conceptual and empirical understanding of data surveillance and data privacy.

2 Polarisation and Information Ethics

In a broader sense, information ethics is concerned with the ethical issues that are raised by Information Technology (Floridi 2008). Although the initial conceptualisation of information ethics emerged from an increasing interest in computer ethics and privacy issues, information technology has widened its scope and objectives. Now, it refers to the role that technology can play in the development of a good society and provide a normative framework for guiding decisions (Turilli and Floridi 2009).

Polarisation is usually understood as "*the tendency of social groups to divide into progressively more extreme factions, each of which regards other groups to be wrong*" (Arvan 2019, p. 87). In that sense, polarisation is much different from mere differences in opinions. Instead, a polarised perspective shows an intense commitment to an ideology, a culture or a political system by demonising and negating 'others' as morally inferior.

Polarisation in the context of information ethics implies extreme positions on the role that technology plays in the development of a good society. While one approach views common good as the foundation of a good society, another views individual rights and liberty as the fundamental moral value when evaluating the ethical decision (Qureshi et al. 2021). In the political philosophy, these two approaches are known as: the ethical approach to the common good and the ethical approach to individual liberty.

2.1 The Ethical Approach to the Common Good

This approach is concerned with finding the moral foundation of a good society (Etzioni 2009). It is based on the premise that society is not composed of atomised individuals living in isolation from each other. Instead, individuals are deeply embedded in their social and political context and social relationships, which gives the meaning to the common good (Mele 2009). Common good refer to goods that are achieved by being a member of a political community (through citizenship), and by actively participating in political discussions, public service, and voluntary actions (Tosun et al. 2016; Walzer 1983). Some examples of common good include public safety, peace and harmony and social stability (Etzioni 2004; Morrison 2012; Sandel 1982). The notion of the common good is a consistent theme in Western and Eastern political philosophy, and has been found in the work of Aristotle, and Confucianism.

According to Aristotle, humans are political by nature, and it is through participating in a political community that they actualise the common good of community safety (Sandel 2005). Confucianism views the existence of common good depend upon the existence of virtuous citizens (Romar 2002) and suggests that by practising virtue ethics, the citizens can promote the common good. However, maintaining and promoting the common good often clashes with individual liberalities (Etzioni 1996; Sandel 2005; Walzer 1990).

2.2 *The Ethical Approach to Individual Liberty*

Protection of individual rights and liberty are the key foundation of liberal democracy (Sandel 2005). The ethics of individual freedom that was developed by Kant (1991) and Rawls (1971) Presupposes individual liberty and autonomy as the foundation of ethical actions. According to Walzer (1983), this perspective believes that society is composed of independent individuals who pursue their interests without interference from others. Liberal thinkers such as Locke (1988) and Mill (2015) place a high value on individual freedom and rights (Becker 2019). They advocated that progress is only possible if individuals are left free to pursue their own personal goals. Consequently, it suggests that policies should be based on the aggregation of individual choices as any other form of authority can diminish individual liberty (Mill 2015). This fear of diminishing liberty often results in a situation where convincing people to sacrifice some of their freedom for 'the common good' becomes difficult (Etzioni 2004).

Privacy is closely interlinked to the notion of autonomy and is the underlying idea of individual freedom (Becker 2019). A violation of privacy can be described as a way of losing control over (or access to) one's personal sphere (Pagallo and Durante 2009). This perspective is exemplified in the recent statements made by Edward Snowden. According to Edward Snowden, "*Because privacy isn't about something to hide. Privacy is about something to protect. That's who you are. That's what you believe in. Privacy is the right to a self*. . . . . *It's why we call it private property. Without privacy, you don't have anything for yourself*" (*quoted in* Schrodt 2016).

These discussions on the importance of privacy and the common good have intensified in the second half of the twentieth century, as patterns of living in societies became more and more individualistic (Becker 2019). However, there are societies that are collectivists and are based on the idea that it is possible to sacrifice individual liberty for the sake of common good (Romar 2002). Generally, the two philosophical positions discussed above are concerned with the notion of an ideal society and provide a guideline to achieve that ideal society. These perspectives also challenge us to find a balance between seeing ourselves as members of the community while respecting and valuing individuals' freedom to pursue their own goals (Pagallo and Durante 2009). In the next section, we apply these theoretical discussions to the social credit system in China.

3 Social Credit System (SCS) in China

The SCS can be divided into the national social credit system and the commercial social credit system. The national SCS is defined as a government-led project for the enhancement of socio-economic creditworthiness by monitoring and regulating citizens' and organisations' conduct (Creemers 2018; Yew 2018). The objective of SCS is to build socio-economic trustworthiness by improving the transparency of legal administration and professional conduct (Yang 2009). There are two key elements of the national SCS: the social credit scores, and red list[1] or blacklist[2] (Statista 2016).

First, the social credit score is an objective index of the credit of an individual or an organisation. To precisely match the credit scores with citizens or businesses, two categories of information are stored in the SCS: the identity information (a unique ID number representing every person and each organisation); and their credit records (automatically created by government bureaus) (Ahmed 2017b; Creemers 2018). More than 75% of credit information is openly displayed to the public and is used for reshaping and encouraging the trustworthy behaviour of people or organisations (Chin and Wong 2016; Hawkins 2017).

Second, the social credit score is an independent index of the incentive mechanism. It provides a quantitative standard for the records of a reward or punishment mechanism by using red-list or blacklist. These lists are the judicial supplement of the SCS. They are used to reward model citizens or punish offenders using administrative and financial mechanisms (Mozur 2019). The Green Channel is used to reward people who are on the red list. This list incentivises the optimisation of administrative services and the decrease of transaction costs. In comparison, if an individual or an organisation cannot meet the minimum credit score, it implies a credibility deficit. These organisations or individuals will be put on the blacklist (Yang 2009; Creemers 2018) and will be penalised (Liang et al. 2018) through various mechanisms such as revoking the right to purchase luxury products (Mistreanu 2018; Creemers 2018).

---

[1] The red list include organizations and individuals with high social credit scores.

[2] Blacklists include two types of lists: (a) the credit blacklist and (b) the dishonest blacklist. It include individuals and organizations with low social credit score.

The national SCS collaborates with the ICT sectors to monitor individual behaviour offline and online (Ahmed 2017b; Cadell and Zhang 2017; Ohlberg et al. 2017). Since 2010, over 500 cities in China have collaborated with ICT businesses to install more than 20 million street cameras, aiming to develop public services and enhance sincere conduct through facial recognition (Meissner 2017). The street cameras providing big data promote top-down surveillance, a predictive-analytic technique to analyse seemingly unrelated data to discover unexpected correlations (Ahmed 2017b).

Compared to the national SCS, the private SCS (private SCS equal to commercial SCS in this paper), led by China's eight technology companies, aims to build sincerity and trust in the economic transactions. It has similar functions to the Fair Isaac Corporation (FICO) that is commonly used for credit score ranking in the United States (Ahmed 2017a). This project is voluntary with less harsh punishments for untruthful behaviours (Kostka 2019) because most of the punishments and rewards of the commercial SCS are limited to market restrictions or preferential treatments of the participating businesses (De-Kloet et al. 2019; Woetzel et al. 2017).

Sesame Credit is a representative of the commercial SCS and the most commonly mentioned form of the private scoring ranking system (Meissner 2017) as well as the most used commercial credit ranking system in China (Kostka 2019). The Sesame Credit is a product of Ant Financial within the Alibaba group, which provides a massive amount of merchant and online consumer data for evaluating customer's credits (Ma 2019). Normally, the data is retrieved from people's transaction histories on the online sales platforms (Alibaba's Taobao), and the records of spending through a phone-based payment system (Alibaba's Alipay) (Pentland 2014). Taobao is the biggest online shopping platform and Alipay is the most widely used phone-based payment system in China (Meissner 2017). Sesame Credit scores are updated once a month, associating a traditional credit ranking system with a commercial loyalty scheme (Diab 2017). It distributes a credit score between 350 and 950 points for each customer, which is founded upon five criteria, including customers' credit history (35%), behavioural trends on finances (25%), abilities to honour agreements (20%), customers' personal information (15%), and their social relationships (5%) (Diab 2017). The systematic ranking system ensures the reliability of the personal credit that can be used by the microfinance institutions to lend money to people, especially to those who do not have official credit records in the banking system.

However, the increasing economic and political significance of big data has created a fear of surveillance capitalism (Zuboff 2015, 2019) and has raised ethical concern around data privacy and individual liberties (Haggerty and Ericson 2000). First, with the expansion of functions of Sesame Credit, people are becoming more concerned about the extent of cooperation between the commercial SCS and the national SCS (Ahmed 2017a). Because of perceived fading separations between governmental and commercial SCSs, there is increasing concern about individual privacy and the potential for its misuse by the Chinese government (Creemers 2018). For instance, since 2017, 381 cities have cancelled deposits in public services departments such as healthcare and social housing if a citizen has high Sesame

Credit scores. It means a high credit score in Commercial SCS enables its owner to have the rights to use green channels which are provided by national SCS with convenient services and reduced market transaction costs (Creemers 2018). Meanwhile, Alibaba Taobao platform does not allow people on the blacklist to have luxury purchases, implying that there is data sharing between the national SCS and the commercial SCS to penalise people in the blacklist (Hatton 2015; Ohlberg et al. 2017; Vanderklippe 2018).

According to the government document, the SCS is being implemented to collect and analyse data on 1.4 billion Chinese citizens and millions of organisations to promote honesty in "government affairs", "judicial credibility", "societal truthfulness", and "commercial integrity" (State Council 2014). The national SCS was unveiled in 2014, and some pieces of the system are already in place. By 2018, 42 pilots government-led SCS pilots had been established, and 12 model cities out of these 48 pilots were selected to illustrate the diversity of credit trials depending on their own situations (De-Kloet et al. 2019). The first example is Shanghai city, which developed the Credit Plus project for evaluating the quality of the technical infrastructure and security arrangements of the ICT industry to encourage local companies to make public credit commitments (Hoffman 2017). The second example is Yiwu city that is the Chinese leading trading city for manufactured products. This city had integrated credit ranking with finance, market supervision, and foreign trade to solve the problem of commercial fraud (Ohlberg et al. 2017). The third example is the Weihai city, providing an efficient path for the improvement of honest conduct. Its local SCS allows citizens to have the initiative in producing unambiguous lists of reward and punishment schemes (Creemers 2018). In short, these cities have taken diverse schemes toward the implementation of local-governments-led SCS, comprising the establishment of red-lists and blacklists in crucial areas and the construction of the information-sharing platform to contribute data-sharing with other national SCS platforms (Kostka 2019).

The social credit score of the population is already being used to make certain decisions. A report by the National Public Credit Information Centre shows that by the end of 2018, approximately 17.45 million "discredited" people were blocked from buying plane tickets by Chinese courts and roughly 5.45 million people were prevented from buying tickets on high-speed trains (Kuo 2019; Smith 2019). Additionally, over 3.59 million Chinese enterprises were added to the blacklist, which excludes them from series of benefits and activities such as receiving financial subsidies; bidding on projects, accessing securities markets, taking part in land auctions and issuing corporate bonds (Huifeng 2019). The Chinese Executive Information Disclosure Network (n.d.) shows that as of July 5th, 2019, approximately 19.3 million people were restricted from air travel because of their lower social credit score. As SCS is an emerging digital system that provides an overall governance framework for 'right and wrong behaviour', its significance in guiding and controlling business and society has been widely debated.

4 Methodology

The SCS provides an exemplary context to understand polarisation around the key principles of information ethics (i.e. the common good vs privacy) and an in-depth understanding of this emerging context can contribute to the theoretical and practical insights on polarisation. In particular, the narratives surrounding the SCS are useful in analysing the key debate in information ethics: what moral principles should guide the implementation and the use of big data projects. Further, the highly polarised nature of social media also helped in understanding the key principles around which the positions of actors differ.

Since the emergence of the SCS, it has become a polarised phenomenon and has been extensively reported on media. To understand the SCS within a broader framework of information ethics, we extracted data from several social media sources. We searched various media articles and reports published from 2018 to 2020, using the following keywords: social credit system, polarisation, common good, freedom, privacy, safety, national security. We retrieved a total of 280 articles. We read through each article and quote and, based on the relevance of the quote to the SCS debate, identified 75 quotes that were usable for this study. Following Riaz et al. (2011), we used quotes as the primary unit of analysis because they provided us with specific statements on the intention, use and implication of SCS.

Our data analysis included three steps: In the first step, we organised quotes based on actors' statements and analysed the content of the quotes to identify first-order codes. In the second step, we merged the first order codes into second-order codes using three criteria: intention, use and implication of SCS. For example, quotes discussing the purpose of the SCS were combined under the second-order theme labelled as intention. In the third step, we looked into the extant literature on the ethical approach to information ethics and the SCS to organise our data. In the next section, we discuss the findings from this analysis.

5 Findings

Our research shows polarisation on the intention and outcome of SCS, which has its roots in the two ethical approaches discussed earlier. On the one side of the spectrum are those who support SCS for promoting common good such as public security, good governance and social fairness. On the other side of the spectrum are those who view SCS as a violation of privacy and civil liberalities. We elaborate on these perspectives in the following paragraphs.

5.1 SCS Promotes Common Good

The analysis of different quotes shows that the SCS promotes common good through three ways: a) SCS builds community harmony and stability [public security], b) SCS creates political trust/good governance c) SCS promotes social fairness.

The supporters of this view see the goal of the SCS is to bridge the trust gap in society through effective monitoring of the government's actions, organisations' activities, and individuals' behaviour. The proponents argue that the Chinese government is using SCS to rebuild the culture of trust, which has been traditionally associated with honesty in China's culture (Smith 2019) and many believe that social trust has deteriorated in recent times. The weakening of the culture of trust has been attributed to increasing competitive behaviour and to a market economy with inadequate controls that have resulted in low quality and fake products, increasing frauds, and outright cheating (Lee 2019).

> *Appeared in the 2000s because the market economy failed to deal with cheaters, fraudsters and promoted fraud and corruption. It came into existences in this changing economic ideology and low-trust environment. It [SCS] is to build up a culture of trust* (Andy Brennan, journalist, China Global Television Network (CGTN) as quoted by Sputnik 2019).

> *Fraud has become ever more common in society, Swindlers have to pay a price* (Lian Weiliang, vice chairman of the National Development and Reform Commission, as quoted in India Today 2016)

> *China's rapid urbanisation associated with the high rate of economic development without any reasonable trust-building measure resulted in Chinese companies losing legitimacy among* Chinese consumers (Wang 2019a).

> *.....Chinese consumers' confidence in companies continued to be eroded due to food-safety scandals such as the milk powder tragedy, and trust between people had fallen so low that no one even dared help an elderly person who had fallen in the road* (Du Liqun, deputy director of the China Credit Research Center, as quoted by Wang 2019b)

> *The term 'credit system' has become popular only in recent years, but the concept of credibility is one the Chinese people have long sought. The goals of our work and the citizens are the same,* (Chu Lidong, deputy director of the Yichun Administration for Industry and Commerce, as quoted by Wang 2019b)

> *.....The root cause for the lack of trust in our society is that the laws are lagging behind the country's development. China must have a credit supervision body and must have a credit law..when law plays its proper role, the government will naturally step back* (Du Liqun, deputy director of the China Credit Research Center, as quoted by Wang 2019a).

This prompted the key figures in the Chinese government to come up with stringent measures to punish individuals and organisations that breach the trust.

> *The effective tool of penalties for acts of bad faith must be fully harnessed. The price to pay for institutional violations, breach of rules and even legal offences now is too low* (Li Keqiang, Premier of China as quoted by Smith 2019).

The Chinese government is using the social credit scores and punishment/ reward schemes to enhance the top-down monitoring and self-supervision of individual and organisational behaviours. The aim is to improve the culture of sincerity.

Supporters of SCS argue that it builds trust in society by monitoring and analysing behaviour through objective indicators (Fourcade and Healy 2017). As the credit score of individuals or organizations is accessible to the public, the fear of 'naming and shaming' further cultivates good behaviour (Hawkins 2017). Therefore, by creating mechanisms to enhance the self-surveillance of personal behaviour, the SCS build trust and improve social safety.

> *We repeatedly remind our customers that using Sesame Credit is voluntary, because Alibaba's data can provide certain kind of proof. It's not 100% accurate, but at least it's one more filter for people to know each other better.* (Zhuan Yirong, Baihe's vice-president, as quoted by Hatton 2015).

Moreover, because the individual and organisational information is aggregated and integrated within and across geographic regions and professional fields by local government, the SCS can enhance self-control and honesty.

> *Without a system, a conman can commit a crime in one place and then do the same thing again in another place. But a credit system puts people's past history on the record. It'll build a better and fairer society* (Wen Quan, blogger, as quoted by Hatton 2015).

Furthermore, the red-list acts as an incentive scheme, and the blacklist acts as a deterrent (Cadell and Zhang 2017). The rewards and punishments have administrative and financial sides, and therefore affect the convenience of individual life and organisational decisions (Mozur 2019). For example, if a business is included on the blacklist, the company and its owner will suffer penalties (such as difficulty in getting project approval, lower credit rating, restriction on buying luxury products), until obligations are fulfilled or debts are paid (Mistreanu 2018).

> *[SCS] won't be Orwellian ... the range of the system must be meticulously restricted ... it should only stay effective in people's economic life and part of their social life where laws and principles are clearly defined and widely recognised* (Zhun 2016).

Therefore, the aims and implementation schemes of the SCSs are to shape and reshape the citizens' behaviours and businesses' activities towards honesty and integrity (Ahmed 2018; Vanderklippe 2018) and apply incentive schemes linked to these scores (Kostka 2019; Chin and Wong 2016). The use of social credit scores and red/blacklist is seen crucial in promoting the top-down supervision and self-supervision (Zhang and Zhang 2016), which is used to build community harmony and stability.

Supporters of SCS suggest that it can create political trust and good governance. The governance encompasses the relationship among various participants in determining the direction and performance of organisations (Carcello 2009). Evidence from 2008 to 2012 showed a growing resentment among Chinese people over corruption. Some forms of corruption were harmful to the public interest and government credibility. For example, buying and selling official positions is one of the forms that the Chinese Communist Party is probably very worried about, because at the core of it is to control the personnel. Furthermore, judicial corruption is also a big issue because it will render any decisions as invalid. Finally, financial corruption, such as the use of power to speculate in financial markets (Ouyang

2013), displayed the ability to control capital, especially in a country where private capital is relatively scarce.

As noted by the president Xi Jinping (2012)

> *Our party only has one goal which is to serve the people whole heartedly. [and] "Under the new circumstances, our Party is facing many severe challenges and problems which need to be solved. In particular, we must make great efforts to solve corruption, isolation from the people, formalism, and bureaucratism among some Party officials* (Xi Jinping, as quoted in BBC News 2012).

Since 2012, Xi Jinping has launched an extensive anti-corruption campaign that has expelled more than a million officials. A BBC study has found that under Mr Xi, more than 170 minister-level and vice-minister-level officials have been sacked and many who were accused of corruption, misconduct and violating Party discipline were jailed (BBC News 2017).

In 2014, the SCS was introduced to build good governance.

> *The Social Credit System emphasises strengthening sincerity in government affairs as well as to provide a mechanism to improve government credibility and establish an honest image of an open, fair, and clean government* (The State Council, as cited in Taylor 2019).

> *Many measures introduced as part of the social trust system are intended to curb official corruption, tackle official dereliction and improve efficiency in enforcing court decisions, ... as well as punish unethical behaviours of professionals such as lawyers, doctors and teachers* (Song 2019).

SCS can promote social fairness by reducing the risk in the transaction (Lyon 2014).

> *The system [SCS] will be set up with an eye toward monitoring the credit records of government agencies, business, social entities, and individuals to ensure civil behaviour to be rule-based across Chinese society* (Taylor 2019).

> *"It (Zhima Credit) is very convenient," "We booked a hotel last night using Sesame Credit and we didn't need to leave a cash deposit"* (Anonymous Female interviewee, as quoted by Hatton 2015).

For these reasons, the supporters of SCS argue that SCS is widely accepted by Chinese citizens. In a recent survey of 2209 people, over 80% of participants strongly supported SCS, and only 1% of participants either strongly or moderately disapprove it (Kostka and Antoine 2019). Further, most respondents believe that the value and benefits drawn from SCS lie in its potential to foster trustworthiness in society (Yew 2018), and 'quality of life' (Kostka 2019).

To summarise the Promotor of the SCS argues that it has a significant implication for the fast-growing economy sector in China. The wider acceptance of the SCS shows citizens's willingness to give up their privacy in exchange for the common good suchs as safety and stability (Kostka 2019; Raghunath 2020)

5.2 SCS Curtail Individual Liberties

Not everyone shares the rosy picture about SCS. Although Chinese people have widely accepted the SCS, it has triggered disagreement and debate on privacy and liberties. Many political figures, academics, and media pundits have labelled it as Big Brother, an Orwellian notion of heightened surveillance and monitoring of citizens, and argue that SCS reveals China's authoritarian streak. SCS is analysed as an integrated tool for datafication, data-driven authoritarianism, and dataveillance. The authoritarianism shows totalitarian tendencies and noticeable privacy infringement by integrating information and technology to develop citizen surveillance (Lee 2018). The head of digital research at Trivium China (a Beijing-based China policy analysis firm) Kendra Schaefer highlighted the purpose of SCS by saying that

> *The real fear of the system isn't the data being taken, but the fear is whether or not the data is being applied by a fair hand* (Kendra Schaefer, the head of digital research at Trivium China , as quoted by Xu 2019).

Critics argue that the SCS promotes totalitarian tendency and curtail individual liberties in three ways: (a) the SCS undermines political freedoms, (b) the SCS undermines individual privacy and autonomy, (c) the SCS enhances social sorting (d) the SCS enhances social sorting.

SCS as a data-driven supervision tool undermines individual privacy and autonomy with an increasing number of privacy infringements. The Chinese government simultaneously has three roles: an enforcer, an evaluator, and a participator in the Social Credit System (Ahmed 2017b). As a result, there is no restriction on the governments to retrieve and use data (Creemers 2017). Hence, the datafication and dataveillance would intensify the digital surveillance of society (Schneier 2015) that ultimately will have negative impacts on privacy protection (Andrejevic and Gates 2014), especially, in the context of limited privacy protection in China.

> *On the outside this system may seem like a way to promote trust and credit worthiness and is supposed to be progressive, but in an authoritarian state, there is no limit to what they have access to, and there is no law to protect those that are harmed* (Hu Jia, Chinese activist, as quoted by Clover 2016).

According to Liu Hu, a Chinese journalist,

> *We need to be cautious on the establishment of [the] social credit system. It is possible it could be used to control the public* (Liu Hu, as quoted by Smith 2019).

Liu Hu was a high-profile target in the early stages of the social credit system for calling out the government on corruption. He was blacklisted and was unable to buy a plane ticket for defaming the government (Smith 2019). SCS has already been used as a tool to force international firms to adopt Chinese values on politically sensitive issues (Zheng 2019).

> *Failure to rectify the errors will be recorded in the airlines' corporate social credit records as 'severely untrustworthy behaviour'* (Xu 2019).

Meanwhile, the way of data collection and analysis will enhance the surveillance capabilities of the SCS.

> *Think about it: personal information would be floating around all over the place, and the individual would be uninformed about any of it, ...wouldn't that be quite scary?* (Wang Xiaolei, deputy director of the People's Bank of China credit rating centre, as quoted by Clover 2016).

With the advancement of the information and communication technology (ICT), the SCS can enhance the power of data owners (Mistreanu 2018; Soo 2018) and undermine individual privacy and autonomy. Based on the governmental control over data in the SCS, the project may be used as a cybernetic mechanism guided by big data (Boyd and Crawford 2012; Creemers 2018). The SCS supervising both online and offline behaviours of citizens cooperates with internet governance (Creemers 2017) and punishments schemes (Hatton 2015; Hoffman 2017), enabling political consensus between citizens and the government to achieve the purpose of authoritarianism (Schneier 2015). Meanwhile, the policy of internet governance permits the Chinese government to build a technologically advanced online censorship system (Qiang 2011; Vanderklippe 2018) to visit personal information for making sure the same political standpoints between citizens and local and central governments (King et al. 2014).

> *I think there is a sense in [the Chinese] government that all this data is being generated on people's mobile phones ... and smart watches and the government thinks 'Hey, I want some of that* (Rogier Creemers, lecturer on Chinese politics at Oxford university, as quoted by Clover 2016).

As noted by Clover (2016),

> *China's internet is fast becoming a laboratory where big data meets big brother, and where the march of technology is combined with profit-driven private companies, authoritarian politics and weak civil liberties is creating a toxic cocktail.*

The emergence of big data through datafication combines the physical identification with the digital surveillance thus increasing the surveillance ability of the Social Credit System compare to the traditional direct supervision (Dencik et al. 2016). Based on this combination, the issue of privacy intrusion is expected to increase, as the invasion of privacy can help the government to control the public ideology consisting of political activities (Galič et al. 2017).

> *By 2020, China's rulers aim to implement an Orwellian system premised on controlling virtually every facet of human life—the so-called 'social credit score'. In the words of that program's official blueprint, it will 'allow the trustworthy to roam everywhere under heaven while making it hard for the discredited to take a single step.'* (Mike Pence, 48th vice-president of United State, as quoted in Matsakis 2019).

The opaque algorithms of the SCS can lead to social sorting, increase the wealth gap and social prejudice. SCS is criticised as a state-wide surveillance apparatus that categorises citizens in a way that could cause discrimination and violate their human rights. The score-gathering algorithms of the SCS are secrets, prohibiting any forms of testing and reviewing to determine how credit scores work (Ahmed 2017a). The algorithm is a type of mathematical model which can automatically calculate social credit scores (Lyon 2014). If the model is opaque, incontestable, and unfettered, it is without any limitation of the algorithmic accountability even if some bias may exist in the value of software designer or programmer (O'Neil 2016; Ananny and Crawford 2016).

> *In theory, there are protections on citizens' data, but in practice there are no controls about how this data may be used... [The policy is] 'a very worrying development [and]...... The plans are certainly comprehensive: Everything from purchasing patterns to search engine histories could be used to decide whether a person is the "trust-breaking" or "trust-keeping" sort.* (Maya Wang, researcher in Human Rights Watch, as quoted by Hawkins 2017).

To summarise, critics are concerned that SCS may create totalitarian tendencies and may breach individuals' privacy under the garb of promoting trust and honesty in the society (Taylor 2019).

6 Discussion and Conclusion

In this paper, we used the media reports on the social credit system and analysed the polarised debates through the framework of information ethics. We use two theoretical approaches in the information ethics, the common good approach and the individual liberty approach to understand the extreme opinions about the intention, use and implication of social credit system. We demonstrated that the supporters of SCS view it as a mechanism to promote social safety, good governance and fairness, while the detractors view it as a tool to enhance government power and a threat to individual liberty and privacy.

By incorporating the framework of information ethics, we provide a fresh perspective to conceptualise polarisation. While social-media-induced polarisation is gaining scholarly attention (Qureshi et al. 2020), there is limited research that explores the link between information ethics and polarisation. Our view is that this link will become increasingly important as digital technology becomes pervasive in the personal, organisational and societal spheres (Qureshi et al. 2018a). We argue for looking at integrative approaches to find a balance between these increasingly polarised ethical values.

In this context, we find the contextual integrity framework advanced by Helen Nissenbaum (2004, 2009) is worth exploring. The contextual integrity framework develops a socially embedded concept of privacy (Becker 2019) and provides guidelines on how data should be collected, used and protected in the digital age (Pagallo and Durante 2009)

The core argument of contextual integrity is that privacy concerns should not be limited to the loss of control over personal information or restricted to the flow of information (Nissenbaum 2009). Instead, privacy discussion should be concerned with the 'inappropriateness' of the flow of information and should ensure that information flows appropriately. According to Nissenbaum (2004), the 'appropriateness' of such system is not determined by an abstract norm or value but is rooted in the context of social structures that have evolved over time and that shape individuals actions and expectations in social situations.

As noted by Nissenbaum

> *We have a right to privacy, but it is neither a right to control personal information nor a right to have access to this information restricted. Instead, it is a right to live in a world in which our expectations about the flow of personal information are, for the most part, met; expectations that are shaped not only by force of habit and convention but a general confidence in the mutual support these flows accord to key organising principles of social life.* (2009, p. 211).

Therefore, the contextual integrity model suggests that when designing a system or technology, the context of information flow and how it affects the interests and preferences of affected parties are important to take into consideration (Pagallo and Durante 2009). In this perspective, the collection, monitoring and tracking of data are allowed as long as they meet the expectations of that context. Furthermore, the key players in the context have the responsibility to ensure the safety of data (Becker 2019).

Based on this model, we provide some recommendations to the polarised debates on privacy and common good in the context of SCS. As noted in the paper, the SCS as an ICT project collects and manages a large volume of data which has the potential to influence common good such as good governance, stability and fairness, as well as individual autonomy and liberties individual autonomy, and liberties. To find the right balance between the common good and individual rights, the designer and enforcers of SCS should take into consideration the technological element and the human element of the system.

a) The technological element of the system refers to the way data is collected, analysed and transmitted. In the context of SCS, there should be an independent governing body to collect, analyse and monitor SCS to prevent any misuse of individual data for political and profit purposes. As the stated goal of SCS is to promote safety, good governance and stability, an independent governing body might be able to address the concern related to privacy and misuse of data.

In addition, we also suggest a gradual implementation of the project. As norms formation is a long and slow process (Qureshi et al. 2016), the government should slow down the project expansion. It will provide more time to experiment and modified the system based on trial and error.

Furthermore, there should be transparency on the way system work. For example, by creating an independent website to explain exactly how the algorithms function, the governing body can increase the trust in the system.

b) The human element in the model is concerned with the interests and preferences of affected parties. As our case study demonstrated, in the current system, individuals have no control over their SCS score, even though their 'reward' and 'punishment' are closely linked to their assigned scores. Additionally, the current SCS score evaluates individuals based on some unspecified criteria. It also includes the behaviour of individuals' close social networks in deciding the score. To make the system accountable to the users, we suggest there should be some provision for the users' engagement (i.e interactive feedback) so that the system is adaptable to changing norms of information sharing (Qureshi et al. 2018b)

As the SCS is at the early stage of implementation, the practices and normative conceptions are still evolving and as such the "contextual integrity" of the system needs further investigation. For example, future research can explore how the social understanding of privacy in China influences the 'context of the interaction' between different parties in the SCS. Researchers can also trace the implementation process of SCS to explore the normative changes over time and how the system conforms to these norms.

At a theoretical level, it would be interesting to explore how the contextual integrity framework addresses the polarisation resulting from conflicting normative values. Particularly, how to determine which ethical value should prevail given the theoretical ambiguity in defining the 'context' (Becker 2019). Through our research, we provide a stepping stone for future research in this emerging area.

References

Ahmed S (2017a) Cashless Society, cached data: security considerations for a Chinese social credit system. Retrieved from https://citizenlab.ca/2017/01/cashless-society-cached-data-security-considerations-chinese-social-credit-system/

Ahmed S (2017b) Consumer protection oversights in the Chinese social credit system. Digital Credit Observatory. Retrieved from http://www.digitalcreditobservatory.org/consumer-protection-oversights-in-the-chinese-social-credit system.html

Ahmed X (2018) Toward a reputation state: the social credit system project of China. Analysis of Collective Decision-Making eJournal. https://doi.org/10.2139/ssrn.3193577

Ananny M, Crawford K (2016) Seeing without knowing: limitations of the transparency ideal and its application to algorithmic accountability. New Media Soc 20(3):973–989. https://doi.org/10.1177/1461444816676645

Andrejevic M, Gates K (2014) Big data surveillance: Introduction. Surv Soc 12(2):185–196. https://doi.org/10.24908/ss.v12i2.5242

Arvan M (2019) The dark side of morality: group polarization and moral epistemology. Philos Forum 50(1):87–115

Auxier B, Rainie L (2019) Key takeaways on Americans' views about privacy, surveillance and data-sharing. Retrieved from https://www.pewresearch.org/fact-tank/2019/11/15/key-takeaways-on-americans-views-about-privacy-surveillance-and-data-sharing/

BBC News (2012) China new leaders: Xi Jinping heads line-up for politburo. https://www.bbc.com/news/world-asia-china-20322288. Accessed on 31 Oct 2020

BBC News (2017) How broad is Xi Jinping's anti-corruption campaign? What is the goal? Retrieved from https://www.bbc.com/zhongwen/simp/chinese-news-41719314

Becker M (2019) Privacy in the digital age: comparing and contrasting individual versus social approaches towards privacy. Ethics Inf Technol 21(4):307–317

Boyd D, Crawford K (2012) Critical questions for big data. Inf Commun Soc 15(5):662–679. https://doi.org/10.1080/1369118X.2012.678878

Brynjolfsson E, Hitt LM, Kim HH (2011) Strength in numbers: how does data-driven decision-making affect firm performance? Available at SSRN 1819486

Cadell C, Zhang S (2017) No more loan rangers? Beijing's waning support for private credit scores. Retrieved from https://www.reuters.com/article/ant-financial-credit/no-more-loan-rangers-beijings-waning-support-for-private-credit-scores-idUSL3N1JO05W

Carcello JV (2009) Governance and the common good. J Bus Ethics 89(S1):11–18. https://doi.org/10.1007/s10551-008-9904-z
Chin J, Wong G (2016) China's new tool for social control: a credit rating for everything. Wall Street J. Retrieved from www.wsj.com/articles/chinas-newtool-for-social-control-a-credit-rating-for-everything-1480351590
Clover C (2016) China: when big data meets big brother, Financial Times 19. Retrieved from https://www.ft.com/content/b5b13a5e-b847-11e5-b151-8e15c9a029fb. Accessed on 28 Oct 2020
Creemers R (2017) Cyber China: upgrading propaganda, public opinion work and social management for the twenty-first century. J Contemp Chin 26(103):85–100
Creemers R (2018) China's social credit system: an evolving practice of control. Retrieved from https://doi.org/10.2139/ssrn.3175792
De-Kloet J, Poell T, Guohua Z, Yiu FC (2019) The platformization of Chinese society: infrastructure, governance, and practice. Chin J Commun 12(3):249–256
Dencik L, Hintz A, Cable J (2016) Towards data justice? The ambiguity of anti-surveillance resistance in political activism. Sociology 3(2):1–12. https://doi.org/10.1177/2053951716679678
Diab R (2017) Becoming-infrastructure: datafication, deactivation and the social credit system. J Crit Libr Inf Stud 1(1):1–23
Etzioni A (1996) The new golden rule: community and morality in a democratic society. Basic Books, New York
Etzioni A (2004) The common good. Polity Press, Cambridge
Etzioni A (2009) The capture theory of regulations—revisited. Society (New Brunswick) 46(4):319–323. https://doi.org/10.1007/s12115-009-9228-3
Floridi L (2008) Information ethics, its nature and scope. In: van den Hoven J, Weckert J (eds) Information technology and moral philosophy. Cambridge University Press, Cambridge, pp 40–65
Fourcade M, Healy K (2017) Seeing like a market. Soc Econ Rev 15(1):9–29
Galič M, Timan T, Koops B (2017) Bentham, Deleuze and beyond: an overview of surveillance theories from the Panopticon to participation. Philos Technol 30(1):9–37. https://doi.org/10.1093/ser/mww033
Haggerty K, Ericson R (2000) The surveillant assemblage. Br J Sociol 51(4):605–622
Hatton C (2015) China 'social credit': Beijing sets up huge system. BBC News. Retrieved from https://www.bbc.com/news/world-asia-china-34592186. Accessed on 31 Oct 2010
Hawkins A (2017) Chinese citizens want the government to rank them. Foreign Policy 24:2107. Retrieved from http://foreignpolicy.com/2017/05/24/chinese-citizens-want-the-government-to-rank-them/
Hoffman SR (2017) Programming China: The Communist Party's autonomic approach to managing state security. Unpublished Doctoral dissertation, University of Nottingham, Nottingham
Hsu H, Chang C, Hsu C, Xhafa F (2017) Big data analytics for sensor-network collected intelligence. ProQuest Ebooks. Academic Press, London
Huifeng H (2019) China's social credit system shows its teeth, banning millions from taking flights, trains. South China Morning Post. Retrieved from https://www.scmp.com/economy/china-economy/article/2186606/chinas-social-credit-system-shows-its-teeth-banning-millions. Accessed on Sept 2020
India Today (2016) An entire life reduced to a 'score': how China plans to give every citizen ratings that could make or break their lives. Retrived from https://www.indiatoday.in/fyi/story/china-scoring-system-348530-2016-10-25. Accessed on 30th Sept 2020
Kant I (1991) Perpetual peace: a philosophical sketch. In: Reiss HS (ed) Political writings, pp 93–130
Kim GH, Trimi S, Chung JH (2014) Big-data applications in the government sector. Commun ACM 57(3):78–85
King G, Pan J, Roberts M (2014) Reverse-engineering censorship in China: randomised experimentation and participant observation. Science 345(6199):891–103. https://doi.org/10.1126/science.1251722

Kostka G (2019) China's social credit systems and public opinion: explaining high levels of approval. New Media Soc 21(7):1595–1593

Kostka G, Antoine L (2019) Fostering model citizenship: behavioral responses to China's emerging social credit systems. Policy Internet 12(3):256–289. https://doi.org/10.1002/poi3.213

Kuo L (2019) China bans 23m from Buying travel tickets as part of 'social credit' system. Retrieved July 7, 2020 from https://www.theguardian.com/world/2019/mar/01/china-bans-23m-discredited-citizens-from-buying-travel-tickets-social-credit-system

Lee K (2018) AI superpowers: China, Silicon Valley and The New World Order. Houghton Mifflin Harcourt, Boston

Lee J (2019) Critics Decry Chinese Social credit system, ignore US credit score scheme. Retrieved from https://sputniknews.com/asia/201902211072640147-Critics-Decry-Chinese-Social-Credit-System-Ignore-US-Scheme/

Liang F, Das V, Kostyuk N (2018) Constructing a data-driven society: China's social credit system as a state surveillance infrastructure. Policy Internet 10(4):415–453

Locke J (1988) Two treatises of government. Cambridge University Press, Cambridge

Lyon D (2014) Surveillance, Snowden, and big data: capacities, consequences, critique. Big Data Soc 1(2):1–13

Ma A (2019) China app shows map of people in debt for social credit system. Retrieved from https://underground.net/china-app-shows-map-of-people-in-debt-for-social-credit-system/

Manyika J, Hunt D, Nyquist S, Remes J, Malhotra V, Medonca L, Auguste B, Test S (2011) Growth and renewal in the United States: retooling america's economic engine. J Appl Corp Financ 23(1):8–19. https://doi.org/10.1111/j.1745-6622.2011.00310.x

Matsakis L (2019) How the West got China's social credit system wrong. Retrieved from https://www.wired.com/story/china-social-credit-score-system/

Meissner M (2017) China's social credit system: a bigdata enabled approach to market regulation with broad implications for doing business in China. Retrieved from https://www.chinafile.com/library/reports/chinas-social-credit-system-big-data-enabled-approach-market-regulation-broad

Mele D (2009) Integrating personalism into virtue-based business ethics: the personalist and the common good principles. J Bus Ethics 88(1):227–244

Mill JS (2015) On liberty, utilitarianism, and other essays. Oxford University Press, Oxford

Mistreanu S (2018) Life inside China's social credit laboratory. The Party's massive experiment in ranking and monitoring chinese citizens has already started. Foreign Policy. Retrieved from https://foreignpolicy.com/2018/04/03/life-inside-chinas-social-credit-laboratory/

Morrison D (2012) The common good. In: Deslauriers M, Destrée P (eds) The Cambridge companion to Aristotle's politics. Cambridge University Press, Cambridge, pp 176–198

Mozur P (2019) One month, 500,000 face scans: how China is using A.I. to profile a minority. New York Times. Retrieved from https://www.nytimes.com/2019/04/14/technology/china-surveillance-artificial-intelligence-racial-profiling.html

Munoz C, Smith M, Patil DJ (2016) Big data: a report on algorithmic systems, opportunity, and civil rights. Retrieved from https://www.whitehouse.gov/sites/default/files/microsites/ostp/2016_0504_data_discrimination.pdf

Nissenbaum H (2004) Privacy as contextual integrity, 79. Wash Law Rev 119(121):154–155

Nissenbaum H (2009) Privacy in context: technology, policy, and the integrity of social life. Stanford University Press.

O'Neil C (2016) Weapons of math destruction: how big data increases inequality and threatens democracy. Crown Publishers, New York

Ohlberg M, Ahmed S, Lang B (2017) Central planning, local experiments. the complex implementation of China's social credit system. Merics Chin Monit 43(1):1–15. https://merics.org/sites/default/files/202004/171212_China_Monitor_43_Social_Credit_System_Implementation.pdf

Ouyang B (2013) Corruption is a serious political problem in China. The New Nork Times. Retrieved from https://cn.nytimes.com/china/20130627/cc27ouyangbin/

Pagallo U, Durante M (2009) Three roads to P2P systems and their impact on business practices and ethics. J Bus Ethics 90(4):551–564

Pentland AS (2014) Social physics: how good ideas spread the lessons from a new science. Penguin, London
Qiang X (2011) The battle for the Chinese Internet. J Democr 22(2):47–61. https://doi.org/10.1353/jod.2011.0020
Qureshi I, Bhatt B, Gupta S, Tiwari AA (2021) Future research directions in polarization. In: Qureshi I, Bhatt B, Gupta S, Tiwari AA (eds) Causes and symptoms of socio-cultural polarization: role of information and communication technologies. Springer
Qureshi I, Kistruck GM, Bhatt B (2016) The enabling and constraining effects of social ties in the process of institutional entrepreneurship. Organ Stud 37(3):425–447
Qureshi I, Fang Y, Haggerty N, Compeau DR, Zhang X (2018a) IT-mediated social interactions and knowledge sharing: role of competence-based trust and background heterogeneity. Inf Syst J 28(5):929–955
Qureshi I, Sutter C, Bhatt B (2018b) The transformative power of knowledge sharing in settings of poverty and social inequality. Organ Stud 39(11):1575–1599
Qureshi I, Bhatt B, Gupta S, Tiwari AA (2020) Call for papers: causes, symptoms and consequences of social media induced polarization (SMIP). Inf Syst J https://onlinelibrary.wiley.com/pb-assets/assets/13652575/ISJ_SMIP_CFP%20(002).pdf
Raghunath N (2020) Teaching and learning guide for: a sociological review of China's social credit systems and Guanxi opportunities for social mobility. Sociol Compass 14(7). https://doi.org/10.1111/soc4.12799
Rawls J (1971) A theory of justice. Harvard University Press, Cambridge, MA
Riaz S, Buchanan S, Bapuji H (2011) Institutional work amidst the financial crisis: emerging positions of elite actors. Organization 18(2):187–214
Romar EJ (2002) Virtue is good business: Confucianism as a practical business ethics. J Bus Ethics 38(1):119–131
Sandel MJ (1982) Liberalism and the limits of justice. Cambridge University Press, Cambridge
Sandel MJ (2005) Morality and the liberal ideal: must individual rights betray the common good? In: Public philosophy: essays on morality in politics. Harvard University Press, Cambridge, MA, pp 147–155
Schneider F (2018) China's digital nationalism. Oxford University Press, Cambridge
Schneier B (2015) Data and Goliath: the hidden battles to collect your data and control your world. Norton & Company, New York
Schrodt P (2016) Edward Snowden just made an impassioned argument for why privacy is the most important right, https://www.businessinsider.com.au/edward-snowden-privacy-argument-2016-9?r=US&IR=T. Accessed on 22 Sept 2020
Smith M (2019) An Orwellian nightmare or a fix for China's trust deficit? The Australian Financial Review. Financial Review. Retrieved from https://www.afr.com/world/asia/an-orwellian-nightmare-or-a-fix-for-china-s-trust-deficit-20190401-p519r9. Accessed on 28 Sept 2020
Song B (2019) The West may be wrong about China's social credit system. Washington Post. https://www.washingtonpost.com/news/theworldpost/wp/2018/11/29/social-credit/?arc404=true. Accessed on 31 Oct
Soo Z (2018) Forget to leash your dog? Chinese credit scoring system for owners means you could lose your pet. South China Morning Post
Sputnik (2019) Critics Decry Chinese Social Credit System, ignore US credit score scheme. Retrived from https://sputniknews.com/asia/201902211072640147-Critics-Decry-Chinese-Social-Credit-System-Ignore-US-Scheme/. Accessed on 30 Sept 2020
State Council (2014) Planning Outline for the Construction of a Social Credit System (2014–2020). Retrieved from https://chinacopyrightandmedia.wordpress.com/2014/06/14/planning-outline-for-the-construction-of-a-social-credit-system-2014-2020/
Statista (2016) Population in China in 2017, by region (in million inhabitants). Retrieved from https://www.statista.com/statistics/279013/population-in-china-by-region/
Taylor, J. (2019) Understanding China's Social Credit System. China Focus. Retrieved July 7, 2020, from http://www.cnfocus.com/understanding-china-s-social-credit-system/

The Chinese Executive Information Disclosure Network (n.d.) Retrieved July 7, 2020, from http://zxgk.court.gov.cn/
Tosun J, Koos S, Shore J (2016) Co-governing common goods: interaction patterns of private and public actors. Polic Soc 35(1):1–12
Turilli M, Floridi L (2009) The ethics of information transparency. Ethics Inf Technol 11(2):105–112
Vanderklippe N (2018) Unpublished Chinese censorship document reveals sweeping effort to eradicate online political content. Retrieved from https://www.theglobeandmail.com/world/article-unpublished-chinese-censorship-document-reveals-sweeping-effort-to/
Van-Dijck J (2014) Datafication, dataism and dataveillance: big data between scientific paradigm and ideology. Surveill Soc 12(2):197–208. https://doi.org/10.24908/ss.v12i2.4776
Walzer M (1983) Spheres of justice: a defense of pluralism and equality. Basic Books, New York
Walzer M (1990) The communitarian critique of liberalism. Political Theory 18(1):6–23
Wang W (2019a) Credit where it's due. Global Times:12–13
Wang W (2019b) New social system aims to bring spirit of trust into society. The Global Times. Retrieved from https://www.globaltimes.cn/content/1142808.shtml. Accessed on 31 Oct 2020
Woetzel J, Seong J, Wei-Wang K, Manyika J, Chui M, Wong W (2017) China's digital economy: a leading global force. Retrieved from https://www.mckinsey.com/global-themes/china/chinas-digital-economy-a-leading-globalforce
Xu J (2019) How social credit system will force firms to toe line. South China Morning Post
Yang G (2009) The power of the Internet in China: citizen activism online. Columbia University Press, New York
Yew C (2018) System-wide effects of credit rating downgrades. Regul Credit Rating Agencies:153–154. https://doi.org/10.4337/9780857939364.00021
Zeng J (2016) China's date with big data: will it strengthen or threaten authoritarian rule? Int Aff 92(6):1443–1462. https://doi.org/10.1111/1468-2346.12750
Zhang K, Zhang F (2016) Report on the construction of the social credit system in China's Special Economic Zones. In: Tao Y, Yuan Y (Comp) Annual report on the development of China's special economic zones. Springer, Singapore, pp 153–171
Zheng S (2019) China harvesting data on global scale, Australian report warns. South China Morning Post. Retrieved from https://www.scmp.com/news/china/diplomacy/article/3033052/china-harvesting-data-global-scale-australian-report-warns?mc_cid=be7c8fd200&mc_eid=ef377d4d77. Accessed 31 Oct 2020
Zhu T, Xiao S, Zhang Q, Gu Y, Yi P, Li Y (2015) Emergent technologies in big data sensing: a survey. Int J Distrib Sens Netw. https://doi.org/10.1155/2015/902982
Zhun L (2016) China's social credit system won't be Orwellian. Global Times. https://www.globaltimes.cn/content/1015248.shtml. Accessed 31 Oct 2020
Zuboff S (2015) Big other: surveillance capitalism and the prospects of an information civilisation. J Inf Technol 30(1):75–89
Zuboff S (2019) The age of surveillance capitalism: the fight for a human future at the new frontier of power. Public Affairs, New York

A Comprehensive Review on Countering Rumours in the Age of Online Social Media Platforms

Amir Ebrahimi Fard and Trivik Verma

Abstract The power of rumour spreading in the age of online social media is intimidating. It can incite to insurrection, denigrate people, and damage financial markets, proving catastrophic for society. Despite widespread scholarly research and practice of developing a constellation of counter-rumour strategies, the massive waves of rumours are still sweeping over individuals, organisations, and societal institutions. To systematically tackle this issue, we present a comprehensive review and an epidemic framework to resolve three challenging aspects of rumour dissemination in online social media. First, we identify and explain the various forms of false and unverified information, relevance, and impact. Second, we address how social media can exacerbate the phenomenon of rumour spreading. Using the framework, the classification of rumour disseminating mechanisms on social media, allows us to develop counter-rumour strategies. Finally, we inspect past strategies employed in addressing rumour dissemination and use the framework to explore parallels between epidemic management and addressing rumour. We identify the highly neglected aspects of the current cumulative rumour response and factors that may be effectively targeted in the future. Our approach might support understanding social media's role in propagating rumours and devising active measures in quelling this epidemic.

Keywords Rumour · Unverified information · Disinformation · Propaganda · Conspiracy theory

1 Introduction

In one of the most famous plays – Henry the Fourth, Part II – Shakespeare writes "rumour is a pipe, blown by surmises, jealousies, conjectures, and of so easy and

A. E. Fard (✉) · T. Verma
Faculty of Technology, Policy and Management, Delft University of Technology, Delft, the Netherlands
e-mail: a.ebrahimifard@tudelft.nl; T.Verma@tudelft.nl

I. Qureshi et al. (eds.), *Causes and Symptoms of Socio-Cultural Polarization*,
https://doi.org/10.1007/978-981-16-5268-4_11

so plain a stop, that the blunt monster with uncounted heads, the still-discordant wavering multitude, can play upon it". His words elegantly express how easy, widespread, and vicious the emergence and circulation of rumours can be. Since he first wrote the play, the phenomenon of rumour spreading is exacerbated and turned into a far-reaching phenomenon to the extent that the World Economic Forum ranked the spread of misinformation as one of the most prominent risks to democracy (Howell et al. 2013).

Although rumour spreading is mostly associated with political contexts due to the excessive use of rumours by political figures to disparage their rivals and critics, this phenomenon's scope is much bigger than politics (Koenig 1985; Allport and Postman 1947; Knopf 1975; DiFonzo 2009). It is a domain-agnostic phenomenon that arises in any circumstance in which meanings are uncertain, questions are unsettled, information is missing, and lines of communications are absent (DiFonzo 2009). From the content perspective, rumours are false or unverified statements about instrumentally important topics. Thus any incident – no matter if it is political or not – could be a rumour-mongering subject. People engage in the rumour process since it attributes a ready-made justification to unexplained events (DiFonzo and Bordia 2007a). It increases the comprehension and understanding of the situation by offering detailed reasoning and clarification. Rumours might also be initiated deliberately as a psychological tool for strategic purposes such as character assassination, influence operations, and financial benefits (DiFonzo and Bordia 2007a, b; Koenig 1985). The dissemination of rumours, whether being intentional or inadvertent, may feed on hate, create fear, and raise false hopes (Knapp 1944). It may tarnish reputation of individuals (Allport and Postman 1947), organisations (Koenig 1985), or even countries (Ellick and Westbrook 2018a), provoke rioting and unrest (Knopf 1975), shake financial markets (Aral 2020), influence decision-making processes (Farrell et al. 2019), and disrupt global aid operations (Vosoughi et al. 2018; DiFonzo and Bordia 2007a).

One of the contributing factors in the escalation of rumour dissemination is polarised beliefs toward rumours (DiFonzo et al. 2013). Polarisation emerges since individuals prefer to interact with those who share similar views and orientations. This phenomenon divides societies into different echo chambers, reinforcing one's belief due to the repeated interactions with like-minded peers (Cota et al. 2019). Within an echo chamber, people are in high consensus and often say and hear similar messages. Research has shown the repetition of a message makes it more believable. Such a setting precipitates in social clusters with heterogeneous views toward a rumour. Such an environment deprives people of opposing views; thus, they increasingly become more confident regarding their echo chamber induced beliefs (Boutyline and Willer 2017; Flaxman et al. 2016).

In this vein, the media's role is crucial as it streamlines communication and increases the rate of reach to the audience (Franks and Attia 2011) (and subsequent exposure to rumours). Thus media could polarise individuals by feeding them with certain content and driving them toward echo chambers. On the other hand, it could expose them to diverse viewpoints, painting a fuller picture on every argument or debate. Research has shown that social media platforms exacerbate polarisation by insulating people from opposing viewpoints (Cota et al. 2019). The size and diversity of social networks (Christakis and Fowler 2009), and automation mechanisms (Li et al. 2020; Shao et al. 2018; Woolley and Howard 2018) play a central role. Besides, other factors such as a lack of media literacy (Guess et al. 2020), minimal supervision (Lazer et al. 2018), low barrier to entry (Tsfati et al. 2020), and the lack of social media regulation (Marsden et al. 2020) facilitate polarisation which subsequently lead to the creation and circulation of rumours.

The escalation of rumour diffusion through social media platforms may lead to severe consequences that can influence political, economic, and social well-being of our society (Vosoughi et al. 2018). For instance, on April 23 of 2013, the Twitter account of *Associated Press* released a tweet saying "Breaking: Two explosions in the White House and Barack Obama has been injured." This tweet went viral by 4000 tweets in less than 5 minutes. This false news spread precipitated a significant drop (to the amount of 140 billion dollars) in the stock market in a single day. Automated trading algorithms immediately began trading based on the potentials and consequences of the white house explosion and the reported death or injury of the U.S. president (Aral 2020). There are plenty of rumour dissemination cases in other domains such as elections (Aral and Eckles 2019), business issues (Farrell et al. 2019), and healthcare (Li et al. 2020) which lead to severe outcomes, that often have a disproportionate impact on the well-being of multiple communities.

In response to the detrimental effects of rumour propagation, a series of confrontation strategies have been devised (Knopf 1975; Ponting 1973; Allport and Postman 1947; DiFonzo and Bordia 2007a). Although taking the potential danger of rumour spreading into account and countering this phenomenon was a significant action, it was often an intermittent effort with ephemeral impacts. There was no long-term plan behind the confrontation strategies. Whenever a major incident happened or was about to happen, rumours started to thrive and then countering techniques were proposed and practised. While this whack-a-mole approach might have worked previously, it could not keep up with the rumour supply and circulation rate due to the sudden growth of social media in the past decade. On the one hand, various stakeholders such as social media platforms, governments, academia, and media organisations collaboratively developed new solutions. On another, lax in policy efforts at multiple social media platforms allowed for more innovative rumour spreading. Although scholars have proposed and practised a constellation of counter-rumour strategies on different scales, the massive waves of rumours still negatively impact individuals, organisations, and societal institutions (Vosoughi et al. 2018). To counter the alarming trend and repercussions of rumour propagation, we need to revise our former tackling approaches by developing a comprehensive understanding of the problem and past counter-strategies.

This chapter reviews three significant domains in the emerging field of rumour studies: the problem, its implications, and strategies for tackling them. The problem definition is a crucial phase as it entails determining what exactly has to be curbed and controlled in rumour propagation. There are different variations of false and unverified information (e.g., fake news, disinformation, misinformation, conspiracy theory, etc.) which are recognised by the scholars as similarly harmful phenomena (Difonzo and Bordia 2007b; Woolley and Howard 2018). We study all aspects within the context of social media – its role and relevance in facilitating a spread – to provide a fuller understanding of the phenomenon. Because of the relatively long period of rumour confrontation in the societies, it is indispensable to obtain an overview of the past counter-rumour strategies and clarify the importance of tackling some rumour variations. It would provide information about the strengths and weaknesses of the rumour responses in the past. Scholars and decisionmakers could utilise that information later in the development of confrontation plan against rumour dissemination.

We organise the rest of the chapter as follows. In Sect. 2, we introduce different forms of false and unverified information. Section 3 investigates social media's role and its features and mechanisms in promoting rumours. Section 4 sets the past counter-rumour strategies in a common framework and evaluate them. Finally, Sect. 5 presents our findings and gives some suggestions for future work.

2 Background

There are many concepts in the English language implying false or unverified information. Terms such as misinformation, disinformation, rumour, urban legend, fake-news, propaganda, and conspiracy theory are just a few of these concepts that intermittently appear in the scientific arena. What academia has experienced regarding the conceptualisation of those terms and their conceptual siblings is an epistemic crisis. Although there are plenty of studies exploring various kinds of false and unverified information from different angles, there is considerable disagreement between proposed definitions. They are often conflated or used interchangeably (Freelon and Wells 2020; O'Connor and Weatherall 2019; Molina et al. 2019; Lazer et al. 2018; Vosoughi et al. 2018). The lack of consensus on conceptualisation would create confusion and drains the community's efforts in countering the surge of false information.

Although the genesis of such information might be deliberate or inadvertent and with different purposes, they primarily disseminate based on similar motives and follow the same dynamical process (i.e. creation and dissemination) (DiFonzo 2009; Difonzo and Bordia 2007b; Difonzo 2018). Regardless of the variations, the dynamics of false and unverified information is similar across the board.

2.1 The Variations of False and Unverified Information

This section investigates rumour, its variants, and its conceptual siblings to understand the differences among variations of false and unverified information. The notion of rumour refers to declarative statements composed of nouns and verb statements that purport to inform, explain, predict and thus provide information (DiFonzo 2009; Bordia et al. 2014). It is a collective process that arises in the collaboration of many. It involves a division of labour among participants, each of whom makes a different contribution (Shibutani 1966). Rumour existence is contingent on its circulation (Bordia et al. 2014), and end of the communication activity equals the death of rumour (Shibutani 1966). A rumour spreads if it relates to, affects, or threatens rumour participants in some way. Rumours are unverified in some context, and they are not accompanied by substantial evidence for at least some group of people (Difonzo and Bordia 2007b). Rumours tend to thrive amid situations that are ambiguous, confusing, uncertain and threatening (DiFonzo 2009). Rumours circulate primarily as a sense-making or threat management mechanism. They offer details and reasons as well as meanings, clarifications, and justifications.

Rumours may take different shapes; however, they evolve into a similar dissemination dynamic which mimics rumour spreading after the first generation of the transmission. Propaganda and fake-news are planted into public deliberately to induce psychological threats and take advantage of the people; however, the audience treats them in the same way they treat rumours. People circulate their impressions, interpretations, or reactions among themselves to make sense of those information (Cook 2020; Difonzo and Bordia 2007b; DiFonzo 2009). Similarly, conspiracy theories and pseudoscience might emerge as a coping strategy among a group of people to manage psychological threats in response to uncertain or threatening situations (Difonzo 2018). Legends, myths, and urban legends are also very similar phenomena; however, their life-cycle is much longer than rumours; hence, we consider them a separate phenomenon. Similarly, Gossip is also a distinct phenomenon in local group levels with a slightly different dynamic. Table 1 summarises those variations and subsequent sections explain them in more detail.

2.1.1 Gossip

Gossip is an evaluative social talk about an individual's personal life. It is a group-level phenomenon which glues down groups and adjusts people's relationships. Gossiping can maintain group cohesiveness, establish, change, maintain group norms, group power structure, and group membership. It can also function as an entertainment mechanism (DiFonzo 2009; DiFonzo and Bordia 2007a). Gossiping is also an effective strategy for intragroup competition (DiFonzo 2009; Fine and Rosnow 1978). Nefarious self-serving motives may drive Gossip to slanderous outcomes. They may break groups apart or taint people's reputation. However, there is benevolent Gossip that functions as a warning against the harmful behaviour of particular individuals. Gossip may also regulate individuals' behaviour regarding the context. Gossip works on group dynamics between friends, not those who do not know each other. It is the signal of affiliation, closeness, and camaraderie (DiFonzo 2009; Fine and Rosnow 1978).

Table 1 Comparison between different forms of false and unverified information (Inspired by DiFonzo and Bordia 2007a)

Context	Evidentiary basis	Perceived importance	Content slanderous	Message theme & structure	Function	Function
Rumour, Ambiguity, danger, threat, or change	Low	High	Maybe	The message is a declarative statement, consisting mostly nouns and verbs.	The message is a declarative statement, consisting mostly nouns and verbs.	Maybe
Gossip, Social network formation and maintenance	Maybe	Low	High	The message is evaluative, informal and refers to individuals.	Allowing groups to become more cohesive and to define their membership, norms, and power structure	High
Legend, Socially cohesive contexts	Low	Low	Low	The narratives pertains to issues that are important for successive generations such as birth, marriage, and death. They have story like structures, including setting plot, characters, climax, and denouement.	To entertain and to convey mores, norms, and cultural truths	High
Propaganda, Threatening situation when much is at stake	Low	High	High	The messages are about supporting or challenging particular viewpoints or ideologies mostly in politics and business. The message structure is composed of fabricated materials as well as manipulated and vivid images, symbols, and slogans.	To simultaneously induce psychological threats and to function as a sense-making and threat management mechanism.	Low
Conspiracy theory, Psychological threats	Low	High	High	The messages follow a narrative about covert and hostile activities of secret and powerful groups.	To cope with threats by providing alternative explanations for events and incidents.	Low
Fake-news, Attention-gaining context	Low	High	High	The messages are emotionally charged and written in narrative style; They are not fact-checked and their source is not verified. In order to draw attentions, elements of (i) threat-related information, (ii) sexually related information, or (iii) elements associated to disgust, are incorporated.	To gain financial benefits by drawing eyeballs.	Maybe
Pseudoscience , Ambiguity and threat	Low	High	Maybe	The message pertains to an issue within the domain of science in a broad sense.	Sense-making and threat management by rejecting the empirical studies and/or promoting fabricated claims	Low
Misinformation , Ambiguity and threat	Low	High	Maybe		For sense-making	Maybe

2.1.2 Legend

Legends are narratives about unusual, humorous, or horrible events with moral lessons[1] (DiFonzo and Bordia 2007a). After being recounted for many years, a prior history of distortion and transformation, legends converge to stable forms and become part of people's folklore and verbal heritage. Legends are immortal because they capture the universal aspects of human character. Legends follow a storytelling framework. They have a setting, plot, characters, climax, and denouement. They function as a mechanism for entertainment and propagation of values and mores. Legends also make sense of the world by conforming to answers to the persistent riddles of life. Legends are about subjects considered important for successive generations. If the legends are about primal forces, cosmology, or religious beliefs, then they are called myths (Allport and Postman 1947; DiFonzo and Bordia 2007a).

2.1.3 Propaganda

Propaganda refers to persuasive tactics devised deliberately by governments or corporations to promote or challenge a particular viewpoint by manipulating symbolic representations (Shibutani 1966; O'Connor and Weatherall 2019). It can occur in computational settings over social media, "using algorithms, automation, and human curation to purposefully manage and distribute misleading information over social media networks" (Woolley and Howard 2018). The computational setting in computational propaganda allows automation which brings scalability and anonymity. Many state and non-state actors use computational propaganda to suppress their oppositions, promote their viewpoints, divert or destroy movements, and create fake trends (Woolley and Howard 2018).

Propaganda may take on particular shapes. One of them is innuendo which functions as a character assassination technique to discredit the reputed individuals. For instance, since early times innuendos tarnished U.S. presidential elections by accusing candidates with illicit sexual relations, racism, brutal treatment of wives, drunkenness and the alleged possession of certain blood types (Allport and Postman 1947). It may also serve as a projection technique to accuse another person of the same things that the accuser is guilty of (Difonzo and Bordia 2007b). One of the most notorious shapes of propaganda rumour is disinformation invented by KGB in 1923. It is black propaganda based on forgeries. Disinformation includes forged and fabricated narratives, letters, documents, photographs, reports, and press releases (Martin 1982; Romerstein 2001). One of the kinds of forgery that is getting increasingly popular is audiovisual (A.V.) manipulation. It includes both

[1] The term "legend" refers to both traditional legends (about knighthood, ogres, witches, sleeping princesses, etc.) and modern or contemporary legends (about dating, technology, organ removal, etc.) Modern/Contemporary legends are also called urban legends which is a misnomer because those narratives do not necessarily occur in an urban environment.

the cutting edge AI-reliant technologies of deepfakes and cheap-fakes; conventional audiovisual manipulation techniques such as speeding, slowing, cutting, re-staging or re-contextualising footage (Paris and Donovan 2019).

2.1.4 Conspiracy Theory

Conspiracy theories are unverified pieces of information circulating about events or incidents initiated for deliberate hostile purposes by a coalition of actors operating in secret. A conspiracy theory assumes predesigned patterns govern the universe, and there is no room for randomness and coincidence. That is why conspiracy theories try to randomly connect the dots and find the secret patterns (Van Prooijen 2018). Conspiracy theories may arise in a variety of subject domains such as scientific research (e.g. global warming is a hoax created by China (Hendricks and Vestergaard 2019)), sport (e.g. referee bribing conspiracy theory (Van Prooijen 2018)), or the government (e.g. deep state conspiracy theory (Benkler et al. 2018)). Among the commonly used conspiracy tactics are contradictory explanations, overriding suspicion, nefarious intent, something must be wrong, persecuted victim, immunity to evidence, re-interpreting randomness (Cook 2020).

2.1.5 Fake-News

The notion of fake-news[2] is defined as "fabricated information that mimics news media contents in form but not in the process and intent". Fake-news outlets do not follow editorial norms and guidelines (Lazer et al. 2018). Such outlets narrate emotionally charged articles that are devoid of fact-checking and source verification; sometimes, pieces have inconsistencies with the registration date (Molina et al. 2019). Although fake-news reports have mostly arisen in a political context, there are plenty of cases in other domains such as vaccination and stock markets (Lazer et al. 2018).

Since the early days of journalism, fake-news found its way into various news outlets (Uberti 2016). Fake-news articles could draw attention easier than real news as there is no constraint for fabrication. We can be as creative as we want to develop appealing, attention-grabbing and memorable articles (Acerbi 2019). More attention means higher readership, leading to a more significant profit margin for the news outlets (Standage 2017). One of the earliest and most successful fake-news articles was the New York Sun's "Great Moon Hoax" of 1835, which claimed there was an alien civilisation on the moon. This fabricated story drew much attention to

[2] In the current political climate, there is a significant disagreement in academia regarding the consumption of the term "fake news" as it became a value-loaded term linked to particular political figures (Vosoughi et al. 2018; Lazer et al. 2018); however, due to the lack of an alternative name and to avoid adding further confusion to the existing fluid terminology, we have elected to retain the term "fake news".

New York Sun to the extent that its circulation reached from 8000 to 19000 copies, which meant overtaking Times of London as the world's bestselling daily newspaper (Standage 2017; Posetti and Matthews 2018).

2.1.6 Pseudoscience

A statement is pseudoscientific if it satisfies three criteria of (i) scientific domain, (ii) unreliability, and (iii) deviant doctrine[3]. The measure of scientific domain entails a pseudoscientific statement to be about an issue within the realm of science.[4] A pseudoscientific statement suffers from a severe lack of reliability and trust. Besides, it has no use for knowledge production nor any practical cases. The deviant doctrine criteria indicate the support of pseudoscientific statement proponents to represent that statement as the most reliable knowledge on the subject matter (Hansson 2017).

Pseudoscience can take two different forms of science denialism, and pseudo-theory promotion (Hansson 2017). Science denialism refers to "the rejection of empirically supported propositions despite scientific consensus and the effort to create the appearance of debate when there is none" (Schmid and Betsch 2019). Some typical examples of denialism are climate change, Holocaust, vaccination, and negative impacts of tobacco (Hansson 2017; Cook 2020). The other category of pseudoscience is pseudo-theory promotion, which refers to the fabrication of a set of claims to advance the pseudoscientist's theory. Sometimes it leads to the rejection of parts of science. Some typical examples of pseudo-theories are astrology, homoeopathy, iridology, Scientology, transcendental meditation, and ancient astronaut theories (Hansson 2017, 2018).

2.1.7 Misinformation

Misinformation is a widespread form of false and unverified information. This concept originates in cognitive psychology and developed by the scholars who were studying misinformation effects on memory formation, visual object classification, children's ability to infer the mental states of others, and performance on multiple-choice tests (Freelon and Wells 2020). The misinformation effect refers to "the distorting effects of misleading post-event information on memory for words, faces, and details of witnessed events" (Frenda et al. 2011). Nevertheless, nowadays, the term has found a much broader yet loose meaning: any kind of deceptive message that might be harmful but spreads inadvertently (Freelon and Wells 2020). If its

[3] To view a statement pseudoscientific, all the three conditions require to be confirmed (Hansson 2017). For example, if a commentary satisfies the first two criteria but not the third one, probably it is fraud in science or mistake in science, but not pseudoscience.

[4] The term "science" implies science in a broad sense which comprises humanities as well.

truthfulness is unverified for an individual and s/he spreads it (without malice), that piece is considered misinformation.

2.2 *Process-Based Perspective*

This section investigates the dynamics of false and unverified information by explaining the emergence and dissemination phases. False and unverified information is initially shared to serve four general purposes of (i) social manipulation, (ii) sense-making and threat management, (iii) social dynamics, and (iv) cultural dynamics. Social manipulation refers to "the purposeful, systematic generation and dissemination of information to produce harmful social, political, and economic outcomes in a target area by affecting beliefs, attitudes, and behaviour" (Mazarr et al. 2019). Planting misleading information into public is a long-standing manipulation strategy when much is at stake (e.g. in wartime, elections, highly competitive markets). False and unverified information can also appear at the time of uncertainty and threat as a coping strategy and "to give meaning to our sensations and to put a context around them, so they gain significance and fit into an understanding that coheres" (DiFonzo 2009). They may also function as a social mechanism to entertain, to supply social information, and to establish, change, or maintain group membership, group power structure, or group norms (DiFonzo and Bordia 2007a). The cultural dynamics is the other purpose of spreading false and unverified information to establish, maintain, or impart cultural mores or values. It also provides answers to the persistent riddles of life (DiFonzo and Bordia 2007a; Allport and Postman 1947).

After the creation of a message on social media – deliberately or inadvertently – the message spreading starts. Humans used to circulate their messages through word of mouth or letter; however, the communication technologies and the emergence of new media facilitated this procedure. Although media is one of the most efficient ways of releasing false and unverified information, not all media outlets are the same. They vary from highly professional ones with codes of conduct, style guides, and journalistic guidelines to those without any policy or standard. Due to the controversial aspects of false or unverified information, they cannot always meet the professional journalism standards and reach credible outlets (Lazer et al. 2018). Sometimes message circulation starts from state-owned media agencies and low credibility news outlets (O'Connor and Weatherall 2019). Stakeholders whose purpose is social manipulation use state-owned media since they operate as the information operation wing of many governments (Ellick and Westbrook 2018b).

Additionally, blogs and low credibility websites may also be the host of non-credible information. They are solely searching for more visits to increase their revenue; therefore, what matters for them is catching eyeballs not complying with journalism norms, and standards (Acerbi 2019). An alternative or complementary channel is online social media platforms. They have a massive user base as well as minimum restrictions for the authorised contents. Thus it can be a perfect environment for any false or unverified information to begin their circulation no matter its purpose (Christakis and Fowler 2009; Lazer et al. 2018).

After releasing false and unverified information, it would be extremely challenging to control its passage and keep it in check, as it forms spontaneously. Its development depends upon fortuitous events, momentary emotional reactions, and the particular interest of those who make up the public. Sometimes, the discussions might be directed and redirected, especially in social manipulation; however, the extent of interventions effectiveness is circumscribed (Shibutani 1966). When false and unverified information goes public, spontaneous discussions, including different communication postures among the people who come across that information, propels it further (DiFonzo and Bordia 2007a). People often participate in those discussions collaboratively by raising questions, providing information, indicating beliefs and opinions, expressing feelings, or suggesting a course of action no matter what is the type of false and unverified information (Bordia and DiFonzo 2004). Thus, whether it is black propaganda to tarnish a presidential candidate or an honest mistake about confusing a firecracker's sound with an explosion, the same dynamic will happen (the scale and life-time of the process depend on a set of internal and external factors). This dynamic process is precisely similar to what occurs in rumour spreading when people engage in the shared sense-making process through interaction with others.

Although the genesis of false and unverified information might be for different reasons, they evolve into a similar dissemination dynamic which mimics rumour spreading after the first generation of the transmission. Propaganda and fake-news are planted into public deliberately to induce psychological threats and take advantage of the people; however, the audience treats them in the same way they treat rumours. People circulate their impressions, interpretations, or reactions among themselves to make sense of those information (Ruths 2019; Difonzo and Bordia 2007b; DiFonzo 2009). Similarly, conspiracy theories and pseudoscience might emerge as a coping strategy among a group of people to manage psychological threats in response to uncertain or threatening situations (Difonzo 2018). Legends, myths, and urban legends are also very similar phenomena; however, their life-cycle is much longer than rumours; hence, we consider them a separate phenomenon. Similarly, Gossip is also a distinct phenomenon in local group levels with a slightly different dynamic.

2.3 Forms of False and Unverified Information

This section draws attention to the message forms in the variations of false and unverified information. As discussed before, rumours, legends, and Gossip are three broad variations of false and unverified information. The least harmful one is a legend and its siblings, namely urban legend and myth. Although they had been rumour once, they are distinct phenomena with crucial differences after years of transmission. Legends' primary goal is to share values and conform to the vacuums of riddles of life. Thus, it is implausible that legends lead to harmful consequences. The other one is Gossip which mainly maintains group-level mechanisms such as cohesiveness, power structure, norms, and membership. However, it may transform into slander based on nefarious self-serving motives. Nevertheless, it is implausible that the impact of gossiping transcends the boundaries of social cliques and reaches more extensive social networks.

The other construct is rumour and its offspring. In a broad sense, rumour functions as a sense-making or threat management mechanism. However, depending on the form of rumour, both sense-making and threat management may take different shapes. In propaganda rumour, it mostly serves a pernicious function. Although there are different types of propaganda rumour, their primary intent is malicious. The conspiracy rumours are also relatively harmful and harass their subjected groups by falsely accusing them. Fake-news rumours might become harmful by promoting appealing yet fabricated materials to lure individuals. The pseudoscientific rumour is a toxic phenomenon that attacks the science institution by tarnishing scientists, scientific evidence, and scientific methods. Misinformation does not inflict any harm wittingly; however, as discussed before, it may appear when uninformed individuals are engaged in the rumour process. Besides, even if misinformation rumour does not take the shape of derogatory rumours and spread with a benign yet inadvertent motive, it may lead to harm (DiFonzo 2009).

Thus among the variations of false and unverified information, the rumour family operates on a large scale, even if they start spreading unwittingly. Without malign intent, they may still lead to severe consequences. Therefore, it is crucial to take the variations of rumour into account and develop a solution to curb and control this phenomenon; otherwise, the repercussions would be inevitable. They may influence political, economic, and social well-being (Vosoughi et al. 2018).

3 Rumour Facilitation Features in Online Social Media Platforms

This section discusses how the introduction of new communication technologies could facilitate message transmission and thus rumour dissemination. The development of communication technologies is a complex and continuous process. Here, we slice up this developing process and take snapshots of a few technologies with significant importance in rumour dissemination.

In the pre-printing era, there was no synchronous and mass communication technology, and the possibility of long-distance message transmission was quite limited (Chakravarthi 1992). Within this period, only local and small-scale communication prevailed. Thus, rumours were also often about local issues and remained within the communities. The invention of the printing press was a turning point in communication technologies as it made mass communication possible (Buringh and Van Zanden 2009). This technology increased the chance of exposure to rumours by *replication* of the same message and sharing them among many people (Standage 2017; Posetti and Matthews 2018; O'Connor and Weatherall 2019).

Another crucial technology was the telephone which introduced *synchronicity* to the communication process. The phone could accelerate and expand the rumour circulation by offering fast *long-distance* communication. The key distinctive features of the printing press and telephone technologies (i.e., synchronicity and mass communication) were incorporated into radio and television and created synchronous mass communication mediums. It was the first time in history that distant live contact with masses became possible. They could also draw more attention because of *multimedia elements*. Besides, compared to written media, the radio and television comprised a wider audience beyond those who could read. Due to the features mentioned above, radio and television were extensively utilised in rumour spreading (Dowe 1997).

The mass spread of rumours began with the emergence of the World Wide Web (WWW) using *distant synchronous/asynchronous multi-lateral communication* (Lehmann 2019). Through the forums, chat rooms, and other WWW-based applications, people could communicate without knowing each other. Such platforms allow individuals to *hide their identities* or use anonymous, or even fake avatar in their profiles (Christakis and Fowler 2009; Hussain 2019). *Minimal supervision* is another feature of the WWW that fostered rumour spreading. Earlier, only a self-selected group of people were linked to media outlets and had access to communication channels. With the advent of a free venue for people to express their thoughts and opinions (in the forums, chat-rooms, their blog or website), WWW created a global platform for people to communicate no matter who they are and how credible their messages (Lazer et al. 2018; Dowe 1997).

The rise of online social media platforms was the landmark in the history of rumour spreading. This technology supports distant multi-lateral communications with different synchronicity modes. Social media is a complex phenomenon that offers novel features in three layers of social, institutional, and technological. From social perspective, it is an enormous hyper-connected network (Christakis and Fowler 2009) pursuing power-law degree distribution (Barabási et al. 2016). The large scale of social networks vastly increases the number of people who might get exposed to rumours. It also increases the chance of creating communities with similar values, beliefs, and interests (Briones et al. 2011; Schor 1995).

This turns social media to an environment with a high potential for polarisation. It allows people who had not any tribune before, find like-minded peers and freely communicate their controversial thoughts quickly. Besides, within social media, high-degree nodes or hubs that play influencers and opinion leaders' role affect the small-world property in the network, which eventually leads to the virality of information and rumours (Barabási et al. 2016; Vosoughi et al. 2018). Furthermore, when a network's size increases, the chance of diversity among the users improves, expanding the scope of potential rumours (Christakis and Fowler 2009).

From the institutional perspective, social media platforms allow their users to participate in information dissemination while leveraging anonymity. It specifically gives a safety margin to the initiators or moderators of inorganic rumours (Fox

2020; McGonagle 2017) since they can "say whatever they want, whenever they want, and yet be shielded by anonymity" (Christopherson 2007). The platforms also enable the democratisation of the content by allowing individuals to consume, create, and distribute their content without governmental control (Tufekci 2017) and with minimal supervision (Lazer et al. 2018). This means people of different ages, education, and nationality are free to share their thoughts, and discuss their ideas about various topics in politics, sport, or trivial daily-basis incidents, to name but a few. They can produce and share whatever content they want as long as it does not violate the platforms guidelines developed at a minimal level not to curtail freedom of speech (Hussain 2019; Roth and Pickles 2020). This policy would lower the barrier to entry for not only those who have not received any training in journalism but also for the ones who bluntly reject the journalistic norms of objectivity and balance (Lazer et al. 2018). The low barrier to entry also contributes to a more polarised community. It allows those who support controversial ideas to easily find their echo chamber and make it bigger and more isolated.

Besides, any attempt to control such an extravagant system is perceived as the censorship, since social media platforms are considered the manifestation of freedom of speech and whatever that restricts this sphere will be interpreted as a violation of freedom of speech. That is why codes of conduct, style guides, and journalistic guidelines in online social media platforms are kept to the minimum level (Ruths 2019). This is an ideal setting for rumour spreading because the information is not verified before releasing into the sphere of online social media.

From a technological perspective, social media is equipped with mechanisms such as recommendation systems and social bots that can easily be used to facilitate the spread of rumours (Woolley and Howard 2018). The recommendation system is a specific type of algorithm used to enhance the user experience by reducing the information overload (Jannach and Jugovac 2019) and helping users find compelling content in large corpora by personalised suggestions (Berkovsky and Freyne 2015; Wagh and Patil 2012). The other automation mechanism in online social media platforms is social bots. They are computer programs that tend to emulate and alter human behaviour and produce content and interact with other humans (Ferrara et al. 2016). Scholars have shown that recommender systems and social bots exacerbate polarisation in social media. Recommender systems drive social media users toward more radical content by deliberately avoiding to expose them with opposing views. Social bots also amplify the spread of information that is pleasing for some people to trap them in echo chambers by inducing certain beliefs. Social bots are primarily active in political contexts (Dandekar et al. 2013; Stella et al. 2018). For instance, research by Dutch newspaper NRC revealed that of over 900 Russian Twitter accounts, listed by the U.S. investigation into Russian meddling in the 2016 elections, as attempting to influence the Dutch debate on Twitter in 2016 and 2017. By far, these accounts focused on amplifying anti-Islam sentiment, and polarising attitudes towards migration and refugees (Hazenburg et al. 2018).

Both social bots and recommendation systems allegedly play a central role in spreading rumours by amplifying the messages with strategic goals and leading people toward rumour rabbit holes, respectively. Some studies show the significant role of bots in the circulation of rumours. They drive rumours by liking, sharing, and searching for information. Notably, they are responsible for a substantial amount of contents during political events such as the 2016 U.S. Presidential election and 2017 French election, to name but a few (Lazer et al. 2018; Woolley and Howard 2018; Shao et al. 2018). On the other hand, there are studies, for example, the most extensive research on the digital spread of rumours, that show the insignificance of social bots compared to humans in the spread of rumours (Vosoughi et al. 2018).

Similarly, in the case of recommendation systems, some studies show the effectiveness of such systems in the circulation of rumours (Matz et al. 2017). In contrast, some others raise doubt about the effectiveness of recommendation systems in the spread of rumours. Although controversial on the surface, all those paradoxical results might be part of a bigger picture (Ruths 2019) which currently does not exist.

4 The Evaluation of Strategies for Countering Rumours

It was merely a century ago that the first systematic efforts against the mass spread of rumours began (Allport and Postman 1947). Since then a variety of techniques have been exercised by media organisations (Fabry 2017), researched at academic institutions (Van Der Linden et al. 2017; Allport and Postman 1947), and recently implemented by social media platforms (Google: How Google Fights Disinformation 2018; Mosseri 2017) and by governments within digital policy frameworks (DW: German justice minister to set up task force on Internet hate speech 2015).

To develop an effective and comprehensive plan to quell rumours and develop novel techniques, it is crucial to be aware of the existing strategies and potential capabilities. We present a review which explores both the targeted and neglected aspects of addressing rumour diffusion. Figure 1 illustrates the variety of prevalent strategies for countering rumours. Those strategies are classified based on their impacts on the components of the communication process. A communication process comprises three major elements of the sender, channel, and receiver in which senders transmit messages to receivers through communication channels. The first group of strategies takes those who initiate rumours into account and restrain them (in case of deliberate rumour spreading). The second group tends to secure communication channels and minimise rumour emergence and circulation within the channels. The purpose of the third group is to protect those who were targeted by the rumours. In the following, we explain the strategies in more detail.

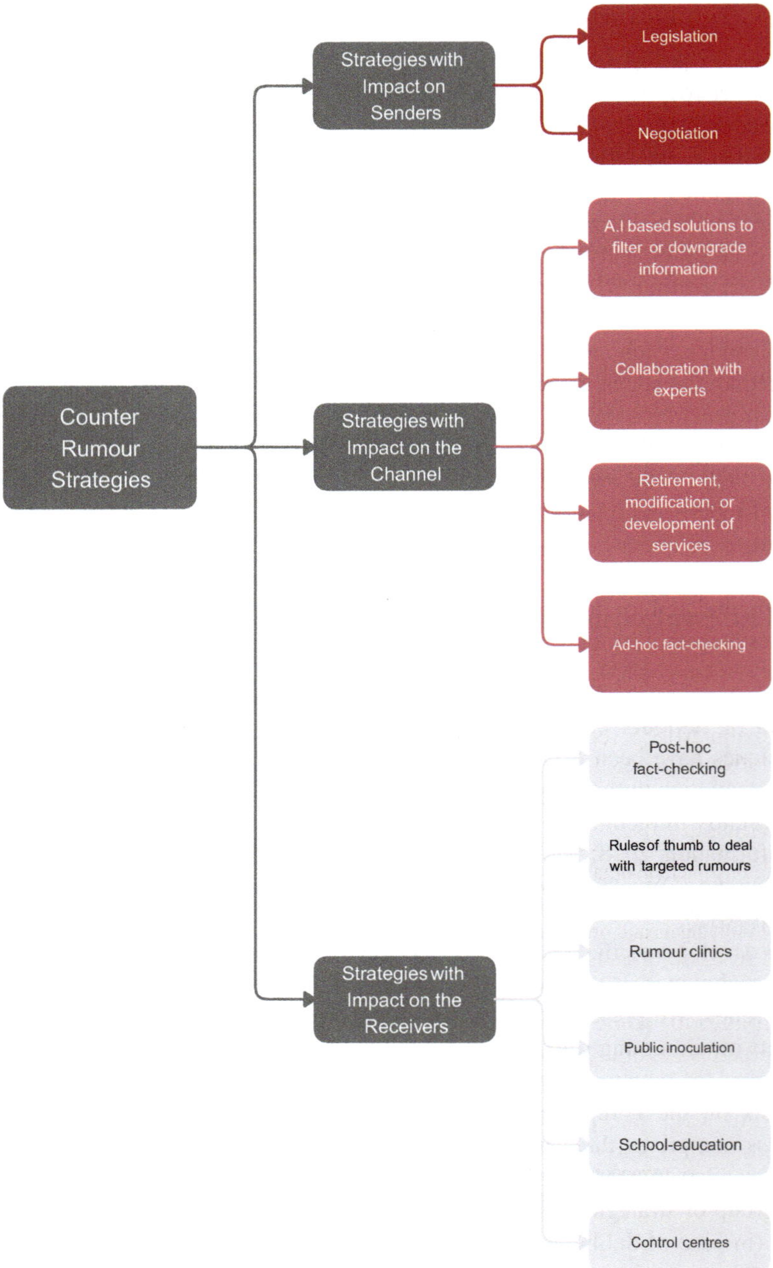

Fig. 1 The classification of counter-rumour strategies

4.1 Strategies with Impact on Senders

In this section, we discuss counter-strategies developed to confront those who deliberately participate in the rumour process. To this end, we propose two main approaches to legislation and political solutions.

4.1.1 Legislation

One of the oldest and most widespread rumour counter-strategies is to take the government's legal action against those who contribute to the rumour spreading. The earliest form of this approach is to protect individuals against baseless defamation and character assassination. Although this is a practical approach to serve this purpose, it could be costly and take a long time. However, on the bright side, legal actions raise awareness by drawing media attention (Farrell et al. 2019). With the growth of online social media platforms, the expansion of legal actions from conventional mediums to online social media gradually started. Germany was among the first countries taking online environments into account (DW: German justice minister to set up task force on Internet hate speech 2015); however, the number of countries with regulations regarding rumour spreading in online environments is increasing (Funke and Flamini 2018).

4.1.2 Negotiation

Social manipulation campaigns are becoming an essential tool for information operations. On the one hand, different governments and organisations use this approach to influence public opinion. On the other hand, platforms and media organisations try to flag such operations and take down the accounts and messages linked to those operations (Fung and Garcia 2019). Reactive measures often seem like a cat and mouse game since new manipulation campaigns keep popping up while platforms adapt to take them down. One of the strategies to confront or limit this spread is negotiating with the offenders and working toward an agreement with them. This tactic is not always a feasible option due to lack of interest from either sides, unknown identity of the offenders, or unrealistic expectations; however, this is a promising approach with meagre cost, and high output (Bodine-Baron et al. 2018).

4.2 Strategies with Impact on the Channel

In this section, we discuss the strategies concerning the protection of communication channels. Media organisations or social media companies propose strategies that aim to make channels rumour-proof and minimise the likelihood of rumour emergence and circulation.

4.2.1 Solutions Based on Artificial Intelligence

The spread of rumours is a rapid, widespread, and profound phenomenon within social media platforms (Vosoughi et al. 2018). One of the most efficient approaches to confront this rampant diffusion is Artificial Intelligence (A.I.). It is a fast and cheap approach, and it can tackle the spread of rumours at scale, and across languages and time zones. A.I. techniques are useful for two primary purposes of content filtering and downgrading.

Filtering
Among the massive streams of information flowing in social media platforms, there are mischievous pieces that could make their way to the platform. Although compared to the information circulating in social media, the volume of such contents is insignificant. They have to be taken down before making public; otherwise, there might be unexpected ramifications. The tremendous amount of circulating information in social media eliminates the option of manual inspection. Instead, platforms benefit from the power of predictive analytics and machine learning. They often first flag the contents that are deemed problematic with high confidence, then those pieces that have a borderline status are sent for human-based evaluation.

Downgrading
Social media platforms are often using a timeline-based design within which there is running list of posts in users main page showing most recent updates from their social network. This list -at least in default setting- does not show contents in chronological order. Platforms use algorithms to show posts in an order that is more appealing for the user. If rumours can game the ranking algorithm and climb up to the top of the list, they likely see them. This dynamic would increase the visibility of rumours which positively affect their circulation rate. To confront this issue, platforms cannot remove rumour related posts as they do not break any law or violate any term; thus they try to identify such posts and relegate them in the timeline (Lyons 2018; Harvey 2018; Google: How Google Fights Disinformation 2018). This action would subsequently reduce rumours spreading chance.

4.2.2 Collaborative Solutions

To protect communication channels from rumours, the collaboration between experts from media organisations, social media platforms, and academia is essential. They all have complementary expertise that would help reduce the chance of rumour emergence and circulation.

Collaboration with Fact-Checkers
One of the biggest concerns for social media platforms is the verification of dubious information. The verification is a difficult problem to address because of two reasons. First, social media platforms purport they cannot arbitrate information truthfulness as they are technology firm and not a media company. Second, the scale of information circulation in social media is massive and conventional methods cannot keep up with information growth. To tackle these issues, social media platforms started to collaborate with fact-checking institutes considered information verification experts. After a primary AI-based screening or receiving reports from users, they sent inappropriate posts to fact-checkers for further assessment. Although this approach can address the first issue, the second problem is still there. The platforms' response to this challenge is to expand the collaboration with fact-checking institutions and turn it into a crowdsourced activity. To this end, they are planning to give a reviewer privilege to particular users and ask them to evaluate flagged social media posts. With this solution, the capacity of fact-checking significantly increases, thus could solve the data volume issue.

Collaboration Between News Outlets and Social Media Platforms
Media literacy and digital journalism are essential in building resilient communication channels against rumours. Social media, along with major media organisations, can promote quality journalism in the digital era. To this end, major social media platforms and news outlets formed partnerships, initiated training programs, and even developed products and services to empower journalists (Mosseri 2017; Policy team: Update on Twitter's review of the 2016 US election 2018; Google News Initiative).

Collaboration with Academia
Tackling large-scale rumours in social media is a recent phenomenon with plenty of unknown and unexplored aspects. A social media platform is an organisation with limited resources which make having a comprehensive understanding of social media rather impossible. On the other hand, universities and scientific institutions are specialised organisations for research. Social media platforms could benefit from cutting edge knowledge without a huge investment in their research and development to collaborate with academia. Such a collaboration is also beneficial for scientific institutions as they would have access to a suitable environment to test old social theories and hypotheses and propose new ones (Al-Tabbaa and Ankrah 2019).

4.2.3 Design Based Solutions

In this category of solutions, the goal is to permanently retire a service, refine a service with issues, or develop new service.

Service Retirement
Sometimes, a service that was initially developed to add value to a business, gradually turns to a source of headache for that organisation. One of the approaches to tackle this issue is to retire the problematic service. Although this might seem like a naive strategy, sometimes the stake of keeping the service open (for modifications) is too high, and the best thing that we can do is to shut down the service as soon as possible. One example of service retirement is Facebook APIs such as Events API, Search API, and App Insights API after Cambridge Analytica scandal (Archibong 2018).

Service Modification
Another approach to deal with problematic services is the modification strategy. Using this approach, the service provider can preserve the service by addressing its shortcomings. One example of this approach is WhatsApp message forwarding limitation policy issued to reduce the rumour diffusion speed (Kastrenakes 2019).

New Service Development
The design and development of new services are essential for the survival and growth of organisations. In the case of rumour response, social media platforms have built services to mitigate the chance of rumour emergence and transmission. They mostly try to put the information in the right context by providing extra information. One of those services is the context button which adds more context to the Facebook posts (Lyons 2018).

4.2.4 Ad-hoc Factchecking

Media organisations are in the front-line of combating rumours. They are on the first tier of the news supply chain, making them responsible for sharing accurate, impartial, and evidence-based information. The significance of the accurate journalism entailed defining an exclusive role in news outlets to inspect information integrity before making public. Later on, this auditing role got a new title of ad-hoc fact-checking it aims to eliminate errors before a piece goes live (Fabry 2017).

4.3 Strategies with Impact on the Receivers

In this section, we discuss strategies to protect people subjugated to rumours. In the following, we discuss six counter-strategies.

4.3.1 Post-hoc Fact-checking

In the previous section, we explained ad-hoc fact-checking as a preemptive counter rumour strategy. Although it is a highly effective approach to confront rumours, it is not always feasible to flag and corrects misleading information beforehand. For instance, during live programs (e.g., presidential debates) it does not make sense to use ad-hoc fact-checking. In such situations, another variant of fact-checking called post-hoc fact-checking is used. It identifies and corrects errors after they go public. Post-hoc fact-checking is less effective than ad-hoc fact-checking as in in the earlier people are already exposed to rumours. Nevertheless, keeping the number of exposed to the minimum has a tremendous impact on tackling rumour diffusion (Graves 2016).

4.3.2 Rule of Thumbs to Deal with Targeted Rumours

When a rumour particularly targets an entity (e.g., an individual, an organisation, a country), the entity's spokesperson should take a stance. Figure 2 displays possible ways of responding to a rumour. Initially, one should decide whether to comment about the rumour or to ignore it. In case of commenting, then there are three avenues they could be followed: (i) Confirmation of the rumour and giving detailed information about it, (ii) Denial of the rumour and giving a rebuttal, or (iii) Withholding to comment about the rumour (DiFonzo et al. 1994).

The other option is to ignore it, which is the weakest quelling strategy. It is doubtful that a rumour dies on its own because something unusual to someone may be deemed as plausible by another person. In other words, even if some people drop the rumour, some others pick it up.

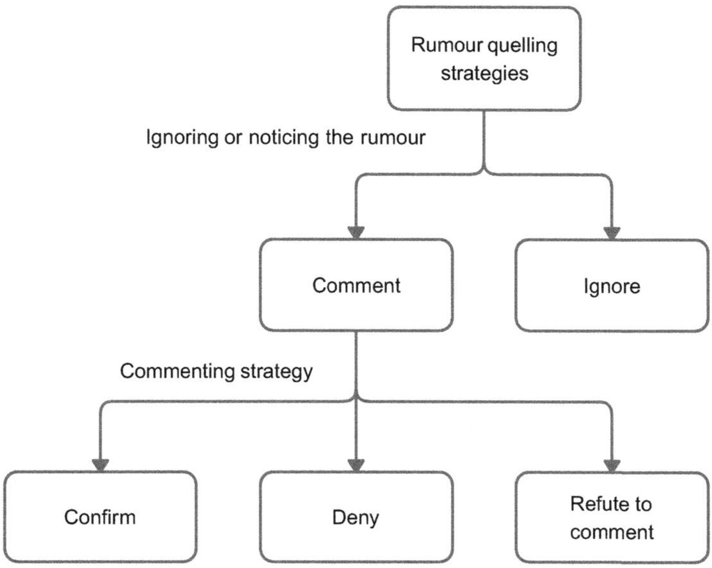

Fig. 2 The classification of counter-rumour strategies. (DiFonzo et al. 1994)

Some rumours are fully or partially truthful. Scholars have shown that confirming the genuine parts of the rumours reduce the chance of rumour transmission. One of the most common strategies to rein in the rumours is denial. There are a few factors that influence denial effectiveness. A denial should be based upon the truth. Denial of a true rumour is a dangerous strategy that may permanently destroy the responsible party's credibility. The denial effectiveness is enhanced when the denial source is trusted and is aligned with the rumour context. It is also crucial to avoid repeating the rumour during the denial. The repetition fosters beliefs to the rumours. The responsible party should also issue the denial as soon as possible rather than after reaching a certain critical mass. Finally, a denial message should deliver a clear, detailed explanation with strong evidence indicating the rumour falsehood and convey to listeners a straightforward course of action about what they should do when they come across the rumour. A no-comment response would work the same as an ignorance strategy, and at worst gives more credence to the rumour. It reinforces the cover-up hypotheses and transfers the message that "we have something to hide" (DiFonzo and Bordia 2007a; DiFonzo 2009; DiFonzo et al. 1994).

4.3.3 Rumour Clinics

The rumour clinic was a workshop composed of experts collecting and analysing major circulating rumours and then training participants about the techniques embedded in those rumours. Although in the beginning, the government was supposed to organise rumour clinics, they stepped back due to the uncertain consequences of sharing and repeating rumours. Despite the initial withdrawal, they could not stand the idea of public rumour revelation, and eventually, in 1943 they could shut down rumour clinics (Allport and Postman 1947; Faye 2007).

4.3.4 Control Centres

In response to widespread rumour circulation during civil right movements in the U.S. in the $1960s$, the government created a telephone service called rumour control centre (RCC) to provide reliable information about floating rumours to the general public. Those who called RCCs could ask about the veracity of rumours and stories they heard, and then RCC staffs could verify that information via police and intelligence units (Young et al. 2014). From an organisational perspective, RCCs were small organisations with a few employees and a simple structure. They only require communication hookups with police and fire departments and other city agencies to get the most recent updates regarding the incidents (Ponting 1973; Knopf 1975). From an institutional perspective, they were counted as governmental agencies (Young et al. 2014). RCCs gradually vanished in the 70s due to the funding and legitimacy issues (Ponting 1973; Faye 2007); however, a digital variant of RCCs has recently been introduced by the Federal Emergency Management Agency

(FEMA) website. This web page provides information about running rumours during disasters. Although it is just a static web page, it is continuously updated by monitoring the circulating rumours in the digital sphere.

4.3.5 Education and Media Literacy

Education is supposed to be highly useful to confront rumour dissemination. By providing knowledge on propaganda techniques and critical thinking, it merely gives a powerful and long-lasting shield against all sorts of misleading information. Open Society Institute calls education "the best all-round solution" and mentions "high-quality education and having more and more educated people is a prerequisite for tackling the negative effects of fake news and post-truth" (Lessenski 2018).

This policy aims to improve media literacy and critical thinking among citizens. It would help them to reflect on the information they receive before believing or sharing them. Despite all the great qualities of education policy, too much emphasis on being critical might backfire and come with unintended consequences of undervaluing respectable and high-quality news outlets (Lazer et al. 2018).

4.3.6 Public Inoculation

Despite shutting down rumour clinics in 1943, the idea of creating immunity against rumours did not die and reframed in public health literature as public inoculation against rumour spreading. As in the rumour clinics, the goal was to create awareness on rumours to not being tricked by them; public inoculation also follows the same idea but with a different style. In biology, inoculation or vaccination refers to the process of training the immune system to produce anti-body by exposing it with a weakened virus. A similar philosophy can be fitting for public inoculation. Still, instead of training the immune system here the idea is to train the brain to build up resistance against rumours (Matz et al. 2017; Van Der Linden et al. 2017).

One of the challenging aspects of public inoculation is its implementation. One of the common strategies in this vein is to resort to media, elites, and thought-leaders to echo inoculation messages (Farrell et al. 2019). It has also shown that serious gaming is a practical approach to inoculate people against rumours (Roozenbeek and van der Linden 2019). Despite the success and effectiveness of public inoculation in countering rumours, it is still considered an experimental solution for rumour confrontation in limited contexts (Roozenbeek and van der Linden 2019). The expansion of this strategy would show its effectiveness in other domains and on a larger scale.

4.4 Evaluation of Strategies

This section first presents a framework for evaluating the counter-rumour strategies, followed by their assessment.

4.4.1 An Evaluation Framework Based on the Spread of Infectious Diseases

The spread of rumours bears many similarities to the evolution and transmission of contagious diseases (Kucharski 2016). Almost half a century ago, Goffman and Newill (Goffman and Newill 1964) directed attention to the analogy between the spread of infectious diseases and disseminating information (Daley and Kendall 1964). They argued that transmission of ideas does not need to be restricted to infectious diseases but is a more general process applied to many contexts. For example, the development of the psychoanalytic movement in the early twentieth century was no less an epidemic than the outbreak of influenza in 1917 and 1918 (Goffman and Newill 1964). This similarity between biological and intellectual epidemics is even caused the same modelling paradigm to be adopted to explain the dynamic of propagation (Daley and Kendall 1964; Moreno et al. 2004).

In epidemiology, control frameworks have proven successful for reining in epidemics (Daley and Gani 2001). It is composed of three mechanisms of (i) education, (ii) immunisation, and (iii) screening and quarantine. The first two are prevention measures that aim to minimise exposure to the disease and give a complete protection to a person against infection. At the same time, the third one has a more interventional nature to reduce the transmission rate.

Education is one of the simplest and cheapest ways to control epidemics by training the public about simple techniques such as wearing masks, washing hands, social distancing, and gargling to reduce the likelihood of exposure to the disease. It is mostly about raising awareness about dos and don'ts regarding a particular condition. For example, in the case of AIDS epidemics, the educational campaigns in February 1987 tried to discourage risk-prone behaviours such as unprotected sex or needle exchange for drug users. The campaign was successful by reducing the spread of the virus in countries where the state organised educational campaigns (Daley and Gani 2001; Leung and Nicoll 2010).

Immunisation through vaccination is one of the most influential and cost-effective strategies to control epidemics (Kato et al. 2011; Daley and Gani 2001; Magnusson 2017). It is referred to as "one of the great public health triumphs of all time" due to achieving landmark gains over a relatively short period. For example, in the case of smallpox, a worldwide vaccination campaign succeeded in eradicating the disease. For instance, the global immunisation program against diphtheria, pertussis, tetanus, poliomyelitis, measles and tuberculosis in 1974, immunised only 5% of the world's children. However, in less than 20 years, more than 90%

of the world's children had received BCG vaccine, and 75–85% had received immunisation against diphtheria, tetanus, pertussis, poliomyelitis and measles (Ruff 1999).

The third approach to control the epidemic is screening and quarantine. It is an interventional approach that plays a role after an epidemic has already started. It is a core public health approach as it can reduce and delay the disease's spread somewhat at the earliest stage. During the epidemics, after screening susceptible individuals, those that pose a risk are quarantined. "Many countries do not attempt these measures because of logistics, and cost-benefit considerations" (Leung and Nicoll 2010; Daley and Gani 2001; Magnusson 2017).

Due to the substantial similarity between the propagation of diseases and the information dissemination from one hand, and a comprehensive framework in disease eradication, this study proposes to adopt the same framework for the rumour confrontation. To this end, the past counter-strategies are set into the epidemic framework to understand which phase of the epidemic control is less emphasised in rumour confrontation.

4.4.2 Effectiveness of Strategies

This section evaluates the counter rumour strategies introduced in the previous section using the epidemic framework. The epidemic framework presents three approaches to control the spread of disease: (i) exposure minimisation, (ii) immunisation or vaccination, and (iii) reducing the transmission rate. In this section, we use the same framework to assess the goal of counter-rumour strategies. As Table 2 displays, rumour counter strategies pursue at least one of the epidemic control approaches.

The role of legislation mitigates the transmission rate and prevents further spread of rumours. It takes punitive measures against those who participate in rumour dissemination. Such measures would make people more careful and cautious about sharing information with their peers. In the political solutions, the goal is to cut the rumour from the source through negotiation by the main sponsors behind the rumours, so it belongs to the strategies with exposure minimisation view.

The A.I. techniques for the filtering and downgrading aim to reduce the visibility of rumours in the online social network by taking down rumour related contents and accounts; thus, they are considered strategies with exposure minimisation approach. If they are used to just flag the misleading contents, they also fall into the third category (reducing the transmission rate). The collaboration between online social media platforms and fact-checking institutes provides information about the truthfulness of the posts circulating on the media. Fact-checking the posts may dissuade people from sharing the news with their network. The collaboration can also improve the accuracy of filtering and downgrading algorithms. The other type of platforms' cooperation is with a media organisation. It would empower professional journalism in the digital era and reduce the likelihood of rumour emergence within news channels. The partnership between platforms and the scientific community would contribute to improving filtering and downgrading techniques

Table 2 Analysis of the quelling strategies against epidemic control framework

		Exposure minimisation	Giving complete protection (vaccination)	Reducing the transmission rate
Rumour counter strategies	Legislation			✓
	Political solution	✓		
	Filtering	✓		✓
	Downgrading	✓		✓
	Collaboration with fact-checking	✓		✓
	Collaboration for media literacy	✓		
	Collaboration in scientific project	✓		
	Service retirement	✓		✓
	Service modification	✓		✓
	New service development	✓		✓
	Ad-hoc fact-checking	✓		
	Post-hoc fact-checking			✓
	Rule of thumbs to deal with targeted rumours			✓
	Rumour clinics		✓	
	Public inoculation		✓	
	Educational policy		✓	
	Control centres			✓

which would eventually minimise the rumour exposure. Within the design-based strategies, the service retirement and the service modifications aim to reduce the rumour appearance and transmission likelihood. The new service development can also serve the same function; however, they are mostly for reducing the rumour transmission among the services that already exist.

The purpose of ad-hoc fact-checking is to prevent mistakes and false information before making public; therefore, it falls into the exposure minimisation category. Post-hoc fact-checking reviews and fixes incorrect information after they go public and decreases the likelihood of rumour transmission. The rule of thumb to deal with targeted rumours is a set of principles that a rumour audience could use to reduce rumour transmission. The rumour clinics and public inoculation try to create immunisation by teaching people how rumours deceive the mind. The purpose of the educational approach is to raise awareness and educate people. It works like a shield for the brain as it aims to train the brain not to be trapped by rumours. Control centres reduce the rumour transmission rate by filling the news channels gap by providing information about the floating rumours.

The introduced counter-measures are exercised intermittently over the past century. Despite tremendous efforts and developing all those strategies, diffusion of rumours not only has not shrunk but also escalated. The quick reactions to the sudden rise of rumours in different periods and the absence of a comprehensive plan are amongst the reasons for the failure of curbing the rumours. Besides, focusing on the rumour exposure minimisation and reducing the rumour transmission rate while neglecting the more effective immunisation approach is another reason for the failure of the current set of strategies against rumour dissemination.

5 Conclusion

The dissemination of large-scale rumour spreading regardless of the purpose could precipitate catastrophic repercussions. This research aims at addressing this challenge by posing three questions: what is a rumour? How does media facilitate its circulation? And how did past counter-rumour strategies perform?

We discuss rumour, Gossip, legend, propaganda, conspiracy theory, fake news, misinformation, and pseudoscience and analyse them from a process-based perspective. We infer that except Gossip and legend – which are fundamentally different regarding the context of emergence, content, and functionality – the rest of false and unverified information variations are other forms of rumour. We also argue legends are improbable to be harmful; gossips might be detrimental, but in small-scales; rumours might become extremely dangerous in large-scale, therefore it is of utmost importance to develop resilience against this phenomenon. The spread of rumours since the pre-printing press till the social media era is taken into account to respond to the second question. The focus was primarily on social media since the spread of rumours scaled-up, diversified, and accelerated during this period. For the third question, we investigated counter-rumour strategies. Based on their impact on different communication components, we classify them into three groups of sender-, channel-, and receiver-related methods. After introducing the strategies, they are assessed based on the proposed epidemic framework. In this framework, strategies are evaluated based on three criteria: exposure dissemination, giving complete protection, and reducing the transmission rate. The analysis shows that the past processes against rumours unevenly cover all aspects of the epidemic framework. Although vaccination is recognised as the most effective approach in controlling the epidemics, there is more emphasis on the other two techniques.

To effectively address the existing gaps in the tackling mass rumour spreading, what is essentially required is a long-term and comprehensive plan covering different variations of rumour spreading and incorporating all aspects of the epidemic framework. This plan mainly focuses on (i) immunisation approach due to its proven effectiveness and (ii) AI-based techniques due to the scale, scope, and speed of rumour spreading in online social media platforms. Besides, we should develop the new generation of strategies for all variations of false and unverified information. Additionally, we must closely monitor social media mechanisms that contribute to the circulation of rumours on a large-scale, such as recommendation systems and social bots.

References

Acerbi A (2019) Cognitive attraction and online misinformation. Palgrave Commun 5(1):1–7

Allport GW, Postman L (1947) The psychology of rumor, 1st edn. Henry Holt and Company

Al-Tabbaa O, Ankrah S (2019) Engineered university-industry collaboration: a social capital perspective. Eur Manag Rev 16(3):543–565

Aral S (2020) The hype machine: how social media disrupts our elections, our economy, and our health-and how we must adapt. Currency

Aral S, Eckles D (2019) Protecting elections from social media manipulation. Science 365(6456):858–861

Archibong I (2018) API and other platform product changes. https://developers.facebook.com/blog/post/2018/04/04/facebook-api-platform-product-changes/

Barabási AL et al (2016) Network science. Cambridge University Press, Cambridge

Benkler Y, Faris R, Roberts H (2018) Network propaganda: manipulation, disinformation, and radicalization in American politics. Oxford University Press, Oxford

Berkovsky S, Freyne J (2015) Web personalization and recommender systems. In: Proceedings of the 21th ACM SIGKDD international conference on knowledge discovery and data mining, pp 2307–2308. https://doi.org/10.1145/2783258.2789995

Bodine-Baron EA, Helmus TC, Radin A, Treyger E (2018) Countering Russian social media influence. RAND Corporation, Santa Monica

Bordia P, DiFonzo N (2004) Problem solving in social interactions on the internet: rumor as social cognition. Soc Psychol Q 67(1):33–49

Bordia P, Kiazad K, Restubog SLD, DiFonzo N, Stenson N, Tang RL (2014) Rumor as revenge in the workplace. Group Org Manag 39(4):363–388

Boutyline A, Willer R (2017) The social structure of political echo chambers: variation in ideological homophily in online networks. Polit Psychol 38(3):551–569

Briones RL, Kuch B, Liu BF, Jin Y (2011) Keeping up with the digital age: how the American red cross uses social media to build relationships. Public Relat Rev 37(1):37–43

Buringh E, Van Zanden JL (2009) Charting the "rise of the west": manuscripts and printed books in Europe, a long-term perspective from the sixth through eighteenth centuries. J Econ Hist 69(2):409–445

Chakravarthi P (1992) The history of communications-from cave drawings to mail messages. IEEE Aerosp Electron Syst Mag 7(4):30–35

Christakis NA, Fowler JH (2009) Connected: the surprising power of our social networks and how they shape our lives. Little, Brown Spark, New York

Christopherson KM (2007) The positive and negative implications of anonymity in internet social interactions: "on the internet, nobody knows you're a dog". Comput Hum Behav 23(6):3038–3056

Cook J (2020) A history of FLICC: the 5 techniques of science denial. https://www.skepticalscience.com/history-FLICC-5-techniques-science-denial.html

Cota W, Ferreira SC, Pastor-Satorras R, Starnini M (2019) Quantifying echo chamber effects in information spreading over political communication networks. EPJ Data Sci 8(1):35

Daley DJ, Gani J (2001) Epidemic modelling: an introduction. Cambridge University Press, Cambridge

Daley DJ, Kendall DG (1964) Epidemics and rumours. Nature 204(4963):1118. https://doi.org/10.1038/2041118a0
Dandekar P, Goel A, Lee DT (2013) Biased assimilation, homophily, and the dynamics of polarization. Proc Natl Acad Sci 110(15):5791–5796
DiFonzo N (2009) The watercooler effect: an indispensable guide to understanding and harnessing the power of rumors. Avery, New York
Difonzo N (2018) Conspiracy rumor psychology. Conspiracy theories and the people who believe them
DiFonzo N, Bordia P (2007a) Rumor psychology: social and organizational approaches. American Psychological Association
Difonzo N, Bordia P (2007b) Rumors influence: toward a dynamic social impact theory of rumor. Frontiers of social psychology. Psychology Press, New York
DiFonzo N, Bordia P, Rosnow RL (1994) Reining in rumors. Organ Dyn 23(1):47–62. https://doi.org/10.1016/0090-2616(94)90087-6
DiFonzo N, Bourgeois MJ, Suls J, Homan C, Stupak N, Brooks BP, Ross DS, Bordia P (2013) Rumor clustering, consensus, and polarization: dynamic social impact and self-organization of hearsay. J Exp Soc Psychol 49(3):378–399
Dowe T (1997): News you can abuse. https://www.wired.com/1997/01/netizen-6/
DW: German justice minister to set up task force on Internet hate speech (2015). https://www.dw.com/en/german-justice-minister-to-set-up-task-force-on-internet-hate-speech/a-18714334
Ellick AB, Westbrook A (2018a) Scopus vs. Web of Science vs. Google Scholar. https://www.nytimes.com/2018/11/12/opinion/russia-meddling-disinformation-fake-news-elections.html
Ellick AB, Westbrook A (2018b) Operation InfeKtion: Russian Disinformation from Cold War to Kanye. https://www.nytimes.com/2018/11/12/opinion/russia-meddling-disinformation-fake-news-elections.html
Fabry M (2017) Here's how the first fact-checkers were able to do their jobs before the Internet. https://time.com/4858683/fact-checking-history/
Farrell J, McConnell K, Brulle R (2019) Evidence-based strategies to combat scientific misinformation. Nat Clim Chang 9(3):191–195. https://doi.org/10.1038/s41558-018-0368-6. http://www.nature.com/articles/s41558-018-0368-6
Faye C (2007) Governing the grapevine: the study of rumor during world war ii. Hist Psychol 10(1):1
Ferrara E, Varol O, Davis C, Menczer F, Flammini A (2016) The rise of social bots. Commun ACM 59(7):96–104
Fine GA, Rosnow RL (1978) Gossip, gossipers, gossiping. Personal Soc Psychol Bull 4(1):161–168
Flaxman S, Goel S, Rao JM (2016) Filter bubbles, echo chambers, and online news consumption. Public Opin Q 80(S1):298–320
Fox J (2020) 'fake news'–the perfect storm: historical perspectives. Hist Res 93(259):172–187
Franks B, Attia S (2011) Rumours and gossip as genres of communication. In: The social psychology of communication. Springer, pp 169–186
Freelon D, Wells C (2020) Disinformation as political communication. Polit Commun 37(2):145–156
Frenda SJ, Nichols RM, Loftus EF (2011) Current issues and advances in misinformation research. Curr Dir Psychol Sci 20(1):20–23
Fung B, Garcia A (2019) Facebook has shut down 5.4 billion fake ac-counts this year. https://edition.cnn.com/2019/11/13/tech/Facebook-fake-accounts/index.html
Funke D, Flamini D (2018) A guide to anti-misinformation actions around the world. https://www.poynter.org/ifcn/anti-misinformation-actions/
Goffman W, Newill VA (1964) Generalization of epidemic theory: an application to the transmission of ideas. Nature 204(4955):225–228
Google News Initiative. https://newsinitiative.withgoogle.com/

Google: How Google Fights Disinformation (2018). https://storage.googleapis.com/gweb-uniblog-publish-prod/documents/How_Google_Fights_Disinformation.pdf
Graves L (2016) Deciding what's true: the rise of political fact-checking in American journalism. Columbia University Press, New York
Guess AM, Lerner M, Lyons B, Montgomery JM, Nyhan B, Reifler J, Sircar N (2020) A digital media literacy intervention increases discernment between mainstream and false news in the United States and India. Proc Natl Acad Sci 117(27):15536–15545
Hansson SO (2017) Science denial as a form of pseudoscience. Stud Hist Philos Sci A63:39–47
Hansson SO (2018) Dealing with climate science denialism: experiences from confrontations with other forms of pseudoscience. Clim Pol 18(9):1094–1102
Harvey D (2018) Serving healthy conversation. https://blog.twitter.com/en_us/topics/product/2018/Serving_Healthy_Conversation.html
Hazenburg H, Van den Hoven M, Cunningham S, Alfano M, Ashgari H, Mumm EE, Fard AE, Rodriguez ET (2018) Micro-targeting and ICT media in the Dutch parliamentary system: Technological changes in Dutch democracy. Technical report. Delft University of Technology
Hendricks VF, Vestergaard M (2019) Fact resistance, populism, and conspiracy theories. In: Reality lost. Springer, pp 79–101
Howell L et al (2013) Digital wildfires in a hyperconnected world. WEF Rep 3:15–94(2013)
Hussain M (2019) An Iranian activist wrote dozens of articles for right-wing outlets. But is he a real person?. https://theintercept.com/2019/06/09/heshmat-alavi-fake-iran-mek/
Jannach D, Jugovac M (2019) Measuring the business value of recommender systems. ACM Trans Manag Inf Syst (TMIS) 10(4):1–23
Kastrenakes J (2019) WhatsApp limits message forwarding in fight against mis-information. https://www.theverge.com/2019/1/21/18191455/whatsapp-forwarding-limit-five-messages-misinformation-battle
Kato F, Tainaka KI, Sone S, Morita S, Iida H, Yoshimura J (2011) Combined effects of prevention and quarantine on a breakout in sir model. Sci Rep 1:10
Knapp RH (1944) A psychology of rumour. Public Opin Q 8(1):22–37. https://doi.org/10.1086/265665
Knopf TA (1975) Rumors, race, and riots. Trans Publ
Koenig F (1985) Rumor in the marketplace: the social psychology of commercial hearsay. Auburn House Publishing Company
Kucharski A (2016) Study epidemiology of fake news. Nature 540(7634):525–525
Lazer DMJ, Baum MA, Benkler Y, Berinsky AJ, Greenhill KM, Menczer F, Metzger MJ, Nyhan B, Pennycook G, Rothschild D, Schudson M, Sloman SA, Sunstein CR, Thorson EA, Watts DJ, Zittrain JL (2018) The science of fake news. Science (New York, NY) 359(6380):1094–1096. https://doi.org/10.1126/science.aao2998
Lehmann S (2019) Fundamental structures in temporal communication networks. In: Temporal network theory. Springer, pp 25–48
Lessenski M (2018) Common sense wanted: resilience to 'post-truth' and its predictors in the new media literacy index 2018. Technical report. Open Society Institute. https://osis.bg/wp-content/uploads/2018/04/MediaLiteracyIndex2018_publishENG.pdf
Leung GM, Nicoll A (2010) Reflections on pandemic (H1N1) 2009 and the international response. PLoS Med 7(10):e1000346
Li HOY, Bailey A, Huynh D, Chan J (2020) Youtube as a source of information on covid-19: a pandemic of misinformation? BMJ Glob Health 5(5)
Lyons T (2018) Hard questions: what's Facebook's strategy for stopping false news? https://newsroom.fb.com/news/2018/05/hard-questions-false-news/
Magnusson R (2017) Advancing the right to health: the vital role of law. World Health Organization, Geneva
Marsden C, Meyer T, Brown I (2020) Platform values and democratic elections: how can the law regulate digital disinformation? Comput Law Secur Rev 36:105373
Martin LJ (1982) Disinformation: an instrumentality in the propaganda arsenal. Polit Commun 2(1):47–64

Matz SC, Kosinski M, Nave G, Stillwell DJ (2017) Psychological targeting as an effective approach to digital mass persuasion. Proc Natl Acad Sci 114(48):12714–12719
Mazarr MJ, Casey A, Demus A, Harold SW, Matthews LJ, Beauchamp-Mustafaga N, Sladden J (2019) Hostile social manipulation present realities and emerging trends. Technical report. RAND National Defense Research Institute, Santa Monica
McGonagle T (2017) "fake news" false fears or real concerns? Neth Q Human Rights 35(4):203–209
Molina MD, Sundar SS, Le T, Lee D (2019) "fake news" is not simply false information: a concept explication and taxonomy of online content. Am Behav Sci:0002764219878224
Moreno Y, Nekovee M, Pacheco AF (2004) Dynamics of rumor spreading in complex networks. Phys Rev E69(6):066130
Mosseri A (2017) Working to stop misinformation and false news.https://newsroom.fb.com/news/2017/04/working-to-stop-misinformation-and-false-news/
O'Connor C, Weatherall JO (2019) The misinformation age: how false beliefs spread. Yale University Press
Paris B, Donovan J (2019) Deep fakes and cheap fakes. Data & Society, New York
Policy team: Update on Twitter's review of the 2016 US election (2018). https://blog.twitter.com/en_us/topics/company/2018/2016-election-update.html
Ponting JR (1973) Rumor control centers. Am Behav Sci 16(3):391–401
Posetti J, Matthews A (2018) A short guide to the history of 'fake news' and disinformation. Int Center J 7
Romerstein H (2001) Disinformation as a kgb weapon in the cold war. J Intel Hist 1(1):54–67
Roozenbeek J, van der Linden S (2019) The fake news game: actively inoculating against the risk of misinformation. J Risk Res 22(5):570–580
Roth Y, Pickles N (2020) Updating our approach to misleading information. https://blog.twitter.com/en_us/topics/product/2020/updating-our-approach-to-misleading-information.html
Ruff T (1999) Immunisation strategies for viral diseases in developing countries. Rev Med Virol 9(2):121–138
Ruths D (2019) The misinformation machine. Science 363(6425):348–348
Schmid P, Betsch C (2019) Effective strategies for rebutting science denialism in public discussions. Nat Hum Behav 3(9):931–939
Schor EL (1995) Developing communality: family-centered programs to improve children's health and well-being. Bull N Y Acad Med 72(2):413
Shao C, Ciampaglia GL, Varol O, Yang K, Flammini A, Menczer F (2018) The spread of low-credibility content by social bots. Nat Commun 9(1):4787. https://doi.org/10.1038/s41467-018-06930-7
Shibutani T (1966) Improvised news. Ardent Media
Standage T (2017) The true history of fake news. https://www.1843magazine.com/technology/rewind/the-true-history-of-fake-news
Stella M, Ferrara E, De Domenico M (2018) Bots increase exposure to negative and inflammatory content in online social systems. Proc Natl Acad Sci 115(49):12435–12440
Tsfati Y, Boomgaarden H, Strömbäck J, Vliegenthart R, Damstra A, Lindgren E (2020) Causes and consequences of mainstream media dissemination of fake news: literature review and synthesis. Ann Int Commun Assoc:1–17
Tufekci Z (2017) Twitter and tear gas: the power and fragility of networked protest. Yale University Press
Uberti D (2016) The real history of fake news. https://www.cjr.org/special_report/fake_news_history.php
Van Der Linden S, Maibach E, Cook J, Leiserowitz A, Lewandowsky S (2017) Inoculating against misinformation. Science 358(6367):1141–1142
Van Prooijen JW (2018) The psychology of conspiracy theories. Routledge, London
Vosoughi S, Roy D, Aral S (2018) The spread of true and false news online. Science 359(6380):1146–1151

Wagh RB, Patil JB (2012) Web personalization and recommender systems: an overview. In: Proceedings of the 18th international conference on management of data, p 114
Woolley SC, Howard PN (2018) Computational propaganda: political parties, politicians, and political manipulation on social media. Oxford University Press, Oxford
Young S, Pinkerton A, Dodds K (2014) The word on the street: rumor, "race" and the anticipation of urban unrest. Polit Geogr 38:57–67

Future Research Directions in Polarization

Israr Qureshi, Babita Bhat, Samrat Gupta, and Amit Anand Tiwari

1 Background

Information communication technologies (ICTs) have the potential to bring the world closer through facilitating communication and social interactions (Hampton and Wellman 2001; Qureshi 2009; Qureshi et al. 2018a). As the twentieth century came to an end and we stepped into the twenty-first century, scholars were optimistic about the power of ICTs to turn the planet into a global village (Wellman et al. 2001; Zhao 2006; Van Alstyne and Brynjolfsson 2005). It was thought that people could express themselves fairly, freely, and safely by using social networking sites and their evolved avatar, social platforms. There were some early cautious voices about these utopian views that highlighted issues of cyber balkanization and fragmentation of online space (Van Alstyne and Brynjolfsson 2005; Zembylas and Vrasidas 2005), but they were few and far between.

These early conversations on the role of ICTs have been influential in shaping the direction and evolution of research in the information systems and communication domain. Since then, one of the important debates in this area has been whether the emerging ICTs are uniting forces, i.e., bring us together, or are polarizing forces, i.e., take us apart? (Kraut et al. 2002; Qureshi et al. 2018a; Wellman et al. 2001). Later in

I. Qureshi · B. Bhat
Australian National University, Canberra, Australia
e-mail: israr.qureshi@anu.edu.au; babita.bhatt@anu.edu.au

S. Gupta (✉)
Information Systems Area, Indian Institute of Management Ahmedabad, Ahmedabad, Gujarat, India
e-mail: samratg@iima.ac.in

A. A. Tiwari
Marketing Management Area, Indian Institute of Management Rohtak, Rohtak, Haryana, India
e-mail: amit.tiwari@iimrohtak.ac.in

I. Qureshi et al. (eds.), *Causes and Symptoms of Socio-Cultural Polarization*,
https://doi.org/10.1007/978-981-16-5268-4_12

this section, we discuss these two perspectives in detail, however first, we propose that the role of ICTs on the society at large should be conceptualized through the lens of pluralistic social cohesion, whether ICTs increase it or decrease it.

Social cohesion (i.e., trust, belonging, and participation in community life) is an important driver of collective action, community resilience, and shared prosperity (Bhatt 2017; Bhatt 2021; Bhatt et al. 2019; Chan et al. 2006; Friedkin 2004; Qureshi et al. 2016, 2018b). Management scholars view it as an enabler of social intermediation, and facilitator of community-driven socioeconomic activities (Kistruck et al. 2013; Pillai et al. 2021a; Qiu et al. 2021). Instead of taking a utopian view that any connectivity and opportunity for social interactions will lead to social cohesion (Neustadtl and Robinson 2002; Robinson et al. 2000; Wellman et al. 2001; Williams 2006), we argue for creating specific mechanisms that mitigate polarization and making dialogic spaces for inter-group conversations (Bhatt et al. 2021; Escobedo et al. 2021; Galdini and De Nardis 2021; Hota and Mitra 2021; Hota et al. 2021; Pandey et al. 2021; Pillai et al. 2021b; Qureshi et al. 2017; Qureshi et al. 2021a, 2021b, 2021c; Shalini et al. 2021). In the following sections, we delve into various communication and social interactions theories that provide core principles and frameworks to understand the role of ICT as uniting and polarizing forces and elaborate on the potential mechanisms that build social cohesion in offline, online spaces.

Media and information richness theory (Daft et al. 1987; Hsieh and Tseng 2017; Parthiban et al. 2020, 2021), channel expansion theory (Carlson and Zmud 1999; DeClerck and Holtzman 2018), the social presence model (Cheung et al. 2011; Rice 1993; Wellman et al. 1996), media symbolism (Liu et al. 2018; Riaz and Qureshi 2017; Trevino et al. 1987), critical mass (Markus 1987; Marwell et al. 1988; Sledgianowski and Kulviwat 2009), the social information processing model (Fulk et al. 1987; Meyer 1994; Rice and Aydin 1991; Rodriguez-Hidalgo et al. 2017; Salancik and Pfeffer 1978), and the reduced social cues model (Evans 2012; Sproull and Kiesler 1986; Walther 1994) provide frameworks for analyzing the effects of ICTs on social cohesion. These theories help us understand the following questions: (a) what factors facilitate the use of particular media for communication, (b) how individuals use those communication channels and how individuals perceive those communication channels, (c) the extent to which reduced social cues help to increase or decrease social cohesion and polarization, and (d) how communication channels constrain the communication itself.

It was argued that ICTs facilitate the development and maintenance of social cohesion because of their potential to provide the benefits of physical networks without the conventional limitations of material resources (meeting rooms and associated equipment), proximity, and temporality. Thus, providing access to a potentially large set of individuals to contact and communicate (Qureshi et al. 2018a; Sledgianowski and Kulviwat 2009). In addition, ICTs carry fewer social context cues than in-person interactions (Daft and Lengel 1986; Sproull and Kiesler 1986), which facilitates the creation of diverse networks, as homophily is less salient (Qureshi et al. 2018a). However, reduced social context cues also have a deregulating effect (Sproull and Kiesler 1986) because communication through ICTs tends to be less formal than written communication (Finholt and Sproull

1990; Fish et al. 1993; Shehata et al. 2015). The fewer social context cues are less appropriate for emotional interactions (Fish et al. 1993; Fox and Moorland 2015; Kiesler and Sproull 1992; Trevino et al. 1990) and may result in social networks that are more instrumental and driven by competence trust rather than generalized trust (Qureshi et al. 2018a). However, the flexibility of communication that ICTs provide could help in creating and maintaining weaker ties, extending ego-centric networks, and providing the possibility to communicate across temporal, geographic, hierarchical, and other social barriers (Constant et al. 1996; Sproull and Kiesler 1986). Early research on ICTs also found that its indiscrete use may result in self-absorption, status equalization, and uninhibited behavior (Sproull and Kiesler 1986). The ICTs can be used as synchronous or asynchronous, and on most occasions, it does not demand instant reciprocity (Cascio 1999; Daft and Lengel 1986; Daft et al. 1987).

While there is agreement on the immediate effects of ICTs on communication and interactions, the long-term or distal outcomes are widely debated. There are two conflicting views about the effects of ICTs on social interactions and their potential for social cohesion and polarization. One view posits that ICTs are integrative and help to connect individuals (Constant et al. 1996; Pickering and King 1995) who lack homophily (Diehl et al. 2016; Qureshi et al. 2018a). Unlike an in-person setting where experts dominate the conversation, ICTs based environment promote participation and involvement of peripheral participants (Eveland and Bikson 1988; Sproull and Kiesler 1986), thus, supporting rich online communities (Jones 1998; Kiesler 1997; Smith and Kollock 1999). Some scholars suggest that ICTs acts as an "ice breaker" by reducing the social overhead inherent in initiating a relationship (Constant et al. 1996) due to their asynchronous, non-proximal, and reduced social cues properties. ICTs also provide a means for maintaining and consolidating existing connections (Lind and Zmud 1995). These characteristics of ICTs help in creating social ties across hierarchies, age groups, genders, ethnicities, space (geography), and time, which result in the rich diversity of an ego-centric network (Qureshi et al. 2018a). The implication of ICTs-based social interactions manifests in ease of making new ties. Therefore, the ego-centric network supported by ICTs tends to grow larger in size in a very short time when compared with conventional ego-centric networks (Qureshi et al. 2018a). This integrative view at times is seen as uncritical of the possibilities ICTs represent for social cohesion.

Another view is that ICTs provide a reduced cues environment that is less suitable for emotional, expressive, or complex communications, and it is responsible for longer decision times, anti-social flaming behaviors, and decreased social involvement (Daft and Lengel 1986; Finholt and Sproull 1990; Fish et al. 1993; Kiesler and Sproull 1992; Lea et al. 1992). Anonymity, invisibility, and lack of other social cues result in disinhibition effect (Tanis and Postmes 2003), which gives rise to a situation that may lead to polarization. Online disinhibition effect is generally defined as an unconstrained behavior in the online environment (Hollenbaugh and Everett 2013; Suler 2004), i.e., online users say and do things that they would not ordinarily do in the in-person environment. Online disinhibition might manifest in a benign manner as self-disclosure, kindness, generosity, and the dispensing of help and advice (Suler 2004). However, it can also result in toxic disinhibition such as rude language, harsh criticisms, hatred, violence, incitement, and verbal attacks (Hollenbaugh and Everett 2013; Sproull and Kiesler 1986). Flaming behavior is one such extreme manifestation of toxic disinhibition. This view primarily sees ICTs as leading to echo chambers that are cohesive within but fractious without. These echo chambers are founding blocks for polarization.

The effects of ICTs on social cohesion and polarization are all the more important due to the rise of digital-native generations that grew up with 24/7 connectivity and access to smartphones (Barak 2018; Grieve 2017). This generation is unlike any past generation in its use of ICTs (Heaney 2007; Ng 2012; Thompson 2013). They are not apprehensive about using online tools; they "hang out" in virtual space, make friends online, and socialize more in virtual space than in physical space (Savage et al. 2006; Sheahan 2005). Understanding how digital natives use ICTs and how it is linked to social cohesion and polarization will be helpful in addressing or at least slowing down the pace of cyberbalkanization (Van Alstyne and Brynjolfsson 2005).

The chapters in this book are an initial attempt at understanding the role of ICTs in leading to polarization. The chapters discussed various aspects of ICT-induced causes and symptoms of socio-cultural polarization. The goal of this book was to bring scholars from disciplines and geography together and contribute to a shared understanding of the role of ICT in socio-cultural polarization. This book broadly covered four themes: methodological developments in polarization, social aspects of polarization; cultural aspects of polarization; and consequences and outcomes of polarization. The chapters in the section on methodological developments discussed various topics such as residential segregation, opinion formation, and polarization due to fake news channels. The chapters in the section on social aspects addressed issues related to political polarization on the causes and mitigation of bushfires in Australia and social polarization due to reservations and affirmative action policies on caste oppression in India (Bhardwaj et al. 2021; Bhatt et al. 2022; Qureshi et al. 2018; Sutter et al. 2022). Further, the cultural aspects of polarization were demonstrated in the cyber-attacks on the literary authors, real-time public sentiment with the Indian government's education policies and subsequent attitudinal shift of social media users, and media bias in reporting of news in the entertainment domain. Finally, this book discusses polarization around the principles of information ethics such as privacy, liberty, and common good in the context of the Chinese social credit system and proposes contextual integrity theory as a theoretical concept to address the ethical concern in big data uses.

2 Future Directions of Research

ICT-induced socio-cultural polarization is a rapidly unfolding multifaceted phenomenon. In the light of emerging complicated challenges such as misinformation, fake news, cyberbullying, trolling, cybercrimes and dark web-driven threats (Ghai et al. 2021; Chiew et al. 2018; McGuire 2019; Van Hee et al. 2018;

Wu et al. 2019), researchers need to shift their focus on developing and testing new frameworks and methodologies while enhancing existing tools and techniques for curtailing the negatives consequences of social technologies. Moreover, the existing technology ecosystem exhibits people's increasing vulnerability towards polarization due to constant exposure to machine learning, deep learning, AI-based social media algorithms (Qureshi et al. 2020). Therefore, future studies need to focus on understanding AI, machine learning, and the role of deep learning in minimizing polarization. To further enrich the understanding of socio-cultural polarization, researchers need to explore vital configurations such as race, language, ethnicity, social status, and more diverse locations. Integration of geo-tags in such studies will provide a realistic view of changing configurations and their causes (Bastos et al. 2018). The findings from these studies could provide new actionable scenarios for policymakers and firms on dynamic neighborhood opinion formation in society.

Further research could also explore how actors are leveraging social media to organize and potentially influence intergroup relations in their constituencies. The connection between online speech and offline harm needs to be investigated. The unprecedented rise in misinformation and fake news dissemination through social media platforms necessitates an in-depth exploration of its root causes and solutions. Since policymakers and government agencies struggle to counter polarization arising due to misinformation (Kyza et al. 2020), more insights on these topics are required. Moreover, studies focusing on actors, content, and behaviors related to sharing inflammatory, offensive, or dangerous content will help develop a thorough understanding of the role of ICT in socio-cultural polarization.

Furthermore, exploring measurement, effects, and processes of affective polarization (whether political, ethnic, religious, or linguistic) could be a promising area of future research. The causal models of polarization driven by informational, demographic, environmental, and institutional factors, especially when related to online networks, need to be studied. Experimental interventions on polarization leading to attitudinal and behavioral measurement advances also need to be investigated in the future.

Finally, social media influencers tend to drive public sentiments (McGregor 2020). Therefore, research on social media influencers' role in polarization and their effectiveness in its mitigation and restoring equilibrium needs to be studied to develop a holistic understanding of polarization.

3 Investigation of Unconventional Cases of Polarization

Mainstream studies on socio-cultural polarization primarily deal with apparent issues related to politics, religion, society, culture, and the environment (Qureshi et al. 2020). This book makes an attempt to uncover hidden aspects of the phenomena of polarization around some of the underexplored issues such as vaccination, social credit system, and National Education Policy. The understanding of socio-cultural polarization around these issues, amongst others, is important as it plays a critical role in the development and growth of nations, especially during crises such as the pandemic. However, in order to develop a deeper understanding of socio-cultural polarization, the polarization around unconventional themes also needs to be explored and understood. For instance, the polarization around e-cigarettes needs to be investigated. Tobacco control experts suggest that e-cigarettes help in getting people out of their smoking habits, however, reports suggest that people are rather getting addicted to it (Smith et al. 2021). Another such example is a controversial debate on red meat consumption. While one side hails high nutritional values of red meat, the other side deems high-risk factors of red meat concerning cancer and diabetes.[1] Other such issues such as the Stop Online Piracy Act (SOPA)[2] have also led to polarization wherein one side sees the act as an attempt to induce information asymmetry while the other side routes it as an effort to stop online piracy.

Such instances of polarization around unconventional issues are widespread across businesses. One such example is research outcomes on the 5G network and its link with cancer: There is much evidence of conflicting studies related to the 5G network causing cancer in humans. Some studies suggest 5G networks don't have sufficient energy to damage DNA.[3] In contrast, other studies with limited evidence indicated that it could cause Glioma (a type of cancer). However, it has been found that studies from both sides are biased and need to be investigated thoroughly (Hardell and Carlberg 2020).

In line with the aforementioned examples, the anti-mask campaigns during the COVID-19 pandemic, polarization in the gaming industry due to adult content and crime-related themes, and eSports' acceptance as a real sport are some of the other examples of non-mainstream polarization that require inquiry from the psychological, technological, social and cultural perspectives. Research on the unconventional cases of polarization in line with the aforementioned examples may help in developing new theories and models for advancing the understanding of the role of ICT in socio-cultural polarization.

4 Further Scope of Methodological Improvements

Humanistic concerns arising from the curtailing of human freedom and development and from racism, sexism, and commodification of the human body are overlooked for the apparent benefits that online systems, including widely used search engines and databases, promise to deliver (Noble 2018; Sarker et al. 2019; Wachter-Boettcher 2017). Therefore, a thorough interrogation of research issues

[1] https://www.healthline.com/nutrition/is-red-meat-bad-for-you-or-good

[2] https://www.congress.gov/bill/112th-congress/house-bill/3261?q=hr3261

[3] https://www.cancerresearchuk.org/about-cancer/causes-of-cancer/cancer-myths/do-mobile-phones-cause-cancer

and methodological developments within the domain of socio-cultural polarization needs to be addressed in future research. The role of ICT in socio-cultural polarization is an evolving area of research. Thus, ICT-induced polarization-related terminology and methodology need constant evaluation and development. While data-driven studies which investigate what is happening by mining relevant data are gaining traction within socio-cultural polarization research, they rarely examine the theoretical paradigms behind the phenomenon.[4] Many such studies focus on data collection and applying data science techniques to the data without explaining why socio-cultural polarization is witnessed and offering a significant contribution to the theoretical context within which polarization is situated (Gupta and Deodhar 2021; Gupta and Kumar 2016; Gupta and Kumar 2020; Gupta and Kumar 2021; Gupta et al. 2016, 2019; Kumar et al. 2017).

Future research avenues should focus on the development of theories to explain major socio-cultural problems and challenges such as political harmony and crisis management. The challenges faced by underrepresented groups based on gender, culture, race, disability, sexual orientation, socioeconomic status in relation to the use/design/development of ICTs need to be investigated to curb socio-cultural polarization. Methodological developments related to the formation and evolution of social media filter bubbles, echo chambers, troll farms, fake news, and other ways in which social media are appropriated for restricting and polarizing the social discourse need to be investigated. The research on the development of methodologies related to collecting and mining user-generated data to examine behavioral aspects of opinion polarization, misinformation propagation, and acculturation is also worth exploring. Methodologies that can measure algorithmic bias inherent in social media, search engines, and AI-based social technologies need to be developed. Furthermore, analysis of the digital divide and exploration of socioeconomic divisions that impact access to or use of technology is a promising avenue of research in the domain of socio-cultural polarization.

5 Conclusion

The aim of this book was to develop a deeper and broader understanding of ICT-induced polarization in the social-cultural domain. The book covers polarization around a range of topics, including affirmative action, residential segregation, Bollywood, bushfires, vaccination, and the social credit system. Through an in-depth investigation of these emerging topics, the book advances our knowledge on the processes, methods, and theories of polarization. It also extends the existing work by identifying the social mechanisms and technological designs to minimize polarization. As such, the book develops systematic knowledge required to under-

[4] https://www.journals.elsevier.com/international-journal-of-information-management/call-for-papers/big-data-theory-building

stand and address large-scale and complex societal challenges and facilitate a deeper understanding of the solutions to the growing issue of polarization in the socio-cultural context.

This book holds significance in developing and developed nations in terms of comparison and learning from challenges and solutions and may spark a broader conversation on the topic of socio-cultural polarization. This book will be useful for scholars from various disciplines, along with engaged organizational leaders, activists, policymakers, and common citizens. We hope that this book will create awareness about the detrimental impact of polarization and provide conceptual and empirical tools for creating cohesive, equitable, and ethical digital spaces.

References

Barak M (2018) Are digital natives open to change? Examining flexible thinking and resistance to change. Comput Educ 121:115–123

Bastos M, Mercea D, Baronchelli A (2018) The geographic embedding of online echo chambers: evidence from the Brexit campaign. PLoS One 13(11):e0206841

Bhardwaj A, Kumar Mishra S, Qureshi I, Kamal Kumar K, Konrad AM, Seidel MDL, Bhatt B (2021) Bridging caste divides: middle-status ambivalence, elite closure, and lower-status social withdrawal. J Manag Stud 58(8):2111–2136

Bhatt B (2017) The role of social enterprises in building inclusive social capital: evidences from multi-case, qualitative field study. Doctoral dissertation, Carleton University

Bhatt B (2021) Ethical complexity of social change: negotiated actions of a social enterprise. J Business Ethics (forthcoming)

Bhatt B, Qureshi I, Riaz S (2019) Social entrepreneurship in non-munificent institutional environments and implications for institutional work: insights from China. J Bus Ethics 154(3):605–630

Bhatt B, Dembek K, Hota PK, Qureshi I (2021) Sharing economy model for the base of the pyramid: an ecosystem approach. In: Qureshi I, Bhatt B, Shukla DM (eds) Sharing economy at the base of the pyramid: opportunity and challenges. Springer Nature, Singapore

Bhatt B, Qureshi I, Sutter C (2022) How do intermediaries build inclusive markets? The role of the social context. J Manag Stud

Carlson JR, Zmud RW (1999) Channel expansion theory and the experiential nature of media richness perceptions. Acad Manag J 42(2): 153–170

Cascio WF (1999) Virtual workplaces: implications for organizational behavior. J Organ Behav 6:1

Chan J, To HP, Chan E (2006) Reconsidering social cohesion: developing a definition and analytical framework for empirical research. Soc Indic Res 75(2):273–302

Cheung CM, Chiu PY, Lee MK (2011) Online social networks: why do students use facebook? Comput Hum Behav 27(4):1337–1343

Chiew KL, Yong KSC, Tan CL (2018) A survey of phishing attacks: their types, vectors and technical approaches. Expert Syst Appl 106:1–20

Constant D, Sproull L, Kiesler S (1996) The kindness of strangers: the usefulness of electronic weak ties for technical advice. Organ Sci 7(2):119–135

Daft RL, Lengel RH (1986) Organizational information requirements, media richness and structural design. Manag Sci 32(5):554

Daft RL, Lengel RH, Trevino LK (1987) Message equivocality, media selection, and manager performance: implications for information systems. MIS Q 11(3):355

DeClerck D, Holtzman S (2018) To text or talk: does communication modality matter when providing criticism to others? Comput Hum Behav 87:109–120
Diehl T, Weeks BE, Gil de Zúñiga H (2016) Political persuasion on social media: tracing direct and indirect effects of news use and social interaction. New Media Soc 18(9):1875–1895
Escobedo MB, Zheng Z, Bhatt B (2021) Socially oriented sharing economy platform in regional Australia: a polanyian analysis. In: Qureshi I, Bhatt B, Shukla DM (eds) Sharing economy at the base of the pyramid: opportunity and challenges. Springer Nature, Singapore
Evans S (2012) Virtual selves, real relationships: an exploration of the context and role for social interactions in the emergence of self in virtual environments. Integr Psychol Behav Sci 46(4):512–528
Eveland JD, Bikson TK (1988) Work group structures and computer support: a field experiment. ACM Trans Office Inf Syst 6(4):354–379
Finholt T, Sproull LS (1990) Electronic groups at work. Organ Sci 1(1):41–64
Fish RS, Kraut RE, Root RW, Rice RE (1993) Video as a technology for informal communication, Association for computing machinery. Commun ACM 36(1):48
Fox J, Moreland JJ (2015) The dark side of social networking sites: an exploration of the relational and psychological stressors associated with Facebook use and affordances. Comput Hum Behav 45:168–176
Friedkin NE (2004) Social cohesion. Annu Rev Sociol 30(1):409–425. https://doi.org/10.1146/annurev.soc.30.012703.110625
Fulk J, Steinfield C, Schmitz J, Power J (1987) A social information processing model of media use in organizations. Commun Res 14(5):529
Galdini R, De Nardis S (2021) Not only for-profit. Sharing solidarity, promoting opportunities. a case study in Rome. In: Qureshi I, Bhatt B, Shukla DM (eds) Sharing economy at the base of the pyramid: opportunity and challenges. Springer Nature, Singapore
Ghai A, Kumar P, Gupta S (2021) A deep-learning-based image forgery detection framework for controlling the spread of misinformation. Inf Technol People
Grieve R (2017) Unpacking the characteristics of Snapchat users: a preliminary investigation and an agenda for future research. Comput Hum Behav 74:130–138
Gupta S, Deodhar S (2021) Understanding digitally enabled complex networks: a plural granulation-based hybrid community detection approach. Inf Technol People
Gupta S, Kumar P (2016) Community detection in heterogenous networks using incremental seed expansion. In: 2016 international conference on data science and engineering (ICDSE). IEEE, pp 1–5
Gupta S, Kumar P (2020) An overlapping community detection algorithm based on rough clustering of links. Data Knowl Eng 125:101777
Gupta S, Kumar P (2021) A constrained agglomerative clustering approach for unipartite and bipartite networks with application to credit networks. Inf Sci 557:332–354
Gupta S, Kumar P, Bhasker B (2016) A rough connectedness algorithm for mining communities in complex networks. In: International conference on big data analytics and knowledge discovery. Springer, Cham, pp 34–48
Gupta S, Kumar P, Perfilieva I (2019) A community detection algorithm based on granulation of links. ALLDATA 2019:41
Hampton K, Wellman B (2001) Long distance community in the network society: contact and support beyond Netville. Am Behav Sci 45(3):476–495
Hardell L, Carlberg M (2020) Health risks from radiofrequency radiation, including 5G, should be assessed by experts with no conflicts of interest. Oncol Lett 20(4):1–1
Heaney J-G (2007) Generations X and Y's internet banking usage in Australia. J Financ Serv Mark 11(3):196
Hollenbaugh EE, Everett MK (2013) The effects of anonymity on self-disclosure in blogs: an application of the online disinhibition effect. J Comput-Mediat Commun 18(3):283–302
Hota PK, Mitra S (2021) Leveraging the power of sharing: the case of a social enterprise at the base of the pyramid. In: Qureshi I, Bhatt B, Shukla DM (eds) Sharing economy at the base of the pyramid: opportunity and challenges. Springer Nature, Singapore

Hota PK, Qiu S, Bhatt B (2021) Ethitrade: countering challenges of sharing economy at the base of the pyramid using technology. In: Qureshi I, Bhatt B, Shukla DM (eds) Sharing economy at the base of the pyramid: opportunity and challenges. Springer Nature, Singapore

Hsieh SH, Tseng TH (2017) Playfulness in mobile instant messaging: examining the influence of emoticons and text messaging on social interaction. Comput Hum Behav 69:405–414

Jones SG (ed) (1998) CyberSociety 2.0: revisiting computer-mediated communication and community. Sage, Thousand Oaks

Kiesler S (ed) (1997) Culture of the Internet. Lawrence Erlbaum Associates, Mahwah

Kiesler S, Sproull L (1992) Group decision making and communication technology. Organ Behav Hum Decis Process 52(1):96

Kistruck GM, Beamish PW, Qureshi I, Sutter CJ (2013) Social intermediation in base-of-the-pyramid markets. J Manag Stud 50(1):31–66

Kraut R, Kiesler S, Boneva B, Cummings J, Helgeson V, Crawford A (2002) Internet paradox revisited. J Soc Issues 58(1):49–74

Kumar P, Gupta S, Bhasker B (2017) An upper approximation based community detection algorithm for complex networks. Decis Support Syst 96:103–118

Kyza EA, Varda C, Panos D, Karageorgiou M, Komendantova-Amann N, Coppolino Perfumi S et al (2020) Combating misinformation online: re-imagining social media for policy-making. Internet Policy Rev 9(4):1–24

Lea M, O'Shea T, Fung P, Spears R (1992) "Flaming" in computer-mediated communication: observations, explanations, implications. In: Lea M (ed) Contexts of computer-mediated communication. Harvester Wheatsheaf, New York, pp 89–112

Lind MR, Zmud RW (1995) Improving interorganizational effectiveness through voice mail facilitation of peer-to-peer relationships. Organ Sci 6(4):445–461

Liu Y, Tan CH, Sutanto J (2018) A media symbolism perspective on the choice of social sharing technologies. Electron Commer Res Appl 29:19–29

Markus ML (1987) Toward a "critical mass" theory of interactive media: universal access, interdependence, and diffusion. Commun Res 14:491–511

Marwell G, Oliver PE, Prahl R (1988) Social networks and collective action: a theory of the critical mass. III. Am J Sociol 94(3):502–534

McGregor SC (2020) "Taking the temperature of the room" how political campaigns use social media to understand and represent public opinion. Public Opin Q 84(S1):236–256

McGuire M (2019) Social media platforms and the cybercrime economy: the next chapter of into the web of profit. Bromium Report

Meyer GW (1994) Social information processing and social networks: a test of social influence mechanisms. Hum Relat 47(9):1013–1047

Neustadtl A, Robinson JP (2002) Social contact differences between Internet users and nonusers in the general social survey. IT Soc 1:73–102

Ng W (2012) Can we teach digital natives digital literacy? Comput Educ 59(3):1065–1078

Noble SU (2018) Algorithms of oppression. NYU Press

Pandey M, Bhati M, Shukla DM, Qureshi I (2021) Resourcing and value creation: a case of sharing economy model at the base of the pyramid. In: Qureshi I, Bhatt B, Shukla DM (eds) Sharing economy at the base of the pyramid: opportunity and challenges. Springer Nature, Singapore

Parthiban R, Qureshi I, Bandyopadhyay S, Bhatt B, Jaikumar S (2020) Leveraging ICT to overcome complementary institutional voids: insights from institutional work by a social enterprise to help marginalized. Inf Syst Front 22(11):1–21. https://doi.org/10.1007/s10796-020-09991-6

Parthiban R, Qureshi I, Bandyopadhyay S, Jaikumar S (2021) Digitally mediated value creation for non-commodity base of the pyramid producers. Int J Inf Manag 56

Pickering JM, King JL (1995) Hardwiring weak ties: interorganizational computer-mediated communication, occupational communities, and organizational change. Organ Sci 6(4):479

Pillai V, Pandey M, Bhatt B (2021a) Social sustainability at BOP through building inclusive social capital: a case study of Drishtee. In: Qureshi I, Bhatt B, Shukla DM (eds) Sharing economy at the base of the pyramid: opportunity and challenges. Springer Nature, Singapore

Pillai, V., Shukla, D. M & Qureshi, I. (2021b). Social intermediation using sharing economy in india: a case study of Farmizen. In I. Qureshi, B. Bhatt & D. M. Shukla (Eds.) Sharing economy at the base of the pyramid: opportunity and challenges, Singapore: Springer Nature.
Qiu S, Xu Z, Bhatt B (2021) The sharing economy platforms in rural China: bridging institutional voids through institutional entrepreneurship. In: Qureshi I, Bhatt B, Shukla DM (eds) Sharing economy at the base of the pyramid: opportunity and challenges. Springer Nature, Singapore
Qureshi I (2009) Influence of computer mediated communication on social capital: a disaggregated approach. Doctoral dissertation, University of Western Ontario, London, Canada
Qureshi I, Kistruck GM, Bhatt B (2016) The enabling and constraining effects of social ties in the process of institutional entrepreneurship. Organ Stud 37(3):425–447
Qureshi I, Pan SL, Zheng Y (2017) Call for papers: digital social innovation. Inf Syst J:1–8
Qureshi I, Fang Y, Haggerty N, Compeau DR, Zhang X (2018a) IT-mediated social interactions and knowledge sharing: role of competence-based trust and background heterogeneity. Inf Syst J 28(5):929–955
Qureshi I, Sutter C, Bhatt B (2018b) The transformative power of knowledge sharing in settings of poverty and social inequality. Organ Stud 39(11):1575–1599
Qureshi I, Bhatt B, Gupta S, Tiwari AA (2020) Call for papers: causes, symptoms and consequences of social media induced polarization (SMIP). Inf Syst J https://onlinelibrary.wiley.com/pb-assets/assets/13652575/ISJ_SMIP_CFP.pdf
Qureshi I, Bhatt B, Shukla DM (2021a) Sharing economy at the base of the pyramid-research framework and future directions. In: Qureshi I, Bhatt B, Shukla DM (eds) Sharing economy at the base of the pyramid: opportunity and challenges. Springer Nature, Singapore
Qureshi I, Bhatt B, Shukla DM (2021b) Overview of sharing economy at the base of the pyramid. In: Qureshi I, Bhatt B, Shukla DM (eds) Sharing economy at the base of the pyramid: opportunity and challenges. Springer Nature, Singapore
Qureshi I, Pan SL, Zheng Y (2021c) Digital social innovation: an overview and research framework. Inf Syst J
Riaz S, Qureshi I (2017) Emergence of a new institutional logic: shaping the institutionally complex field of community radio in India. In: Seidel SL, Greve HR (eds) Emergence: research in the sociology of organizations, pp 383–418
Rice RE (1993) Media appropriateness: using social presence theory to compare traditional and new organizational media. Hum Commun Res 19(4):451–484
Rice RE, Aydin C (1991) Attitudes toward new organizational technology: network proximity as a mechanism for social information processing. Admin Sci Q 36(2):219
Robinson JP, Kestnbaum M, Neustadtl A, Alvarez A (2000) Mass media use and social life among Internet users. Soc Sci Comput Rev 18:490–501
Rodríguez-Hidalgo C, Tan ES, Verlegh PW (2017) Expressing emotions in blogs: the role of textual paralinguistic cues in online venting and social sharing posts. Comput Hum Behav 73:638–649
Salancik GR, Pfeffer J (1978) A social information processing approach to job attitudes and task design. Admin Sci Q 23(2):224
Sarker S, Chatterjee S, Xiao X, Elbanna A (2019) The sociotechnical perspective as an 'axis of cohesion' for the IS discipline: recognizing its historical legacy and ensuring its continued relevance. MIS Q 43(3):695–719
Savage SB, Collins-Mayo S, Cray G, Mayo B (2006) Making sense of generation Y: the world view of 15-to 25-year-olds. Church House Publishing
Shalini, Manoharan, B, Parthiban R, Qureshi I, Bhatt B, Rakshit K (2021) Digital technology-enabled transformative consumer responsibilisation: a case study. Eur J Market (forthcoming)
Sheahan P (2005) Generation Y: surviving (and thriving) with generation Y at work. Hardy Grant Publishing, Richmond
Shehata AMK, Ellis D, Foster A (2015) The impact of information and communication technologies on informal scientific communication: a naturalistic inquiry approach. Libr Rev 64(6–7):428–445
Sledgianowski D, Kulviwat S (2009) Using social network sites: the effects of playfulness, critical mass and trust in a hedonic context. J Comput Inf Syst 49(4):74–83

Smith MA, Kollock P (eds) (1999) Communities in cyberspace. Routledge, London
Smith KE, Ikegwuonu T, Weishaar H, Hilton S (2021) Evidence use in E-cigarettes debates: scientific showdowns in a 'wild west' of research. BMC Public Health 21(1):1–16
Sproull L, Kiesler S (1986) Reducing social context cues: electronic mail in organizational communications. Manag Sci 32(11):1492–1512
Suler J (2004) The online disinhibition effect. Cyberpsychol Behav 7(3):321–326
Sutter C, Bhatt B, Qureshi I (2022) What makes resource provision an effective means of poverty alleviation? A resourcing perspective. Organ Sci. https://doi.org/10.1287/orsc.2021.1570
Tanis M, Postmes T (2003) Social cues and impression formation in CMC. J Commun 53(4):676–693
Thompson P (2013) The digital natives as learners: technology use patterns and approaches to learning. Comput Educ 65:12–33
Trevino LK, Lengel RH, Daft RL (1987) Media symbolism, media richness, and media choice in organizations: a symbolic interactionist perspective. Commun Res 14(5):553–574
Trevino L, Lengel R, Bodensteiner W, Gerloff E, Muir N (1990) The richness imperative and cognitive style. Manag Commun Q 4:176–197
Van Alstyne M, Brynjolfsson E (2005) Global village or cyber-balkans? Modeling and measuring the integration of electronic communities. Manag Sci 51(6):851–868
Van Hee C, Jacobs G, Emmery C, Desmet B, Lefever E, Verhoeven B et al (2018) Automatic detection of cyberbullying in social media text. PLoS One 13(10):e0203794
Wachter-Boettcher S (2017) Technically wrong. WW Norton & Company
Walther J (1994) Anticipated ongoing interaction versus channel effects on relational communication in computer-mediated interaction. Hum Commun Res 20(4):473–501
Wellman B, Salaff J, Dimitrova D, Garton L, Gulia M, Haythornthwaite C (1996) Computer networks as social networks: collaborative work, telework, and virtual community. Annu Rev Sociol 22(1):213–238
Wellman B, Quan-Haase A, Witte J, Hampton K (2001) Does the Internet increase, decrease, or supplement social capital? Social networks, participation, and community commitment. Am Behav Sci 45(3):436–455
Williams D (2006) On and off the'Net: scales for social capital in an online era. J Comput-Mediat Commun 11(2):593–628
Wu L, Morstatter F, Carley KM, Liu H (2019) Misinformation in social media: definition, manipulation, and detection. ACM SIGKDD Explor Newsl 21(2):80–90
Zembylas M, Vrasidas C (2005) Globalization, information and communication technologies, and the prospect of a 'global village': promises of inclusion or electronic colonization? J Curric Stud 37(1):65–83
Zhao S (2006) Do Internet users have more social ties? A call for differentiated analyses of Internet use. J Comput-Mediat Commun 11(3):844–862

Index

A
ABP news, 222, 223, 225
Academia, 255, 256, 260, 270, 271
Acculturation, 165
Active citizenship, 145
Activism, 143
Act of terrorization, 164
Adaptations, 36, 37, 82, 125, 126
Adaptive models, 59
Adaptive networks, 16, 54, 58, 59, 67
Ad-hoc fact-checking, 268, 272, 273, 278
Administrative costs, 234
Affirmative action, 16, 133–146, 288, 291
Agenda setting theory, 11
Agent-based model, 30, 33, 45
Agent's mobility, 31
Agent's opinion, 33, 41, 42, 45, 46
AI-based social technologies, 291
AI-based techniques, 279
Algorithm-based content promotion, 14
Algorithmic accountability, 246
Algorithmic filtering, 156
Algorithmic input, 13, 14
Algorithms, 13, 14, 45, 65, 74, 78, 86, 88, 154, 156, 183–185, 187, 245–247, 255, 259, 266, 270, 277, 289, 291
Alternative views, 226
Aluminium sector, 121
Ambient temperature, 123, 124
Anti-mask campaigns, 290
Anti-reservation protests, 141
Anti-vaccination, 52, 53, 55, 68
Anti-vaccine communities, 68
Anti-vaxxers, 9, 56, 58
Application Programming Interface (API), 62, 90, 189, 190, 272
Arson emergency, 116, 118, 121
Artificial intelligence (AI), 156, 270
Artistic suicide, 165
Atrocities, 138, 143
Attitude polarization, 180–182, 184, 187
Attitudinal change, 16, 189, 190, 192–202
Audio-visual manipulation, 260
Australian bushfire, 16, 117
Autism, 53–55
Autonomy, 205, 216, 244, 245, 247
Axelrod model, 31

B
Backlash, 136
Behavioural trends, 238
Bengaluru Rain, 92, 95
Biased narrative, 74
Biases, 3, 11, 15, 16, 31, 32, 47, 57, 78, 86, 92, 144, 145, 211–226, 246, 288, 291
Big data, 12, 178, 233, 234, 238, 240, 245, 288
Binary opinion state, 29, 47
Biodiversity, 115, 116, 119
Bipolar division, 225
Blacklists, 237, 239, 242
Blacks, 134, 135, 137, 139, 146
Bollywood, 15, 16, 211–226, 291
Bollywood drug probe, 221–223
Bondage, 136
Book burning, 153
Bots, 53, 185, 266, 267, 280
Bounded confidence, 58, 62

I. Qureshi et al. (eds.), *Causes and Symptoms of Socio-Cultural Polarization*,
https://doi.org/10.1007/978-981-16-5268-4

Bureaucratism, 243
Burning, 119, 122–125, 153, 161
Business continuity plan, 61

C
Caste, 16, 134, 135, 138–146, 152, 155, 157–159, 162, 163, 165, 167, 179, 288
Caste rift, 167
Celebrities, 10, 55, 212, 213, 216–218
Censorial inspection, 153
Censorship, 10, 15, 16, 151–171, 266
  law, 157, 158, 170
  system, 266
  of writing, 164
Central agent, 34
Channel, 2, 3, 7, 8, 14, 16, 73–111, 134, 143, 160, 164, 212, 213, 218–220, 222, 237, 239, 262, 265, 267, 269–272, 277–279, 286, 288
Cheating, 186, 241
Chinese apps, 92, 95
Circulation of uncensored literature, 157
Civilizational values, 79
Civil liberties, 245
Civil protests, 79
Classification of tweets, 190
Climate change, 9, 10, 116–118, 120–127, 178, 179, 261
Clinical trials, 63, 64
Cloud computing, 187
Clustering, 32, 39, 43, 47, 219–221
  algorithm, 46, 183
  output, 222–224
Clutches of censorship, 165
Coal, 116, 121, 122, 125, 126
Coal mining, 117, 121, 125
Coefficient of infection, 84
Coefficient of news, 90, 91
Cognitive dissonance, 11
Cognitive & motivational process, 179, 181, 186
Cohesion, 1–3, 17, 119, 120, 123, 286–288
Collaboration, 125, 257, 268, 270, 271, 277, 278
Collaborative problem solving, 1
Collaborative solutions, 270–271
Colonial interests, 138
Commodification, 290
Common good approach, 17, 235–236, 247
Common opinion, 90
Communal riots, 159, 165
Communal tension, 157, 165
Communication process, 2, 11–12, 265, 267
Communication technologies, 262
Community, 1, 54, 76, 116, 137, 152, 183, 236, 255, 286
  harmony, 241, 242
  immunity, 56
  logic, 123
  resilience, 122, 126, 286
  safety, 236
Compartmental models, 80
Complete protection, 276, 278, 279
Complex social networks, 59
Computational propaganda, 259
Computer ethics, 235
Concept of “carnival,” 163
Conditional entropy, 41
Confirmation bias, 11, 57
Confirmation of rumour, 273
Conforming opinions, 8
Confucianism, 236
Consensus, 12, 54, 56, 58, 60–62, 65, 67, 75, 80, 85–88, 90, 91, 93, 94, 96, 97, 116, 126, 245, 254, 256, 261
  formation, 54, 59–62, 65, 66, 69, 80, 82, 89, 90, 92
  score, 88
Conspiracy, 5, 184, 260, 263, 279
Conspiracy theory, 17, 52, 57, 134, 255–258, 260
Content analysis, 189–191, 197, 198, 204
Content consumption, 3
Context of mobility, 32
Contextual integrity, 17, 246–248, 288
Continuous opinion variable, 32
Control frameworks, 276, 278
Controversial books, 156, 159
Controversial issues, 80
Controversial topics, 16
Controversies, 16, 54, 65, 152, 157–159, 167, 168, 171, 179, 212, 213, 216–218, 221, 223, 225, 226
Convergence of opinion, 86
Convergence parameter, 60, 69
Cooked up stories, 91
Coordinated online attacks, 160
Corruption, 7, 241–244
Countering rumours, 253–280
Counter-rumour strategies, 255, 256, 268, 272, 273, 276, 277, 279
Coverage bias, 214
COVID Tally, 92, 95
COVID-19 vaccine, 9, 16, 51–69
Credit ranking, 238, 239, 242, 245
Credit scores, 237–239, 241, 242, 245, 246

Creditworthiness, 237
Crimeware-as-a-Service, 7
Criminal offense, 6
Crisis management, 291
Critical thinking, 275
Cultivation theory, 11
Cultural dynamics, 262
Cultural segregation, 45
Culture-based content, 3
Cyber-attack, 152, 288
Cyber-attacks on literary work, 16
Cyberbalkanization, 12, 13, 15, 171, 288
Cyberbullying, 4–6, 168, 288
Cybercrime, 4, 6–7, 288
Cybercriminals, 6, 7
Cybernetic mechanism, 245

D
Dalit power, 167
Danger, 52, 124, 155, 171, 179, 255, 258
Dangerous content, 289
Darbhanga Bus accident, 92
Dark web, 4, 7, 288
Data cleaning, 62–90
Datafication, 234, 244, 245
Data preparation process, 62
Data privacy, 234, 235, 238
Data-sharing, 239
Dataveillance, 244
Deep learning, 289
Defamation of dominant ideologies, 151
Degree of polarization, 16, 45, 54, 65
Delhi riots 2020, 159
Deliberately stoked controversy, 168
Democracy, 1, 8, 9, 127, 138, 142, 146, 155, 179, 214, 215, 234, 254
Democratic authority, 118
Democratic discussions, 169
Democratic values, 8
Democratisation, 266
Democratisation of censorship, 157
Denial of rumour, 273, 274
Density function, 88, 90, 185
Density of empty spaces, 31, 33, 35
Deprivation, 138, 141, 142, 146
Descriptive analysis, 189, 190, 192, 197
Design based solution, 271–272
Deterrent, 242
Digital, 2, 5, 6, 17, 74, 117, 143, 153, 154, 160, 161, 169, 184, 198, 219, 233, 239, 244–246, 267, 271, 274, 275, 277, 291, 292
  culture, 153, 166
  India campaign, 74
  journalism, 271
  literacy, 191, 198, 207
  technologies, 2, 154, 171, 246
Digital-native, 288
Disastrous consequences, 116, 214
Discipline, 226, 243, 288, 292
Discrimination, 30, 135, 138–143, 145, 146, 160, 234, 245
Discrimination forms, 30
Discriminatory policies, 141
Discursive censorship, 153
Disinformation, 6, 76, 77, 118, 255, 256, 259, 267, 270
Distrust, 53, 56, 117, 127, 178, 184
Diverse ideologies, 142
Diversity of discourse, 7
Divide and rule, 138
Divisive agenda, 6
Domestically manufactured vaccines, 56
Domestic energy, 116
Dominant economic logic, 126
Dominant race, 136
Double-edged sword, 2, 127
Downgrading, 270, 277, 278
Drought, 120, 123, 124
Dubious narrative, 168
Dynamical co-evolution, 16, 54
Dynamic behavior, 36
Dynamics of polarization, 73–111

E
Echo chamber, 1, 8, 9, 12, 14, 16, 28, 29, 32, 46, 52, 54–58, 67, 68, 74, 79, 80, 91, 116, 118, 126, 127, 134, 135, 152, 154, 169–171, 178, 179, 184, 186, 198–202, 215, 225, 254, 266, 288, 291
E-cigarettes, 290
Ecology, 116, 125
Economic impact, 68
Economic mobility, 139
Economy, 7, 52, 61, 65, 97, 115, 116, 119, 121, 126, 127, 141, 207, 241, 243
Ecosystem, 3, 115, 116, 119, 120, 125, 289
Eco-terrorism, 116
Education, 2, 3, 15, 16, 28, 137–144, 161, 166, 177–207, 266, 275, 276, 288, 289
Education excellence, 191, 198, 204
Effect of polarization, 167, 181, 186
Ego-centric network, 287
Electoral communication, 127
Empty site, 31, 33–36, 38

Energy industry, 121
Entertainment domain, 225, 226, 288
Environmental issues, 16, 116
Environmentalists, 116, 120, 123–127
E-petition, 4
Epidemic framework, 277, 279
Epidemiological modeling, 16, 74, 80–85, 87, 90
Epistemic crisis, 256
Epistemic power, 216, 217
Epistemological shift, 137
Equality and justice, 16
Equilibrium, 10, 35, 289
Equitable relief, 135
Erdős–Rényi random network model, 59, 85
Erroneous belief, 77
Ethical values, 246, 248
Ethnic polarization, 31
Evaluation framework, 276–277
E-voting, 4
Exclusionary nationalist discourses, 154
Export economy, 121
Exposure dissemination, 279
Exposure minimisation, 277–279
Extreme case, 40, 45
Extreme views, 1, 15, 17, 67
Extremism, 17, 183

F
Fabrication, 214, 260, 261
Fact-checking, 260, 271–273, 277, 278
Fact-checking institutes, 271, 277
Facts, 55, 76, 77, 80, 91, 92, 94, 96, 117, 118, 123, 134, 135, 142, 154, 155, 162, 163, 165, 171, 213, 214, 218, 219, 224
Fake channel population, 92
Fake news, 15–17, 68, 74, 76–78, 80–87, 89–93, 95, 96, 110–111, 121, 127, 153–155, 166, 168, 171, 218, 226, 255–258, 260–261, 264, 275, 279, 288, 289, 291
Fake news channels, 73–111, 288
Fake products, 241
False and unverified information, 256–264, 280
False information, 76, 77, 278
False story, 162
Farmers protest, 92
Film censorship, 10
Filter bubble, 13, 154, 181, 186, 291
Filtering, 156, 270, 277, 278
Filtering and downgrading techniques, 277
Final configuration, 35–45
Financial inclusion, 234
Fire services, 124
Flaming, 12, 127
Flaming behaviors, 287, 288
Flammable materials, 122
Followers, 53, 56, 78, 92, 134
Followership, 14
Foreign manufactured vaccines, 56
Formalism, 243
Fragmentation, 12, 28, 45, 46, 182, 285
Fragmented opinion, 82–83
Fragmented opinion cluster, 60
Frauds, 6–7, 134, 155, 239, 241, 261
Freedom of speech, 13, 155, 157, 164, 266
Free Speech, 153, 156, 168
Frequency distribution, 224
Fringe group, 167
Fundamental rights, 159

G
Game theory, 10, 30
Gaming platforms, 5
Gatekeeping, 214
Genome sequence, 66
Geographical divides, 127
Ghettoization, 13
Gilgit Baltistan, 92, 95
Global decarbonisation, 125
Global Village, 156, 161, 169, 170, 285
Global warming, 125, 260
Good governance, 4, 17, 240, 241, 243, 246, 247
Gossip, 17, 212, 218, 257, 258, 263, 264, 279
Government policies, 77, 96, 179, 180, 187, 198–202
Greenhouse gas emissions, 125
Greenhouse gases, 121
Group polarization, 181–183
Group support system (GSS), 181, 182
Gun laws, 8, 9

H
Happy agent, 34
Harmful smoke, 119
Hashtag classification, 191
Hate messages, 77
Hatred, 5, 11, 76, 118, 167, 288
Health, 2–4, 6, 52, 53, 56, 57, 66, 77, 80, 91, 92, 94–96, 115, 116, 119, 123, 166, 217, 275–277

Healthcare, 2, 3, 9, 28, 53, 54, 58, 68, 178, 238, 255
Health-related information, 77
Heatwaves, 123
Heinous crimes, 143
Herd behavior, 12
Herding behaviour, 81
Hermeneutic approach, 153
Heterodox, 138
Heterogeneous beliefs, 31
High-tech users, 145
Hindustan Times, 222, 224, 225
Historical injustice, 146
Homogeneous group, 118
Homophilic effect, 67
Homophilic structure, 8, 215
Homophily, 12, 68, 215, 286, 287
Honesty, 239, 241, 242, 246
Human development, 138, 140
Human dignity, 146
Human interference, 125
Hybrid logic, 16, 126, 127

I

ICT-enabled feedback mechanisms, 2
ICT-enabled services, 3
ICT platforms, 3, 134, 146, 155
Ideal society, 237
Identity theft, 6
Ideological identity, 9
Ideological polarization, 154, 182
Ideological rhetoric, 161
Ideological segregation, 13
Ideologies, 1, 7, 8, 10, 11, 78, 80, 84, 126, 134, 138, 142, 151, 153, 164, 165, 170, 171, 214, 235, 241, 245, 258
Immigration, 8
Immune system, 63, 275
Immunisation, 55–57, 276–278
Immunisation approach, 279
Incentive mechanism, 237
Income-level membership, 28
India China war, 92, 95
Indian Express, 168, 222, 224, 225
India Today, 157, 222, 224, 241
India TV, 222, 224, 225
Indirect cost, 119
Individual conformity, 156
Individualization, 32
Individual liberty approach, 17, 236–237, 246
Individual mobility preferences, 47
Inefficient testing, 63
Inequality, 8, 28, 37, 135, 140, 144, 145, 158, 179
Infected, 59, 82–85, 87, 89, 92, 96
Infected category, 83, 92
Infodemic, 52, 77
Informal institutions, 146
Informational bubble, 8
Information and communication technology (ICT), 1–7, 9, 10, 12–17, 55, 133–146, 151–171, 178, 202, 212, 234, 238, 239, 245, 247, 285–291
Information campaigns, 96
Information chaos, 1
Information ethics, 15, 17, 233–248, 288
Information exposure, 67
Information monopolies, 164
Information sharing, 73, 79, 239, 248
Information societies, 1, 213
Information technology identity construction, 181, 186
Infrastructure, 17, 28, 122, 123, 239
Initial configuration, 35
Initial random configuration, 35, 36
Innuendos, 163, 259
Institutional power, 216, 217
Intellectual fascism, 160
Interest-agnostic content, 14
Intergovernmental Panel on Climate Change (IPCC), 124
Intermediate value, 38, 40, 44
Internal biases, 213, 215
Internet governance, 245
Iron ore, 121
Irreconcilable attitudes, 117
Iterations, 36, 38, 60–62, 65–67, 69, 86, 88, 90–94, 96, 98, 120
Iterative process, 60

J

Job creation, 9
Journalism standards, 262

K

K-means clustering, 220
K-means hierarchical clustering, 219

L

Land management practices, 123
Law governing censorship, 158
Legend, 17, 163, 167, 256–259, 263, 264, 279

Legislation, 30, 55, 135, 269, 277, 278
Legitimization, 146
Level of fakeness, 93
Lexicon sentiment analysis, 219
Life and health, 91, 94
Life-threatening news, 80
Life threat factor, 92
Like-minded individuals, 12, 32, 79
Like-minded users, 10, 14
Linguistic conventions, 85
Literary censorship, 15, 16, 151–171
Literary censorship's trajectory, 157
Literature ban, 151
Literature-based folklore, 162
Local alignment, 42, 43
Local clustering, 39
Local clustering configurations, 43
Local majority, 37, 38, 82
Lockdown, 57, 66, 68
Long-distance communication, 265
Lower barrier to entry, 255, 266
Lower weighted feature, 42
Lsqnonlin function, 87, 89

M
Machine learning, 62, 219, 270, 289
Machine learning algorithm, 14
Mainstream media, 143, 145
Majority of sites, 44
Malware, 6
Marginalization, 137, 165
Marginalized cultural practices, 165
Marginal representation, 141
Marginal sections, 139, 146
Market restrictions, 238
Masquerading, 77
Mass communication, 3, 12, 264, 265
MATLAB, 87–89
Measles-Mumps-Rubella (MMR), 54, 55
Measles outbreak, 55
Measure of overlapping, 41
Media, 2, 52, 74, 116, 134, 152, 177, 212, 240, 254, 286
  bias, 15, 16, 211–226, 288
  campaign, 2, 68, 136, 159
  framing, 215
  literacy, 127, 144, 255, 271, 275, 278
  propaganda, 158
Mediating technologies, 142
Medical hoax, 54
Mental health, 2, 6, 57, 77
Meta-theoretical analysis, 180, 182, 188
Micro-blogging platform, 13
Microfinance institutions, 238
Microsoft Azure, 62, 65, 90
Minimalists, 123, 126
Minimal supervision, 255, 265, 266
Minorities, 28, 31, 134–136, 138, 146, 160, 165, 182, 234
Misconduct, 243
Misinformation, 4–5, 9, 10, 15–17, 52–54, 57, 58, 66, 68, 74, 76, 77, 96, 127, 154, 166, 168, 218, 254–256, 258, 261–262, 264, 279, 289, 291
Mistrust, 5, 74
Mitigation strategies, 125, 126
Mobile technology, 199
Mobility dynamics, 15, 29
Mobilization, 143
Mob lynching, 166
Moral principles, 240
Motivated reasoning, 11, 118
Multicultural patterns, 31
Multiliteracies, 145
Multimedia-based learning, 4
Multimodal communication, 144
Multimodal media production, 144
Murders, 79, 145, 215
Muted group theory, 10
Mutual information, 41–42, 45, 46
Mutual information indexes, 41, 42, 46
Myth-making, 162

N
Naming and shaming, 242
National education policy, 15, 16, 206, 207, 289
National Education Policy 2020 (NEP 2020), 16, 177–207
National Herald India, 221, 224, 225
Natural disasters, 57, 115, 119, 120, 123
Natural Language Processing (NLP), 65
NDTV, 90, 91, 95, 222–225
Negative beliefs, 117
Negative impact, 6, 58, 96, 119, 244, 261
Negative sentiment, 213, 221, 222
Negotiation, 9, 126, 269, 277
Neighboring agent, 34, 37, 42, 43, 45
Neighbourhood attribute, 47
Neighbourhood composition, 29, 34, 41, 45, 46
Nepal attacks, 92, 95
Network simulation, 58–62, 83, 85–88, 90
News 18, 222, 224
News channels, 8, 73–111, 134, 212, 213, 218–220, 222, 277, 278, 288
New service development, 272, 278

News feed, 13, 14
News/information filtering, 270
News satire, 76
Nitish Kumar oath, 92, 95
No-compromise mentality, 8
Non-mixed neighbourhoods, 38–41, 44, 45
Normative conceptions, 248
Normative framework, 235
Northern states of India, 142
Nuclear power, 126
Number of agents, 33, 36
Number of locations, 36
Number of moves, 36
Number of subscribers, 84, 87, 88
Number of views, 82, 84, 87

O
Online abuse, 169
Online bubble, 168
Online communities, 287
Online discourse, 16, 54, 65
Online disinhibition, 287
Online opinion formation, 51–69
Online public discourse, 65
Online social media platforms, 253–280
Online uproar, 159
Opinion cluster, 41–44, 46, 60
Opinion dynamics, 30, 32, 58, 68, 181, 186
Opinion evolution model, 54
Opinion formation, 11, 16, 27–48, 51–69, 75, 82, 85, 86, 90, 98, 288, 289
Opinion polarization, 28, 30, 46, 184, 186, 291
Opinion-reinforcing information, 11
Opinion state, 15, 29, 30, 46, 47
Oppression, 16, 144, 171, 288
Organisational decisions, 242
Organized violence, 160
Orthodox, 138
Overlap index, 43–45

P
Pandemic, 2, 52, 54, 56, 57, 63, 67–69, 76, 77, 79, 83, 145, 160, 290
Parody, 96, 97
Partisan bias, 47
Partisan division, 185
Partisan information, 185
Partisan narratives, 171
Partisan news, 7, 8
Patriarchal structures, 144
Pedagogy, 137, 144, 145
Penalties, 127, 241, 242
People centric, 2
Perceived credibility, 217
Perceived polarization, 184
Periodic boundary conditions, 33
Peripheral information processing, 213
Personal information, 6, 238, 245–247
Persuasive algorithm, 13, 14
Persuasive arguments, 30, 181, 182
Phishing, 6
Physical segregation, 47
Physical separation, 28, 46
Polarity scores, 59–61, 86, 88, 90
Polarization, 2, 28, 52, 74, 116, 146, 152, 178, 213, 235, 254, 286
  of opinion, 152, 159
  score, 178
  theories, 180, 184, 212, 290, 291
  of users, 87–88
Polarization-censorship relationship, 153
Polarized, 7, 9, 11, 12, 14, 28, 29, 32, 45, 46, 52, 54, 60, 66, 68, 78, 79, 167, 169, 170, 183, 186, 213–215, 224–226
  debates, 7, 215
  neighbourhoods, 31, 45, 46
  network, 183
  public opinion, 6, 11, 76, 142, 171, 184, 197–200, 215, 224, 269
  views, 11
Polarizing views, 78
Policy, 2, 66, 77, 116, 135, 160, 179, 234, 255, 288
  gridlock, 116, 126
Policymaking, 9, 122
Political agendas, 9
Political communication, 184
Political conviction, 156
Political debate, 67, 79
Political deprivation, 142
Political discourse, 145, 183
Political divides, 116
Political elites, 117, 121
Political frames, 117
Political harmony, 291
Political ideologies, 7, 10, 80, 142, 171
Politically sensitive issues, 244
Political mileage, 68
Political polarization, 9, 31, 47, 78, 80, 115–127, 179, 180, 288
Political segregation, 47
Political trust, 241, 242
Political weapon, 155
Politicking, 117
Pollution, 119
Popular demand, 153

Post-disaster reconstruction, 119
Post-hoc fact-checking, 272–273, 278
Post-pandemic world, 2
Post-university life, 141
Precautionary measures, 58
Predictive analytics, 238, 270
Prejudice, 3, 7, 170, 212, 245
Prejudiced groups, 170
Pre-liberalization, 142
Presidential election, 77, 134, 155, 215, 217, 259, 267
Privacy, 154, 166, 233–248, 288
  infringements, 244
  intrusion, 234, 245
  issues, 235
  protection, 244
Privatization, 142
Process definition, 78
Productivity, 119, 145, 234
Profiling and scoring systems, 234
Progressive Writers Movement, 158
Propaganda, 5, 17, 76, 158, 164, 256–260, 263, 264, 275, 279
Propaganda-based mentality, 5
Proportion of neighbourhoods, 38–40, 44–46
Protracted social conflict, 11
Pro-vaccine groups, 68
Pseudo-code, 86
Pseudoscience, 17, 257, 258, 261, 263, 279
Pseudoscientific statement, 261
Psychological threats, 257, 258, 263
Psychosocial lives, 12
Public health, 52, 56, 275–277
Public inoculation, 275, 278
Public morality, 153, 159
Public opinions, 6, 11, 12, 16, 76, 142, 144, 171, 178, 179, 184, 187, 197–200, 215, 224, 269
Public policy, 143, 179
Public safety, 234, 236
Public services, 48, 236, 238
Public spheres, 142, 143, 146, 161, 178, 183
Punishment mechanism, 237

Q
Quelling strategies, 273, 278

R
Race, 11, 61, 63, 66, 67, 134–137, 144, 146, 165, 289, 291
Race-based slavery, 134
Racial and caste oppression, 16
Racial discrimination, 145
Racial disparity, 2
Racial residential segregation, 47
Random binary encounters, 59, 60
Random network-theory, 74
Ranking system, 14, 238
Rate of infection, 85
Recommendation system, 14, 266, 267, 280
Red-lists, 237, 239, 242
Red meat consumption, 290
Reducing transmission rate, 277–279
Regulators, 96
Relief and recovery activities, 127
Religious fundamentalists, 169
Religious polarization, 169
Religious sentiments, 159
Reparations, 62, 64, 133–146
Republic World, 90, 91, 95, 222, 224
Reservation policy, 15, 16, 133–146
Residential segregation, 15, 27–48, 288, 291
Residential space, 29, 33, 35, 42, 44, 46
Restricted plurality of voices, 164
Retribalization, 154, 161, 169
Reward system, 127
Right to privacy, 247
Riots, 12, 31, 79, 159, 165
Role of censorship, 152
Role of ICTs, 1–17, 142, 143, 152, 153, 285, 286, 288–291
Rumour, 17, 53, 76, 79, 82, 167, 218, 253–280
  clinics, 274, 275, 278
  confrontation, 256, 275, 277
  counter-strategies, 269, 277, 278
  diffusion, 255, 267, 272, 273
  dissemination, 254–256, 264, 275, 279
  exposure minimisation, 278, 279
  propagation, 255
  spreading, 254, 255, 257, 263, 265–267, 269, 270, 275, 279
  studies, 255
Rumour control centre (RCC), 274
Rumour-mongering, 254
Rumour-proof channels, 270

S
Satisfaction of agent, 34, 46
Schelling model, 29–32
Schelling opinion, 15, 27–48
Schelling's model of segregation, 32
Science denialism, 261
Screening and quarantine, 276, 277
Seasonal bushfires, 116, 119, 120
Secondary comments, 62

Second-order themes, 120, 240
Security, 6, 122, 239–241
Seed comments, 62
Segregation index, 47
Segregation patterns, 39, 44
Segregation process, 28, 30, 36, 47
Selective exposure, 12, 67, 185, 215
Self-censorship, 170
Self-confirming newsfeeds, 169
Self-control, 242
Self-quarantine rules, 57
Self-reinforcing mythological bubble, 156
Self-supervision, 241
Semiotic domain, 144
Sense-making, 257, 258, 262–264
Sensitivity analysis, 60, 69, 86
Sensory emotive Web, 177
Sentiment, 7, 53, 85, 88, 157, 159, 165, 178, 213, 218–223, 266, 288, 289
  analysis, 62, 68, 218, 221, 226
  scores, 16, 62, 65, 85, 86, 88, 90, 213, 219–221
Sentimental leaning, 220
Service modification, 272, 278
Service retirement, 272, 278
Short-sighted policies, 125
Simple interaction rules, 32
Single dominant opinion, 32
SIS curve, 89
SIS model, 82, 83, 87
Skepticism, 11
Slavery, 134, 136, 137, 144
Snowball sampling method, 189, 202
Social activists, 164
Social and ideological polarization, 154
Social awareness campaigns, 68
Social behaviour, 58, 67, 82, 85, 184
Social bots, 266, 267, 280
Social capital, 123, 141
Social cohesion, 1–3, 17, 123, 286–288
Social Comparison Theory (SCT), 181, 182
Social connectedness, 179, 186
Social credit system (SCS), 233–248, 288, 291
Social cues, 286, 287
Social development, 139
Social diversity, 28
Social dynamics, 32, 262
Social flaming, 127
Social fragmentation, 28, 45, 46
Social housing, 238
Social identity theory, 11
Social illusion, 145
Social inequality, 144
Social influence, 15, 28, 29, 31, 32, 36, 45–47, 59
Social innovation, 3
Social institutions, 17, 146, 265
Social interactions, 4, 60, 83, 127, 178, 285–287
Social intermediation, 3, 286
Social justice, 1, 138, 140–142, 144, 145
Social manipulation, 262, 263
Social manipulation campaigns, 269
Social media, 2, 52, 74, 117, 142, 152, 177, 212, 240, 254, 288
  abuse, 164
  analytics, 179, 180, 189, 198, 202
  campaign, 2, 68, 159
  data, 15, 184, 189
  induced toxic debates, 169
  influencers, 5, 55, 289
  platform, 53, 55, 56, 59, 69, 74, 76, 78, 79, 96, 97, 127, 142, 146, 162, 187, 188, 200, 201, 203, 253–280
  sanctions, 127
  slander, 152, 160
  sources, 240
  technologies, 178
  vilification, 152, 153, 168
Social media-enabled interactions, 200
Social media induced polarization (SMIP), 16, 53, 67, 68, 177–207, 218, 246
Social network analysis, 184
Social network-based polarization, 182
Social networking site, 164, 178, 183, 187, 188, 198, 285
Social networks, 8, 12–15, 53, 59, 60, 127, 183–185, 187, 198, 215, 247, 255, 258, 264, 265, 270, 277
Social platforms, 4, 285
Social polarization, 288
Social power, 216
Social prejudice, 245
Social rank, 138
Social roots, 139
Social segregation, 29, 30, 143
Social sorting, 244, 245
Social spheres, 142
Social stability, 236
Social stigma, 141, 162
Social structures, 247
Social systems, 122
Societal implications, 200
Societal inequality, 8
Societal taboo, 163
Socio-cultural beliefs, 33
Socio-cultural environment, 2

Socio-cultural life, 163
Socio-cultural polarization, 7, 15, 31, 46, 152, 155, 200, 201, 288–292
Socio-economic trustworthiness, 237
Socio-environmental cost, 119
Socio-political-cultural issues, 165
Socio-psychological beliefs, 13
Socio-psychological roots, 10
Spatially close agents, 41, 46
Spatial patterns, 30, 38, 39, 42, 43, 45
Spatial political segregation, 47
Spatial segregation, 30
Spiral of silence, 12
Spread of fake information, 76
Spread of fake news, 5, 74, 77, 96, 127
Spread of misinformation, 4–5, 9, 52, 54, 58, 66, 68, 77, 127, 168, 254
Square lattice, 33
Stable dynamical scenario, 32
Standard deviations, 36, 39, 40, 42, 91–93, 96, 220
State definition, 78
Statistical models, 58, 59, 85
Stimulated controversies, 158
Stop Online Piracy Act (SOPA), 290
Strategies for countering rumours, 267–279
Subcultural identity, 163
Sub-humanization, 146
Subscribers, 16, 74, 82, 84, 87, 88, 108, 143
Subversion of power, 163
Surveillance capitalism, 234, 238
Susceptible, 80, 82–85, 87, 89, 92, 157, 277
Susceptible Exposed Infected Skeptic model (SEIZ model), 82
Susceptible Infected Recovered model (SIR model), 82
Susceptible Infected Recovered Susceptible model (SIRS model), 83
Susceptible Infected Susceptible model (SIS model), 82, 83, 87, 88
Susceptible position, 84
Sustainability logic, 125–126
Synchronicity, 265
System-justifying tendencies, 122

T

Tailgating, 6
Technological artifacts, 2
Technology-based social change, 2
Technology-mediated, 143
Tendency of agents, 40
Term frequency-inverse document frequency (TF-IDF), 219, 221
Text analysis, 90
Threat management, 257, 258, 262, 264
Threshold tolerance, 37
Times Now, 222, 224
Tolerance level, 60, 85, 86
Tolerance parameters, 58, 59
Tolerance threshold, 29, 46
Total absence, 40
Totalitarian tendencies, 244
Total local grouping, 40
Toxic gases, 121
Traditionalists, 116, 120–123, 126, 127
Train the brain, 275, 278
Transaction costs, 237, 239
Transfer coefficient, 90, 91
Transfer coefficient values, 87
Transfer dynamics, 83
Transparency, 4, 57, 127, 197, 237, 247
Trend of censorship, 162
Tribal echo-chamber, 171
Troll farms, 291
Trolls, 5, 6, 53, 57, 160
True news, 73–111
Trust, 1, 4, 117, 118, 169, 217, 241–244, 246, 247, 261, 286, 287
Trusted source, 78
Twitter, 13, 16, 46, 69, 74, 78–80, 95, 97, 121, 127, 134, 156, 160, 164, 178, 179, 183–186, 188–190, 197, 201–204, 216, 255, 266, 271
Twitter data stream, 188
Two-dimensional matrix, 222

U

Unbiased information, 224
Uncontrolled fires, 122
Unhappy agent, 34–36, 38
Uninhibited behavior, 287
Unofficial censorship, 157, 170, 171
Unsupervised segmentation, 220
Unverified information, 5, 17, 255–264, 279, 280
Upper castes, 139, 141, 146, 152, 167
Urbanisation, 241
User engagement, 13, 53
Users' behavior, 66, 184
U-shape relationship, 77

V

Vaccination, 9, 13, 52–56, 58, 67, 68, 179, 217, 260, 261, 275–279, 289, 291
Vaccination rates, 54–56

Vaccine acceptance, 9
Vaccine development, 51–69
Vaccine hesitancy, 52, 53, 56, 68
Vaccine legislation, 55
Vaccine safety, 53
Values of tolerance, 35, 86
Variability, 90, 94, 96
Variations of rumour, 264, 279
Veracity of content, 174
Verifiable facts, 76
Viewers, 3, 16, 62, 87, 88, 108
Violence, 11, 12, 79, 152, 160, 165, 166, 170, 288
Virtual and online publication, 160
Virtual communities, 57
Virtual media, 178
Virtue ethics, 236
Virtue signalling, 156
Voter model, 30, 83

W
Water quality, 119
Weather conditions, 123, 124
Web 5.0, 177
Web-driven threats, 288
Webservice, 4
Wellbeing, 80
White body supremacy, 134
Whites, 136, 146
Wildfire, 115, 116
Wildlife staff, 124
Wild protests, 169
Withholding to comment, 273
Women empowerment, 2
Workplace environment, 183

Y
YouTube, 3, 14, 59, 62, 67, 73–111, 143, 145, 184
  channels, 16, 74, 75, 87, 88, 95, 143, 160
  videos, 53, 54, 59, 61–63, 65, 66, 68, 75, 87–88, 92

Z
ZEE news, 87, 90, 91, 95, 222–225

GPSR Compliance

The European Union's (EU) General Product Safety Regulation (GPSR) is a set of rules that requires consumer products to be safe and our obligations to ensure this.

If you have any concerns about our products, you can contact us on ProductSafety@springernature.com

In case Publisher is established outside the EU, the EU authorized representative is:

Springer Nature Customer Service Center GmbH
Europaplatz 3
69115 Heidelberg, Germany

Batch number: 10732090

Printed by Printforce, the Netherlands